OPPORTUNITIES AND CHALLENGES OF WORKPLACE DIVERSITY

Theory, Cases, and Exercises

OPPORTUNITIES AND CHALLENGES OF WORKPLACE DIVERSITY

Theory, Cases, and Exercises

Kathryn A. Cañas

University of Utah

Harris Sondak

University of Utah

Upper Saddle River, New Jersey 07458

Library of Congress Cataloging-in-Publication Data

Opportunities and challenges of workplace diversity : theory, cases, and
exercises / [edited by] Kathryn A. Cañas, Harris Sondak.
  p. cm.
 Includes bibliographical references and index.
 ISBN-13: 978-0-13-134306-1
 ISBN-10: 0-13-134306-8
 1. Diversity in the workplace—United States. 2. Diversity in the
workplace—United States—Case studies. I. Cañas, Kathryn A. II. Sondak,
Harris.
 HF5549.5.M5O67 2008
 658.3008—dc22

                                                          2006103491

Senior Acquisitions Editor: Michael
Ablassmeir
VP/Editorial Director: Jeff Shelstad
Product Development Manager:
Ashley Santora
Assistant Editor: Keri Molinari
Editorial Assistant: Kristen Varina
Marketing Manager: Anne Howard
Marketing Assistant: Susan Osterlitz
Associate Director, Production Editorial:
Judy Leale
Managing Editor: Renata Butera
Production Editor: Kelly Warsak

Permissions Coordinator: Charles Morris
Associate Director, Manufacturing:
Vinnie Scelta
Manufacturing Buyer: Michelle Klein
Director of Design: Christy Mahon
Art Director: Jayne Conte
Composition: Techbooks
Full-Service Project Management:
Penny Walker/Techbooks
Printer/Binder: R.R.D./Harrisonburg
Cover Printer: R.R.D./Harrisonburg
Typeface: 10/12 Times Ten Roman

Credits and acknowledgments borrowed from other sources and reproduced, with
permission, in this textbook appear on appropriate page within text.

Pearson Education LTD.
Pearson Education Singapore, Pte. Ltd
Pearson Education, Canada, Ltd
Pearson Education–Japan

Pearson Education Australia PTY, Limited
Pearson Education North Asia Ltd
Pearson Educación de Mexico, S.A. de C.V.
Pearson Education Malaysia, Pte. Ltd.

10 9 8 7 6 5 4 3
ISBN-13: 978-0-13-134306-1
ISBN-10: 0-13-134306-8

Brief Contents

Contents

Preface

DIVERSITY AND THE WORKPLACE: CREATING A DIALOGUE OF OPPORTUNITY

In this text we create a dialogue of opportunity about the topic of workplace diversity with scholars, managers, consultants, and students. We examine the intersections of diversity and the workplace as we embrace diversity's complexities—including its benefits, challenges, and paradoxes. Having a diverse workplace is indeed a business opportunity, but only when its complexities are managed successfully, which requires that they are both acknowledged and understood. Without understanding diversity as a complex phenomenon, it is difficult to gain a comprehensive understanding of what it means to manage a diverse workforce effectively. In essence, we hope to contribute a significant and unique perspective to today's conversation about diversity in the workplace by encouraging and engaging in open dialogue.

As we discuss diversity as an opportunity, we hope to help our readers become more effective and responsible organizational members. The underlying argument supported throughout our discussion is that organizations that manage their diverse workforce effectively will have a competitive advantage over organizations that do not. That is, we believe that managing diversity well will lead to increased organizational performance. A diverse workforce is more likely to gain a competitive advantage when diversity is implemented systemically; that is, it must be understood and valued as an essential component of every aspect of the organization rather than incorporated sporadically within it. Organizations that are able to accomplish this will have more opportunity to excel in all areas.

Three-Tiered Structure for Understanding

Our discussion unfolds in three stages: First, we offer both a theoretical and a legal understanding of diversity; second, we provide detailed case studies of U.S. businesses that have both managed and mismanaged diversity; third, we incorporate multiple exercises that help students examine diversity on both personal and organizational levels.

In Part I, "Uncovering the Complexities of Workplace Diversity," our goal is to help explain the complexities of workplace diversity from both managerial and legal perspectives. Managers in today's dynamic workplace need to understand how these two perspectives interact—specifically, how one informs the other in the context of a complex workplace. In the first of the two opening essays in this part, we examine diversity from a managerial point of view and discuss the following important considerations for understanding diversity in American business: the changing U.S. demographics, multiple alternative definitions of diversity and important principles to acknowledge when defining diversity; four paradigms or approaches for diversity management; and the complexities of the business case for diversity. In the second essay, P. Corper James outlines the legal aspects of managing diversity in his explication of the classes of people protected by law, the legal definition of sexual harassment, the Americans with Disabilities Act (ADA), and the Age Discrimination in Employment Act (ADEA). In addition, he offers general legal advice for both managers and employers on the topic of diversity management.

In Part II, "Managing and Mismanaging: Case Studies on American Businesses," we illustrate organizational successes and mistakes of American businesses. This section reflects our belief that understanding diversity is facilitated through detailed examination of real case studies. Our collection of comprehensive case studies focuses on how familiar organizations have grappled with diversity management. Our examples of organizations include Augusta National, Mothers Work, Texaco, Wells Fargo, Ford, Tom's of Maine, Cracker Barrel, General Motors, and IBM; we discuss how these organizations have managed diversity issues related to gender, race and national origin, age, religion and spirituality, sexual orientation, and disabilities in the workplace.

In Part III, "Developing Three Essential Skills," our goal is to encourage our readers to examine their own relationship with diversity, assess how organizations manage diversity, and better understand the intersection of diversity and work. These exercises invite students to engage in energized, intelligent dialogue on the many complexities of diversity in the workplace.

Terms and Concepts that Frame Our Discussion

Diversity

A primary objective of our text is to illuminate the complexities of diversity. We understand *diversity* as a matrix of dynamic and interrelated identity groups that operate on multiple dimensions including *primary* and *secondary* personal characteristics and *organizational contexts*.[1] These dimensions are continuously interacting as they unite to represent a person in his or her entirety. Primary dimensions—those that most profoundly define us—include gender, race and national origin, age, religion and spirituality, sexual orientation, and disabilities. Secondary dimensions—often just as significant as the primary dimensions but more likely to change—include military experience, parental status, educational background, social location/economic status, and geographic origin and location. Organizational contexts—which are specifically related to the workplace—include work content/field, formal and informal status, division/department, work location, and union affiliation. While all dimensions are significant when defining oneself, we choose to focus mostly on the primary dimensions of diversity, although a number of the secondary dimensions are discussed throughout the articles, essays, cases, and exercises.

In addition to understanding diversity as having three interrelated dimensions, we believe that the following five principles are critical to understanding the complexities of diversity: Diversity is expansive but not without boundaries; diversity is fluid and dynamic; diversity is based on both similarities and differences; diversity is rooted in nonessentialist thought; and diversity is directly related to how one approaches work. In our opening essay we offer a detailed explanation of each of these principles in addition to delineating other definitions of diversity by a variety of diversity scholars.

Affirmative Action, Valuing Diversity, Diversity Management

Diversity scholars often articulate three stages to understanding how workplace diversity has changed over time: *affirmative action*, *valuing diversity*, and *diversity management* (or *managing diversity*). The phrase *valuing diversity* is a movement beyond the affirmative action position of amending wrongs done in the past to those Americans—most specifically African Americans and women—who have been underrepresented in positions of organizational power. Diversity initiatives that represent the second stage, valuing diversity, are, according to scholar and consultant R. Roosevelt Thomas, "designed to enhance the individual's awareness, understanding and acceptance of differences between people." And "in contrast to diversity management, valuing differences does not involve the changing of corporate culture and systems."[2]

Diversity management represents a movement beyond valuing diversity and a managerial approach in which diversity is viewed as both a competitive advantage and the right thing to do; diversity is linked to strategic goals and is understood as directly influencing the way employees approach work. Thomas describes this stage as "a holistic approach to creating a corporate environment that allows all kinds of people to reach their full potential in pursuit of corporate objectives."[3] Further, he explains that managing diversity approaches diversity from a management perspective, that is, how best to manage the company's human resources given the fact that those resources are now far more diverse than in earlier times. It is not about leveling the playing field to give minorities and women an extra advantage; it's about maximizing the contributions of all employees.[4]

The focus of our text is primarily on the third stage, managing diversity, because we believe it is this framework that American businesses should strive toward. We do not ignore the other stages, however, and we provide discussions of affirmative action and valuing diversity in the opening essays.

Dominant and Nondominant Groups

Underlying any discussion of diversity in American business, whether affirmative action, valuing diversity, or diversity management, is the recognition that some groups have had and continue to have more power than others. Those with power represent the *dominant* group and control the construction and dissemination of knowledge, make decisions, and allocate burdens and rewards and thus hold the more influential positions in the workplace. White men have historically held most positions of power in the workplace and thus typically constitute the dominant group in most organizations. In addition, there are groups of people, located on the periphery of power, who have historically been disempowered or *nondominant*. These less powerful groups of people include, but are not limited to, women, people with disabilities, older workers, people of color, people of different ethnicities, and gay, lesbian, bisexual, and transgendered people.

Although less powerful, subordinate groups often possess the ability—especially when working together—to negotiate successfully with the dominant group. And although we focus largely on the nondominant groups of people in our discussion of diversity, we believe white men constitute a critically important component of managing diversity because, as organizational leaders, they often have the ability to make decisions that directly affect the role of diversity in the workplace. Moreover, we often forget that white men are themselves a diverse group—whether, for example, in terms of age, religion, sexual orientation, disability, or parental status. Further, unless both the dominant and nondominant groups work together, it is impossible for diversity to become a competitive advantage in the workplace.

Prejudice and Discrimination

An important objective of this text is to encourage the readers to reflect on the ways in which diversity affects them. While using this textbook, we hope that students will gain a better understanding of how they may be prejudiced, often unknowingly, against groups of people they may view as different, seeing them through preconceived notions as lesser or deficient in some way. In addition, we hope that students will understand, specifically from the case study section, that discrimination—denying opportunities, resources, or access to a person because of his or her group members—is, unfortunately, often a business reality. The case studies that illustrate discrimination represent uniquely helpful resources, because organizations that have made serious mismanagement errors can provide powerful lessons.

Stereotyping and Essentializing

Other significant, interrelated concepts that encourage self-reflection include *stereotyping* and *essentializing*. We ask our readers the question: What are the potential effects of stereotyping and essentializing in the workplace? Stereotypes are particularly powerful, as they are formed when we ascribe exaggerated beliefs or generalizations to people based on their group identities rather than seeing each person as an individual (e.g., a professor might expect all athletes to be irresponsible students). Stereotypes are common and often arise from incomplete or incorrect information and restricted experience with a particular group of people.

Just as serious is assuming that a characteristic or set of characteristics is the essence—the essential nature—of all members of a group (e.g., people might expect that women are, by nature, better nurturers than men). Although it may be a human tendency to stereotype or essentialize others, it is important to remember both the inaccuracy of doing so and the potentially devastating effects of these generalizations on individuals' realities in their daily lives.

Instructor's Manual

Because the majority of our textbook is based on teaching diversity through case studies, we have dedicated much of the instructor's manual to the same. To enhance students' learning, each case study is accompanied by a detailed Teaching Note and set of PowerPoint slides. The instructor's manual also includes example syllabi, responses to discussion questions, comprehensive exercise instructions, and suggestions for individual and group assignments.

Acknowledgments

We thank many people for their assistance with this project, which would not have succeeded if not for their contributions. We would like to acknowledge the Pearson/Prentice Hall editorial, production, and permissions team for their professionalism throughout the project. Our gratitude goes to the reviewers for their valuable comments and suggestions: Joseph Ofori-Dankwa, Saginaw Valley State University; Ranjna Patel, Bethune Cookman College; Eleanor H. Buttner, University of North Carolina–Greensboro; George R. Maughan, Indiana State University; Marian C. Schultz, University of West Florida; Jane Hass Philbrick, Savannah State University; Bennie L. Osborne, Florida International University; Shawnta S. Friday, Florida A&M University; Nicholas J. Chabra, University of North Carolina–Greensboro; Nancy Bertaux, Xavier University; Rachna Nagi-Condos, American River College; and Christina Stamper, Western Michigan University. In addition, we extend our appreciation to our research assistant, University of Utah alumna Melissa Greensides, who has been with us since the inception of our project. Our deepest appreciation is extended to our families and friends; without them, nothing would have been possible or worthwhile. Dr. Cañas thanks Servando and Carol Cañas, Lance Pearson, Luke Cañas Pearson, Rhea Rose Cañas Pearson, Susan Cañas Gregoire, and Whitney King. Dr. Sondak especially thanks his parents, Fraser Nelson, and Neah Bois.

About the Authors

Dr. Kathryn A. Cañas is a member of the Management Department in the David Eccles School of Business at the University of Utah. Her teaching currently includes courses on managing diversity, business communication, and pedagogical theories and practices on both undergraduate and graduate levels. Her teaching has included courses on rhetorical criticism and theory, public speaking and persuasion, interpersonal communication and coaching, written communication, gender and communication, and writing for publication. She has presented a number of papers at national and regional conferences and recently published the essay "Demonizing Democracy: The Strange Career of Lani Guinier" in *New Approaches to Rhetoric*. Her professional association memberships include the Management Communication Association and the Association for Business Communication.

Dr. Cañas received her B.A. in English and communication from Boston College, her M.A. in speech communication from Indiana University, and her Ph.D. in communication from the University of Utah. For more information, please visit her Web site at *www.business.utah.edu/~mgtkc/*.

E-mail: *mgtkc@business.utah.edu*

Dr. Harris Sondak is a member of the Management Department in the David Eccles School of Business at the University of Utah. His teaching includes courses on groups, negotiations, creating and maintaining business relationships, managing conflict in organizations, competitive strategy, managing diversity, organizational behavior, consulting, and business ethics and leadership. He has taught these subjects to executives, Ph.D. candidates, M.B.A. students, and undergraduates from around the world. Dr. Sondak's research investigates the psychology of allocation decisions, negotiation, group process and decisions, and procedural justice and ethics. His research has been published in a number of leading academic journals. Dr. Sondak has served as a reviewer, a member of the editorial board, and as the associate editor for scholarly publications.

Dr. Sondak received his BA in philosophy from the University of Colorado and his M.S. and Ph.D. in organizational behavior from Northwestern University. He was a member of the faculty of the Fuqua School of Business at Duke University and has been a visiting faculty member at the International Institute for Management Development (IMD) in Lausanne, Switzerland, the Graduate School of Business, Stanford University, and the Indian School of Business in Hyderabad, India. For more information, please visit his Web site at *www.business.utah.edu/~mgths/*.

E-mail: *sondak@business.utah.edu*

Notes

1. Our definition is based on a combination of definitions from Marilyn Loden, Lee Gardenswartz, and Anita Rowe. Their definitions are found in Loden, *Implementing Diversity* (New York: McGraw-Hill, 1996); and Gardenswartz and Rowe, *Diverse Teams at Work: Capitalizing on the Power of Diversity* (New York: McGraw-Hill, 1994).

2. R. Roosevelt Thomas, Jr. *Beyond Race and Gender: Unleashing the Power of Your Total Work Force by Managing Diversity* (New York: AMACOM, 1991), 169.

3. Ibid., 167.

4. Ibid., 168.

OPPORTUNITIES AND CHALLENGES OF WORKPLACE DIVERSITY

Theory, Cases, and Exercises

PART I
UNCOVERING THE COMPLEXITIES OF WORKPLACE DIVERSITY

In this first part, "Uncovering the Complexities of Workplace Diversity," our goal is to explore the complexities of workplace diversity from both managerial and legal perspectives. In the essay "Diversity in the Workplace: A Theoretical Perspective" we examine diversity from a managerial point of view and discuss the following important considerations for understanding diversity in American business: the changing U.S. demography; multiple alternative definitions of diversity and important principles to acknowledge when defining diversity; four paradigms or approaches for diversity management; and the complexities of the business case for diversity.

In the essay "Diversity in the Workplace: A Legal Perspective" P. Corper James outlines the legal aspects of managing diversity in his explication of the classes of people protected by law, the legal definitions of sexual harassment, the Americans with Disabilities Act (ADA), and the Age Discrimination in Employment Act (ADEA). In addition, he offers general legal advice for both managers and employers on the topic of diversity management.

1

DIVERSITY IN THE WORKPLACE: A THEORETICAL PERSPECTIVE

D iversity training has become a multibillion-dollar industry. Corporate America invests in a wide variety of diversity summits, workshops, toolkits, books, training videos, e-learning programs, executive coaching sessions, and leadership academies. As companies embrace diversity initiatives, they publicly declare their allegiance to promoting diversity as a business strategy.

American Express, for example, maintains that "the connection between the diversity of our workforce and our overall performance quality is clearly valued."[1] Marriott International enthusiastically describes its commitment to diversity as "absolute" and asserts that strong diversity management "is the only way to attract, develop, and retain the very best talent available. It is the only way to forge the business relationships necessary to continue our dynamic growth."[2] Similarly, Deloitte & Touche asserts, "Diversity is a business priority critical to our success," and the "future will belong to those companies that fully appreciate and value diversity."[3] Boldly claiming that "diversity is who we are," Starbucks describes diversity as "a way of life" and "the core of our culture and a foundation for the way we conduct business."[4]

Although there is a clear movement in corporate America to embrace diversity in the workplace, not so clear is the public acknowledgment and dialogue about the challenges associated with managing diversity. We intend to address this need by discussing not only the benefits of diversity but also its complexities. Managing diversity is a sometimes difficult process with often uncertain results. Even skilled managers with the best intentions can fail to anticipate and resolve the problems that managing diversity presents.

For example, consider the case of Xerox, long a progressive leader in diversity management. The company has won a long string of diversity-related awards and has been rated as one of the top 10 companies in hiring minorities, women, people with disabilities, and gay and lesbian employees by *Fortune, Forbes, Working Mother, Latino Style,* and *Enable Magazine.*[5] Xerox's approach to managing diversity has been clear and consistent; chairman and chief executive officer Anne M. Mulcahy states: "Diversity breeds creativity. Maybe it's because people with different backgrounds challenge each other's underlying assumptions, freeing everybody from convention and orthodoxy."[6]

Nonetheless, diversity management at Xerox has had its problems. Xerox employees "fashioned a workplace display of African American dolls with nooses around their necks, igniting a lawsuit against the company in 2002."[7] In addition to this complaint, lawsuits also alleged the following: White employees and supervisors regularly referred to Xerox as "the ghetto" because the company hired so many minority employees; a

Dr. Kathryn A. Cañas and Dr. Harris Sondak, The University of Utah photograph of an African American female employee was doctored by a white supervisor to portray her as a prostitute; a book with hundreds of offensive racial jokes and pictures was copied and bound on Xerox equipment by employees and distributed throughout the company; and evidence was found that suggested the clear lack of promotional opportunity and equal pay for African Americans.[8] Although Xerox has been a model of diversity management for over 40 years, it recently was charged with blatant, systemic discrimination of African Americans.

Nor does managing diversity effectively guarantee positive business results. Denny's is an exemplary case of how a company can transition from being the "bad boy" of diversity to becoming a laudable model of diversity management. After being besieged with racial discrimination lawsuits in the 1990s, in 2004 the restaurant chain was impressively ranked 37th in DiversityInc's "Top 50 Companies for Diversity" list and 5th in *Fortune's* "Best Companies for Minorities" list. The implementation of Denny's highly acclaimed diversity management program demonstrated both "how fast and far a company can progress with an aggressive strategy and strong leadership" and "the limits of what diversity can deliver."[9] CEO and president Nelson Marchioli has never been able to quantify the financial benefits from the millions of dollars invested in Denny's diversity transformation; in fact, Denny's reported a net loss of $11.6 million for the first half of 2004.[10]

Despite such paradoxes, many business leaders view diversity as a strategic business imperative. The central claim of the business case for diversity is that managing diversity is good for the bottom line. This view maintains that a diverse workforce creates a competitive advantage as it decreases costs while enhancing creativity, problem solving, recruitment of the best talent, marketing strategies, overall productivity, leadership effectiveness, global relations, and organizational flexibility.[11]

Although the business case argument represents a significant position on workforce diversity, it fails to illuminate the complexities of diversity and diversity management. We concur with the conclusion of an important research project on diversity that "organizations that invest their resources in taking advantage of the opportunities that diversity offers should outperform those that fail to make such investments."[12] But this research also suggests that diversity becomes an exciting business opportunity only when it is managed effectively at all levels of an organization and understood in light of both its advantages and disadvantages.

The purpose of this essay is to help students understand the complexities of diversity management through five steps. We (1) provide evidence that managing diversity is a necessity of contemporary business by illuminating the ever-changing demographics of the American workforce; (2) consider alternative frameworks for defining and understanding diversity; (3) examine different approaches that organizational leaders can use to manage diversity; (4) describe the business case for diversity, which argues that diversity contributes to the bottom line; and, finally, (5) discuss the challenges, counter-arguments, and paradoxes associated with the business case philosophy.

STEP 1: EXAMINING WORKPLACE DEMOGRAPHY

Although there are differing opinions about diversity management, one aspect of diversity cannot be disputed: The American workforce and management are becoming increasingly heterogeneous. As we look at statistical changes in U.S. demographics in general and the workplace in particular, we begin to understand why diversity management is a compelling issue for American business.

National Demographic Changes

According to the U.S. Census Bureau, the proportion of whites in the United States will decline from approximately 79 percent of the population in 2010 to 72 percent in 2050.[13] Latinos, by contrast, will grow from about 16 percent to 25 percent of the population, numbering more than 100 million in 2050.[14] The African American population will grow from 40 million in 2010 to 61 million in 2050, or about 15 percent of the population; and the Asian American population will more than double, from 14 million in 2010 to 33 million in 2050, which will be about 8 percent of the population.[15]

In addition, according to the 2000 U.S. census, 4.1 million people, or 1.5 percent of the total U.S. population, self-reported as Native American and Alaska Native alone or in combination with one or more races.[16] The bureau also reported that the number of Arabs and Arab Americans in the United States doubled since 1980, growing from 610,000 in 1980 to 1.2 million in 2000.[17] Another increasing population comprises the 15 million gay men and lesbians in the United States.[18]

Workplace Demographic Changes

Just as the national population is becoming more diverse so, too, is the workforce changing. A record number of women are entering the U.S. workforce, for example. According to the Bureau of Labor Statistics, women now account for 46.6 percent of today's workers,[19] and many analysts predict that women in the workforce will soon become the majority. Richard Judy, director of the Center for Workforce Development at the Hudson Institute, stated: "By 2020, the female share [of the workforce] will have increased gradually to about 50 percent."[20]

Despite their increased numbers, women and minorities still receive a disproportionately low share of the rewards allocated by U.S. businesses. Women occupy only about 8 percent of executive vice president positions (and above) at Fortune 500 companies.[21] African Americans and Latinos represent approximately 25 percent of the U.S. population yet hold fewer than 5 percent of senior-management positions.[22]

Moreover, a study of the pay gap between men and women found that women psychologists earn 83 cents to the male dollar; women college professors earn 75 cents to the male dollar; and women lawyers and judges earn 69 cents to the male dollar.[23] Thus, although it has been argued that choice of occupation affects overall pay rates, even within particular occupations men are paid more than women. Even in some occupations where women historically predominate, men are paid more.[24]

Nondominant groups continue to suffer discrimination beyond low pay. In the case of women, for example, pregnancy discrimination complaints filed with the federal Equal Employment Opportunity Commission (EEOC), for example, jumped 39 percent from fiscal year 1992 to 2003, even as the birth rate declined.[25] In the case of gay and lesbian workers, nearly two out of five say they consistently face some form of hostility or harassment on the job.[26]

Whereas other groups have made gains in access to jobs, people with disabilities have lost ground, as the number entering the workforce seems to have decreased overall in the last decade, even with the passing of the Americans with Disabilities Act (ADA) in 1990.[27] Moreover, only 35 percent of people with disabilities report being employed full or part time, compared with 78 percent of those who do not have disabilities.[28] This disadvantage persists despite the numbers of people who are or are likely to become disabled. In fact, U.S. workers have approximately a 30 percent chance of becoming disabled for at least 90 days at some point during their working years.[29]

The older worker is also changing the landscape of the American workplace. Douglas Holbrook, a member of the AARP's board of directors, explains that "[a]s of July 2004, more than 23 million persons aged 55 and older were in the labor force.... In recent years, labor force participation rates have been rising even among persons in their late 60s and 70s—beyond the age of traditional retirement."[30]

The increasing intersection between religion or spirituality and the workplace is an additional contemporary workplace phenomenon. As more people become open about their spirituality—95 percent of Americans say they believe in God, and 48 percent say they talk about their religious faith at work according to the Gallup Organization—it is not surprising, then, that there are more than 10,000 Bible and prayer groups in workplaces that meet regularly, and there are many annual conferences on religion and the workplace.[31] And yet, while employees embrace combining religion and work, the EEOC reports a 29 percent spike since 1992 in the number of religious-based discrimination charges.[32]

Purchasing Power Trends

As demographics shift, so do market and purchasing power trends. For example, the combined buying power of African Americans, Asian Americans, and Native Americans in 2007 will more than triple its 1990 level of $453 billion, to almost $1.4 trillion.[33] In addition, Latino spending is expected to reach almost 10 percent of the nation's overall spending by 2008, up from approximately 5 percent in 1990.[34] Furthermore, the buying power of the gay and lesbian market is projected to reach $608 billion by 2007, a cumulative increase of more than 34 percent from 2002 figures.[35]

Although this discussion represents only a glimpse of demographic changes and trends, the dynamic quality of the American workforce is clear. Realizing that the diversity of the workforce is increasing encourages the development of a framework for understanding and defining diversity. Unless businesses develop a strategy for managing a more diverse workforce and for developing managerial talent from within many different groups, organizational effectiveness is likely to fall short.

WHAT DO YOU THINK?
What do you believe is the most significant demographic change facing the American workplace? Why?

STEP 2: DEFINING DIVERSITY

In managing diversity, it is helpful to know what *diversity* means. A number of scholars, practitioners, and organizations have defined diversity in various ways. We present some of these definitions in this section, moving from the more simple approaches to those that are more complex and comprehensive.

Society for Human Resource Management (SHRM)

The Society for Human Resource Management (SHRM), a leading professional association, recognizes that although diversity "is often used to refer to differences based on ethnicity, gender, age, religion, disability, national origin and sexual orientation," it also encompasses an "infinite range" of "unique characteristics and experiences" including, among others, the way one communicates, one's height and weight, and speed of learning and comprehension.[36]

Taylor H. Cox, Jr.

Taylor H. Cox, Jr., associate professor in the University of Michigan Business School and founder of Taylor Cox and Associates Inc., a well-known diversity management research and consulting firm, defines diversity as "the variation of social and cultural identities among people existing together in a defined employment or market setting." Offering further explanation, Cox maintains that social and cultural identities are "personal affiliations" such as gender, race, national origin, religion, age, and work specialization that have "significant influence on people's major life experiences."[37] Employment and market settings refer to systems that go beyond businesses and include, for example, churches, schools, factory work teams, industrial customers, baseball teams, and military units.[38]

Marilyn Loden

Marilyn Loden, a nationally recognized organizational change consultant, emphasizes the importance of an expansive and all-encompassing definition of diversity, because when any group—white men, for example—is excluded, managing diversity may create division rather than inclusion. She maintains that to "avoid widescale opposition," corporations should define diversity such that "everyone's diversity is valued."[39] For Loden, diversity reflects "important human characteristics that impact individuals' values, opportunities, and perceptions of self and others at work."[40] Loden's widely embraced model of diversity, as represented in Figure 1-1, explicates diversity as having both primary and secondary dimensions.

The primary dimensions of diversity—age, ethnicity, gender, mental/physical abilities, race, and sexual orientation—are "interlocking segments of a sphere" that represent the core of an individual's identity. Secondary dimensions, which are "more mutable, less visible to others around us, and more variable" include work style, geographic origin and present location, income, work experience, military experience, family status, religion, native language, communication style, organizational role and level, and education.[41] Loden explains that because the secondary dimensions are more dynamic, their power is "less constant" and "more individualized than is true for the core dimensions."[42] In effect, the primary and secondary dimensions give definition to people's lives "by contributing to a synergistic, integrated whole—the diverse person."[43]

Anita Rowe and Lee Gardenswartz

Anita Rowe and Lee Gardenswartz, human resource experts on managing workforce diversity, embrace Loden's definition of diversity but add two additional dimensions, as

FIGURE 1-1 The Diversity Wheel

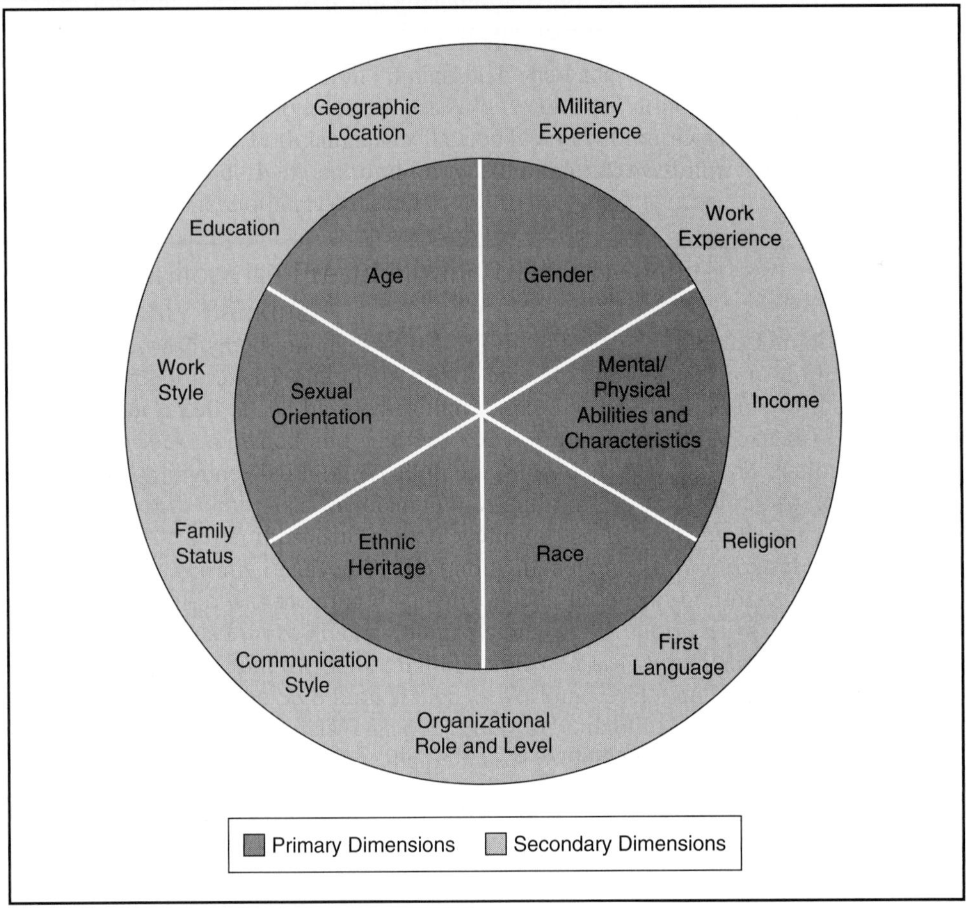

Loden Associates designs innovative models such as the diversity wheel to facilitate understanding of a broad range of primary and secondary dimensions of diversity.

Source: From *Implementing Diversity* © 1996. Irwin Professional Publishing.

represented in Figure 1-2—one, personality, in the center, and the other, organizational membership, on the periphery. According to Rowe and Gardenswartz, at the center of the diversity model is personality, which is "the innately unique aspect" that "permeates all other layers" and unites them.[44] The next layer is represented by "internal dimensions" (Loden's primary dimensions). Following the internal dimensions are the external dimensions, which are "brought to bear by society and one's experiences in the world" (Loden's secondary dimensions).[45] The outermost layer consists of organizational dimensions such as union affiliation, management status, functional level/classification, work content/field, seniority, division/department, and work location. In sum, these four layers of diversity come together to form one's "diversity filter."[46]

R. Roosevelt Thomas, Jr.

R. Roosevelt Thomas, Jr., CEO of R. Thomas & Associates, Inc. and founder and president of The American Institute for Managing Diversity, maintains that diversity is

FIGURE 1-2 Four Layers of Diversity

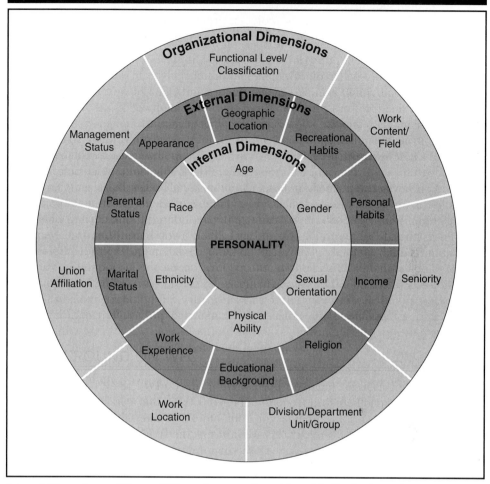

Internal Dimension and External Dimensions are adapted from Marilyn Loden and Judy Rosener, *Workforce America!* (Business One Irwin. 1991).

Source: From *Diverse Teams at Work.* Gardenswartz & Rowe (Irwin, 1995).

"any mixture of items characterized by differences and similarities."[47] Thomas states that when business leaders make decisions, they must deal with both differences and similarities simultaneously. In addition, Thomas emphasizes that diversity must be viewed as all-inclusive insofar as "if you are concerned about racism, you include all races; if you're concerned about gender, you include both genders; or if you're concerned about age issues, you include all age groups."[48]

David A. Thomas and Robin J. Ely
David A. Thomas and Robin J. Ely, Harvard Business School faculty members, link diversity directly to its impact on work as they define diversity as "the varied perspectives and approaches to work that members of different identity groups bring."[49] Diversity is thus "not simply a reflection of the cosmetic differences among people,

such as race and gender; rather, it is the various backgrounds and experiences that create people's identities and outlooks."[50]

Thomas and Ely explain how diverse groups bring not only their "insider information" but also "different, important, and competitively relevant knowledge and perspectives about how to actually do work," for example, how to set and achieve goals, design organizational processes, frame tasks, communicate, and work effectively in teams. If an organization truly embraces the value of diversity, it will allow diverse employees to challenge basic assumptions about an organization's inner workings. This freedom will enable employees to "identify more fully with the work they do," thereby "setting in motion a virtuous circle."[51]

WHAT DO YOU THINK?

What are the important dimensions of diversity that might matter at work or in your classroom?

What would you like other people to know about you in terms of the important dimensions of diversity?

What stereotypes do you think others have about the social categories you belong to?

A Framework for Understanding Diversity

Building on the various definitions we have reviewed, we believe that diversity is most usefully represented within the context of the following principles: (1) Diversity is expansive but not without boundaries; (2) diversity is fluid and dynamic; (3) diversity is based on both similarities and differences; (4) diversity is rooted in nonessentialist thought; and (5) diversity is directly related to how one approaches work.

Diversity Is Expansive but Not Unbounded

The principle that diversity is expansive but has boundaries challenges two commonly held, contrary assumptions about diversity. Too narrow is the assumption that diversity is limited to one's gender and skin color. We include other dimensions of diversity in our conception, for example, single parents, bilingual employees, and people who embrace spirituality. Too broad, however, are definitions that tend to depict diversity as lacking any type of boundary. When organizations are described as having infinite layers of diversity—for example, one's division/department, or work location—diversity gets overextended.

Many such distinctions are inherent in almost any imaginable organizational or social structure and context; if the concept of diversity were to include every characteristic of every individual in any workplace, it would lack both clarity and usefulness. We want to tie the notion of diversity to the people and groups of people who work in organizations, and we want to have the ability to distinguish between more or less diverse organizations and groups. We think that understanding an individual's experience is important, but that is true for management in general, not just for managing diversity.

Diversity Is Fluid and Dynamic

Often overlooked are diversity's characteristics of fluidity and dynamism. Although diversity affiliations are often portrayed as absolute and clearly distinct, they are, we believe, fluid, continuous, and indefinite. Consider race, for example. The U.S. Census Bureau identifies race as a "socio-political" construct rather than a scientific one. Thus, it should not be surprising that people's conception of race is complex and variable. About 6 percent of Americans say that they do not belong to any of the races identified by the bureau, and more than 2 percent say they belong to at least two races simultaneously.[52] As organizational scholar Deborah R. Litvin explains: "The categories constructed through the discourse of workforce diversity as natural and obvious are hardpressed to accommodate the complexity of real people."[53]

In addition, the lines of diversity overlap, as most individuals associate themselves with a number of social category dimensions. For example, a disabled woman of Christian Lebanese descent might define herself in terms of various constellations of gender, religion, national origin, or disability. Also, employees often move in and out of diversity categories—a single parent may get married, a gay man may come out, an able-bodied employee may have an accident and become disabled, or an employee may newly require a flexible schedule to care for an ailing parent.

Diversity Is Based on Both Similarities and Differences

Diversity's dynamic quality is often ignored because of our tendency to define ourselves in terms of who and what we are not—our differences. Thus, we believe that organizations should reconceptualize diversity so that it is understood in terms of both differences and similarities. In this approach to diversity, affiliations will no longer represent rigid categories; individuals will view themselves as having qualities in common rather than narrowly defining themselves in terms of how they differ, and the advantages of diversity can be realized while its potential disadvantages can be avoided or minimized.[54]

Furthermore, organizations must consider that not only do people identify with multiple dimensions of diversity simultaneously but the combinations of their multiple demographic categories influence group processes and outcomes. Demographic category memberships may be aligned by individuals or not; when they are, they create deeper divisions within groups than when they are not. Thus, when a number of dimensions of diversity line up they can create strong "faultlines" in a group.[55] For example, consider the workgroup represented in Figure 1-3. In Panel A, the group is divided along categories of sex, race, age, and function, so that a strong faultline separates the men from the women (also, the whites from the Asians, the young from the midcareer, and the finance analysts from the marketers). In Panel B, however, no strong subgroups are likely to form, because the dimensions of diversity are not aligned. The strength of faultlines, and not just the amount of diversity in a group, may affect group morale, conflict, and performance.[56]

Diversity Is Rooted in Nonessentialist Thought

When defining one's diversity in terms of specific categories like race or age, it is easy to fall into the trap of essentialist thinking. Categorizing people or inviting them to categorize themselves can lead to essentializing—making the assumption that a characteristic, or set of characteristics, is the essential nature of all members of a group.

| FIGURE 1-3   Examples of Strong and Weak Faultlines |

A: Strong Faultline

Group Member	Sex	Race	Age	Functional Expertise
1	Male	White	26	Finance
2	Male	White	30	Finance
3	Male	White	27	Finance
4	Female	Asian	47	Marketing
5	Female	Asian	53	Marketing

B: Weak Faultline

Group Member	Sex	Race	Age	Functional Expertise
1	Male	White	53	Finance
2	Male	White	30	Marketing
3	Male	Asian	27	Finance
4	Female	White	47	Marketing
5	Female	Asian	26	Finance

Essentialism, as discussed by Litvin, is damaging because it "encourages individuals to immediately attribute their colleagues' thoughts and behaviors to their demographic category membership."[57]

An example of essentialist thinking is presuming that because someone is a woman, it is in her nature to want children. Although it may be true that most women have at least one child,[58] it is not the case that maternal desires are necessarily part of what it means to be a woman. Other examples of essentializing include assumptions such as the following: All Asian Americans are strong quantitative thinkers; all women use a relationship-based communication style; and all men are persuaded by hard facts rather than emotional appeal. It is important to remember the differences (and similarities) among individuals within a group and not just the differences (and similarities) between groups. Although it is much easier to simply categorize people as members of groups, a nonessentialist framework transcends such generalizations while encouraging us to see the complexities of each individual.

Diversity Is Directly Related to How One Experiences Work

In discussions of workplace diversity, it seems obvious that diversity should be examined in the context of how it informs the way in which one approaches his or her job. The reality, however, is that diversity is often incorporated superficially in an organization, for instance, simply mentioned in a mission statement or articulated as a value and pursued only in terms of numbers of diverse employees, when it should, by contrast, be considered in terms of its direct relation to how employees perceive and perform their work and interact with both their colleagues and those outside their organizations. As explained by Thomas and Ely, companies that effectively manage diversity have developed "an outlook on diversity that enables them to incorporate employees' perspectives into the main work of the organization and to enhance work by rethinking primary tasks and redefining markets, products, strategies, missions, business practices, and even cultures."[59]

> ## WHAT DO YOU THINK?
> What principles are the most important in defining and understanding diversity? Why?

In sum, these five principles provide a guideline for developing a representative framework for understanding diversity. Organizational leaders have struggled not only to define diversity but also to formulate an approach to direct and shape their philosophy on diversity and to help them implement diversity initiatives.

STEP 3: UNDERSTANDING LEADERSHIP-BASED ORGANIZATIONAL PARADIGMS FOR MANAGING DIVERSITY

According to Thomas and Ely, since before the civil rights era, organizational and political leaders have embraced various paradigms, or approaches, for understanding and managing diversity. These paradigms include the resistance paradigm, the discrimination-and-fairness paradigm, the access-and-legitimacy paradigm, and the integration-and-learning paradigm. Working in tandem with these paradigms are the rhetorics of resistance, affirmative action, valuing diversity, and diversity management.

Although these paradigms developed, in turn, from prior to the civil rights era (resistance) to the present day (integration/learning), we believe that they should not be seen as a continuous trend toward improved diversity management in American business. To assume that one approach has built on another and that progress has been made through this history does not account for the diversity paradoxes that often exist in today's workplace. An example of one such diversity paradox is that many progressive organizations incorporate diversity management systemically and integratively yet still contain pockets of serious resistance against diversity. Thus, although we generally discuss the following approaches chronologically, their manifestations in real organizations do not always follow such a clear, progressive trajectory.

The Resistance Paradigm

The resistance paradigm represents an approach based on the rejection and evasion of diversity and diversity initiatives. Although this perspective was more commonly expressed in the United States prior to the civil rights movement, it continued into the 1970s and beyond. For many years, management in a number of industries and occupations consisted of largely homogeneous groups of white men; diversity remained misunderstood and unappreciated.[60] Much of the workforce was made up of immigrants and/or ethnic minorities, but in an effort to maintain privilege, established majorities among both managers and blue-collar workers resisted changes in workplace demographic diversity—particularly in terms of color of skin and gender—because of outright prejudice or because they believed that minority groups might gain power and influence, which they wanted to avoid.[61]

The Rhetoric of Resistance

As the resistance paradigm upholds diversity as more of a threat than an opportunity, the rhetoric of resistance takes the form, for example, of "defiant assertions that changes are inefficient or unacceptable to shareholders because they increase costs and reduce profits."[62]

Exemplifying this rhetoric is the case of Cracker Barrel Restaurants and its founder Dan Evins, who established the company in 1969. In January 1991 when Evins was president, chief executive officer, and chairman of the board, Cracker Barrel blatantly discriminated against gay men and lesbians working in its restaurants. Reflecting the rhetoric of resistance, Cracker Barrel maintained that because it was "founded upon a concept of traditional American values" it was deemed "inconsistent with our concept and values and ... with those of our customer base, to continue to employ individuals ... whose sexual preferences fail to demonstrate normal heterosexual values which have been the foundation of families in our society."[63]

WHAT DO YOU THINK?
What other organizations can you identify that exemplify the resistance paradigm and, as a result, the rhetoric of resistance?

The Discrimination-and-Fairness Paradigm
Organizations that experience moderate pressures to incorporate diversity often embrace the discrimination-and-fairness paradigm. This approach, often adopted in the late 1960s and 1970s, is based on accommodating the legal responsibilities of diversity, specifically in terms of federal mandates. The underlying philosophy of this paradigm is described by Thomas and Ely as follows: "Prejudice has kept members of certain demographic groups out of organizations" and "[a]s a matter of fairness and to comply with federal mandates, we need to work toward restructuring the makeup of our organizations to let it more closely reflect that of society."[64]

The strength of this approach is that it makes efforts to recruit and, to some extent, to retain diverse employees, but this model treats all people within a given social demographic category as being the same. In other words, the paradigm's weakness is that it does not "allow employees to draw on their personal assets and perspectives to do their work more effectively."[65] Unsurprisingly, organizations that embrace this paradigm have no real strategy for managing diversity, since they believe that the minority view should "conform to the expectations of the organization's existing culture."[66]

The Rhetoric of Affirmative Action
Expressed in the discrimination-and-fairness paradigm is the rhetoric of affirmative action, which is grounded in moral and social responsibility with the goal of amending wrongs done in the past to those Americans—minorities and women in particular—who have been underrepresented in positions of organizational and political power.[67] The phrase "affirmative action" was first used in 1961 when President Kennedy issued an executive order that created the Committee on Equal Employment Opportunity and mandated that employers spending federally provided funds "take affirmative action" to ensure that hiring and employment practices were free of racial bias.[68]

Then, in 1965, President Lyndon Johnson issued an executive order requiring federal contractors to "take affirmative action to ensure that applicants are employed, and that employees are treated during employment without regard to their race, creed, color, or national origin."[69] In 1967 Johnson expanded the order to include affirmative action requirements to benefit women.

Although it was created as a temporary remedy to "level the playing field" for all Americans, affirmative action became, for many, synonymous with rhetoric such as "preferential treatment" and "quotas," which worked quickly to discredit the policy's original sentiment. Affirmative action has been strongly challenged in both political and judicial contexts. In a historic 2003 case involving the University of Michigan's admissions policies, the Supreme Court upheld the right of universities to continue to consider race as one element when selecting their students. In this situation, the Court found that affirmative action furthered "a compelling interest in obtaining the educational benefits that flow from a diverse student body."[70]

WHAT DO YOU THINK?
What other organizations can you identify that exemplify the discrimination-and-fairness paradigm and, as a result, a rhetoric of affirmative action?

The Access-and-Legitimacy Paradigm

Companies operating from the access-and-legitimacy paradigm, common in the 1980s and early 1990s, emphasize bottom-line reasons for incorporating diversity. In this approach, companies "accept and celebrate differences so they can better serve their diverse pool of customers."[71] The underlying philosophy of this paradigm is that because of diverse demographics in various markets, "new ethnic groups are quickly gaining consumer power," so organizations need "a demographically more diverse workforce to help . . . gain access to these differentiated segments." Employees with multilingual skills, for example, will help organizations to understand and serve customers better, thereby gaining "legitimacy" with them.[72]

On the positive side, this model creates opportunities for people from less represented groups to enter new positions in business because their diversity is, at least on some levels, valued by the organization. The paradigm's most serious limitation is obvious: When a business regards employees' experience as useful only to gain access to narrow markets, those employees are, and may feel, marginalized. In effect, the work of diverse employees is pigeonholed rather than integrated systemically throughout the organization.

The Rhetoric of Valuing Diversity

The rhetoric of valuing diversity, as used in the access-and-legitimacy paradigm, extends beyond the rhetoric of affirmative action by embracing "awareness, education, and positive recognition of the differences among people in the workforce."[73] Leaders who use this rhetoric are not just trying to satisfy federal guidelines under antidiscrimination law but rather are claiming to value the contributions that diverse employees make in an effort to create an inclusive work environment.

Andrea Jung has impressively leveraged diversity as a competitive advantage since she became CEO of Avon in 1999. Today, the once-struggling Avon boasts not only increased profits and innovations but also having more women in management positions than any other Fortune 500 company; in addition, people of color make up a third of Avon's workforce.[74] The company's famous direct-selling method now has a corps of 3.9 million independent sales representatives worldwide, many of whom are women of color selling products to a diverse clientele. Furthermore, Avon has been actively developing Latina-geared cosmetics called *Eres Tu (It Is You)* and has launched ad campaigns featuring women of color, including sisters Venus and Serena Williams, and Salma Hayek. John Fleming, regional vice president for Avon West, sums up Avon's diversity philosophy: "Avon is committed to diversity. The marketplace is becoming more and more diverse each year, thus the diversity we see in the marketplace must be reflected in our representative ranks and in our management ranks."[75]

WHAT DO YOU THINK?

What other organizations can you identify that exemplify the access-and-legitimacy paradigm and, as a result, a rhetoric of valuing diversity?

The Integration-and-Learning Paradigm

The integration-and-learning paradigm, which largely emerged in the 1990s, reflects characteristics of both the discrimination-and-fairness paradigm and the access-and-legitimacy paradigm but goes beyond them by embracing the business case for diversity and incorporating "employees' perspectives into the main work of the organization."[76] Leaders who adopt this approach recognize that employees frequently make decisions and choices at work that draw on their identity-group affiliations.[77] Executives expect that having a diverse workforce and management team will lead to better decisions and an enhanced bottom line.

Organizational leaders who adopt this paradigm are proactive about learning from diversity, encourage people to use their cultural experience at work, fight forms of dominance and subordination based on demographic categories, and ensure that conflicts related to diversity are acknowledged and resolved with sensitivity.[78] In addition, when using this approach, leadership "must recognize both the learning opportunities and the challenges that the expression of different perspectives presents for an organization."[79]

The Rhetoric of Diversity Management and Beyond

The rhetoric of diversity management, as expressed in the integration-and-learning paradigm, is different from both the rhetoric of affirmative action and the rhetoric of valuing diversity, specifically because it maintains that effective diversity management creates not only a competitive advantage in consumer markets but an environment in which differences are "valued and allowed to influence positively [organizational members'] experience in and contribution to the work of the organization."[80]

Louis V. Gerstner, Jr., the CEO of IBM from 1995 to 2002, embraced a rhetoric of diversity management and was the catalyst for IBM's philosophical shift from "minimizing differences to amplifying them and to seizing on the business opportunities they present."[81] Gerstner and IBM's vice president of Global Workforce Diversity, Ted Childs, created eight diversity task forces made up of the following demographic executive-led constituencies: Asians, African Americans, gay/lesbian/ bisexual/transgender (GLBT) individuals, Hispanics, white men, Native Americans, people with disabilities, and women. After receiving feedback from these constituencies, Gerstner was better equipped to manage diversity systemically at IBM. And, IBM indeed looks different today than it did in 1995 with, for example, a 370 percent increase in the number of female executives worldwide, a 733 percent increase of GLBT executives, and a tripling of the number of executives with disabilities. According to Thomas, IBM succeeded in managing diversity because it had put in place four "pillars of change": IBM demonstrated leadership support, engaged employees as partners, integrated diversity with management practices, and linked diversity goals to business goals.[82]

WHAT DO YOU THINK?

What other organizations can you identify that exemplify the integration-and-learning paradigm and, as a result, a rhetoric of diversity management?

Although the rhetoric of diversity management presents a progressive way of understanding diversity in the workplace, this approach has not been thoroughly examined. While the business case argument has been assumed to be true by many organizations and commentators, managers still have little evidence of the effect of their diversity initiatives on the profitability of their businesses; and because of the emotion and passion often associated with diversity issues, this critically important discussion has—on many levels—been inadvertently avoided or actively silenced. As a result, we acknowledge counterarguments, challenges, and paradoxes associated with the business case.

STEP FOUR: DESCRIBING THE BUSINESS CASE FOR DIVERSITY

For the past decade, proponents of the business case for diversity have maintained that a diverse workforce yields a competitive advantage in terms of reducing costs, winning the competition for talent, and driving business growth. The business case is problematic, however. Before we discuss these problems, we briefly present each of the main components of the business case for diversity.

Cost Savings

The business case suggests that by embracing the value of diversity and diversity management, an organization will reduce costs and create a competitive advantage.[83] For example, if employees believe they are respected, they will stay with the company longer while maintaining strong accountability and productivity. The Society for Human Resource Management (SHRM) reminds us of the commonsense argument that a company's return on investment "is reduced when commitment and productivity are lost because employees feel disregarded, time is wasted with conflicts and misunderstandings, and money is spent on legal fees and settlements."[84] The business case for diversity assumes that managing diversity will lead to lower turnover among women and minorities, higher commitment from them, and fewer lawsuits. Lowering these factors should reduce costs to the company and, in turn, raise profits.

Turnover

Diversity scholars have noted the problem of high turnover rates for diverse employees—especially women and African Americans. Studies suggest that organizations have not been as successful in managing women and racio-ethnic minorities as they have white men.[85] In fact, the turnover rate for African Americans in the U.S. workforce is 40 percent higher than the rate for whites,[86] and women have higher turnover rates than men at all ages, not just during their childbearing years.[87]

The trend for women is particularly disturbing, as large numbers of highly qualified women are dropping out of mainstream careers. There are "pull" and "push" factors facing women who are choosing to leave the workplace. The pull factors include caring for both young children and elderly parents; the push factors include unsatisfying, unstimulating jobs that lack opportunity and exist in organizational cultures that uphold rigid policies, lack flexibility, and do little to thwart the glass ceiling effect.[88]

Commitment and Absenteeism

Scholars tend to agree that the absentee rate for women and nonwhite men is higher than it is for white males.[89] In many cases, family responsibilities, including child and elder care, are key factors underlying such high absenteeism.[90] Unsurprisingly, a Gallup poll found that mothers employed full time would prefer part-time employment, flexible hours, or telecommuting.[91] Companies are beginning to respond to work/family balance issues by offering changes in benefits, day care facilities, and flexible hours. With such changes, there is some evidence to suggest that organizational commitment and job satisfaction improve, absenteeism rates decline, and work efficiency increases.[92]

Discrimination Lawsuits

If a company invests in diversity training, it seems reasonable to suggest that the result will be an awareness of difference, and better interpersonal and intergroup relations, and thus fewer charges of discrimination.

Winning the Competition for Talent

An organization with a strong reputation for managing its diverse workforce will be more likely to attract and recruit the most talented workers. It is, therefore, a competitive advantage to be ranked in one of the "top diversity lists," such as *Fortune*'s "Best Companies for Minorities," *DiversityInc*'s "Top Companies for Diversity," or *Working Mother*'s "The 100 Best Companies for Working Mothers List." In addition, it is now common for talented recruits to "ask about an organization's diversity initiative and factor that into their employment decision."[93]

Driving Business Growth

Marketplace

In light of the increasingly global and diverse consumer market, one commonly heard business case argument is that the "cultural understanding" needed to market to specific demographic niches "resides most naturally in marketers with the same cultural background."[94] In fact, some scholars suggest that "[i]n some cases, people from a minority culture are more likely to give patronage to a representative of their own group" and "[f]or at least some products and services, a multicultural sales force may facilitate sales to members of minority culture groups.[95]

Creativity and Problem Solving

There is evidence to suggest that heterogeneous groups perform well in terms of making well-considered decisions.[96] When employees feel that their diverse backgrounds and perspectives are recognized and appreciated, the quality of creativity and problem solving is likely to improve. Researchers have suggested that "minority views can stimulate consideration of non-obvious alternatives in task groups" and that "persistent exposure to minority viewpoints stimulates creative thought processes."[97] Diverse workforces have the potential to solve problems better because of several factors: a greater variety of perspectives brought to bear on the issue; a higher level of critical analysis of alternatives; and because there is a lower probability of groupthink, a higher probability of generating creative solutions.[98] As explained by SHRM: "[E]mployees from varied backgrounds can bring different perspectives, ideas and solutions, as well as devise new products and services, challenge accepted views and generate a dynamic synergy that may yield new niches for business opportunity."[99]

Flexibility and Global Relations

According to the business case, the skills of flexibility and adaptability that are learned in a diverse workplace will extend generally and enhance the employee's ability to communicate across national and organizational cultures. Thus, diverse companies should be more able to compete successfully in a complex and global economy. Research suggests, for example, that companies with greater diversity make better business partners and merge more smoothly with other companies. The transition is less difficult for diverse companies because they are familiar with accepting the differences among people and within cultures.[100] Scholars argue that this characteristic of adaptability will enhance a company's ability to communicate more effectively when faced with developing and maintaining relations internationally.[101]

WHAT DO YOU THINK?
Which dimensions of the business case for diversity are the most persuasive? Why?

STEP 5: ACKNOWLEDGING THE ARGUMENTS CHALLENGING THE BUSINESS CASE FOR DIVERSITY

We believe that the business case for diversity represents an important yet early step toward understanding the intersection of diversity and the workplace. To consider the complexities of this relationship, we illuminate several assumptions underlying the business case and some questions about them.

Assumption: A Diverse Workforce Will Increase Overall Productivity

One of the most credible voices challenging the business case for diversity is Thomas A. Kochan, professor of management and codirector of the Institute for Work and Employment Research at MIT Sloan School of Management. Kochan maintains that "The diversity industry is built on sand. . . . The business case rhetoric for diversity is simply naïve and overdone. There are no strong positive or negative effects of gender or racial diversity on business performance."[102] This statement is based on the findings of a 5-year research project led by the Diversity Research Network and published in the journal *Human Resource Management.*

Unfortunately, perhaps, one cannot simply assume that a diversity program will benefit an organization; in fact, "[p]oorly managed diversity programs can be as harmful as well-run ones can be beneficial."[103] And, adding even more complexity, "[e]ven when diversity is managed well, the results are mixed. The best organizations can overcome the negative consequences of diversity, such as higher turnover and greater conflict in the workplace, but that still does not mean that there are [necessarily] positive outcomes."[104]

Assumption: The Results of Diversity Efforts Are Easy to Measure

Human resources executives often do not demand documented evidence proving the bottom-line value of diversity initiatives because, in many cases, it is both difficult and costly to obtain. Kochan explains that "it's easier to create activities and get credit for doing something than it is to create metrics and measures and hold people accountable."[105] According to Laura Liswood, senior advisor to Goldman Sachs on diversity issues and a scholar at the University of Maryland's Academy of Leadership, it is difficult to create valid measures of increased organizational performance because of diversity: "There is a connection between diversity and financial success, but typical profit-and-loss systems don't capture the benefits that diversity creates."[106] It is one thing to measure diversity in terms of recruitment, promotion, or turnover rates; but it is entirely different to measure the full strategic or financial impact of diversity initiatives.

Assumption: Diverse Employees Embrace Diversity Initiatives

With very little discussion of potential resistance from diverse employees, it is often assumed that they will embrace a company's diversity plan. And when diversity programs are designed to empower diverse employees from a number of different affiliations, it is indeed curious that, as one study found, "[m]any employees, even women and other minority groups, think corporate diversity programs benefit only black employees."[107] Also intriguing is that, in the same study, African American employees also were critical of corporate diversity efforts.[108]

Assumption: Diversity Training Adds Value to an Organization

Diversity training programs are often questioned and have even been charged with hampering an organization's efforts to understand diversity and use it as a business advantage.[109] Diversity training can indeed have negative effects by raising expectations; for example, diversity training may increase "the minorities' anger and frustration" while increasing "the white males' isolation and exclusionary behavior."[110] Training programs aimed at addressing subtle forms of discrimination and exclusion often do not lead to long-term changes in behaviors.[111] Instead, "group members and leaders must be trained to deal with group process issues, with a focus on communicating and problem-solving in diverse teams."[112]

It is paradoxical that despite large investments in diversity training (it is an estimated $8 billion industry), the total number of discrimination charges filed with the EEOC have increased steadily since 1996—hitting a 7-year high in 2002—within the categories of race, sex, national origin, religion, age, and disability.[113] This trend may represent increased dissatisfaction because of organizational failures despite the efforts of managers and consultants, or increased expectations; alternatively, increased awareness of these issues may simply have made it easier to recognize problems and enter complaints. In other words, factors leading to the increase of filings with the EEOC may include real failure, higher expectations, or increased awareness.

Assumption: Diverse Employees Are More Likely to Capitalize on Diverse Markets

One of the most frequently made business case arguments is that by hiring diverse employees, organizations will be able to capitalize on diverse markets. This claim rests on the assumption that customers desire to be served by those who physically resemble themselves. Evidence to support this argument, however, is lacking. The Diversity Research Network, for example, "finds no consistent evidence that most customers care whether the salespeople who serve them are of the same race or gender."[114] In short, there is no clear proof that diversity causes better market performance. Indeed, the relationship between diversity and performance may be the reverse: Better-performing companies may simply attract the best talent among all groups of workers.[115]

Assumption: The Relationship between White Men and Diversity Is Clearly Articulated

Some diversity scholars use an expansive definition of diversity so that no group—especially white men—feels excluded, whereas other scholars fail even to address the relationship between the dominant group that is white men and diversity. Sondra Thiederman, president of Cross-Cultural Communications, a San Diego–based consulting firm for workplace diversity and cross-cultural business practices, believes that one common mistake that diversity advocates make is failing to incorporate the majority population in their strategies.[116] According to DiversityInc.com, the role of the diversity manager is to help the white-male employee understand and embrace the diversity movement by reassuring him that he is not the enemy; helping him see his position of privilege; and explaining how diversity is not only a societal value but also a competitive advantage.[117] Another approach is to invite white-male employees to become part of the organization's diverse culture by, for example, participating in a diversity-strategy group, mentoring and coaching people from nondominant groups, or organizing the minority development programs or minority recruitment.[118]

Most discussions of diversity neglect any recognition of the diversity within the "white male" category. When looked at from a nonessentialist perspective, white-male employees may affiliate themselves just as strongly with their religion, sexual orientation, parental status, or age, as with their race. For example, white men may experience discrimination because they are Jewish, gay, a single parent, or an older worker. Lost in the business case rhetoric is a discussion of the multiple layers of diversity within the category white male, a clear method for making the white male voice legitimate in the conversation about managing diversity, and acknowledgment that white males also represent a protected class under the category "color of skin" as defined by the federal government.

WHAT DO YOU THINK?

Are there other assumptions underlying the business case for diversity that should be addressed?

Summary and Conclusion

The U.S. workforce is more diverse than ever before and will become more so with increasing globalization. The widely believed business case for diversity holds that managing diversity well can lead to improved organizational performance. This may be true, but it is clear that managing diversity poorly can lead to disastrous results. If managers lead a diverse organization poorly, they will engender high levels of interpersonal conflict and low levels of group cohesion, employee morale, and organizational commitment. There are no easy solutions to managing effectively in general, let alone managing a diverse workforce effectively. Managers should recognize the complexity of this task and embrace it as a learning opportunity for themselves and their organizations.

In sum, managing diversity well depends on many of the same skills as managing effectively in general. In this essay we have introduced students to the need to manage diversity, alternative models for thinking about how to do so, and some of the complex issues that make that task challenging. Management is difficult, fraught with much uncertainty, and recognizing the complexities that increase that uncertainty is important in helping students learn how to recognize effective management and become effective organizational members and managers.

Notes

1. American Express, "Diversity: Business Formula for Success," http://www10. americanexpress.com/sif/cda/page/0,1641, 13345,00.asp.
2. Marriott International's statement on diversity, http://marriott.com/corporateinfo/ culture/Diversity.mi.
3. Deloitte & Touche, "About Diversity & Inclusion," http://www.deloitte.com/dtt/ section_node/0,1042,sid%3D2271,00.html.
4. Starbucks, "Diversity: Diversity Is Who We Are," www.starbucks.com/aboutus/ SB-DIVERSITY-FIN.pdf.
5. Xerox, "Diversity: Making All the Difference," www.xerox.com/diversity.
6. Ibid.
7. Fay Hansen, "Diversity's Business Case Doesn't Add Up," *Workforce.com,* April 2003, www.workforce.com/archive/ feature/23/42/49/index.php.
8. Ibid.
9. Irwin Speizer, "Diversity on the Menu," *Workforce Management,* November 2004, 41–45, www.workforce.com/archive/ feature/23/88/37/index.php
10. Ibid.
11. Discussions of the business case for diversity can be found at www.shrm.org/.
12. Thomas Kochan and others, "The Effects of Diversity on Business Performance: Report of the Diversity Research Network," *Human Resource Management* 42 (Spring 2003): 3–21.
13. U.S. Census Bureau, "U.S. Interim Projections by Age, Sex, Race, and Hispanic Origin," March 18, 2004.
14. Ibid.
15. Ibid.
16. U.S. Census Bureau, http://www.census. gov/, DiversityInc Factoids & Style Guide, 26.
17. Ibid., 33.
18. Witeck-Combs and Harris Interactive, *DiversityInc Factoids & Style Guide,* 27.
19. U.S. Bureau of Labor Statistics, *Monthly Labor Review,* April 2001.
20. "Shifting Demographics," www.diversityinc. com/members/1694.cfm.
21. Betsy Morris, "How Corporate America Is Betraying Women," *Fortune,* January 10, 2005, 66.
22. Management Leadership for Tomorrow, *DiversityInc Factoids & Style Guide,* 76.

23. Morris, "How Corporate America Is Betraying Women," 70.

24. Ibid.

25. Stephanie Armour, "Pregnant Workers Report Growing Discrimination," *USA Today,* February 16, 2005, www.usatoday.com/money/workplace/2005-02-16-pregnancy-bias-usat_x.htm.

26. Harris Interactive and Witech-Combs, *DiversityInc Factoids & Style Guide,* 82.

27. David C. Stapleton and Richard V. Burkhauser, eds; *The Decline in Employment of People with Disabilities: A Policy Puzzle* (Kalamazoo, Michigan: W.E. Upjohn Institute Research, 2003).

28. "Landmark Disability Survey Finds Pervasive Disadvantage: 2004 N.O.D./Harris Survey Documents Trends Impacting 54 Million Americans," June 25, 2004. http://www.nod.org/. For more information, see http://www.adaportal.org; http://www.ilr.cornell.edu/ped/DisabilityStatistics/; http://www.dsc. ucsf.edu/main.php; http://www.worksupport.com/Main/factsres.asp.

29. Health Insurance Association of America, http://www.employerhealth.com/HER_sample_pages/sp3411.htm.

30. Douglas Holbrook, "Breaking the Silver Ceiling: A New Generation of Older Americans Redefining the New Rules of the Workplace; Testimony before the Senate Special Committee on Aging," September 20, 2004, http://www.aarp.org/research/ press/testimony/Articles/a2004-09-22-aging.html.

31. Michelle Conlin, "Religion in the Workplace: The Growing Presence of Spirituality in Corporate America," *Business Week,* November 1, 1999, http://www.businessweek.com/archives/1999/b3653001.arc.htm.

32. Conlin, "Religion in the Workplace," http://www.businessweek.com/archives/1999/b3653001.arc.htm.

33. Selig Center for Economic Growth, http://www.selig.uga.edu/; *DiversityInc Factoids & Style Guide,* 88.

34. Ibid., 92.

35. Witech-Combs Communications, *DiversityInc Factoids & Style Guide,* 96.

36. SHRM's definition of diversity is available at www.shrm.org/diversity/definingdiversity.asp.

37. Taylor Cox, Jr., *Creating the Multicultural Organization: A Strategy for Capturing the Power of Diversity* (San Francisco: Jossey-Bass, 2001), 3–4. See also, Cox, *Cultural Diversity in Organizations: Theory, Research & Practice* (San Francisco: Berrett-Koehler, 1993).

38. Cox, *Creating the Multicultural Organization,* 3–4.

39. Marilyn Loden, *Implementing Diversity* (New York: McGraw-Hill, 1996), 13.

40. Ibid., 14.

41. Ibid., 15.

42. Ibid., 15.

43. Ibid., 16.

44. Lee Gardenswartz and Anita Rowe, *Diverse Teams at Work: Capitalizing on the Power of Diversity* (New York: McGraw-Hill, 1994), 32.

45. Ibid., 32.

46. Ibid.

47. R. Roosevelt Thomas, Jr., *Redefining Diversity* (New York: AMACOM, 1996), 5. See also, R. Thomas, Jr., *Beyond Race and Gender: Unleashing the Power of Your Total Work Force by Managing Diversity* (New York: AMACOM, 1991).

48. R. Thomas, Jr., *Redefining Diversity,* 7–8.

49. David A. Thomas and Robin J. Ely, "Making Difference Matter: A New Paradigm for Managing Diversity," in *Harvard Business Review on Managing Diversity* (Boston: Harvard Business School Publishing Corp., 2001), 36.

50. Kali Saposnick, "Managing Diversity as a Key Organizational Resource: An Interview with David Thomas," *Leverage Points,* no. 37, Pegasus Communications (2003), www.pegasus.com.com/levpoints/thomasint.html.

51. Thomas and Ely, "Making Difference Matter," 36–37.

52. U.S. 2000 Census Bureau, http://www.census. gov/prod/cen2000/dp1/2kh00.pdf.

53. Deborah R. Litvin, "The Discourse of Diversity: From Biology to Management," *Discourse and Organization* 4, no. 2 (1997): 202.

54. Jeffrey T. Polzer, Laurie P. Milton, and William B. Swann, Jr. "Capitalizing on Diversity: Interpersonal Congruence in Small Work Groups," *Administrative Science Quarterly* 47 (June 2002): 296–325.

55. Dora C. Lau and Keith J. Murnigham, "Demographic Diversity and Faultlines: The Compositional Dynamics of Organizational Groups," *Academy of Management Review* 23 (1998): 325–40.

56. Sherry M. B. Thatcher, Karen A. Jehn, and Elaine Zanutto, "Cracks in Diversity Research: The Effects of Diversity Faultlines on Conflict and Performance," *Group Decision and Negotiation* 12 (2003): 217–41.

57. Litvin, "*The Discourse of Diversity,*" 204, 207.

58. Barbara Downs, "Fertility of American Women: June 2002," *Current Population Reports,* October 2003, 20–548, http://www.census.gov/prod/2003pubs/p20-548.pdf.

59. Thomas and Ely, "Making Difference Matter," 48.

60. Parshotam Dass and Barbara Parker, "Strategies for Managing Human Resource Diversity: From Resistance to Learning," *Academy of Management Executive* 13 (1999): 68–80.

61. Ibid.

62. Ibid.

63. John Howard, "The Cracker Barrel Restaurants," in Kathryn A. Cañas and Harris Sondak, *The Opportunity of Workplace Diversity: Theory, Cases, and Exercises* (New Jersey: Prentice Hall, 2006). For more information on how Cracker Barrel changed its discrimination policy in 2002, see "Cracker Barrel Ends Discrimination Policy," http://gay.com/news/article.html?2002/12/05/4; and "HRC Praises Cracker Barrel's Decision to Prohibit Discrimination Based on Sexual Orientation," http://tgcrossroads.org/news/archive.asp?aid=513.

64. Thomas and Ely, "Making Difference Matter," 38.

65. Ibid.

66. Saposnick, "Managing Diversity as a Key Organizational Resource." www.pegasus.com/levpoints/thomasint.html.

67. "How Is a Diversity Initiative Different from My Organization's Affirmative Action Plan?" SHRMOnline, http://www.shrm.org/diversity/diversityvsaffirmaction.asp.

68. More information on Executive Order 10925 is available at http://www.eeoc.gov/abouteeoc/35th/thelaw/eo-10925.html; http://teachingamericanhistory.org/library/index.asp?document=541; and http://www.infoplease.com/spot/affirmativetimeline1.html.

69. More information on Executive Order 11246 is available from http://www.dol.gov/esa/regs/compliance/ofccp/fs11246.htm; http://www.elinfonet.com/11246sum.php; and http://www.now.org/nnt/08-95/affirmhs.html.

70. Borgna Brunner, "Bakke and Beyond: A History and Timeline of Affirmative Action," http://www.infoplease.com/spot/affirmative1.html. For more on this issue, see "U.S. Supreme Court Rules on University of Michigan Cases," http://umich.edu/news/Releases/2003/Jun03/supremecourt.html, and "Split Ruling on Affirmative Action," http://www.npr.org/news/specials/michigan.

71. Saposnick, "Managing Diversity as a Key Organizational Resource," www.pegasus.com/levpoints/thomasint.html.

72. Thomas and Ely, "Making Difference Matter," 44.

73. "How Is a Diversity Initiative Different from My Organization's Affirmative Action Plan?" SHRMOnline, http://www.shrm.org/diversity/diversityvsaffirmaction.asp.

74. Linda Bean, "Avon: Diversity Key to Rebuilding an Ailing Brand," *DiversityInc.com,* December 6, 2004, www.diversityinc.com/members/10704.cfm.

75. "110 Years of Direct Selling Success," MinorityCareer.com: Online Employment Opportunities Resource, http://www.minoritycareer.com/features2.html.

76. Thomas and Ely, "Making Difference Matter," 47.

77. Ibid., 49.

78. Ibid., 34.

79. Ibid., 52–54.

80. Saposnick, "Managing Diversity as a Key Organizational Resource," www.pegasus.com/levpoints/thomasint.html.

81. David A. Thomas, "Diversity as Strategy," *Harvard Business Review,* September 2004, 100.

82. Ibid., 104–107.

83. Peter Wright, Stephen P. Ferris, Janine S. Hiller, and Mark Kroll, "Competitiveness through Management of Diversity: Effects on Stock Price Valuation," *Academy of Management Journal* 38 (1995): 272–87.

84. "What Is the 'Business Case' for Diversity?" SHRMOnline, http://shrm.org/diversity.businesscase.asp.

85. Taylor H. Cox and Stacy Blake, "Managing Cultural Diversity: Implications for Organizational Competitiveness, *Academy of Management Executive* 5 (1991): 45–56.

86. Gail Robinson and Kathleen Dechant, "Building a Business Case for Diversity," *Academy of Management Executive,* 11, no. 3, (1997): 21–31.

87. Felice N. Schwartz, "Management Women and the New Facts of Life," *Harvard Business Review,* January 1989, 65–76.

88. Sylvia Ann Hewlett and Carolyn Buck Luce, "Off-Ramps and On-Ramps: Keeping Talented Women on the Road to Success," *Harvard Business Review,* March 2005, 43.

89. Robinson and Dechant, "Building a Business Case for Diversity," 231.

90. Ibid.

91. Hudson Institute. *Opportunity 2000: Creative Affirmative Action Strategies for a Changing Workforce* (Indianapolis, IN: Hudson Institute, 1988).

92. S. A. Youngblood and K. Chambers-Cook, "Child Care Assistance Can Improve Employee Attitudes and Behavior," *Personnel Administrator,* February 1984, 93–95.; J. S. Kim and A. F. Campagna, "Effects of Flextime on Employee Attendance and Performance: A Field Experiment," *Academy of Management Journal* 24 (1981): 729–41.

93. Norma Carr-Ruffino, *Diversity Success Strategies* (Boston: Butterworth-Heinemann, 1999), 11. See also, Carr-Ruffino, *Making Diversity Work* (New Jersey: Prentice Hall, 2005).

94. Robinson and Dechant, "Building a Business Case for Diversity," 233.

95. Cox and Blake, "Managing Cultural Diversity: Implications for Organizational Competitiveness," 47.

96. Warren E. Watson, Kamalesh Kumar, and Larry K. Michaelsen, "Cultural Diversity's Impact on Interaction Process and Performance: Comparing Homogeneous and Diverse Task Groups," *Academy of Management Journal* 36 (1993); P. L. McLeod and S. A. Lobel, "The Effects of Ethnic Diversity on Idea Generation in Small Groups," *Academy of Management Best Paper Proceedings,* 1992, 227–31; W. E. Watson, K. Kumar, and L. K. Michaelsen. "Cultural Diversity's Impact on Interaction Process and Performance: Comparing Homogeneous and Diverse Task Groups," *Academy of Management Journal* 36 (1993): 590–602.

97. Cox and Blake, "Managing Cultural Diversity: Implications for Organizational Competitiveness," 47.

98. Carr-Ruffino, *Diversity Success Strategies,* 13.

99. "What Is the 'Business Case' for Diversity?" SHRMOnline, http://shrm.org/diversity.businesscase.asp.

100. Sherry Kuczynski, "If Diversity, Then Higher Profits?" *HRMagazine* 44, no. 13 (1999): 69.

101. Robinson and Dechant, "Building a Business Case for Diversity," 235; Carr-Ruffino, *Diversity Success Strategies,* 13.

102. Hansen, www.workforce.com/archive/feature/23/42/49/index.php.

103. Kuczynski, "If Diversity, Then Higher Profits?" 69.

104. Thomas Kochan and others, "The Effects of Diversity on Business Performance: Report of the Diversity Research Network," *Human Resource Management* 42 (Spring 2003): 3–21. See also, A. S. Tsui, T. D. Egan, and C. A. O'Reilly, "Being Different, Relational Demography and Organizational Attachment," *Administrative Science Quarterly* 37 (1992): 549–79.

105. Hansen, www.workforce.com/archive/feature/23/42/49/index.php.

106. Ibid.

107. Martha Frase-Blunt, "Thwarting the Diversity Backlash," *HR Magazine,* June 2003, 137.

108. Ibid., 138.
109. Shari Caudron, "Training Can Damage Diversity Efforts," *Personnel Journal* 72 (April 1993): 50–62, http://www.workforce.com/archive/feature/22/20/86/index.php; Patricia L Nemetz and Sandra L Christensen, "The Challenge of Cultural Diversity: Harnessing a Diversity of Views to Understand Multiculturalism," *Academy of Management Review* 21 (April 1996): 434–62.
110. Ibid.
111. Thomas Kochan and others, "Effects of Diversity on Business Performance," 4.
112. Hansen, www.workforce.com/archive/feature/23/42/49/index.php.

113. Ibid.
114. Thomas Kochan and others, "Effects of Diversity on Business Performance," 16.
115. Kuczynski, "If Diversity, Then Higher Profits?" 68.
116. Frase-Blunt, "Thwarting the Diversity Backlash," 138.
117. Jordan T. Pine, "Getting White Men to Buy In: Corporate America's Biggest Challenge," *DiversityInc.com,* December 11, 2001, www.diversityinc.com/members/1939.cfm.
118. Yoji Cole, "White Men Can Be Diversity Leaders, Too," *DiversityInc.com,* October 11, 2002, http://www.diversityinc.com/members/3657.cfm.

2 | DIVERSITY IN THE WORKPLACE: A LEGAL PERSPECTIVE

There was a time when "diversity in the workplace" was a contradiction in terms. In fact, until the federal government required businesses and organizations to become more diverse by enacting legislation prohibiting employment discrimination and harassment, there was almost no incentive to hire a diverse staff.

Workplace discrimination and harassment law has evolved to include prohibitions against various types of conduct directed at specific groups of people. In the 40 years since the enactment of the prohibition of unlawful discrimination, common beliefs surrounding discrimination law have emerged. Whereas most people in today's society are aware that certain forms of discrimination and harassment in the workplace violate the law, they are often surprised to find that many types of discrimination and harassment, while impolite, are not illegal, and that in many cases an employee has no legal recourse for being mistreated.

Many parts of the law are simple and easy to understand. For example, a person cannot be treated differently or poorly in the workplace based on his or her age, as long as the employee is over 40. The analysis for such an "age-based" claim is not much more complicated than that. However, many parts of discrimination and harassment law are very difficult to digest and comprehend. For example, not only is the Americans with Disabilities Act (ADA) difficult for employers and employees to understand, but very few attorneys can explain all its nuances, and the federal courts have struggled for years to determine its proper scope and interpret its difficult language. For that reason, in this essay I spend more time on some issues than on others. The cases chosen as examples for this essay are often the seminal cases in each category but are sometimes just among the most interesting. The cases represent, in some way, the foundation of some particular piece of the law and sometimes the surprising and interesting claims and findings that result.

The demographics of the American workforce, and how an employer can run his or her business, changed with the passage of Title VII of the Civil Rights Act of 1964.[1] The Civil Rights Act of 1964 is the most sweeping and important civil rights legislation ever enacted in this country. The act applies to employers with 15 or more employees, because, it is assumed, that companies of that size are likely to engage in interstate commerce and therefore be subject to federal regulation.

With the passage of Title VII, the United States Congress intended to eliminate both employment discrimination as well as the broader economic and social effects of discrimination. However, gathering enough votes to pass Title VII was a difficult task.

P. Corper James, J. D., Woodbury & Kesler, Salt Lake City, Utah

The notes and legislative history of the act show that it was "sold" to skeptical members of Congress and the public as a sound economic policy, not as an important social or moral policy. According to congressional leaders at the time: "The failure of our society to extend job opportunities to the Negro is an economic waste. The purchasing power of the country is not being fully developed."[2]

Title VII outlaws discrimination in hiring, promoting, and the general treatment of employees. In addition, the law has since been expanded to include protection for vendors and patrons of businesses. When Title VII was first proposed, it included protection against discrimination based on race, national origin, color of skin, and religion. It did not originally include protection against gender-based discrimination.

In an attempt to kill Title VII, Representative Howard W. Smith from Virginia included a ban on gender discrimination. Smith assumed that the inclusion would encourage fellow representatives to oppose the legislation. Congress passed Title VII despite the amendment, and gender became a part of the law. Women's groups such as the National Women's Party had unsuccessfully lobbied for the inclusion of gender in Title VII, and Smith, in an attempt to kill the law, ironically accomplished what they could not.

ADMINISTRATION OF THE LAW

Title VII is administered by the Equal Employment Opportunity Commission (EEOC), an independent executive agency consisting of five presidentially appointed members who serve 5-year terms. Violations of Title VII are brought to the EEOC through agency investigation and individual complaints. A complaint or "charge" must be filed with the EEOC within 180 days after the occurrence of the alleged unlawful employment practice, unless there is a state or local organization operating under a similar state or local statute, in which case the claim can be placed with that organization.

If the claim is filed with a state or local agency, an EEOC claim may be filed up to 300 days after the alleged discrimination occurs, or 30 days after the local proceedings end, whichever occurs first. The investigating organization determines whether the charge has merit, or is "meritorious." If the charge is deemed meritorious, the EEOC attempts conciliation with the offending organization. If the charge is deemed nonmeritorious or no conciliation has been reached within 180 days, the EEOC notifies the person who filed the complaint in a "right to sue" letter. The charging party then has 90 days after receiving the letter to bring a civil action in federal court under Title VII.

AMENDMENTS TO TITLE VII

Title VII was expanded in 1967 with the Age Discrimination in Employment Act (ADEA), 29 United States Code, Sections 621–634; in 1974 with the Vietnam Veterans Readjustment Assistance Act of 1974, 38 United States Code, Section 2011; in 1978 with the Pregnancy Discrimination Act; and in 1990 with the ADA, 42 United States Code, Section 12101.

Today there are eight "protected classes." The protected classes comprise people that the United States Supreme Court and the United States Congress have determined have suffered a disproportionate share of discrimination as a result of their status as members of the protected class. Individuals within protected classes are therefore entitled to bring a federal lawsuit against an employer if they believe that they have been subjected to different or poor treatment in the workplace as a result of their protected class status. However, before an individual may file a lawsuit in federal court, he or she must first file a claim with the EEOC.

THE PROTECTED CLASSES

Race

Title VII does not specifically define race, and distinguishing among races is a difficult task. In general, people choose their race based on the categories found on federal or state employment applications. The general categories are familiar to most Americans: Caucasian/White, Asian, African American/Black, Pacific Islander/Native Hawaiian, American Indian/Alaskan Native. For the purposes of Title VII and employment discrimination, an employer may not treat an employee or applicant differently or poorly on the basis of race, generally based on those federal categories.

GRIGGS V. DUKE POWER CO.

An early case entitled *Griggs v. Duke Power Co.*[3] illustrates how Title VII can be applied in the workplace. It also illustrates how employers may try to circumvent the act. In *Griggs,* a North Carolina power company required employees to have a high school diploma or to pass a standardized general intelligence test as a condition of employment or transfer to jobs that were categorized as more than general labor. Traditionally, African American employees were not promoted beyond the general labor class of jobs. The company argued that the intelligence test was required for all employees regardless of race and therefore the company's policy did not violate Title VII. The United States Supreme Court determined that even though the test requirements were neutral on their face in terms of race, the requirements were not related to a "legitimate business purpose" and had an unfair impact on African Americans. In essence, the court held that the power company was unable to demonstrate how compliance with the requirements translated to successful performance of the jobs. As a result, the court ruled that the requirements were a violation of Title VII. ■

WHAT DO YOU THINK?

What was the power company really trying to do? How can a company demonstrate that employment screening procedures serve legitimate business purposes?

National Origin

National origin is a large and somewhat general category that includes a person's country of birth, ethnicity, ancestry, or culture. Although race and national origin may seem to be the same, they are in fact different. There are many people of the same race but from different cultures, ethnicities, and countries. For example, not all Americans are Caucasians, and not all Hispanics were born in Mexico. An employer cannot treat an employee or applicant differently or poorly based on his or her country of birth, ethnicity, ancestry, or culture.

FRAGANTE V. HONOLULU

In *Fragante v. Honolulu,*[4] a Filipino applicant was rejected despite good qualifications and scores on a preemployment exam. The applicant spoke English with a thick Filipino accent. The position required the clerk to deal with 330 angry, English-speaking customers per day by telephone. The applicant sued claiming national origin discrimination. The federal appeals court ultimately held that the requirement that clerks be able to communicate effectively in English was necessary to the job and thus was a bona fide occupational qualification that satisfied a legitimate business purpose under Title VII. Therefore, the city's rejection of the applicant was not a violation of Title VII. ■

WHAT DO YOU THINK?

Under this rule, when can a company discipline, terminate, or refuse to hire an employee?

Color of Skin

Color of skin can be distinguished from race and national origin. Two people may be from the same country and of the same race, but may still have different colors of skin. Title VII makes it illegal for an employer to treat an employee or applicant differently or poorly based on his or her color of skin—regardless of the color. Some people struggle with this category because this classification does not apply to only one color of skin; it applies to all colors of skin.

EQUAL EMPLOYMENT OPPORTUNITY COMMISSION V. TRAILWAYS, INC.

In *Equal Employment Opportunity Commission v. Trailways, Inc.,*[5] an African American employee filed a discrimination charge with the EEOC based on color of skin and race alleging that his employer's prohibition of beards had a disparate impact on African Americans who suffer from a disease known as pseudofolliculitis barbae (PFB). For people with PFB, shaving can cause serious physical consequences including infection and facial scarring. The EEOC found for the employee and brought the lawsuit against the company claiming that PFB is a condition unique to African Americans and based on their color of skin, and that therefore the company's policy had a disparate impact on African American employees. The court found for the EEOC and held that the evidence demonstrated that the 25 percent of the male African American workforce who suffer from the condition were effectively excluded from the company's job market as a class because of their color of skin and this racial trait. ■

On a related note, the commonly used term *reverse discrimination* is often used in circumstances in which there is discrimination against a person identified in a majority group. Reverse discrimination is a social construct that has no legal application. Title VII applies to all people regardless of status as a member of a majority or a minority group.

Religion

Religion could be considered the first protected class given the role religious freedom played in the early stages of the founding of the United States. According to Title VII, the religion category includes all aspects of religious observance and practice, as well as belief. Title VII defines belief broadly to include almost any belief system, or lack of belief in any particular traditional belief system, including agnosticism and atheism. In the employment context, an employer may not treat an employee or applicant differently or poorly because of his or her beliefs. In addition, the act requires that an employer accommodate an employee's or applicant's observance of his or her religious beliefs when reasonable. An accommodation is reasonable when it does not cause undue hardship on the employer's business.

CORPORATION OF THE PRESIDING BISHOPRIC OF THE CHURCH OF JESUS CHRIST OF LATTER-DAY SAINTS V. AMOS

In *Corporation of the Presiding Bishopric of the Church of Jesus Christ of Latter-Day Saints v. Amos,*[6] two individuals fired from their jobs with church-owned corporations for failure to live by certain church standards brought an action for religious discrimination. In *Amos,* the United States Supreme Court upheld a provision exempting religious organizations from Title VII's prohibition against discrimination in employment on the basis of religion. The holding of the *Amos* case means that churches can discriminate on the basis of religion in favor of their own members. ■

WHAT DO YOU THINK?
What impact do you think the Court's ruling has had on religious universities such as Brigham Young University or the University of Notre Dame?

Age
The ADEA prohibits employers from discriminating against employees based on age. The act applies only to workers age 40 and over.

GENERAL DYNAMICS LAND SYSTEMS, INC. V. CLINE

In *General Dynamics Land Systems, Inc. v. Cline,*[7] the United States Supreme Court upheld an amended collective bargaining agreement that eliminated the company's obligation to provide health benefits to retired employees, except for current workers at least 50 years old. Workers under 40 sued under Title VII. The court held that workers under 40 did not have a claim, holding that Title VII is not designed to stop an employer from favoring an older employee over a younger one. ∎

WHAT DO YOU THINK?
Do workers who are under the age of 40 have any recourse against age-based discrimination? Should they?

Veterans

In the employment context, this protection applies only to Vietnam veterans and disabled veterans.[8] The statutes that have been enacted likely protect only those two groups of veterans, since those groups have had the most difficulty assimilating into the workforce. Of course, in the future the courts could expand the class to include a wider scope of veterans.

UNITED STATES V. BOARD OF TRUSTEES OF ILLINOIS STATE UNIVERSITY

In *United States v. Board of Trustees of Illinois State University,*[9] the federal court held that a hiring program adopted to circumvent a lawful veterans' preference program violated Title VII. Under the program, veterans were given preference points on an employment exam that allowed many to be hired. The majority of the veterans that applied for and received jobs were white males. The university attempted to alter the system to promote the hiring of more women and minorities. The federal court held that the university's attempt to alter the system amounted to discrimination against white males and that the veterans' preference was lawful. This case illustrates a virtual exception to Title VII. In this case, despite the fact that the veterans' preference law created a disparate impact on women and minorities, the court held that that preference was lawful. ∎

Disability

In 1991, the ADA became the single most important employment law of its generation. The ADA includes protection from discrimination based on a disability as well as requirements for employers and those offering other public facilities regarding access and accommodations for disabled employees, vendors, and patrons.

- The ADA defines a disability as a physical or mental impairment that substantially limits one or more major life activities.
- "Impairment" is defined as a diagnosable physiological, mental, or psychological disorder or condition.

- "Substantially limits" is defined as limited more than the average person based on the nature and severity of the condition, and the duration of the condition.
- "Major life activities" are defined as those things necessary to live, such as walking, talking, breathing, seeing, hearing, learning, sitting, standing, lifting, sleeping, working, and caring for oneself.

If an employee is substantially limited in one or more of the major life activities, he or she may qualify as disabled. If the employee qualifies as disabled, he or she qualifies for protection under the three primary functions of the ADA: disability discrimination, reasonable accommodation, and access.

Disability Discrimination

The definition of discrimination based on disability is broader in scope than the other protected classes. An employee has a claim for discrimination if he or she (1) has a current disability, (2) has a record or history of a disability, or (3) is regarded as or perceived to be disabled. For example, an employee may be subjected to discrimination for a medical condition that he or she used to suffer from but has successfully treated or overcome. Mental and emotional disabilities and other medical conditions that are associated with social taboos generally fall into this category. Likewise, an employee may suffer discrimination based on a perceived disability. As with other protected classes, an employer may not discriminate against an employee, applicant, vendor, or patron based on a disability.

LANMAN V. JOHNSON COUNTY

In *Lanman v. Johnson County*,[10] decided in December 2004, a deputy sheriff sued the employing county alleging there was a hostile work environment in violation of the ADA after she had been called "crazy" and "nuts" and been asked "are you off your medication" and several other questions regarding her mental health. The court ruled that although an action could be brought under the ADA, the jokes and comments directed toward her did not fit within the "perceived disability" category of the ADA, since the comments were more likely a sign of personality conflicts and simple rude behavior and not evidence that her employer regarded her as "substantially limited in one or more major life activities." Simply rude or boorish behavior, while obviously not recommended in the workplace, is not illegal. ■

Reasonable Accommodation

If an individual is able to perform the essential functions of his or her job, with or without an accommodation, but there are barriers owing to disability, the employee may request an accommodation from his or her employer. Accommodations provided by employers range from a customized piece of equipment such as telecommunications devices for the deaf (TDD) or Braille machines, to raised or lowered desks, flexible schedules, or similar accommodations. An accommodation can come in any form as long as it is reasonable and not unduly burdensome for the employer. Unduly burdensome accommodations include those that are very costly and/or fundamentally alter the nature or operation of the employer's business. An employer may also deny an accommodation request that is a direct threat to the safety and health of employees.

All businesses should have a comprehensive procedure in place for dealing with accommodation requests. Employers should also beware that owing to the broad scope of disability discrimination, it is never appropriate for them to approach an employee about a perceived disability or unilaterally to recommend some type of accommodation. Disabled individuals must be the ones who request accommodations. Once an employee requests an accommodation or identifies that he or she is having difficulty performing the functions of the job owing to some medical condition, the ADA requires the employer to try to accommodate that employee.

PGA TOUR, INC. V. MARTIN

In *PGA Tour, Inc. v. Martin*,[11] the United States Supreme Court ruled that allowing golfer Casey Martin to ride in a golf cart owing to his disability was a reasonable accommodation, since it did not fundamentally alter the nature of the event. The Court's analysis included a discussion about the nature of the competition and the potential advantage gained by a cart user. ■

WHAT DO YOU THINK?

Does a golf cart give a golfer an advantage over competitors who are required to walk?

TOYOTA MOTOR MANUFACTURING, KENTUCKY, INC. V. WILLIAMS

In *Toyota Motor Manufacturing, Kentucky, Inc. v. Williams*,[12] the United States Supreme Court held that an assembly line worker was not substantially limited in the major life activity of performing manual tasks owing to her carpal tunnel syndrome. Although her condition affected her ability to do her job, it did not restrict her from engaging in activities that are central to most people's daily lives, and therefore she did not qualify as disabled. To some people's surprise, this case makes clear that although an employee may be unable to do a particular job, that inability does not necessarily mean that he or she is substantially limited in any major life activity. ■

Access

The ADA drastically altered the American business landscape with new accessibility requirements far broader than those imposed by the Rehabilitation Act of 1973. The ADA includes strict requirements for businesses, universities, sports stadiums, and virtually any other public place with regard to ramps, door width, parking, and accessible restrooms and facilities. The ADA takes the original economic philosophy of Title VII—particularly that the purchasing power of a large group of Americans is not being utilized—and extends it from the workplace to the marketplace, capitalizing on the "purchasing power" of disabled persons.

Sex/Gender

This category includes protection based not only on being male or female but also based on pregnancy and against sexual harassment.

Pregnancy Discrimination

Pregnancy discrimination was added in 1978 and protects women from being treated differently or poorly based on pregnancy, childbirth, or related medical conditions. In essence, an employer must treat a pregnant woman like anyone else who may need temporary accommodations for medical reasons.

Sexual Harassment

Sexual harassment evolved as a subcategory of gender discrimination. Prohibitions against sexual harassment, and the ADA, have had the greatest impact on the American workplace. Sexual harassment comes in two forms: quid pro quo and hostile work environment.

Quid Pro Quo Sexual Harassment   Quid pro quo is a Latin term that means "this for that." Quid pro quo sexual harassment occurs when a supervisor promises or confers benefits in return for sexual favors, or when a supervisor adversely affects an employee's status based on the employee's rejection of the sexual advances. For a situation to constitute quid pro quo sexual harassment, the perpetrator must maintain a position of power over the victim, and the victim must suffer some tangible employment action as a result of the harassment. An employer cannot promote, or demote, an employee based on his or her acceptance or rejection of sexual advances. Conditioning employment status on the acceptance of sexual advances is a violation of Title VII.

BURLINGTON INDUSTRIES, INC. V. ELLERTH

In *Burlington Industries, Inc. v. Ellerth,*[13] the United States Supreme Court distinguished between "quid pro quo" and "hostile work environment" sexual harassment when it ruled that a female employee who had been subject to a supervisor's sexual advances even though no tangible employment action had yet resulted may still have a hostile work environment claim. In today's workplace most supervisors are aware that soliciting sexual favors in exchange for job status is inappropriate and illegal, therefore making hostile environment cases much more prevalent. ■

Hostile Work Environment Sexual Harassment   Hostile work environment sexual harassment has less to do with job status and more to do with the job environment. An employee may make a claim for hostile work environment based on sexual jokes, comments, e-mails, or pictures in the workplace. Because hostile work environment sexual harassment is about the work environment, the relative employment positions of the perpetrator and victim are irrelevant. A supervisor can harass a subordinate, a subordinate can harass a supervisor, and coworkers of equal status can harass each other. In fact, since the focus of these claims is on the environment, a visitor, vendor, or patron of a business can assert a harassment claim if he or she is subjected to a hostile work environment. To prevail on a sexual harassment claim, a claimant must demonstrate each of the following:

1. ***He or she has been subjected to conduct that is sexual in nature.***   Employers who are trying to prevent this kind of conduct should not have difficulty defining "sexual in nature." Common sense dictates the difference between a sexual and a nonsexual pat on the back or comment about a coworker's appearance. Items or conduct of a sexual nature found in the workplace can be visual, physical, or verbal. Examples of visual materials might include photographs, calendars, e-mails, Web sites, and gestures that are sexual in nature. Examples of physical conduct include any touching, petting, patting, or grabbing that is sexual in nature. Examples of verbal conduct include jokes, comments, and stories that are sexual in nature. Cautious employers will attempt to keep any items or conduct that might be construed as sexual in nature out of the workplace.

2. ***The sexual conduct must be severe and/or pervasive.***   The law states that the sexual conduct must alter the work environment to the point that the victim can no longer remain in the workplace. Pervasive conduct is ongoing, widespread, or repetitive to the point that is has created a hostile environment. The mildest sexual jokes and comments can become pervasive over time to create a hostile work environment. In contrast, one incident can constitute hostile work environment harassment if it is severe enough. To be considered substantially severe, one incident almost always has to include sexual touching of some type. Regardless of the conduct, if it is relatively minor and has not altered the environment to the point that the victim can no longer come to work, the conduct will not rise to the level of sexual harassment.

3. ***The sexual conduct must be unwelcome and/or unwanted.***   Sexual conduct is not inherently unlawful. In fact, it is unlawful only when it is unwelcome or unwanted. The problem, of course, is that supervisors and coworkers often do not know when someone is going to be offended by a joke or comment. To prevail, a claimant must have in some way demonstrated his or her disapproval of the sexual conduct. A claimant may manifest unwelcomeness in a variety of ways, including telling the joke teller that his or her jokes are offensive, not participating, walking away, or reporting the conduct to a supervisor. The best rule to adopt is that since it is impossible to know how someone will react to sexual conduct, it is better to prohibit the conduct in the workplace altogether.

ELLISON V. BRADY

In *Ellison v. Brady,*[14] a federal appeals court established a "reasonable woman" standard, stating that the focus should be on the perspective of the victim. In *Ellison,* an employee was frightened by her coworker's subtle advances and strange love notes. The court held that a reasonable woman could have had a similar reaction and found that her perception was therefore reasonable. Other courts have extended the standard of reasonableness to all parties, male or female, claiming sexual harassment. Courts now generally call the standard the "reasonable person, similarly situated" standard. The standard evaluates the reasonableness of a person's claim based on who the claimant is, and how other, similarly situated people might react in the same situation. Thus, the standard prevents any outrageous, bad-faith claims from progressing in the courts. ■

Gender is no longer relevant to sexual harassment. Anyone can harass or be harassed; gender is not relevant to a sexual harassment claim. According to the law, a man can sexually harass another man just as he can sexually harass a woman. Likewise, a woman can sexually harass a man or another woman.

ONCALE V. SUNDOWNER OFFSHORE SERVICES, INC.

In *Oncale v. Sundowner Offshore Services, Inc.,*[15] the United States Supreme Court stated that same-gender sexual harassment qualifies under Title VII. In *Oncale,* a heterosexual male employee worked on an all-male crew on an oil platform in the Gulf of Mexico. The employee was subjected to humiliating sex-related actions by several male coworkers. The court held that the gender of the harassers and the harassed was irrelevant under Title VII and that the employee could bring an action under Title VII. ■

WHAT DO YOU THINK?
Does the *Oncale* finding challenge your stereotypes of sexual harassment?

When discussing sexual harassment, or any kind of harassment including racial, religious, or any other unlawful discrimination based on a protected class, it is important to remember that a party's intent is irrelevant. It is never an adequate defense to say "I was trying to be funny" or "I was trying to be friendly." The only relevant factor is how the affected person perceives the joke or comment. Since it is impossible to predict how people will respond to sexual or racial jokes or comments, such topics are better left out of the workplace.

In sum, any other classifications such as marital status, political affiliation, and weight are not protected classes. This means that an employer may discriminate against employees based on political affiliation, and the employees have no recourse in a federal or state court. Of course, such behavior by the employer will nevertheless likely affect the business negatively, such as through bad publicity or by word of mouth.

ADVICE FOR MANAGERS

Have a Title VII Policy and Procedure
Employers have a relatively simple and powerful defense against any Title VII claim. Developing a thorough, well-articulated equal opportunity policy, in conjunction with a complaint and investigation procedure, is the most important step a company can take to protect itself from any Title VII charge. The company or organization should require supervisors to adhere strictly to its policies and procedures and provide periodic training for supervisors and subordinates. A company's ability to demonstrate that

it has a policy that it follows and that it trains employees regularly will protect employers from losing most Title VII cases.

Be Clear about the "Legitimate Business Purpose" Concept

Of course, nothing can prevent an employee from making an internal complaint or filing a complaint with EEOC. Almost every company with more than 15 employees will at some point be asked to respond to a charge of unlawful discrimination or harassment. A company's first defense is that the company has a policy in place, the company followed the policy, and the employees were aware of the policy. A company may also defend itself with the "legitimate business purpose" concept. A company can do almost anything, including discriminate based on a protected class, if it can show it did so for a legitimate business purpose or out of business necessity.

For example, a construction company will not be required to hire a disabled person who cannot lift more than 25 pounds if the essential functions of the job include regularly lifting more than 25 pounds. In such a case the company is discriminating by not hiring the applicant based on his or her disability; however, the company has a legitimate business purpose for doing so. But again, companies must beware: What constitutes a "legitimate business purpose" and "essential functions of the job" are hotly contested issues. A company can get itself into trouble with definitions that are either too broad or too narrow in scope.

Develop Objective Job Criteria

Perhaps most important, a company can act in accord with the intent and language of Title VII by making all its hiring and firing decisions based on objective job criteria. How an employee performs his or her job should be the only factor in determining that employee's status. Companies should be blind to race, religion, gender, disability, or any other protected category. New hires, promotions, demotions, and terminations should be made without regard to any of the characteristics identified in the protected classes.

Do Not Retaliate

Title VII includes a provision that protects any employee from retaliation for lodging a complaint of discrimination or harassment. An employee cannot be demoted or terminated for filing a complaint or lawsuit. To be protected, the employee need not prevail on his or her complaint but rather must demonstrate a reasonable, good-faith belief that the complaint was valid. Under this provision, a company can find itself in trouble even if it wins a discrimination or harassment claim. Imagine a scenario in which an employee complains that he or she is being sexually harassed. The company immediately responds by investigating the claim, disciplining the alleged harassers, and preventing another incident. Or, imagine that the company conducts an investigation and finds that the allegations are not serious enough to warrant any action or discipline. In other words, in either case, the company does exactly what it is supposed to do. However, another problem arises if the complaint creates hard feelings that lead to a negative reaction. Imagine that one of the alleged harassers is a supervisor and that this person is so upset about the complaint that he or she scales back the complaining employee's job duties until the employee is fired 6 weeks later. Under these circumstances, the company may have a hard time defending itself against a retaliation claim.

ADVICE FOR EMPLOYEES

Follow Policies and Procedures

Employees have rights under Title VII, but they also have responsibilities. To prevail on a legal complaint or charge of discrimination or harassment, an employee must show that he or she at least generally followed all policies and procedures. This principle is important for two reasons. First, part of any analysis into a discrimination or harassment complaint is determining whether the employee followed the company's complaint procedure. Second, being a cooperative and productive employee makes it difficult for an employer to demonstrate a legitimate, nondiscriminatory reason for any discriminatory conduct.

Most companies have written policies and procedures in an employee handbook or other official company documents. Most employees also receive policy and procedure information and training at an orientation. If employees perform their job and follow any complaint guidelines, they increase their chances with any charge or complaint.

Behave Reasonably

Employees have a simple way to avoid being the subject of a Title VII allegation and to respond appropriately to unwanted conduct: Behave reasonably and professionally. It is not that difficult to determine when jokes or comments contain content that is "sexual in nature." Likewise, employees engaging in conversations pertaining to protected class issues should be respectful. Title VII is not intended to be a code of conduct that prohibits certain topics of discussion; it is intended to prevent members of protected classes from being treated differently or poorly based on protected-class status in the employment context. Realistically, employees will engage in personal conversations with each other on a wide variety of topics.

Although many lawyers would recommend to their corporate clients that all issues subject to Title VII protections not be discussed at all in the workplace, such a hope is, of course, not realistic; what managers should insist on, however, is that all organizational members be respectful in their discourse and avoid jokes, derogatory terms, and stereotypes. Likewise, an employee who is offended by a joke, comment, or other conduct should immediately report it to a supervisor or speak to the instigator. A little common sense and consideration is the best approach to any difficult workplace scenario.

A WORD ABOUT AFFIRMATIVE ACTION

Affirmative action is not a component of Title VII and does not generally affect the private sector. It does, however, affect government organizations and universities. One could argue that Title VII and affirmative action are opposites. Traditionally, affirmative action included preferences and quotas in interviewing and hiring, whereas Title VII outlawed differentiating between those who are part of a protected class and those who are not. By 2005 the two were more in harmony. Affirmative action currently requires government employers and state actors to actively recruit and reach out to minority candidates but does not allow quotas or preferences.[16]

THE FUTURE OF TITLE VII

There are many examples in the media of businesses and organizations that seem to struggle with managing a diverse workforce and have repeatedly dealt with Title VII claims; there are also many organizations that are flourishing under the law. However, the companies or organizations involved are not necessarily obvious ones.

For example, the Oakland Raiders football team is known for its commitment to excellence, rabid fans, and colorful collection of players. Not as well known, however, is that for more than 40 years, the Oakland Raiders have pioneered workplace diversity. The Raiders were the first to draft an African American quarterback in the first round of the amateur draft (Eldridge Dickey); the first to employ a Hispanic American quarterback (Tom Flores); and the first to hire a Hispanic American head coach (Tom Flores). Further, the team was the first in the NFL in the modern era to hire an African American head coach (Art Shell) and the first to boast a female chief executive officer (Amy Trask). The Raiders were also the first U.S. sports franchise to launch a separate alternative-language (Spanish) Web site and have since added German and Mandarin language sections to its Web site for its German and Chinese fans. The Raiders lead by example in the National Football League, and thousands of other organizations do likewise in their own business sectors.

The Raiders' approach is smart and effective because the American workplace is going to become only more diverse as the country's demographics continue to change. It is more important than ever for employers to understand when their or their employees' conduct is unlawful and how to protect themselves from the unwanted cost and scrutiny of a Title VII lawsuit. Accomplishing these goals is challenging, in part because employment discrimination law is fluid. Not only do the relevance and application of the various protected classes change over time, the categories themselves change.

For example, prior to September 11, 2001, the protection against discrimination based on national origin was rarely an issue. In the post 9/11 world, national origin litigation has become more prevalent, and relevant, as people of Middle Eastern descent have lately been discriminated against more frequently. Also, sexual orientation is not a federally protected class, but it is a protected class in varying degrees in several states and is protected by hundreds of businesses through company policy. Many believe that sexual orientation will eventually receive federally protected class status.

However Title VII changes in the future, it will continue to be an important law that protects employees from discriminatory workplace conduct and therefore fosters workplace diversity.

Notes

1. *U.S. Code* 2000 et seq.
2. *U.S. Code Cong. & Admin. News,* 88th Congress, 2nd sess., 1964, 2513–2517.
3. 401 U.S. 424 (1971).
4. 888 F.2d 591 (9th Cir. 1989).
5. 530 F. Supp. 54 (D. Colo. 1981).
6. 483 U.S. 327 (1987).
7. 540 U.S. 581 (2004).
8. See Vietnam Era Veterans' Readjustment Assistance Act of 1974, 38 *U.S. Code* 793, 794.
9. 944 F.Supp. 714 (C.D. Ill. 1996).
10. 2004 WL 3017258 (10th Cir.).
11. 532 U.S. 661 (2001).
12. 534 U.S. 184 (2002).
13. 524 U.S. 742 (1998).
14. 924 F.2d 872 (9th Cir. 1991).
15. 523 U.S. 75 (1998).
16. See *Gratz v. Bollinger,* 539 U.S. 244 (2003).

PART

II

MANAGING AND MISMANAGING

Case Studies on American Businesses

In this second part, "Managing and Mismanaging: Case Studies on American Businesses," we illustrate organizational mistakes and successes of U.S. businesses. This section reflects our belief that understanding diversity is facilitated through detailed examination of real case studies.

Our collection of comprehensive case studies focuses on how familiar organizations have grappled with diversity management. In particular, we consider seven dimensions of diversity and how organizations address them: gender (Augusta National and Mother's Work); race and national origin (Texaco and Wells Fargo); age (Ford Motor Co.); religion and spirituality (Tom's of Maine); sexual orientation (Cracker Barrel); disabilities (BOOST, General Motors, and IBM). We also include a case study about an exemplary organization (IBM). In addition to these cases, we have included timely *New York Times* articles and critical essays that further explore the complexities of each of these topics.

CHAPTER

3 ‖ GENDER

The federal government protects the rights of both men and women in the workplace under the protected class gender. In this chapter the focus is on women in the workplace, specifically because they are increasingly present and visible in the workforce and are often faced with a challenging set of circumstances as they attempt to balance work and family, advance up the corporate ladder, and function successfully in arenas traditionally dominated by men.

Objectives

- To examine the relationship between women and the workplace.

- To examine the complexities of women's experiences in the workplace.

- To examine why women often choose to leave their careers and how they face a variety of obstacles when attempting to reenter the workplace.

- To examine claims of gender discrimination in both public and private organizations.

Preview Questions

- Do women face special obstacles to advancing their careers?

- What can organizations do to make their female employees more productive at work and more satisfied as members of the organization?

- Are there circumstances under which either public or private organizations should be allowed to discriminate openly against women?

Some Important Dates

1839 Mississippi becomes the first state to grant women the right to hold property in their own name, with their husband's permission.

1869 The first women's suffrage law in the United States is passed in the territory of Wyoming.

1872 Susan B. Anthony is arrested in Rochester, New York, for trying to vote.

1890   Wyoming becomes the first state to grant women the right to vote in all elections.

1900   Every state has passed legislation modeled after New York's Married Women's Property Act (1848), granting married women some control over their property and earnings.

1920   The Nineteenth Amendment to the U.S. Constitution is ratified. It declares: "The right of citizens of the United States to vote shall not be denied or abridged by the United States or by any state on account of sex."

1963   The Equal Pay Act is passed by Congress, promising equitable wages for the same work, regardless of the race, color, religion, national origin, or sex of the worker.

1964   Title VII of the Civil Rights Act passes and includes a prohibition against employment discrimination on the basis of race, color, religion, national origin, or sex.

1969   In *Bowe v. Colgate-Palmolive Company,* 416 F. 2d 711 (7th Cir. 1969), the Seventh Circuit Court of Appeals rules that women meeting the physical requirements can work in many jobs that had previously been for men only.

1974   *Cleveland Board of Education v. LaFleur,* 414 U.S. 632 (1974), determines it is illegal to force pregnant women to take maternity leave on the assumption they are incapable of working in their physical condition.

1978   The Pregnancy Discrimination Act bans employment discrimination against pregnant women.

1981   The U.S. Supreme Court rules that excluding women from the draft is constitutional.

1997   Elaborating on Title IX of the Education Amendments of 1972 to the Civil Rights Act of 1964 (the first comprehensive federal law to prohibit sex discrimination against students and employees of educational institutions), the Supreme Court rules that college athletics programs must actively involve roughly equal numbers of men and women to qualify for federal support.

MORGAN STANLEY SETTLES BIAS SUIT WITH $54 MILLION

Morgan Stanley agreed yesterday to pay $54 million to settle a sex discrimination case rather than stand trial on the federal government's accusation that it denied equal pay and promotions to women in a division of its investment bank.

The settlement, which could cover as many as 340 women, is the second largest the Equal Employment Opportunity Commission has reached with a company

it sued and is the first with a major securities firm.

It came minutes before a lawyer for the agency would have switched on a projector and laid out the statistical evidence against the firm, and it averted the possibility that a jury could find Morgan Stanley, one of the most prestigious firms on Wall Street, guilty of sex discrimination. Testimony in the case was expected

---

Patrick McGeehan, New York Times (Late Edition (East Coast)), New York, N.Y.: Jul 13, 2004. pg. A. 1.
Copyright New York Times Company Jul 13, 2004.

to include some salacious details about trips to strip clubs and allegations of sexual harassment.

Immediately after the jury of eight women and four men filed into a federal courtroom in Lower Manhattan, Judge Richard M. Berman entered and told them an agreement had just been struck. Judge Berman, who had pressed the two sides to settle for more than two years, called the settlement a "watershed in safeguarding and promoting the rights of women on Wall Street."

The settlement came after a weekend of negotiating that involved Morgan Stanley's chairman and chief executive, Philip J. Purcell, and the chairwoman of the commission, Cari M. Dominguez.

In a statement, Mr. Purcell said: "We are proud of our commitment to diversity and would like to thank the E.E.O.C. staff for working with us to conclude this matter in such a positive way."

Along with paying the money to settle complaints, Morgan Stanley, which did not admit to any wrongdoing under the settlement, agreed to spend $2 million on diversity programs overseen by an outside monitor to improve the chances that women will succeed there, according to a consent decree the company signed with the commission. The company also must provide antidiscrimination training for managers and employees in the division that deals in stock trading for institutional clients.

Some other big Wall Street firms have been defending themselves against complaints of discrimination over the last eight years. Merrill Lynch and Smith Barney have paid more than $200 million combined to women who worked in their brokerage operations. A panel of arbitrators recently found that Merrill had engaged in sexual discrimination and awarded $2.2 million to one of its former brokers.

Elizabeth Grossman, the lead trial lawyer for the commission, said outside the courthouse yesterday that "discrimination is very much a problem" in the securities industry today. "I expect that we will hear more from women on Wall Street and from racial minorities on Wall Street," she said.

Morgan Stanley officials have fervently denied accusations of harassment and unequal treatment of women in its operations. But some Wall Street executives and lawyers said Morgan Stanley did not want to take the chance that the commission could persuade the jury that some of the allegations were valid.

"I don't think Morgan Stanley would have settled unless there was an element of truth there," said Muriel Siebert, a longtime brokerage executive who was the first woman to own a seat on the New York Stock Exchange. "There had to be something there or they wouldn't come up with $54 million."

Ms. Siebert said the outcome should cause directors of all Wall Street firms to question whether their employees are facing discrimination, but she acknowledged that $54 million would not do much financial harm. To Morgan Stanley, which earned more than $1 billion last quarter, that amount is "nothing," Ms. Siebert said.

"It may spill off their coffee cups in the morning," she said.

The $54 million settlement is the second-biggest sex discrimination settlement with the E.E.O.C. behind the $81 million that Publix Super Markets agreed to pay in 1997.

At least $12 million of the money to be paid by Morgan Stanley will go to one woman, Allison K. Schieffelin. Ms. Schieffelin, 42, was a successful bond saleswoman for Morgan Stanley, earning more than $1.3 million a year, when she first complained that she had been denied a promotion to managing director because

(continued)

of her sex. The commission took up her cause, eventually filing suit against the company on Sept. 10, 2001, under federal civil rights laws. The commission is charged with enforcing those laws in the workplace.

Ms. Schieffelin, who said in interviews with *The New York Times* in 2002 that she had sacrificed her personal life to get ahead at Morgan Stanley, was scheduled to testify first for the commission. She was eager to tell of the treatment she had endured and witnessed on the trading floor at Morgan Stanley's headquarters near Times Square, followed by the testimony of more than 20 other women with similar complaints, some involving behavior that could have proved embarrassing to the company.

In one instance, Ms. Schieffelin said, she arranged a group dinner with an important client at an exclusive restaurant in New York, only to be escorted into a cab afterward while her male co-workers took the client to a strip club. Ms. Schieffelin, who contacted the commission in 1998 to complain, was fired in 2000.

She contended that the firing was a retaliatory act, but Morgan Stanley officials countered that Ms. Schieffelin was fired for insubordination after turning hostile and disrespectful toward her supervisor, a woman who had recently received the promotion Ms. Schieffelin sought.

Other women who had worked in the division were prepared to recount more salacious tales, according to court filings. Some senior executives of the division were also expected to take the witness stand. As the prospect of that public spectacle approached, Morgan Stanley officials grew keener to settle.

On Sunday, Mr. Purcell called Ms. Dominguez, a commission spokesman said. They talked twice by phone in the evening, with the second conversation lasting until almost midnight, the spokesman said.

Lawyers continued the negotiation into early morning and told the judge of a prospective agreement about 9:30 a.m. The consent decree was signed in a room behind the judge's bench about 1 p.m., the time Ms. Grossman and Morgan Stanley's lead lawyer, Emily Nicklin, were scheduled to make their opening statements.

Judge Berman thanked Mr. Purcell and Ms. Dominguez for becoming involved. After he announced the terms of the settlement to a crowd of more than 120 people in a courtroom that seats about 75, Ms. Grossman and Ms. Nicklin stood elbow to elbow fielding questions from reporters. Ms. Grossman repeatedly said that Morgan Stanley would become "a much better place for women to work."

Without granting that Morgan Stanley had treated women unfairly, Ms. Nicklin, a partner in the law firm of Kirkland & Ellis, said, "Diversity is always enhanceable."

Ms. Dominguez, who twice appeared in court, along with Mr. Purcell, in earlier attempts to reach a settlement, praised the firm in a prepared statement. "With this settlement, Morgan Stanley has taken an important leadership step in adopting progressive programs to promote diversity that should serve as a model for the financial services industry," it said.

The settlement ended the first phase of resolving the disputes between the company and women who worked in the division since 1995, including Ms. Schieffelin. Of the $54 million, $40 million will be set aside for women who qualify to make claims under the consent decree.

Morgan Stanley will have 10 days to contact all of the women who have worked in the division since 1995 and invite them to make claims. Lawyers in the case said they could not estimate how many of about 340 eligible women might file claims.

Those claims will be considered by a special master, Abner Mikva, who is a former federal judge. After hearing them all, he will decide how much of the $40 million, if any, each woman will receive.

Ms. Schieffelin will file a claim in that process, her lawyer, Wayne N. Outten, said. He would not say how much of the $40 million she would seek, but an actuary Mr. Outten hired in preparation for trial estimated her lost income to be $33 million to $72 million.

Ms. Schieffelin declined to comment yesterday beyond praising the agreement

as "a great settlement that's good for everybody."

Donald Kempf, Morgan Stanley's chief legal officer, made it clear that the company did not think she should get any of the money. It was the commission's decision to give $12 million to Ms. Schieffelin, he said.

"We had zero input," Mr. Kempf said, standing in the courtroom long after the judge, the jury and the crowd had dispersed.

ESSAY: OFF-RAMPS AND ON-RAMPS
Keeping Talented Women on the Road to Success

Throughout the past year, a noisy debate has erupted in the media over the meaning of what Lisa Belkin of the *New York Times* has called the "opt-out revolution." Recent articles in the *Wall Street Journal,* the *New York Times, Time,* and *Fast Company* all point to a disturbing trend—large numbers of highly qualified women dropping out of mainstream careers. These articles also speculate on what might be behind this new brain drain. Are the complex demands of modern child rearing the nub of the problem? Or should one blame the trend on a failure of female ambition?

The facts and figures in these articles are eye-catching: a survey of the class of 1981 at Stanford University showing that 57 percent of women graduates leave the work force; a survey of three graduating classes at Harvard Business School demonstrating that only 38 percent of women graduates end up in full-time careers; and a broader-gauged study of MBAs showing that one in three white women holding an MBA is not working full-time, compared with one in 20 for men with the same degree.

The stories that enliven these articles are also powerful: Brenda Barnes, the former CEO of PepsiCo, who gave up her megawatt career to spend more time with her three children; Karen Hughes, who resigned from her enormously influential job in the Bush White House to go home to Texas to better look after a needy teenage son; and a raft of less prominent women who also said goodbye to their careers. Lisa Beattie Frelinghuysen, for example—featured in a recent *60 Minutes* segment—was building a very successful career as a lawyer. She'd been president of the law review at Stanford and went to work for a prestigious law firm. She quit after she had her first baby three years later.

Sylvia Ann Hewlett (cwlp@centerforwork-lifepolicy.org) is the founder and president of the Center for Work-Life Policy, a New York–based not-for-profit organization. She also heads up the Gender and Public Policy Program at the School of International and Public Affairs at Columbia University in New York. Her most recent book is Creating a Life (Miramax Books, 2002). Carolyn Buck Luce (carolyn.buck-luce@ey.com) is the global managing partner for Ernst & Young's health sciences industry practice in New York. She is the cochair for the Center for Work-Life Policy's Hidden Brain Drain task force.

Sylvia Ann Hewlett and Carolyn Buck Luce, *Harvard Business Review*, March 1, 2005 (HBR OnPoint Enhanced Edition), DOI: 10.1225/9416.

These stories certainly resonate, but scratch the surface and it quickly becomes clear that there is very little in the way of systematic, rigorous data about the seeming exodus. A sector here, a graduating class there, and a flood of anecdotes: No one seems to know the basic facts. Across professions and across sectors, what is the scope of this opt-out phenomenon? What proportion of professional women take off-ramps rather than continue on their chosen career paths? Are they pushed off or pulled? Which sectors of the economy are most severely affected when women leave the workforce? How many years do women tend to spend out of the workforce? When women decide to reenter, what are they looking for? How easy is it to find on-ramps? What policies and practices help women return to work?

Early in 2004, the Center for Work-Life Policy formed a private sector, multiyear task force entitled "The Hidden Brain Drain: Women and Minorities as Unrealized Assets" to answer these and other questions. In the summer of 2004, three member companies of the task force (Ernst & Young, Goldman Sachs, and Lehman Brothers) sponsored a survey specifically designed to investigate the role of off-ramps and on-ramps in the lives of highly qualified women. The survey, conducted by Harris Interactive, comprised a nationally representative group of highly qualified women, defined as those with a graduate degree, a professional degree, or a high-honors undergraduate degree. The sample size was 2,443 women. The survey focused on two age groups: older women aged 41 to 55 and younger women aged 28 to 40. We also surveyed a smaller group of highly qualified men (653) to allow us to draw comparisons.

Using the data from the survey, we've created a more comprehensive and nuanced portrait of women's career paths than has been available to date. Even more important, these data suggest actions that companies can take to ensure that female potential does not go unrealized. Given current demographic and labor market trends, it's imperative that employers learn to reverse this brain drain. Indeed, companies that can develop policies and practices to tap into the female talent pool over the long haul will enjoy a substantial competitive advantage.

WOMEN DO LEAVE

Many women take an off-ramp at some point on their career highway. Nearly four in 10 highly qualified women (37 percent) report that they have left work voluntarily at some point in their careers. Among women who have children, that statistic rises to 43 percent.

Factors other than having children that pull women away from their jobs include the demands of caring for elderly parents or other family members (reported by 24 percent) and personal health issues (9 percent). Not surprisingly, the pull of elder care responsibilities is particularly strong for women in the 41 to 55 age group—often called the "sandwich" generation, positioned as it is between growing children and aging parents. One in three women in that bracket have left work for some period to spend time caring for family members who are not children. And lurking behind all this is the pervasiveness of a highly traditional division of labor on the home front. In a 2001 survey conducted by the Center for Work-Life Policy, fully 40 percent of highly qualified women with spouses felt that their husbands create more work around the house than they perform.

Alongside these "pull" factors are a series of "push" factors—that is, features of the job or workplace that make women head for the door. Seventeen percent of

FIGURE 3-1   How Many Opt Out?

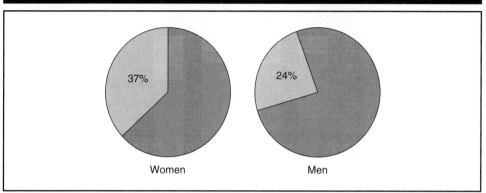

In our survey of highly qualified professionals, we asked the question, "Since you first began working, has there ever been a period where you took a voluntary time out from work?" Nearly four in ten women reported that they had—and that statistic rises to 43% among women who have children. By contrast, only 24% of highly qualified men have taken off-ramps (with no statistical difference between those who are fathers and those who are not).

women say they took an off-ramp, at least in part, because their jobs were not satisfying or meaningful. Overall, understimulation and lack of opportunity seem to be larger problems than overwork. Only 6 percent of women stopped working because the work itself was too demanding. In business sectors, the survey results suggest that push factors are particularly powerful—indeed, in these sectors, unlike, say, in medicine or teaching, they outweigh pull factors. Of course, in the hurly-burly world of everyday life, most women are dealing with a combination of push and pull factors—and one often serves to intensify the other. When women feel hemmed in by rigid policies or a glass ceiling, for example, they are much more likely to respond to the pull of family.

It's important to note that, however pulled or pushed, only a relatively privileged group of women have the option of not working. Most women cannot quit their careers unless their spouses earn considerable incomes. Fully 32 percent of the women surveyed cite the fact that their spouses' income "was sufficient for our family to live on one income" as a reason contributing to their decision to off-ramp.

Contrast this with the experience of highly qualified men, only 24 percent of whom have taken off-ramps (with no statistical difference between those who are fathers and those who are not). When men leave the workforce, they do it for difference reasons. Child-care and elder-care responsibilities are much less important; only 12 percent of men cite these factors as compared with 44 percent of women. Instead, on the pull side, they cite switching careers (29 percent), obtaining additional training (25 percent), or starting a business (12 percent) as important reasons for taking time out. For highly qualified men, off-ramping seems to be about strategic repositioning in their careers—a far cry from the dominant concerns of their female peers.

For many women in our study, the decision to off-ramp is a tough one. These women have invested heavily in their education and training. They have spent years accumulating the skills and credentials necessary for successful careers. Most are not eager to toss that painstaking effort aside.

LOST ON REENTRY

Among women who take off-ramps, the overwhelming majority have every intention of returning to the workforce—and seemingly little idea of just how difficult that will prove. Women, like lawyer Lisa Beattie Frelinghuysen from the *60 Minutes* segment, who happily give up their careers to have children are the exception rather than the rule. In our research, we find that most highly qualified women who are currently off-ramped (93 percent) want to return to their careers.

Many of these women have financial reasons for wanting to get back to work. Nearly half (46 percent) cite "having their own independent source of income" as an important propelling factor. Women who participated in focus groups conducted as part of our research talked about their discomfort with "dependence." However good their marriages, many disliked needing to ask for money. Not being able to splurge on some small extravagance or make their own philanthropic choices without clearing it with their husbands did not sit well with them. It's also true that a significant proportion of women currently seeking on-ramps are facing troubling shortfalls in family income: 38 percent cite "household income no longer sufficient for family needs" and 24 percent cite "partner's income no longer sufficient for family needs." Given what has happened to the cost of homes (up 38 percent over the past five years), the cost of college education (up 40 percent over the

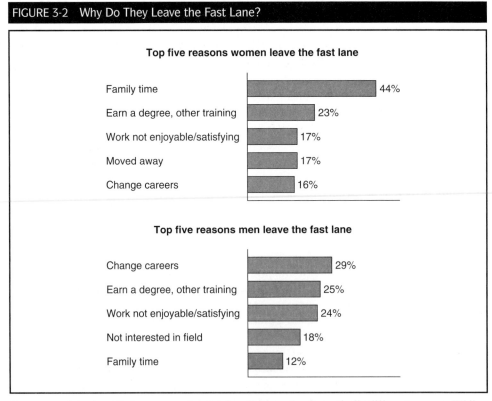

FIGURE 3-2   Why Do They Leave the Fast Lane?

Top five reasons women leave the fast lane

Family time	44%
Earn a degree, other training	23%
Work not enjoyable/satisfying	17%
Moved away	17%
Change careers	16%

Top five reasons men leave the fast lane

Change careers	29%
Earn a degree, other training	25%
Work not enjoyable/satisfying	24%
Not interested in field	18%
Family time	12%

Our survey data show that women and men take off-ramps for dramatically different reasons. While men leave the workforce mainly to reposition themselves for a career change, the majority of women off-ramp to attend to responsibilities at home.

past decade), and the cost of health insurance (up 49 percent since 2000), it's easy to see why many professional families find it hard to manage on one income.

But financial pressure does not tell the whole story. Many of these women find deep pleasure in their chosen careers and want to reconnect with something they love. Forty-three percent cite the "enjoyment and satisfaction" they derive from their careers as an important reason to return—among teachers this figure rises to 54 percent and among doctors it rises to 70 percent. A further 16 percent want to "regain power and status in their profession." In our focus groups, women talked eloquently about how work gives shape and structure to their lives, boosts confidence and self-esteem, and confers status and standing in their communities. For many off-rampers, their professional identities remain their primary identities, despite the fact that they have taken time out.

Perhaps most interesting, 24 percent of the women currently looking for on-ramps are motivated by "a desire to give something back to society" and are seeking jobs that allow them to contribute to their communities in some way. In our focus groups, off-ramped women talked about how their time at home had changed their aspirations. Whether they had gotten involved in protecting the wetlands, supporting the local library, or rebuilding a playground, they felt newly connected to the importance of what one woman called "the work of care."

Unfortunately, only 74 percent of off-ramped women who want to rejoin the ranks of the employed manage to do so, according to our survey. And among these, only 40 percent return to full-time, professional jobs. Many (24 percent) take part-time jobs, and some (9 percent) become self-employed. The implication is clear: Off-ramps are around every curve in the road, but once a woman has taken one, on-ramps are few and far between—and extremely costly.

THE PENALTIES OF TIME OUT

Women off-ramp for surprisingly short periods of time—on average, 2.2 years. In business sectors, off-rampers average even shorter periods of time out (1.2 years). However, even these relatively short career interruptions entail heavy financial penalties. Our data show that women lose an average of 18 percent of their earning power when they take an off-ramp. In business sectors, penalties are particularly draconian: In these fields, women's earning power dips an average of 28 percent when they take time out. The longer you spend out, the more severe the penalty becomes. Across sectors, women lose a staggering 37 percent of their earning power when they spend three or more years out of the workforce.

Naomi, 34, is a case in point. In an interview, this part-time working mother was open about her anxieties: "Every day, I think about what I am going to do when I want to return to work full-time. I worry about whether I will be employable—will anyone even look at my résumé?" This is despite an MBA and substantial work experience.

Three years ago, Naomi felt she had no choice but to quit her lucrative position in market research. She had just had a child, and returning to full-time work after the standard maternity leave proved to be well-nigh impossible. Her 55-hour week combined with her husband's 80-hour week didn't leave enough time to raise a healthy child—let alone care for a child who was prone to illness, as theirs was. When her employer denied her request to work reduced hours, Naomi quit.

After nine months at home, Naomi did find some flexible work—but it came at a high price. Her new freelance job as a consultant to an advertising agency barely covered

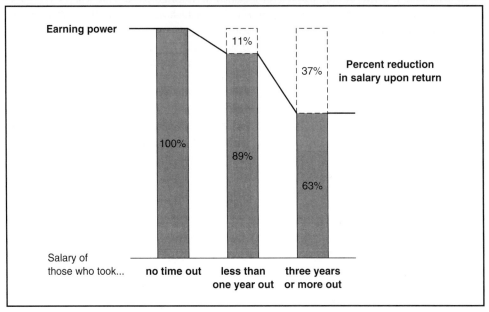

FIGURE 3-3   The High Cost of Time Out

Earning power

11%

37%   **Percent reduction in salary upon return**

100%

89%

63%

Salary of those who took...

no time out   **less than one year out**   **three years or more out**

Though the average amount of time that women take off from their careers is surprisingly short (less than three years), the salary penalty for doing so is severe. Women who return to the workforce after time out earn significantly less than their peers who remained in their jobs.

the cost of her son's day care. She now earns a third of what she did three years ago. What plagues Naomi the most about her situation is her anxiety about the future. "Will my skills become obsolete? Will I be able to support myself and my son if something should happen to my husband?"

The scholarly literature shows that Naomi's experience is not unusual. Economist Jane Waldfogel has analyzed the pattern of earnings over the life span. When women enter the workforce in their early and mid twenties they earn nearly as much as men do. For a few years, they almost keep pace. For example, at ages 25 to 29, they earn 87 percent of the male wage. However, when women start having children, their earnings fall way behind those of men. By the time they reach the 40-to-44 age group, women earn a mere 71 percent of the male wage. In the words of MIT economist Lester Thurow, "These are the prime years for establishing a successful career. These are the years when hard work has the maximum payoff. They are also the prime years for launching a family. Women who leave the job market during those years may find that they never catch up."

TAKING THE SCENIC ROUTE

A majority (58 percent) of highly qualified women describe their careers as "non-linear"—which is to say, they do not follow the conventional trajectory long established by successful men. That ladder of success features a steep gradient in one's 30s and steady progress thereafter. In contrast, these women report that their "career paths have not followed a progression through the hierarchy of an industry."

Some of this nonlinearity is the result of taking off-ramps. But there are many other ways in which women ease out of the professional fast lane. Our survey reveals that 16 percent of highly qualified women work part-time. Such arrangements are more prevalent in the legal and medical professions, where 23 percent and 20 percent of female professionals work less than full-time, than in the business sector, where only 8 percent of women work part-time. Another common work-life strategy is telecommuting; 8 percent of highly qualified women work exclusively from home, and another 25 percent work partly from home.

Looking back over their careers, 36 percent of highly qualified women say they have worked part-time for some period of time as part of a strategy to balance work and personal life. Twenty-five percent say they have reduced the number of work hours within a full-time job, and 16 percent say they have declined a promotion. A significant proportion (38 percent) say they have deliberately chosen a position with fewer responsibilities and lower compensation than they were qualified for, in order to fulfill responsibilities at home.

DOWNSIZING AMBITION

Given the tour of women's careers we've just taken, is it any surprise that women find it difficult to claim or sustain ambition? The survey shows that while almost half of the men consider themselves extremely or very ambitious, only about a third of the women do. (The proportion rises among women in business and the professions of law and medicine; there, 43 percent and 51 percent, respectively, consider themselves very ambitious.) In a similar vein, only 15 percent of highly qualified women (and 27 percent in the business sector) single out "a powerful position" as an important career goal; in fact, this goal ranked lowest in women's priorities in every sector we surveyed.

Far more important to these women are other items on the workplace wish list: the ability to associate with people they respect (82 percent); the freedom to "be themselves" at work (79 percent); and the opportunity to be flexible with their schedules (64 percent). Fully 61 percent of women consider it extremely or very important to have the opportunity to collaborate with others and work as part of a team. A majority (56 percent) believe it is very important for them to be able to give back to the community through their work. And 51 percent find "recognition from my company" either extremely or very important.

These top priorities constitute a departure from the traditional male take on ambition. Moreover, further analysis points to a disturbing age gap. In the business sector, 53 percent of younger women (ages 28 to 40) own up to being very ambitious, as contrasted with only 37 percent of older women. This makes sense in light of Anna Fels's groundbreaking work on women and ambition. In a 2004 HBR article, Fels argues convincingly that ambition stands on two legs—mastery and recognition. To hold onto their dreams, not only must women attain the necessary skills and experience, they must also have their achievements appropriately recognized. To the extent the latter is missing in female careers, ambition is undermined. A vicious cycle emerges: As women's ambitions stall, they are perceived as less committed, they no longer get the best assignments, and this lowers their ambitions further.

In our focus groups, we heard the disappointment—and discouragement—of women who had reached senior levels in corporations only to find the glass ceiling still in place, despite years of diversity initiatives. These women feel that they are languishing and have not been given either the opportunities or the recognition that would allow them to realize their full potential. Many feel handicapped in the attainment of their goals. The result is the vicious cycle that Fels describes: a "downsizing" of women's ambition that becomes a self-fulfilling prophecy. And the discrepancy in ambition levels between men and women has an insidious side effect in that it results in insufficient role models for younger women.

REVERSING THE BRAIN DRAIN

These, then, are the hard facts. With them in hand, we move from anecdotes to data—and, more important, to a different, richer analytical understanding of the problem. In the structural issue of off-ramps and on-ramps, we see the mechanism derailing the careers of highly qualified women and also the focal point for making positive change. What are the implications for corporate America? One thing at least seems clear: Employers can no longer pretend that treating women as "men in skirts" will fix their retention problems. Like it or not, large numbers of highly qualified, committed women need to take time out. The trick is to help them maintain connections that will allow them to come back from that time without being marginalized for the rest of their careers.

Create Reduced-Hour Jobs

The most obvious way to stay connected is to offer women with demanding lives a way to keep a hand in their chosen field, short of full-time involvement. Our survey found that, in business sectors, fully 89 percent of women believe that access to reduced-hour jobs is important. Across all sectors, the figure is 82 percent.

The Johnson & Johnson family of companies has seen the increased loyalty and productivity that can result from such arrangements. We recently held a focus group with 12 part-time managers at these companies and found a level of commitment that was palpable. The women had logged histories with J&J that ranged from eight to 19 years and spoke of the corporation with great affection. All had a focus on productivity and pushed themselves to deliver at the same level they had achieved before switching to part-time. One women, a 15-year J&J veteran, was particularly eloquent in her gratitude to the corporation. She had had her first child at age 40 and, like so many new mothers, felt torn apart by the conflicting demands of home and work. In her words, "I thought I only had two choices—work full-time or leave—and I didn't want either. J&J's reduced-hour option has been a savior." All the women in the room were clear on one point: They would have quit had part-time jobs not been available

At Pfizer, the deal is sweetened further for part-time workers; field sales professionals in the company's Vista Rx division are given access to the same benefits and training as full-time employees but work 60 percent of the hours (with a corresponding difference in base pay). Many opt for a three-day workweek; others structure their working day around children's school hours. These 230 employees—93 percent of whom are

FIGURE 3-4   How Ernst & Young Keeps Women on the Path to Partnership

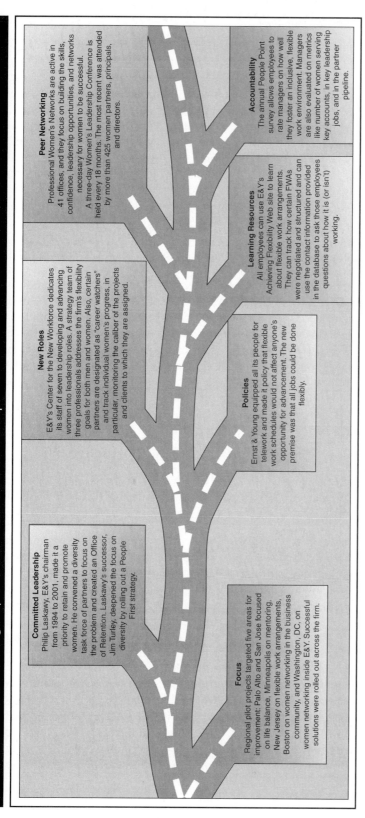

Committed Leadership
Philip Laskawy, E&Y's chairman from 1994 to 2001, made it a priority to retain and promote women. He convened a diversity task force of partners to focus on the problem and created an Office of Retention. Laskawy's successor, Jim Turley, deepened the focus on diversity by rolling out a People First strategy.

Focus
Regional pilot projects targeted five areas for improvement: Palo Alto and San Jose focused on life balance, Minneapolis on mentoring, New Jersey on flexible work arrangements, Boston on women networking in the business community, and Washington, DC, on women networking inside E&Y. Successful solutions were rolled out across the firm.

New Roles
E&Y's Center for the New Workforce dedicates its staff of seven to developing and advancing women into leadership roles. A strategy team of three professionals addresses the firm's flexibility goals for both men and women. Also, certain partners are designated as "career watchers" and track individual women's progress, in particular, monitoring the caliber of the projects and clients to which they are assigned.

Policies
Ernst & Young equipped all its people for telework and made it policy that flexible work schedules would not affect anyone's opportunity for advancement. The new premise was that all jobs could be done flexibly.

Peer Networking
Professional Women's Networks are active in 41 offices, and they focus on building the skills, confidence, leadership opportunities, and networks necessary for women to be successful. A three-day Women's Leadership Conference is held every 18 months. The most recent was attended by more than 425 women partners, principals, and directors.

Learning Resources
All employees can use E&Y's Achieving Flexibility Web site to learn about flexible work arrangements. They can track how certain FWAs were negotiated and structured and can use the contact information provided in the database to ask those employees questions about how it is (or isn't) working.

Accountability
The annual People Point survey allows employees to rate managers on how well they foster an inclusive, flexible work environment. Managers are also evaluated on metrics like number of women serving key accounts, in key leadership jobs, and in the partner pipeline.

In the mid-1990s, turnover among female employees at Ernst & Young was much higher than it was among male peers. Company leaders knew something was seriously wrong; for many years, its entering classes of young auditors had been made up of nearly equal numbers of men and women—yet it was still the case that only a tiny percentage of its partnership was female. This was a major problem. Turnover in client-serving roles meant lost continuity on work assignments. And on top of losing talent that the firm had invested in training, E&Y was incurring costs averaging 150% of a departing employee's annual salary just to fill the vacant position.

E&Y set a new course, marked by several important features outlined here. Since E&Y began this work, the percentage of women partners has more than tripled to 12% and the downward trend in retention of women at every level has been reversed. E&Y now has four women on the management board, and many more women are in key operating and client serving roles. Among its women partners, 10% work on a flexible schedule and more than 20 have been promoted to partner while working a reduced schedule. In 2004, 22% of new partners were women.

working mothers—remain eligible for promotion and may return to full-time status at their discretion.

Provide Flexibility in the Day

Some women don't require reduced work hours; they merely need flexibility in when, where, and how they do their work. Even parents who employ nannies or have children in day care, for example, must make time for teacher conferences, medical appointments, volunteering, child-related errands—not to mention the days the nanny calls in sick or the day care center is closed. Someone caring for an invalid or a fragile elderly person may likewise have many hours of potentially productive time in a day yet not be able to stray far from home.

For these and other reasons, almost two-thirds (64 percent) of the women we surveyed cite flexible work arrangements as being either extremely or very important to them. In fact, by a considerable margin, highly qualified women find flexibility more important than compensation; only 42 percent say that "earning a lot of money" is an important motivator. In our focus groups, we heard women use terms like "nirvana" and "the golden ring" to describe employment arrangements that allow them to flex their workdays, their workweeks, and their careers. A senior employee who recently joined Lehman Brothers' equity division is an example. She had been working at another financial services company when a Lehman recruiter called. "The person who had been in the job previously was working one day a week from home, so they offered that opportunity to me. Though I was content in my current job," she told us, "that intriguing possibility made me reevaluate. In the end, I took the job at Lehman. Working from home one day a week was a huge lure."

Provide Flexibility in the Arc of a Career

Booz Allen Hamilton, the management and technology consulting firm, recognized that it isn't simply a workday, or a workweek, that needs to be made more flexible, it's the entire arc of a career.

Management consulting as a profession loses twice as many women as men in the middle reaches of career ladders. A big part of the problem is that, perhaps more than in any other business sector, it is driven by an up-or-out ethos; client-serving professionals must progress steadily or fall by the wayside. The strongest contenders make partner through a relentless winnowing process. While many firms take care to make the separations as painless as possible (the chaff, after all, tends to land in organizations that might employ their services), there are clear limits to their patience. Typically, if a valued professional is unable to keep pace with the road warrior lifestyle, the best she can hope for is reassignment to a staff job.

Over the past year, Booz Allen has initiated a "ramp up, ramp down" flexible program to allow professionals to balance work and life and still do the client work they find most interesting. The key to the program is Booz Allen's effort to "unbundle" standard consulting projects and identify chunks that can be done by telecommuting or shorts stints in the office. Participating professionals are either regular employees or alumni that sign standard employment contracts and are activated as needed. For the professional, it's a way to take on a manageable amount of the kind of work they do best. For Booz Allen, it's a way to maintain ties to consultants who have already proved their merit in a challenging profession. Since many of these talented women will eventually return to full-time consulting employment, Booz Allen wants to be their employer of choice—and to keep their skills sharp in the meantime.

When asked how the program is being received, DeAnne Aguirre, a vice president at Booz Allen who was involved in its design (and who is also a member of our task force), had an instant reaction: "I think it's instilled new hope—a lot of young women I work with no longer feel that they will have to sacrifice some precious part of themselves." Aguirre explains that trade-offs are inevitable, but at Booz Allen an off-ramping decision doesn't have to be a devastating one anymore. "Flex careers are bound to be slower than conventional ones, but in ten years' time you probably won't remember the precise year you made partner. The point here is to remain on track and vitally connected."

Remove the Stigma

Making flexible arrangements succeed over the long term is hard work. It means crafting an imaginative set of policies, but even more important, it means eliminating the stigma that is often attached to such nonstandard work arrangements. As many as 35 percent of the women we surveyed report various aspects of their organizations' cultures that effectively penalize people who take advantage of work-life policies. Telecommuting appears to be most stigmatized, with 39 percent of women reporting some form of tacit resistance to it, followed by job sharing and part-time work. Of flexible work arrangements in general, 21 percent report that "there is an unspoken rule at my workplace that people who use these options will not be promoted." Parental leave policies get more respect—though even here, 19 percent of women report cultural or attitudinal barriers to taking the time off that they are entitled to. In environments where flexible work arrangements are tacitly deemed illegitimate, many women would rather resign than request them.

Interestingly, when it comes to taking advantage of work-life policies, men encounter even more stigma. For example, 48 percent of the men we surveyed perceived job sharing as illegitimate in their workplace culture—even when it's part of official policy.

Transformation of the corporate culture seems to be a prerequisite for success on the work-life front. Those people at or near the top of an organization need to have that "eureka" moment, when they not only understand the business imperative for imaginative work-life policies but are prepared to embrace them, and in so doing remove the stigma. In the words of Dessa Bokides, treasurer at Pitney Bowes, "Only a leader's devotion to these issues will give others permission to transform conventional career paths."

Stop Burning Bridges

One particularly dramatic finding of our survey deserves special mention: Only 5 percent of highly qualified women looking for on-ramps are interested in rejoining the companies they left. In business sectors, that percentage is zero. If ever there was a danger signal for corporations, this is it.

The finding implies that the vast majority of off-ramped women, at the moment they left their careers, felt ill-used—or at least underutilized and unappreciated—by their employers. We can only speculate as to why this was. In some cases, perhaps, the situation ended badly; a woman, attempting impossible juggling feats, started dropping balls. Or an employer, embittered by the loss of too many "star" women, lets this one go much too easily.

It's understandable for managers to assume that women leave mainly for "pull" reasons and that there's no point in trying to keep them. Indeed, when family overload and the traditional division of labor place unmanageable demands on a working woman, it does appear that quitting has much more to do with what's going on at home than what's going on at work. However, it is important to realize that even when pull factors seem to be dominant, push factors are also in play. Most off-ramping decisions are conditioned by policies, practices, and attitudes at work. Recognition, flexibility, and the opportunity to telecommute—especially when endorsed by the corporate culture—can make a huge difference.

The point is, managers will not stay in a departing employee's good graces unless they take the time to explore the reasons for off-ramping and are able and willing to offer options short of total severance. If a company wants future access to this talent, it will need to go beyond the perfunctory exit interview and, at the very least, impart the message that the door is open. Better still, it will maintain a connection with off-ramped employees through a formal alumni program.

Provide Outlets for Altruism

Imaginative attachment policies notwithstanding, some women have no interest in returning to their old organizations because their desire to work in their former field has waned. Recall the focus group participants who spoke of a deepened desire to give back to the community after taking a hiatus from work. Remember, too, that women in business sectors are pushed off track more by dissatisfaction with work than pulled by external demands. Our data suggest that fully 52 percent of women with MBAs in the business sector cite the fact that they do not find their careers "either satisfying or enjoyable" as an important reason for why they left work. Perhaps not surprisingly, then, a majority (54 percent) of the women looking for on-ramps want to change their profession or field. And in most of those cases, it's a woman who formerly worked in the corporate sphere hoping to move into the not-for-profit sector.

Employers would be well advised to recognize and harness the altruism of these women. Supporting female professionals in their advocacy and public service efforts serves to win their energy and loyalty. Companies may also be able to redirect women's desire to give back to the community by asking them to become involved in mentoring and formal women's networks within the company.

Nurture Ambition

Finally, if women are to sustain their passion for work and their competitive edge—whether or not they take formal time out—they must keep ambition alive. Our findings point to an urgent need to implement mentoring and networking programs that help women expand and sustain their professional aspirations. Companies like American

Express, GE, Goldman Sachs, Johnson & Johnson, Lehman Brothers, and Time Warner are developing "old girls networks" that build skills, contacts, and confidence. They link women to inside power brokers and to outside business players and effectively inculcate those precious rainmaking skills.

Networks (with fund-raising and friend-raising functions) can enhance client connections. But they also play another, critical role. They provide the infrastructure within which women can earn recognition, as well as a safe platform from which to blow one's own horn without being perceived as too pushy. In the words of Patricia Fili-Krushel, executive vice president of Time Warner, "Company-sponsored women's networks encourage women to cultivate both sides of the power equation. Women hone their own leadership abilities but also learn to use power on behalf of others. Both skill sets help us increase our pipeline of talented women."

ADOPT AN ON-RAMP

As we write this, market and economic factors, both cyclical and structural, are aligned in ways guaranteed to make talent constraints and skill shortages huge issues again. Unemployment is down and labor markets are beginning to tighten, just as the baby-bust generation is about to hit "prime time" and the number of workers between the ages of 35 to 45 is shrinking. Immigration levels are stable, so there's little chance of relief there. Likewise, productivity improvements are flattening. The phenomenon that bailed us out of our last big labor crunch—the entry for the first time of millions of women into the labor force—is not available to us again. Add it all up, and CEOs are back to wondering how they will find enough high-caliber talent to drive growth.

There is a winning strategy. It revolves around the retention and reattachment of highly qualified women. America these days has a large and impressive pool of female talent. Fifty-eight percent of college graduates are now women, and nearly half of all professional and graduate degrees are earned by women. Even more important, the incremental additions to the talent pool will be disproportionately female, according to figures released by the U.S. Department of Education. The number of women with graduate and professional degrees is projected to grow by 16 percent over the next decade, while the number of men with these degrees is projected to grow by a mere 1.3 percent. Companies are beginning to pay attention to these figures. As Melinda Wolfe, head of global leadership and diversity at Goldman Sachs, recently pointed out, "A large part of the potential talent pool consists of females and historically underrepresented groups. With the professional labor market tightening, it is in our direct interest to give serious attention to these matters of retention and reattachment."

In short, the talent is there; the challenge is to create the circumstances that allow businesses to take advantage of it over the long run. To tap this all-important resource, companies must understand the complexities of women's nonlinear careers and be prepared to support rather than punish those who take alternate routes.

Discussion Questions

1. Why do women leave careers after having invested heavily in developing the skills that would help them succeed in those careers?
2. Would men leave their careers if they had a spouse who was earning enough to support their family?

3. What would employers have to do to allow women who leave their jobs to return and catch up to where they would have been had they not left? How would these policies affect those who do not take time off from work?
4. Why do more women professionals work part-time than their counterparts in business?
5. What are the costs and benefits to a company of providing full benefits and training to those employees who work part-time?
6. What risks do they take when employees make use of their companies' work-life policies? Are these risks the same for men and women?
7. Are women more likely to leave a job because it is uninteresting or unenjoyable than men? Why?

The complete statistical findings from this research project, and additional commentary and company examples, are available in an HBR research report entitled "The Hidden Brain Drain: Off-Ramps and On-Ramps in Women's Careers" (see www.womenscareersreport.hbr.org).

CASE STUDY: AUGUSTA NATIONAL GOLF CLUB
Membership for Women or Staying the Course?

It was early November of 2002, and William Johnson—known to friends and associates as "Hootie"—chairman of the venerable Augusta National Golf Club, had just finished his last interview with one of several national news organizations. Speaking candidly about the club's membership policies, Mr. Johnson had requested that his comments not be published until the following week. He also talked about how actions that had taken place over the previous seven or eight months would affect the 2003 Masters Golf Tournament, a competition that many people regard as the most prestigious golf event in North America, but one that was now shrouded in controversy.

THE FIRST SIX MONTHS

On Sunday, April 14, 2002, golfing phenomenon Tiger Woods had won the Masters Golf Tournament for the third time, having previously finished first in 1997 and 2001. News of his accomplishment—three victories by age 26, and two in a row—made headlines the world over. It was also during the 2002 Masters that Lloyd Ward, the chief executive of the United States Olympic Committee and an

This case was prepared by Research Assistants Ray B. Swart, Ashish K. Singh, and Andrew Nelson under the direction of James S. O'Rourke, Concurrent Professor of Management, as the basis for class discussion rather than to illustrate either effective or ineffective handling of an administrative situation.

Eugene D. Fanning Center for Business Communication, Mendoza College of Business, University of Notre Dame.

African American member of the Augusta National Golf Club, commented to reporters that he was advising the leaders of the club to admit a woman, and to do it soon. Mr. Ward said that he would work from within Augusta to lobby for women, adding, "Inclusion does not just mean people of color."[1] Little did Mr. Ward know (or anyone else for that matter) that his innocuous remarks would be the impetus for even more attention-grabbing headlines in the near future.

Martha Burk, Ph.D., Chair of the National Council of Women's Organizations read Mr. Lloyd's comments and decides to take action. On June 12, Ms. Burk writes a letter to William "Hootie" Johnson, Chairman of Augusta, telling him that "the NCWO knows that Augusta National and the sponsors of the Masters do not want to be viewed as entities that tolerate discrimination against any group, including women." She then urged him to open their membership to women immediately, so that it would not be issue when the tournament [the Masters] is staged next year.[2]

On July 8th, Mr. Johnson wrote Ms. Burk a brief, three sentence response, in essence stating that as a distinctly private club, Augusta cannot talk about its membership practices with those outside the organization, and that he found her letter's references to discrimination, allusions to the sponsors and setting of deadlines to be both offensive and coercive. The next day, Mr. Johnson issues a public press release lashing out at Ms. Burk and the NCWO. In that statement, he said that Augusta "will not be bullied, threatened or intimidated. Our membership alone decides our membership—not any outside group with its own agenda. There may well come a day when women will be invited to join our membership but that timetable will be ours and not at the point of a bayonet."[3]

On July 30th, the NCWO sent letters to the CEOs of the television sponsors of the Masters—Citigroup, Inc., the Coca-Cola Company, General Motors Corporation (with a separate letter addressed to the general manager of the Cadillac Motor Division) and IBM Corporation—requesting that they suspend sponsorship of the tournament, since it is owned, controlled and produced by Augusta National Incorporated, an organization that discriminates against women by excluding them from membership.[4] A letter was also sent to Tim Finchem, Commissioner of the Professional Golfers Association (PGA) asking the PGA Tour to adhere to its written policy on discrimination (the PGA will not cosponsor an event with a club having discriminatory policies) by withdrawing recognition of any kind from the Masters Golf Tournament. Curiously, the letter does acknowledge that the Masters Tournament is not an "official" part of the PGA Tour.[5]

In mid-August, Mr. Finchem replied to the NCWO, saying that they were correct in identifying the Masters as an event not co-sponsored by the Professional Golfers Association, and as such, the PGA would be unable to require Augusta National to implement the PGA's host club policy with respect to the Masters.[6]

Leah C. Johnson, Director of Public Affairs for Citigroup, also replied to the NCWO, stating that, with regard to their comments about the Masters Golf Tournament, Citigroup had communicated its views privately to the management of the club.[7] Finally, Rick Singer, Director of Worldwide Sponsorship Marketing for IBM, wrote to Ms. Burk and the NCWO, saying that IBM did not view sponsorship of the Masters as contradictory to the company's long-standing commitment to diversity and support for women in business.[8] Within days, Ms. Burk sent a follow-up letter to Samuel J. Palmisano, CEO of IBM, telling him that Mr. Singer's letter was not responsive to points raised in the NCWO's initial complaint. Specifically, the NCWO wanted answers to two specific questions:

1. *"Is IBM's policy on sex discrimination different from its policy on race discrimination?"*
2. *"How does IBM reconcile its sponsorship of the Masters with its written policies against gender discrimination, and specifically those policies against sponsoring recreational activities and organizations that discriminate on the basis of gender?"*[9]

IBM did not respond to the second letter.

On August 30th, in response to Ms. Burk's letters to the tournament's television sponsors, Mr. Johnson issued a press release, saying that the Augusta National Golf Club would not request the participation of any media sponsors for the 2003 Masters Golf Tournament. Instead, the telecast will be sponsored by the separately incorporated "Masters Tournament." In his statement, Mr. Johnson said that because the NCWO's true target is Augusta National, the sponsors should not be put in the position of having to deal with the NCWO's pressure.[10] After reading the press release, Martha Burk said, "I think they're (Augusta National) doing what they can to avoid having a woman member. They're willing to pay a lot of money to continue to discriminate. That's what it comes down to."[11]

On the following day, August 31st, the NCWO announced that it would focus its attention on the CBS Television Network and on September 18th, sent a letter to Sean McManus, the President of CBS Sports, requesting that the network suspend broadcasting the Masters Tournament. In her letter, Ms. Burk stated that if CBS Sports were to continue broadcasting the Masters Golf Tournament, it would be acting irresponsibly as a Federal Communications Commission licensee and as a corporate citizen because, she wrote, "use of the airways is not an entitlement; the FCC licenses broadcasters to operate in the public interest and broadcasters are mandated to act responsibly."[12]

On September 19th, Sean McManus responded to Ms. Burk in a letter from CBS Sports, saying that, as a sports television programmer serving millions of men and women who eagerly anticipate and avidly watch the network's Masters broadcast each year, CBS intended to cover the Masters, just as it has done for the past 46 years. To not do so, he said, would be a disservice to fans of this major championship.[13]

AUGUSTA NATIONAL GOLF CLUB AND THE MASTERS TOURNAMENT

Located at what is now the corner of Washington and Berckmans Roads in Augusta, Georgia, Augusta National Golf Club was founded in 1932 and was designed by Bob Jones and Alister MacKenzie. Augusta's membership is limited to around 300 persons and is one of the most exclusive private clubs in the world. Play on the course is allowed only from October to May. Membership in Augusta National is by invitation only and there are currently no female members, although women played more than 1,000 rounds on the course last year, many more than were allowed at some other male-only clubs. Information about club membership is not easy to obtain, but as the controversy surrounding the club's exclusionary policies began making headlines, some details began to emerge. The average member age, according to *USA Today,* is 72 and they come mainly from old-line industries: banking and finance, oil and gas, manufacturing and distributing. New members are nominated by existing members and are determined partly by how many current members die or leave. The waiting list is said to be about 300 with the chairman having the final say on who gets invited to join. Annual membership fees are in the $25,000-to-$50,000 range, with the chairman having control of the club's purse strings.[14] Augusta National admitted its first African-American member in 1990, purportedly thanks to an inside effort led by Mr. Johnson before the club could become a target of protests.

The first Masters Tournament was held at Augusta in March of 1934, and was hosted by Bob Jones and Clifford Roberts, who served as chairman of both the club and tournament for another 43 years until his death in 1977. Originally called the Augusta National Invitation Tournament, the name was changed to the Masters in 1939. Beginning in 1940, the Masters has been held during the first full week of April on an annual basis (with the exception of 1943, 1944 and 1945 because of World War II).[15] Steeped with tradition, the Masters is the first of golf's four Major Championships to be played each calendar year. The other three majors, in order of play, are the United States Open, the British Open, and the PGA Championship. The Masters is also the only Major Championship to be played at the same venue every year. In keeping with Mr. Jones' and Mr. Roberts' original concept for the tournament, the Masters is still an invitation-only event, and as such, it has the smallest playing field of any of the four Major Championships.

Each year, the winner of the Masters is presented with a green jacket. That jacket must remain at Augusta National, with the exception of the first 12 months during which the champion may take it home with him. The total purse distributed to the playing field in 2002 was $5.5 million with another $3.3 million going to charity. Award-winning columnist Ron Green Sr., who has covered golf for five decades, describes the emotional impact of the tournament on those who compete there: "The Masters has brought men to tears of joy and tears of sorrow. It has been a defining event in the lives of champions and it has scarred its victims for life."[16]

Augusta National operates the Masters independent from any golf organization. The club gets most of its money from an annual television contract with CBS Sports and sales from its souvenir store at the course. It is estimated that these "public" sources of revenue amount to about $20 million, an amount that is greater than the $15 million generated by membership dues (if the published but unconfirmed figures are accurate). Mr. Johnson has said, "Augusta National and the Masters—while happily entwined—are quite different. One is a private golf club. The other is a world-class sports event of great public interest. It is insidious to attempt to use one to alter the essence of the other."[17] Ms. Burk responded by saying, "The Masters, in my mind, is not tied at the hip to this club. An event of this profile could be held somewhere else."[18] She also adds that a private club that hosts a public event like the Masters is not really private.

THE COLUMBIA BROADCASTING SYSTEM

The Columbia Broadcasting System was founded in 1927, and is currently owned by Viacom, Inc. The CBS Television Network has aired the Masters Golf Tournament on a one-year contract every year since 1956. The financial agreement between the Masters and CBS Sports has been kept private, and the contract is regarded as unique in comparison both to other sporting events and to other golf tournaments. Rather than bidding on the right to broadcast the tournament and then covering their costs by selling advertising time, the Augusta National Golf Club essentially covers CBS's production costs. CBS is then permitted to show just four minutes of commercial advertisements an hour. With so little commercial time for sale, the Masters has never been a moneymaker for CBS. Analysts have estimated that, in 2002, fees paid to CBS were approximately $5 million, as compared to an average price range of $8–$20 million for other popular golf tournaments. There is some speculation that the club may be forced to lower the fee even further and make up the cost difference by raising ticket prices and selling more merchandise. However, CBS regards its broadcast of the Masters as a privilege, as it is traditionally the highest rated televised golf tournament of the year.

THE SPONSORS

Each of the television sponsors of the Masters Golf Tournament has a corporate policy forbidding gender discrimination. Ms. Burk and the NCWO acknowledged this fact in each of the letters sent to the companies, asking them to suspend their sponsorship of the Masters television broadcast.

Citigroup Corporation

Citigroup Corporation (originally known as The Travelers) has been a sponsor of the broadcast for many years. Ms. Burk praised Citigroup for the creation of its corporate division, Women and Company, and acknowledged that they had been chosen as one of the "100 best companies for working mothers" in 2001.[19]

The Coca-Cola Company

Coca-Cola has been a sponsor of the tournament for only one year. In her letter to Coca-Cola's chairman and chief executive, Ms. Burk applauded the company's November 2000 agreement to engage an outside panel to monitor pay and promotion of minority and women workers.[20] In a non-public manner, Coca-Cola's CEO Douglas Daft had tried to influence Augusta National's policy with seemingly little effect. The company's talks with both Augusta National and the NCWO were reported to be friendly and non-contentious.

IBM Corporation

IBM (formerly International Business Machines) has been a sponsor of the Masters for only one year, as well. In her letter to IBM, Ms. Burk pointed out that their decision to continue sponsoring the Masters broadcast directly contradicted their actions regarding race discrimination issues involved with the PGA Championship, held at Shoal Creek Golf Club in Alabama in 1990.[21] IBM withdrew its sponsorship when it was revealed that Shoal Creek discriminated against African-Americans.

Cadillac Motor Division, General Motors Corporation

General Motors' Cadillac Division has a long history of sponsoring the Masters broadcast. A press report from Cadillac spokesman Jeff Kuhlman noted that since Cadillac is the official car of the Masters Tournament and not the Augusta National Golf Club, sponsorship would continue.[22]

THE PROFESSIONAL GOLFERS ASSOCIATION

The Professional Golfers Association (PGA) of America was founded on April 10, 1916, in New York with 35 charter members. Since its inception, the PGA has grown into the largest sports organization in the world with more than 27,000 dedicated men and women golf professionals who promote the game of golf to everyone, everywhere. The PGA conducts some 40 tournaments a year for PGA Professionals, but the Masters Golf Tournament is not an event cosponsored by the PGA Tour. The PGA Tour does require that host clubs of their cosponsored events, with whom they have contractual relationships, maintain membership policies under which membership is not restricted on the basis of race, religion, sex or national origin.[23]

THE NATIONAL COUNCIL OF WOMEN'S ORGANIZATIONS

The NCWO is the nation's oldest and largest coalition of women's groups. Its 160 member organizations represent women from all socioeconomic and demographic groups, and collectively represent more than seven million women nationwide. NCWO member organizations include grassroots, research, service, media and legal advocacy groups. They work together to advocate change on many issues of importance to women, including equal employment opportunity, economic equity, media equality, education, job training, women's health and reproductive issues, as well as the specific concerns of mid-life and older women, girls and young women, women of color, business and professional women, homemakers and retired women. NCWO decisions are made by a simple majority vote at bi-monthly meetings where each dues-paying organization has one vote. An eight-member Steering Committee publicizes and implements these decisions. When the Council is not in session, the Chair is authorized to speak for the Council if the policy issue is clear.[24]

NEW VOICES ARE HEARD

Clifford Roberts, who ran the Augusta National Golf Club with an iron fist for 45 years, actively recruited corporate chiefs as members from the club's inception. (It is important to note that Augusta National has only individuals as members, not corporations or organizations). The CEOs appreciated having a golf club to visit in the winter, even though many of them did not golf there frequently. The local Augusta members are said to appreciate that. Many of the prominent CEOs of large national companies are still viewed as outsiders. Confrontations are not usually welcome or well received. Prudence and discretion reign.[25]

In late September of 2002, Ms. Burk began sending letters to CEOs and other prominent members of Augusta National, asking them to explain why they belong to a club that has no female members. "We'll ask them for on-the-record statements about how they reconcile membership in the club with their corporate codes of conduct and their marketing practices to women," said Ms. Burk.[26] A few club members, speaking on the condition of anonymity, said that they had become distressed by the confrontational approach taken by Mr. Johnson. This loosely knit faction could be characterized as an outer circle that lives and works outside of Georgia, choosing to communicate with one another more frequently as the dispute escalated. Some have said they will press their case to various members privately.[27]

On October 4th, Sanford I. Weill, chairman and chief executive of Citigroup, becomes the first corporate executive to openly offer his support to the women's organization. A Citigroup statement signed by Leah C. Johnson, Director of Public Affairs, sent to the NCWO said that Mr. Weill had "expressed his views to the Augusta National Golf Club and will continue to engage in what he hopes will be a constructive dialogue on this issue, toward an objective that he believes we share with your organization. However, he respectfully intends to keep this dialogue private."[28]

Within a few days, members Lloyd Ward, the chief executive of the United States Olympic Committee, and Kenneth I. Chenault, the chief executive of American Express, also offered their support for the inclusion of women as members at Augusta. In a letter to Martha Burk, Mr. Ward said, "I am committed to breaking down barriers which exclude women from membership at Augusta in the weeks and months ahead."[29] And in a statement released through American Express, Mr. Chenault said, "I believe women should be admitted as members of the Augusta National Golf Club. I have made my views known within the club because I believe that is the most effective and appropriate way to bring about a change in membership policy."[30] Ms. Burk said in an interview that she was gratified by Mr. Ward's letter because "it's strongly worded and puts a short time frame on the issue."[31] Ms. Burk also said that she believed that the position taken by these men would lead more Augusta members to push for the admission of women. The Augusta National Golf Club offered no public announcement with regard to these latest revelations.

WILL THE REAL "HOOTIE" JOHNSON PLEASE STAND UP?

William "Hootie" Johnson, 71, is a native of Augusta, Georgia who attended his first Masters when he was four and has been the chairman of the Augusta National Golf Club since 1998. His recent actions concerning female membership seem to be an enigma. Four years earlier, Mr. Johnson brokered a deal in which South Carolina became the first major college to name its business school after a woman, New York investment banker Darla Moore. He also invited the University of South Carolina women's golf team to play at Augusta. I. S. Leevy Johnson, one of three African Americans elected to the South Carolina state legislature in 1970 with Mr. Johnson's backing, speaking about female membership at Augusta said, "I think it's inevitable. If anything, I think this controversy has delayed it. In my opinion, [Mr. Johnson] was already trying to do it on the inside."[32]

Martha Burk, 61, Chair of the National Council of Women's Organizations, has made it clear that her battle with the Augusta National Golf Club is not, in any way, a legal issue. As a private club, Augusta has the legal right to set its own policies, but Ms. Burk indicated that they have the moral imperative to do better. When asked why Augusta National and why now, Ms. Burk said, "Because it's the home of the Masters, it is highly symbolic. It reminds women of the glass ceiling and unequal pay and all the reasons women are running second in America."[33] Ironically, Ms. Burk's brothers and cousins called her "Hootie" as a youngster. "It is strange how that worked out," she says.[34]

THE FINAL WORD?

On November 12th, Mr. Johnson's remarks to the press were finally published. He adamantly affirmed his stance against admitting a woman to the Augusta National Golf Club anytime in the near future. In an Op-Ed article appearing in *The Wall Street Journal,* Mr. Johnson wrote, "If we wish to open all private organizations to men and women, as Ms. Burk and [the] NCWO wish to do with Augusta National, the end is near for many uncontroversial and long-standing private groups. Women's colleges like Smith and Wellesley, historically black colleges like Spelman, the Girls Scouts of America, the Junior League, fraternities and sororities would all have to be dissolved or radically changed from the single-sex profile that has become an essential part of their character and, indeed, the reason they are sought after. Do they, too, 'discriminate'?"[35] Mr. Johnson goes on to say, "Whether, or when, we have women as members is something that this club will decide alone, and in private. It is for others to decide, from where they stand, whether threat-based tactics are appropriate. But from here, it feels like some things are worth defending, and sometimes that means taking a stand. In my mind and in my heart, I know this is one of them."[36] When asked if Augusta National would try to proceed with the [Masters] tournament as usual, Mr. Johnson responded: "No, we won't try. We will proceed. And will succeed."[37]

Martha Burk reacted quickly and with dismay to Johnson's position. "If the decision stands not to admit a woman before next year's Masters, then it's a slap in the face to Augusta members who have spoken out asking for this discrimination to end."[38] Ms. Burk also said, "I hope cooler heads and rationality will prevail and they will come down on the side of fairness, regardless of what [Mr.] Johnson thinks. These guys are not Boy Scouts or Girl Scouts, they're adult human beings, many of them CEOs of the largest U.S. corporations."[39]

In a statement made several weeks earlier Ms. Burk said, "It's not our goal to aggravate Augusta National. Our goal is to get the club membership open to women—period. Some members of that community would like to characterize us as strident, which we are not. We are, however, resolved. And we all know there's only one way for this story to end. It's just a matter of time."[40]

And what of those members Ms. Burk refers to? The members who said they had expressed their views directly to Mr. Johnson or his allies at the club in recent weeks were civilly told to back off on the issue, that their opinions were out of touch with the rest of the membership. With an agreement that they not be identified, one member said, "A few of us were made to feel like we should keep to ourselves on this subject, or maybe consider whether we belonged at Augusta National."[41] Another said, "I was told that maybe I did not understand the history and tradition of Augusta National as well I should."[42] A third member observed that, "Some of us find this all needlessly embarrassing, but I believe we are a distinct minority. We are being told that maybe we don't understand the way things are done and why, that this is a thing of principles, important principles, as they see them. It's a strong, defiant attitude."[43]

When asked for his reaction to several members' saying they want to see a woman member at Augusta, Mr. Johnson would only say, "I'm not going to talk about member issues. Those are private matters to be dealt with from within."[44]

"What [Mr. Johnson] means by that," one anonymous member said, "is that those members have been or will be firmly reminded that they are violating a club policy by speaking out. They will be reminded that that is not the way things have been done around our club for decades and decades."[45]

Discussion Questions

1. What are the basic business issues in the case?
2. Should women be invited to join Augusta National Golf Club? If so, when?
3. Who are the key stakeholders in this case? Does anyone have a stake in the outcome of this dispute other than the principals whose views have been aired in the media?
4. Should the NCWO continue to press this issue? If so, how?
5. What are the implications for both Augusta National and the NCWO?
6. What problems might prominent Augusta National members (CEOs, for example) face?
7. What other courses of action could have been pursued by key individuals?

CASE STUDY: MOTHERS WORK INC.

Brand Image and Accusations of Employment Discrimination

INTRODUCTION

On June 27, 2003, Rebecca Matthias, the COO of the world's largest maternity clothing company, Mothers Work, Inc., called an urgent meeting with her top executives: Dan Matthias, Mothers Work's chairman, Sheryl Roth Rogers, vice president of marketing, Mona Astra Liss, Mothers Work's publicity director and Frank Mullay, vice president of stores. The five administrative personnel were gathered to discuss

This teaching note was prepared by Research Assistants Carolyn E. Billick and Lusiena H. C. Wong under the direction of James S. O'Rourke, Concurrent Professor of Management, as the basis for class discussion rather than to illustrate either effective or ineffective handling of an administrative situation.

Eugene D. Fanning Center for Business Communication, Mendoza College of Business, University of Notre Dame.

how the company would address a recent lawsuit filed against Mothers Work, Inc. by a former district manager, Cynthia Papageorge. Papageorge has accused Mr. Mullay of firing her three years earlier because of her gender and pregnancy.

Mothers Work, Inc. has already settled two similar discriminatory complaints (one of which was filed by Papageorge's boss, Jane Dowe). Papageorge's case, however, has been embraced by the media and damage to Mothers Work's reputation could ensue. Women's rights groups issued statements of disapproval within days of the lawsuit's filing. For example, Serrin Foster, the president of Feminists for Life, declared, " 'It is mind blowing to think that a company named Mothers Work that profits from selling apparel to pregnant women would terminate [women's employment] simply because of their maternity.' "[46]

Rebecca Matthias is renowned for her support of women in the workplace, as her company was founded on the premise that women can be both professionals and mothers. The Mothers Work corporate officers must now determine how their $500 million maternity clothing company should react to allegations that it discriminates against pregnant women.

Matthias has earned degrees from MIT, Columbia University, and the University of Pennsylvania. She is the author of *Mothers Work: How a Young Mother Started a Business on a Shoestring and Built It into a Multi-Million Dollar Company*. Matthias serves on the Board of Trustees at Drexel University and Hahnemann MCP Medical University and is a member of the Board of Overseers of the School of Arts and Science at the University of Pennsylvania.[49] On September 16, 2003, Rebecca Matthias was recognized by the United States Small Business Administration at the National Entrepreneurial Conference in Washington, D.C. for her success with Mothers Work.[50]

CORPORATE COMMUNICATION AT MOTHERS WORK

No Corporate Communication division exists at Mothers Work, so many of the communications tasks are undertaken by Rebecca Matthias and Publicity Director Mona Astra Liss. Liss is responsible for all of Mothers Work's fashion publicity in print and in broadcast. She organizes Mothers Work's fashion shows and other activities promoting the Mothers Work maternity lines. One of Ms. Liss's initiatives was the creation of A Pea in a Pod's celebrity program. Famous women such as Cindy Crawford, Sarah Jessica Parker, Toni Braxton, and Claudia Schiffer showcased Mothers Work maternity wear while pregnant.

Ms. Liss has written for *The New York Times, The Washington Post, People,* and *US Weekly* and has been featured on the Today Show, Oprah and E! Entertainment. She is currently working with cable television channel, TBS Superstation, to provide maternity clothing advice to pregnant women. Ms. Liss has been a very prominent individual known for promoting Mothers Work clothing and products.[51]

WOMEN IN THE WORKFORCE

Since 1950, the increase in the percentage of working women has been overwhelming. In 1999 about 60 percent of females 16 years of age and older were in the workforce, an increase of 20 percent since the turn of the 20th century.

Women also accounted for 85 percent of the total increase in the number of workers with more than one job for periods between 1989 and 1999. Labor force participation for women continues to be highest in the 35–44 age groups.[52]

Women are working harder as with all Americans. The average full time worker works about 43 hours per week. For married working women, the amount of hours increased from 41 hours in 1989 to 46 hours in 1998.[53] In addition, women also have to take care of their families and so in a way, they are working "double shift." Balancing between a career and a family can be difficult. As the number of women entering the workforce continues to rise, more businesses are offering services and information to help women find jobs or to better their understanding maternity rights. A good example of such an information source would be "*The 100 Best Companies for Working Mothers List 2003,*"[54] a magazine published by Working Mothers.

PREGNANCY DISCRIMINATION

The Pregnancy Discrimination Act of 1978 was passed as an amendment to Title VII of the Civil Rights of 1964. The act states that "women affected by pregnancy, childbirth, or related medical condition shall be treated the same for all employment-related purposes, including receipt of benefits under fringe benefit programs, as other persons not affected but similar in their ability or inability to work."[55]

Despite the protection offered by the legal system against pregnancy discrimination in the work place, the number of pregnancy-related discrimination cases is on the rise. Pregnancy discrimination complaints nationwide jumped 10 percent last year to just over 4,700 cases, according to the Equal Employment Opportunity Commission (EEOC). Such complaints have increased by approximately 40 percent since 1992.[56]

Lawyers, enforcement officials and workers' advocates believe that the increase is partly a symptom of widespread layoffs. According to Will Hannum, an Andover, Mass., attorney who represents employers in labor matters, the shaky economy has exacerbated the situation as companies try to cope with pressures that sometimes force them to choose which employees to keep on the payroll.[57]

THE FAMILY MEDICAL LEAVE ACT

The Family Medical Leave Act (FMLA) was passed by the Congress of the United States and signed into law in 1993. That legislation guarantees employees of companies up to 12 weeks of unpaid leave annually for certain medical reasons or for the birth or adoption of a child.

To be eligible, the employer must have 50 or more employees who have worked for the employer at least 12 months and 1,250 hours in the last year. The FMLA requires that employers reinstate employees to their former job or an equivalent job at the end of the leave, and must maintain any group health insurance coverage under the same conditions of coverage and cost-sharing arrangement as if the employee were working during the leave.[58]

MASSACHUSETTS MEDICAL LEAVE ACT

Besides the Family Medical Leave Act, residents of Massachusetts (the state in which Papageorge filed her lawsuit) receive additional protection from the Massachusetts Maternity Leave Act (MMLA). The MMLA requires that an employee on leave be restored to her previous or a similar position upon her return to employment following leave. That position must have the same status, pay, length of service credit and seniority as the position the employee held prior to the leave.[59]

The MMLA also requires that a maternity leave not affect an employee's right to receive vacation time, sick leave, bonuses, advancement, seniority, length of service credit, benefits, plans or programs for which she was eligible at the date of her leave, and any other advantages or rights of her employment incident to her position. Such maternity leave, however, need not be included in the computation of such benefits, rights and advantages.[60]

An employee returning from the leave does not have greater rights in terms of benefits or work conditions over other employees who have been working while the prior employee was on leave. The employer is also not required to reinstate a returning employee to her previous position if other employees of the same caliber and length of service have been laid off during her leave period due to economic conditions or operation changes.

Nothing in the MMLA shall be construed to affect any bargaining agreement, employment agreement, or company policy providing benefits that are greater than, or in addition to, those required under the statute. An employer may grant a longer maternity leave than required under the MMLA. However, if the employer does not intend for full MMLA rights to apply to the period beyond eight weeks, the employer must communicate it clearly to the employee in writing prior to the commencement of the leave.[61]

PAPAGEORGE'S "CONDITION"

Cynthia Papageorge began working for Mothers Work, Inc. in 1997 as a district manager for stores in Massachusetts, Connecticut, and Rhode Island.[62] In October of 1999, Papageorge was 37 weeks pregnant with her first child when Mothers Work vice president, Frank Mullay, inspected four of Papageorge's stores unannounced. Mullay found deficiencies in the stores' housekeeping, made several references to Papageorge's pregnancy and even suggested that Cynthia could not meet her job requirements as a result of her "condition."

The lawsuit claims that within several days of the random store inspection, Mullay ordered Papageorge's supervisor, Jan Dowe, to fire Papageorge on the grounds that Papageorge was pregnant. In an affidavit, Dowe stated she refused to fire Papageorge after company officials told Dowe it would be illegal to let Papageorge go. Dowe met with Mullay and informed him of the illegality of his proposal. He responded with, " 'There are ways of getting around the law.'"[63] Six months later, Papageorge was released after requesting medical leave for a shoulder injury, which was unrelated to her pregnancy. Dowe was also fired for inadequate job performance after taking maternity leave.

Mark Itzkowitz, Papageorge's lawyer has claimed, "'It seems that pregnant women are subject to termination by virtue of their pregnancy. That position was made known in meetings with managers at Mothers Work. The other women [from the other three lawsuits] were terminated for the same reason.'"[64]

Discussion Questions

1. What facts in this case appear to be the most important to you?
2. Who are the key stakeholders in this case? How will a verdict for or against Papageorge affect the parties?
3. What actions (if any) should Mothers Work, Inc. take? What message should the company send to the public? Who is Mothers Work's target audience?
4. What are the critical issues of this case? Which issues should Mothers Work confront first?
5. Since there is no Corporate Communications department, who should deliver Mothers Work's message? What media should Mothers Work use to convey its position?
6. This lawsuit has not received much media attention (since the original filing of the suit). Why do you think this is the case?

Appendix A

MOTHERS WORK INC.

FIGURE 3-6

Copyright 2003 Yahoo! Inc.   http://finance.yahoo.com/

References

1. Pennington, Bill, and Dave Anderson. "Some at Augusta National Quietly Seek a Compromise," *The New York Times*, September 29, 2002, Section 8, pp. 1, 6.

2. Letter from Martha Burk to William Johnson. June 12, 2002. Available from http://www.womensorganizations.org/news/augustaletter.pdf.

3. Letter from William Johnson to Martha Burk. July 8, 2002. Available from http://www.womensorganizations.org/news/augustaletter.pdf.

4. Press Release: "Statement By Hootie Johnson" The Golf Central Newsroom, July 9, 2002, http://www.womensorganizations.org/news/position04_press.htm.

5. Letters from Martha Burk to Sanford Weill, Douglas Daft, G. Richard Wagoner, Mark LaNeve and Samuel Palmisano. July 30, 2002. Available from http://www.womensorganizations.org/news/.

6. Letter from Martha Burk to Tim Finchem. July 30, 2002. Available from http://www.womensorganizations.org/news/august%20letter.

7. Letter from Tim Finchem to Martha Burk. August 20, 2002. Available from http://www.womensorganizations.org/news/august%20letter.

8. Letter from Leah C. Johnson to Martha Burk. August 22, 2002. Available from http://www.womensorganizations.org/news/august%20letter.

9. Letter from Rick Singer to Martha Burk. August 15, 2002. Available from http://www.womensorganizations.org/news/august%20letter.

10. Letter from Martha Burk to Samuel Palmisano. August 20, 2002. Available from http://www.womensorganizations.org/news/august%20letter.

11. Press Release: "Statement by Hootie Johnson." August 30, 2002. Available from http://www.womensorganizations.org/news/augusta%20press%20.

12. Ferguson, Doug. AP Golf Writer. "Women's group targets CBS," *USA Today,* August 31, 2002. Available from http://www.usatoday.com/sports/golf/masters.

13. Letter from Martha Burk to Sean McManus. September 18, 2002. Available from http://www.womensorganizations.org/news/augusta_CBS.pdf.

14. Letter from Sean McManus to Martha Burk. September 19, 2002. Available from http://www.womensorganizations.org/news/augusta_CBS.pdf.

15. McCarthy, Michael, and Erik Brady. "Privacy becomes public at Augusta," *USA Today,* September 27, 2002. Available

from http://www.state.ma.us/mcad/maternity2.html

17. Green, Ron Sr. "It Is Still Augusta National Golf Club," April 8, 2002. Available from http://www.golfweb.com/u/ce/multi/0,1977,5209104,00.html.

18. Press Release: "Statement by Hootie Johnson." The Golf Central Newsroom, July 9, 2002. Available from http://www.womensorganizations.org/news/position04_press.htm.

19. Ferguson, Doug. Associated Press Golf Writer. "Augusta Chairman Lashes Out at Group." July 9, 2002. Available from http://www.radicus.net/news/wed/cn/Aglf-augusta-national.

20. Letter from Martha Burk to Sanford Weill. July 30, 2002. Available from http://www.womensorganizations.org/news/august.

21. Letter from Martha Burk to Douglas Daft. July 30, 2002. Available from http://www.womensorganizations.org/news/august%20letter.

22. Letter from Martha Burk to Samuel Palmisano. July 30, 2002. Available from http://www.womensorganizations.org/news/august%20letter_IBM.pdf.

23. Letter from Martha Burk to G. Richard Wagoner. July 30, 2002. Available from http://www.womensorganizations.org/news/august%20letter.

24. http://www.pga.com.

25. http://www.womensorganizations.org.

26. Pennington, Bill. "At Ever-Contrary Augusta, Even Ike Didn't Hold Sway," *The New York Times,* October 10, 2002, pp. C21, C24.

27. McCarthy, Michael. "Group Takes Augusta Golf Fight to Companies," *USA Today,* July 17, 2002. Available from http://www.usatoday.com/sports/golf/masters/2002.

28. Pennington, Bill, and Dave Anderson. "Some at Augusta National Quietly Seek a Compromise," *The New York Times,* September 29, 2002, Section 8, pp. 1, 6.

29. Fabrikant, Geraldine, and Richard Sandomir. "Executive Speaks Up For Women At Augusta," *The New York Times,* October 5, 2002, pp. B1, B21.

30. Sandomir, Richard. "U.S.O.C. Chief Backs Women at Augusta," *The New York Times,* October 8, 2002, pp. C21, C25.

31. "A Welcome to the Club," *the New York Times,* October 9, 2002, p. C17.

32. Sandomir, Richard. "U.S.O.C. Chief Backs Women at Augusta," *The New York Times,* October 8, 2002, pp. C21, C25.

33. Newberry, Paul. Associated Press. "Hootie Johnson: Complex Man at Center of Masters Dispute." Available from http://pga.com/Newsline/Industry.

34. Blauvelt, Harry. "Burk Not Afraid to Take on Status Quo," *USA Today,* October 9, 2002. Available from http://www.usatoday.com/sports/golf/masters/2002.

35. Blauvelt, Harry.

36. Johnson, William. "Why I'm Teed Off," *The Wall Street Journal,* November 12, 2002, p. A20.

37. Johnson, William.

38. Brown, Clifton. "At Club in Augusta, Policy of Chairman Remains 'Men Only'," *The New York Times,* November 12, 2002, pp. A1, C24.

39. Brown, Clifton.

40. Comments made by Martha Burk to *The Washington Post,* November 12, 2002. Available from http://www.now.org/issues/wfw/111202augusta.html.

41. Davis, Barker. "Burk Keeps Swinging Away at Golf's Augusta," *The Washington Times,* October 23, 2002. Available from http://www.washtimes.com/national/20021023_13631490.thm

42. Pennington, Bill, and Clifton Brown. "Members of Club Who Favor Change Told to Back Off," *The New York Times,* November 13, 2002, pp. C19, C22.

43. Pennington, Bill, and Clifton Brown.

44. Brown, Clifton. "At Club in Augusta, Policy of Chairman Remains 'Men Only'," *The New York Times,* November 12, 2002, pp. A1, C24.

45. Pennington, Bill and Clifton Brown. "Members of Club Who Favor Change Told to Back Off," *The New York Times,* November 13, 2002, pp. C19, C22.

46. Steven Ertelt, "Maternity Store Sued for Pregnancy Discrimination After Employee Fired ," 30 June 2003, http://www.prolifeinfo.com/nat19.html.

47. Wharton Entrepreneurial Programs, "Profiting from Pregnancy," <K"http://

www.wep.wharton.upenn.edu/maternity.html < "http://www.wep.wharton.upenn.edu/maternity.html>.

48. Tom Belden, "Mother Work Includes Serving as Role Model," 18 September 2003, <http://www.philly.com/mld/inquirer/6797380.htm>.

49. Wharton Entrepreneurship Conference, <http://www.whartonentreconf.org/wec/bios.asp#matthias>.

50. Mothers Work, Inc., "US Small Business Administration (SBA) Honors Rebecca Matthias, President & COO of Mothers Work," 16 September 2003 <http://biz.yahoo.com/prnews/030916/phtu022_1.html> (17 November 2003).

51. http://tbssuperstation.com/hostedmovies/expert/0,14005,7721,00.html.

52. http://www.roadandtravel.com/businessandcareer/careers/dyk_womworkers.htm

53. Ibid.

54. http://www.workingmother.com/oct03/100BestList.shtml

55. http://womensissues.about.com/library/weekly/aa062901a.htm

56. http://www.reddingemployment.com/news/business/past/20031005bus075.shtml

57. http://www.reddingemployment.com/news/business/past/20031005bus075.shtml

58. http://www.people.virginia.edu/~jhv3q/EmpLaw2001/fmla_summary.htm

59. http://www.state.ma.us/mcad/maternity2.html

60. Ibid.

61. http://www.state.ma.us/mcad/maternity2.html

62. Theo Emery, "Maternity Co. Fires Pregnant Woman," 27 June 2003, <http://www.cbsnews.com/stories/2003/06/27/national/printable560715.shtml.< 18 November 2003.

63. Burrelle's Information Services: CBS News Transcripts, in *LexisNexis,* <http://80-web.lexis-nexis.com.lib_proxy.nd.edu/universe/document?_m=e32f03b65dd39d7f69819adda18510b3&_docnum=2&wchp=dGLbVtbzSkVA&_md5=a4ecbf93dbc25c150d9cdba78c08e739>.

64. Steven Ertelt, "Maternity Store Sued for Pregnancy Discrimination After Employee Fired," 30 June 2003, http://www.prolifeinfo.com/nat19.html (18 November 2003).

4 | RACE AND NATIONAL ORIGIN

Race, as a protected class, is defined in accordance with the following categories as determined by the U.S. government: Caucasian/White, Asian, African American/Black, Pacific Islander/Native Hawaiian, American Indian/Alaskan Native. National origin is also a protected class and is defined as a person's country of birth, ethnicity, ancestry, or culture.

Objectives

■ To examine the relationship between people of different races/national origins and the workplace.

■ To examine the claim that minority employees should be mentored very differently than their white counterparts.

■ To examine how an organizational leader responded to a diversity management crisis in an effort to protect corporate image and improve stakeholder relations.

■ To examine how creating relationships within racial and national groups can be critical to success in business.

Preview Questions

■ Should organizational leaders modify their mentoring style when mentoring minority employees?

■ How should an organization respond to a diversity crisis—should it take a short-term approach and simply settle the lawsuit, or should it take a long-term approach and make diversity systemic throughout the organization?

■ Should organizations adapt to the values of different cultures when making business transactions or apply a universal set of standards?

Some Important Dates

1619 First African slaves arrive in Virginia.
1789 U.S. Constitution is ratified with a clause that equates a slave to three fifths of a white citizen and includes a provision that slave trade will end within 20 years.

1798–1808	Decade of greatest U.S. importation of African slaves, totaling approximately 200,000.
1819	U.S. law equates slave trading with piracy, punishable by death.
1857	U.S. Supreme Court rules slavery legal in the Dred Scott case.
1861	The Civil War begins.
1863	Emancipation Proclamation, issued in 1862 by President Lincoln to free slaves in Confederate territory, goes into effect.
1865	Thirteenth Amendment, passed and ratified in the same year, abolishes slavery; first historical black colleges and universities form.
1868	Fourteenth Amendment grants African Americans full U.S. citizenship and equal civil rights.
1870	Fifteenth Amendment grants African American men the right to vote.
1873–83	Supreme Court cases weaken key postwar civil rights laws and constitutional amendments; states can now reinstitute discriminatory laws.
1884	"Jim Crow" laws appear throughout southern and western states to segregate African Americans in education, travel, and public accommodations.
1896	Supreme Court deals a blow to integrated education in *Plessy v. Ferguson,* reinforcing the "separate but equal" concept.
1950–52	Five cases are filed in Kansas, Delaware, South Carolina, Virginia, and the District of Columbia to challenge the constitutionality of segregated education.
1952	Supreme Court consolidates five cases into *Oliver Brown et al. v. the Board of Education of Topeka, Kansas.*
1954	Supreme Court unanimously declares that separate educational facilities are "inherently unequal" and violate the Fourteenth Amendment, which guarantees all citizens "equal protection of the laws."
1963	Equal Pay Act is passed by Congress, promising equitable wages for the same work, regardless of the race, color, religion, national origin, or sex of the worker.
1964	Title VII of the Civil Rights Act passes including a prohibition against employment discrimination on the basis of race, color, religion, national origin, or sex.

ABERCROMBIE & FITCH BIAS CASE IS SETTLED

Abercrombie & Fitch, one of the nation's trendiest retailers, settled race and sex discrimination lawsuits yesterday, agreeing to alter its well-known collegiate, all-American—and largely white—image by adding more blacks, Hispanics, and Asians to its marketing materials.

After a federal judge in San Francisco approved the class-action settlement yesterday, the two sides announced an agreement that calls for Abercrombie & Fitch to pay $40 million to several thousand minority and female plaintiffs. Abercrombie also agreed to hire 25 diversity recruiters and a vice president for diversity and to pursue benchmarks so that its hiring and promotion of minorities and women reflect its applicant pool.

Steven Greenhouse, *New York Times.* (Late Edition—Final), New York, NY: November 17, 2004.
Copyright 2004 New York Times Company Nov 17, 2004.

In an unusual step, the settlement calls for Abercrombie to increase diversity not just in hiring and promotions, but also in its advertisements and catalogs, which have long featured models who were overwhelmingly white and who seemed to have stepped off the football field or out of fraternities or sororities. Plaintiffs' lawyers said they insisted that the company agree to add more diversity to its marketing materials so as not to discourage minorities from applying for jobs.

In another unusual move, the settlement requires Abercrombie to stop focusing on predominantly white fraternities and sororities in its recruitment. Many Abercrombie workers have said that company employees were often told to go to college campuses and to urge good-looking fraternity and sorority members to apply for jobs.

When Abercrombie was sued in June 2003, several Hispanic, black, and Asian plaintiffs complained that when they applied for jobs, they were steered not to sales positions out front, but to low-visibility, back-of-the-store jobs, stocking, and cleaning up.

"Abercrombie had a back-of-the-bus mentality," said Kimberly West-Faulcon, Western regional counsel for the NAACP Legal Defense and Education Fund. "Now instead of hiring them in the back of the store, they will have diversity recruiters. It sends a message to young people that we're moving past this kind of thing."

Bill Lann Lee, the plaintiffs' lead lawyer and former director of the Justice Department's civil rights division, said Abercrombie had refused to hire many minority students who had impressive work and school records. He added that the percentages of minority and women managers at Abercrombie were far below industry averages.

"We're talking about discrimination being visited on some of the best and the brightest within their community," Mr. Lee said.

He applauded the settlement, approved yesterday by Judge Susan Illston of Federal District Court. "The import of this settlement is that a major American company has stepped forward and become a model," Mr. Lee said.

Abercrombie, which did not admit guilt, agreed to hire a monitor, to provide diversity training to all managers who do hiring, and to revise performance evaluations for managers, making progress in diversity goals a factor in bonuses and compensation. The settlement also called for $7.2 million in lawyers' fees.

In a statement, Mike Jeffries, Abercrombie's chairman, said: "We have, and always have had, no tolerance for discrimination. We decided to settle this suit because we felt that a long, drawn-out dispute would have been harmful to the company and distracting to management."

Several industry analysts said the settlement would help Abercrombie's marketing. The company has 700 stores and 22,000 employees and had $1.7 billion in sales last year.

"Their profile, their image is going to evolve," said Robin S. Murchison, a retail analyst with Jefferies & Company. "It will still be the cool kids. You can walk onto any Ivy League campus and there's a lot more going on than Waspy-looking guys and girls. I think they'll tap into that. I actually think it will work to their advantage."

In an interview yesterday, Carla Grubb, a 21-year-old black plaintiff who is a student at California State University at Bakersfield, said that after she applied for a sales job at an Abercrombie store, she was hired to dust, clean windows, and vacuum.

"I was always doing cleaning—they said I was a good window washer," said

(continued)

Ms. Grubb, who later landed a job elsewhere repairing computers. "I should have received the same treatment as everybody else. It made me feel bad. No one should be judged by the color of their skin."

Senior executives often face the challenge of helping promising employees of color break through the glass ceiling. An in-depth study reveals that minority protégés should be mentored very differently than their white counterparts.

ESSAY: THE TRUTH ABOUT MENTORING MINORITIES
Race Matters

Diversity has become a top priority in corporate America. Despite the best intentions, though, many organizations have failed to achieve racial balance within their executive teams. Some have revolving doors for talented minorities, recruiting the best and brightest only to see them leave, frustrated, and even angered by the barriers they encounter. Other companies are able to retain high-potential professionals of color only to have them become mired in middle management. Still others have minorities in their executive ranks, but only in racialized positions, such as those dealing with community relations, equal employment opportunity, or ethnic markets.

In my research on the career progression of minorities at U.S. corporations, I have found that whites and minorities follow distinct patterns of advancement. Specifically, promising white professionals tend to enter a fast track early in their careers, whereas high-potential minorities take off much later, typically after they have reached middle management. I've also found that the people of color who advance the farthest all share one characteristic—a strong network of mentors and corporate sponsors who nurture their professional development.

PATTERNS OF MOVEMENT

In a 3-year research project, I studied the career trajectories of minority and white professionals at three major U.S. corporations. The most striking aspect of my findings was the consistency of the data. White professionals who eventually became executives—a group I'll henceforth refer to simply as "white executives"—usually entered a fast track in Stage 1, whereas both white and minority professionals who later plateaued in middle management, and minorities who eventually became executives, all inched along during that period. In Stages 2 and 3, the careers of minorities who ultimately became executives took off, surpassing those of the plateaued managers.

This stark difference in the career trajectories of white and minority executives suggests that companies implicitly have two distinct tournaments for access to the top jobs. In the tournament for whites, contenders are sorted early on, and only those deemed most promising proceed to future competition. In the tournament for

David A. Thomas, Harvard Business School.

minorities, the screening process for the best jobs occurs much later. This and other differences have important implications for minority professionals—and for the people mentoring them through the different stages.

Stage 1

According to my research, a pernicious result of the two-tournament system was that many high-potential minorities became discouraged when they failed to be fast-tracked early in their careers. They became demotivated—and deskilled, especially when they saw their white colleagues receive plum assignments and promotions. As a result, their performance fell to a level that matched their modest rewards.

But some minorities—those who eventually became executives—avoided that fate. What kept them motivated and prepared to take advantage of opportunities that arrived belatedly? A common thread among them was their relationships with mentors. Even though the minority executives were not on an obvious fast track, influential mentors were investing in them as if they were, which helped prevent them from either ratcheting down their performance or simply leaving the organization.

This is not to say that the minorities in the study who became executives did not experience their share of disappointments; they did. But they evaluated themselves in terms of personal growth, not external rewards. Committed to excellence, they found the process of learning new skills rewarding. In general, minority executives made early career choices that placed them at the leading edge of the work they liked. They were more enthusiastic about the work itself and less concerned with how quickly—or slowly—they were climbing the corporate ladder. In fact, two minority executives in the study actually took demotions to transfer from staff jobs into operations, where they saw a better match for their skills and a greater opportunity for professional growth. Stage 1 was thus a time for minority executives to gain the three *C*'s: confidence, competence, and credibility.

In contrast, minority professionals who subsequently plateaued in middle management tended to make their decisions based on perceived fast-track career opportunities, not on the actual work. They were more prone to take salary and title promotions that offered little increase in management responsibility.

Interestingly, minority executives were promoted to middle management only slightly faster than minority plateaued managers, but with much greater job continuity. They were much less likely to have changed departments, made lateral moves, or transferred away from core positions. Surprisingly, they even received, on average, fewer promotions within a given level than did minorities who failed to make it past middle management. A close inspection of the data, however, revealed that the promotions of minority managers offered little real expansion of responsibilities, as compared with the promotions of minority executives.

Minority executives attributed much of their later success to their immediate bosses, other superiors, and peers who helped them develop professionally. Of course, such developmental relationships are important for everybody climbing the corporate ladder, regardless of race, but what distinguished minority executives from white executives and plateaued managers was that they had many more such relationships and with a broader range of people, especially in the early years of their careers. Within the first three years at the organization, minority executives had established at least one developmental relationship, usually with a boss or a boss's boss. These mentors provided critical support in five ways.

First, the relationships opened the door to challenging assignments that allowed the minority executives to gain professional competence. Second, by putting the future executives in high-trust positions, the mentors sent a message to the rest of the organization that these people were high performers, thus helping them gain confidence and establish their credibility. Third, the mentors provided crucial career advice and counsel that prevented their protégés from getting sidetracked from the path leading to the executive level. Fourth, the mentors often became powerful sponsors later in the minority executives' careers, recruiting them repeatedly to new positions. Fifth, the mentors often protected their protégés by confronting subordinates or peers who leveled unfair criticism, especially if it had racial undertones. For example, a superior-performing African American in the study had a laid-back style that detractors said was an indication of his slacking off, playing on the stereotype that blacks are lazy. The mentor directly challenged the detractors by pointing out that his protégé was the leading salesperson in the division.

In summary, in Stage 1, the winners in the white tournament earned fast promotions into middle management. In the minority tournament, the signals sent to winners were more subtle, taking the form of rich mentoring relationships, challenging assignments, and expanded responsibilities, which showed the rest of the organization that these people merited future investment. (Winners of the white tournament also received those benefits, but the most obvious prizes in that contest were fast promotions.)

Stage 2

Once minority executives entered middle management, they typically had to wait another 10 to 15 years before reaching the executive level. But Stage 2 was usually where their careers took off. And without exception, the minority executives in the study vividly recalled that their initial middle-management jobs were critical to their eventual success. Interestingly, few of the white executives felt that way, perhaps because they did not regard their jobs in early Stage 2 as big opportunities to prove themselves in the same way that their minority counterparts did.

In Stage 2, minority executives continued to increase their functional knowledge, allowing them to deepen and broaden their foundation of the three *C*'s. When leading others, minority executives often were able to influence subordinates who might otherwise have been resistant, owing to the sheer technical or functional competence they had acquired in Stage 1. Through that process, they were able to enhance their managerial skills and judgment. Stage 2 was also an important period for the minority executives to apply their existing skills to complex situations, which then helped them demonstrate their potential and extend their credibility within the larger organization. Thus, they were able to expand their network of relationships, including those with mentors and sponsors, beyond the boundaries of their original functional groups. By the end of Stage 2, every minority executive in the study had at least one influential executive as a mentor, and many were highly regarded by several executives who acted as sponsors.

The split between minority executives and plateaued managers became more pronounced in Stage 2. Minority executives still received fewer promotions than minority plateaued managers, but they reached upper middle management in less time because their promotions were bigger and more significant. The assignment patterns of the minority managers continued to be unfocused: They had more job changes—either by department, location, or function (especially changes from line to staff jobs)—and they tended to serve in fix-it roles involving the same kind of challenges over and over, with no opportunity to acquire new skills.

Stage 2 was also when the careers of minority and white executives began to converge—their experiences, assignments, and pace of advancement became increasingly similar. There were still, however, some notable differences. Compared with their white counterparts, minority executives were twice as likely to change functions, twice as likely to take on special projects or taskforce assignments, three times as likely to take a turnaround assignment, almost twice as likely to change locations, and four times as likely to report a big success. In many ways, these differences are a reversal of what occurred in Stage 1, in which white executives had markedly more opportunities to prove themselves than minority executives did. For that reason, Stage 2 can be thought of as a catching-up and breaking-out period for minority executives.

Interestingly, although minority and white executives had a similar number of developmental relationships in Stage 2, minority executives were far more likely to have powerful corporate-level executives as sponsors and mentors. In reviewing their careers, minority executives usually described a senior person who had been watching their progress during this period without their full awareness.

Stage 3

The climb from upper middle management to the executive level required a broad base of experience—well beyond a functional expertise. In Stage 3, people took on issues specific to working across functional boundaries, and that change encouraged them to think and act more strategically and politically.

To distinguish oneself as executive-level material in Stage 3, an individual needed highly visible successes that were directly related to the company's core strategy.

Minority executives in Stage 3 continued developing their network of highly placed mentors and sponsors. An individual's relationship with his executive boss, in particular, became crucial; it played a central role in helping each minority executive break through to the highest level. Furthermore, in Stage 3 the minority executives reported developing at least two new relationships with other executives. In contrast, most of the minority plateaued managers did not establish any new developmental relationships during that time.

The networks of minority executives were also much more diverse than those of the minority managers. For example, African American managers who plateaued relied either almost exclusively on members of their own racial group for key developmental support or predominantly on whites. In contrast, those who reached the executive level, especially the most successful among them, had built genuine, personal long-term relationships with both whites and African Americans.

The careers of minority and white executives continued to converge in Stage 3, especially with regard to developmental relationships. Clearly, it was impossible to make it to the executive level, regardless of race, without the active advocacy of an immediate boss and at least one other key sponsor or mentor. Nevertheless, as was the case in Stage 2, minority executives tended to have a higher proportion of their developmental relationships with the corporate elite than did white executives.

In summary, during Stages 2 and 3, the careers of minority executives became clearly differentiated from those of plateaued managers, and in Stage 3, the career trajectories and experiences of minority and white executives finally converged.

MENTORING CHALLENGES

A key finding of this research is that professionals of color who plateaued in management received mentoring that was basically instructional; it helped them develop better skills. Minority executives, by contrast, enjoyed closer, fuller developmental relationships with their mentors. This was particularly true in people's early careers, when they needed to build confidence, credibility, and competence. That is, purely instructional mentoring was not sufficient; protégés needed to feel connected to their mentors.

Specifically, a mentor must play the dual role of coach and counselor: Coaches give technical advice—explaining how to do something—whereas counselors talk about the experience of doing it and offer emotional support. Both are crucial.

Many people, however, do not approach mentoring from a developmental perspective. They do not understand how to work with subordinates, especially minorities, to prepare them for future opportunities. My own experience and the findings of other studies suggest that organizations can change this situation by educating managers about their developmental role and by teaching them how to mentor effectively.

Cross-Race Issues

This education process must include an awareness of the inherent difficulties of mentoring across race. A significant amount of research shows that cross-race (as well as cross-gender) relationships can have difficulty forming, developing, and maturing. Nevertheless, the mentoring of minority professionals must often be across race, as it was for most of the minority executives in my study. And to develop the personal connections that are the foundation of a good mentoring relationship, the participants must overcome the following potential obstacles.

Negative Stereotypes

Mentors must be willing to give their protégés the benefit of the doubt: They invest in their protégés because they expect them to succeed. But a potential mentor who holds negative stereotypes about an individual, perhaps based on race, may withhold that support until the prospective protégé has proven herself worthy of investment. (Such subtle racism may help explain why none of the minority professionals in my study had been fast-tracked. Whites were placed on the fast track based on their perceived potential, whereas people of color had to display a proven and sustained record of solid performance—in effect, they often had to be overprepared—before they were placed on the executive track.)

Moreover, when a person of color feels that he won't be given the benefit of the doubt, he behaves in certain ways—for example, he might not take risks he should for fear that if he fails, he will be punished disproportionately.

Identification and Role Modeling

Close mentoring relationships are much more likely to form when both parties see parts of themselves in the other person: The protégé sees someone whom he wants to be like in the future. The mentor sees someone who reminds him of himself years ago.

This identification process can help the mentor see beyond a protégé's rough edges. But if the mentor has trouble identifying with her protégé—and sometimes differences in race are an obstacle—then she may not be able to see beyond the protégé's weaknesses. Furthermore, when the mentoring relationship is across race, the mentor will often have certain limitations as a role model. That is, adoption of the behavior of the mentor by the protégé may produce different results. In my study, an African American participant recounted how his white mentor encouraged him to adopt the mentor's more aggressive style. But when the protégé did so, others labeled him an "angry black man."

Skepticism about Intimacy

At companies without a solid track history of diversity, people may question whether close, high-quality relationships across race are possible. Does the mentor, for example, have an ulterior motive, or is the protégé selling out his culture?

Public Scrutiny

Because cross-race relationships are rare in most organizations, they tend to be more noticeable, so people focus on them. The possibility of such scrutiny will often discourage people from participating in a cross-race relationship in the first place.

Peer Resentment

A protégé's peers can easily become jealous, prompting them to suggest or imply that the protégé does not deserve whatever benefits she has received. Someone who fears such resentment might avoid forming a close relationship with a prospective mentor of another race. Of course, peer resentment occurs even with same-race mentorships, but it is a much greater concern in cross-race relationships because of their rarity.

Not surprisingly, many cross-race mentoring relationships suffer from "protective hesitation": Both parties refrain from raising touchy issues. Protective hesitation can become acute when the issue is race—a taboo topic for many mentors and protégées. People believe that they aren't supposed to talk about race; if they have to discuss it, then it must be a problem. But that mind-set can cripple a relationship. Consider, for example, a protégé who thinks that a client is giving him a difficult time because of his race but keeps his opinion to himself for fear that his mentor will think he has a chip on his shoulder. Had the protégé raised the issue, his mentor might have been able to nip the problem early on. The mentor, for instance, might have sent the protégé to important client meetings alone, thereby signaling that the protégé has the backing of his mentor and the authority to make high-level decisions.

In other words, relationships in which protégé and mentor openly discuss racial issues generally translate into greater opportunity for the protégé. To encourage and foster that type of mentoring, organizations can teach people, especially managers, how to identify and surmount various race-related difficulties. It should be noted that when the complexities of cross-race relationships are handled well, they can strengthen a relationship. For one thing, if a mentor and protégé trust each other enough to work together in dealing with touchy race-related issues, then they will likely have a sturdy foundation to handle other problems. In fact, people have reported that race differences enabled them to explore other kinds of differences, thus broadening the perspectives of both parties. That education is invaluable because people who can fully appreciate the uniqueness of each individual are more likely to be better managers and leaders.

Network Management

As discussed earlier, one of a mentor's key tasks is to help the protégé build a large and diverse network of relationships. The network must be strong enough to withstand even the loss of the mentor.

My research has shown that the most effective network is heterogeneous along three dimensions. First, the network should have functional diversity; it should include mentors, sponsors, role models, peers, and even people toward whom the protégées themselves might be developing mentoring relationships. Second, the network should have variety with respect to position (seniors, colleagues, and juniors) as well as location (people within the immediate department, in other departments, and outside the organization). And third, the network should be demographically mixed in terms of race, gender, age, and culture.

A network of relationships becomes vulnerable when it lacks any one of the dimensions. For example, if a person's network is limited to her organization, she will find it difficult to find employment elsewhere. However, people of color have the tendency to draw on a network from primarily outside their organizations. Such support can be invaluable, but it will provide little help when that individual is being considered for a highly desirable in-house assignment. Establishing a diverse network is just the start—a person's network must be replenished and modified continually.

CREATING THE ENVIRONMENT FOR SUCCESS

Many mentors of minority professionals assume that their job begins and ends with the one-on-one relationships they establish with their protégées. This is hardly true. Mentors, especially those at the executive level, must do much more by actively supporting broader efforts and initiatives at their organizations to help create the conditions that foster the upward mobility of people of color.

Organizations should provide a range of career paths, all uncorrelated with race, that lead to the executive suite. Ideally, this system of movement would allow variation across all groups—people could move at their own speed through the three stages based on their individual strengths and needs, not their race. Achieving this system, however, would require integrating the principles of opportunity, development, and diversity into the fabric of the organization's management practices and human resource systems. And an important element in the process would be identifying potential mentors, training them, and ensuring that they are paired with promising professionals of color.

Discussion Questions

1. What are the differences between instructional and developmental mentoring?
2. Why might race be an obstacle to identification between mentor and protégé?
3. Why are necessary conversations about race between mentor and protégé so often difficult?
4. When might a focus on the work itself, rather than on a position's perceived ability to further one's career, be helpful to an ambitious manager?
5. Why is a diverse network of supporters particularly significant for the advancement of minority executives?

CASE STUDY: TEXACO, INC.
Racial Discrimination Suit (A)

Amidst pending allegations that Texaco had consistently failed to promote blacks in certain employee groups because of their race and had "fostered a racially hostile environment,"[1] Texaco was hit with yet another allegation. As reported by *The New York Times* on November 4, 1996, Texaco executives were taped discussing a $520 million lawsuit which was filed by six employees in 1994 on behalf of almost 1,500 other minority workers at the firm. In these discussions, "senior Texaco managers made disparaging comments about minorities and discussed destroying documents related to [the] class-action discrimination suit."[2]

Texaco Chief Executive Officer, Peter I. Bijur, now faced a major corporate crisis in just his sixth month at the helm of Texaco. "The tape recording is [the latest] piece of evidence in [the] anti-discrimination lawsuit brought against the company in two years."[3] Texaco's history of hiring and promoting minorities was less than exemplary, even for the oil industry. The written transcripts of the audiotape, as provided to the courts by an ex-Texaco executive, containing racial slurs and stating intentions to destroy evidence, threatened to exacerbate Texaco's already mounting minority-related issues. The once hardly-noticed racial discrimination suit, Roberts v. Texaco, quickly began to attract media and public attention.

THE CHARGE

Among the many questions immediately facing Texaco's CEO, Peter Bijur, were these: what action should he take on behalf of the company in response to the newly released tapes? What would the best approach be in managing this public-relations disaster? Should employees be addressed separately from the public sector? Is racial discrimination part of the Texaco culture? What, if any, steps can be taken to minimize future discrimination practices? Are reparations necessary? If so, how should it be addressed?

TEXACO, INC. BACKGROUND

"Texaco Inc., originally known as The Texas Company, was founded in 1902 in Beaumont, Texas, by oilman 'Buckskin' Joe Cullinan and New York investor Arnold Schlaet."[4] In 1996, the time of the case, Texaco ranked #11 on the

This case was prepared by Research Assistants Tanya Goria, DeWayne Reed, and Dan Skendzel under the direction of James S. O'Rourke, Concurrent Associate Professor of Management, as the basis for class discussion rather than to illustrate either effective or ineffective handling of an administrative situation. Information was gathered from corporate as well as public sources.

Eugene D. Fanning Center for Business Communication, Mendoza College of Business, University of Notre Dame. Copyright ©2000. Eugene D. Fanning Center for Business Communication. All rights reserved. No part of this publication may be reproduced, stored in a retrieval system, used in a spreadsheet, or transmitted in any form by any means—electronic, mechanical, photocopying, recording, or otherwise—without permission.

Fortune 500 (Exhibit 1) list and employed more than 27,000 people worldwide.[5] Within the petroleum industry, Texaco ranked third behind Exxon and Mobil. At year's end in 1996, Texaco had assets of $27 billion and revenues of more than $45 billion.[6]

The company's recent employee history had been less than ideal. *The Wall Street Journal* reported that:

> Texaco had been a snakepit of disappointed middle management since the 1980s. . . . It went from 11 layers of management to five, dumping tens of thousands of employees over the next decade. Last year [1996], in fact, was the first in a long time that Texaco's payroll grew instead of shrank.[7]

Middle management discontent may have been an issue, but Texaco claims to have been working earnestly toward a more integrated work force, despite the layoffs. In a November 1996 interview on *Nightline,* Texaco CEO Peter Bijur offered this assessment of Texaco's employment figures: "16.6 percent of our U.S. work force of 27,426 were minorities in 1991, while as of last June, 22.3 percent of our 19,554 employees were minorities. Of those employees, the percentage of minorities in supervisory, management, and executive positions was 6.8 percent in 1989, and 9.5 percent in 1994."[8]

In early 1996, the Equal Employment Opportunity Commission (EEOC) reviewed the lawsuit against Texaco and found that black workers seeking promotion were chosen "at rates significantly below that of their non-black counterparts."[9] The EEOC's finding also support the results of a study of one Texaco division by the Department of Labor. They discovered that minority employees took up to twice as many years as white workers to win promotions and ordered Texaco to pay compensation and revised its company-wide appraisal system.

Another survey, carried out for a rival oil company, found that the proportion of highly paid black workers at Texaco was consistently below the industry average. White senior managers at Texaco outnumbered their black counterparts by more than 80 to one.

THE MEETING

During a 1994 meeting between Texaco finance department manager Richard Lundwall and other Texaco finance department managers, recordings were made by Lundwall allegedly detailing derogatory remarks being made by the department managers concerning Texaco's African-American employees. "The transcript filed by Plaintiffs of the pending discrimination lawsuit against Texaco contains four instances of remarks with apparent racial connotations: (1) a statement characterizing African-Americans as "f****** n****rs"; (2) a statement, 'you know how black jelly beans agree,' followed by other remarks relating to jelly beans; (3) references to an event at which African-Americans allegedly sat through the playing of the United States National Anthem and then standing for a song presented as the Black National Anthem; and (4) references to Hanukkah and Kwanzaa."[10] Further comments included: "All the black jelly beans seem to be glued to the bottom of the bag."[11]

The behavior captured on tape revealed discrimination issues within the culture at Texaco. The term "black jelly beans" was used on the tape and Bob Ulrich, an attendee of the meeting and one of the individuals who used the term, through his attorney Jonathan Rosner, stated that the reference on the tape was not in any way intended to be a racial slur. Rosner pointed out that the term "jelly bean" is not, in and of itself, known to be a derogatory term, and Ulrich had no reason to think that the reference carried any such connotations.

Rosner also observed that Ulrich's reference to jelly beans was prompted by a speech given by an African-American at a conference at which the speaker, advocating integration and opposing separatist philosophies, illustrated his remarks by using jars of jelly beans as an analogy for racial integration. "While Ulrich could not remember the name of the speaker to whom he referred, Dr. R. Roosevelt Thomas, Jr. was identified as the probable source of the remarks alluded to by Ulrich. Dr. Thomas is the founder and former President of the American Institute for Managing Diversity, at Morehouse College in Atlanta, Georgia.[12]

PUBLIC OUTCRY

The public was outraged when it received the initial reports that top executives within Texaco had made derogatory remarks about its African-American employees. Those derogatory remarks seemed to validate the public thought, feeling and insecurity surrounding Corporate America. At a time when affirmative action was being questioned, and the issues of prejudice and injustice were being debated, tangible evidence was offered that the "good ole boys" network, "glass ceilings" and many other negative Corporate America caricatures did in fact exist. This incident was specific to Texaco, but the public sentiment reflected a wider scope of discriminatory issues.

Rev. Jesse Jackson quickly became the voice of the black community, calling for a boycott of all Texaco products. The public responded by cutting up Texaco credit cards, and boycotting independent Texaco dealers. Wall Street recognized the potentially disastrous effects on business and adjusted its stock price accordingly. Texaco stock traded at $99^{5/8}$ at the opening on November 4th, 1996, and dropped to 97 by the end of trading that day.

UNRESOLVED ISSUES

At the time of the case, Texaco, Inc. appeared to have disproportionately lower levels of minorities in roles of authority as compared to whites. Also it should be noted that the discrimination lawsuits that the tape supported were pending prior to the meeting in 1996. The U.S. EEOC had begun an investigation into the employment practices of Texaco prior to the taping of the conversation. These and other unresolved issues appeared to support the notion that Texaco had substantive discrimination problems that management would have to address directly.

Questions

1. What are the critical issues surrounding the newly released tapes?
2. How should Peter Bijur and Texaco respond to the allegations? How should the company respond to the publicity?
3. Should the employees be addressed separately from the general public? How can Texaco mend fences with minority employees and customers?
4. What would be an effective corporate strategy in dealing with encouraging diversity in the workplace.

CASE STUDY: TEXACO, INC.
Racial Discrimination Suit (B)

Roughly one week after *The New York Times* story of Texaco's racial discrimination fiasco hit the street, the company's stock price had tumbled to $95^{3/8}$.

Texaco's reaction to the debacle was swift. On learning of the allegations of misconduct, the company hired Michael Armstrong, a Manhattan lawyer with Kirkpatrick & Lockhart. Armstrong conducted an extensive independent investigation into the affair that included a review of Texaco's diversity and equal-opportunity policies.

On November 4, 1996, the day *The New York Times* story broke, the company issued a press release stating that "if these allegations are true, they represent an outrageous violation of the company's core values and principles. Any such conduct is deplorable and will never be tolerated by Texaco."[13] (Exhibit 1)

The company also vowed to take appropriate disciplinary action against those employees proved guilty. The two managers caught on tape, who at the time still worked for Texaco, were quickly suspended (with full pay) pending the results of the investigation. Subsequently, the two decided to leave the firm and Richard Lundwall and Bob Ulrich were stripped of benefits.[14]

Peter Bijur, Chairman and CEO since only July of 1996, personally authored a letter on November 4, 1996, addressed to Texaco employees explaining the

This case was prepared by Research Assistants Tanya Goria, DeWayne Reed, and Dan Skendzel under the direction of James S. O'Rourke, Concurrent Associate Professor of Management, as the basis for class discussion rather than to illustrate either effective or ineffective handling of an administrative situation. Information was gathered from corporate as well as public sources.

Eugene D. Fanning Center for Business Communication, Mendoza College of Business, University of Notre Dame. Copyright ©2000. Eugene D. Fanning Center for Business Communication. All rights reserved. No part of this publication may be reproduced, stored in a retrieval system, used in a spreadsheet, or transmitted in any form by any means—electronic, mechanical, photocopying, recording, or otherwise—without permission.

allegations against the firm and outlining Texaco's investigation into the matter (Exhibit 2). In the letter, Bijur expressed his deep anger and sadness at the alleged incident and re-affirmed Texaco's policy toward the highest ethical and moral standards. "My personal commitment to you is to intensify our efforts to eliminate this [discriminatory] behavior from the workplace," said Bijur. He took further action by broadcasting a message to all employees via satellite on that same day. "We care about each and every employee," he said. "I care deeply."[15]

Behind the scenes, Bijur was also getting the Board of Directors involved in the process. "We had several board and executive committee meetings," said Bijur. Through these meetings, Bijur was able to express Texaco's position and listen to the board's counsel and guidance. The support of the board of directors, according to Bijur, was a crucial ingredient in moving to end the lawsuit quickly.

Additionally, Bijur began to meet with shareholder groups and influential individuals. For example, he met with the Interfaith Center on Corporate Relations, (which is a group of religious shareholders), the New York State Comptroller, and the New York City Comptroller.

Over the course of the next three weeks, Bijur would make himself available for interviews with *The New York Times, Business Week,* and *NBC Nightly News,* among others. Throughout these interviews, he did not attempt to evade questions or deny the reality of the situation. His message was two-pronged: to relate the company's embarrassment about the incident; and to tell Texaco's side of the story—namely that racial discrimination was not commonplace at Texaco and that the company had been making strides to improve minority presence in past years.

"I do not think there is a culture of institutional bias within Texaco," said Bijur. "I think we've got a great many very good and decent human beings, but that unfortunately we mirror society. There is bigotry in society. There is prejudice and injustice in society. I am sorry to say that, and I am sorry to say that probably does exist within Texaco. I can't do much about society, but I certainly can do something about Texaco."[16]

In a November 6, 1996, statement, Bijur publicly outlined a six-step plan aimed at "moving quickly to right these [discriminatory] wrongs (Exhibit 3)." The CEO vowed that Texaco senior executives would visit every major company location in the U.S. to meet with employees and apologize for the embarrassing incident. He also pledged to refocus on the company's core values through the creation of a special committee of board members that would review human resource and diversity programs.

On November 12, 1996, Bijur met with Rev. Jesse Jackson and other black leaders in an effort to stave off a planned boycott of Texaco products and to reassure minorities that Texaco did not condone discrimination in any form. Rev. Jackson emerged from the meeting only to reaffirm the nationwide boycott and picketing of Texaco service stations scheduled to begin four days later, on November 16, 1996.[17]

Three days after Bijur met with Jackson, Texaco settled the Roberts v. Texaco lawsuit filed on behalf of 1,400+ minority employees. Under the settlement, Texaco agreed to pay $115 million in cash plus expenses and salary adjustments to the plaintiffs. In total, the settlement was valued at $176 million. In addition, the company agreed to create an Equality and Tolerance Task Force to determine potential improvements in Texaco's human resources programs, and to monitor the progress of these programs. In a company press release announcing the deal, Bijur said, "with this litigation behind us, we can now move forward on our broader, urgent mission to make Texaco a model of workplace opportunity for all men and women."[18] (Exhibit 4)

On November 15, 1996, Bijur also authored a statement for Texaco employees explaining the lawsuit settlement and the company's reasoning for reaching such an agreement. He again used this format to reassure employees of Texaco's commitment to fairness and equal opportunity (Exhibit 5). In a subsequent interview, Bijur would state, "I made the judgement that we needed to accelerate the settlement process. And those discussions on settlement commenced almost immediately."[19]

Texaco had also signed an agreement with Judge A. Leon Higginbotham Jr., chief judge emeritus of the U.S. Court of Appeals for the 3rd Circuit, to guide it through its review of human resource and diversity policies and practices.[20] The result of this review was Texaco's Workforce Diversity Plan, which it unveiled in mid-December 1996. To help achieve its goal of attracting and retaining a highly capable workforce, among other things, Texaco said it would in 1997:

- Enhance the interviewing, selection, and hiring skills of its managers;
- Expand its overall college recruitment;
- Use search firms with a record of recruiting from a wide, diverse range with key competencies for Texaco.

Based on our review, we have set . . . initiatives that are well balanced and beneficial to all our employees and bring us a critical competitive advantage," said Bijur. "The goals of our program were set by determining what the demographics of Texaco's workforce are likely to be in the year 2000. And, to be clear, these are goals—they are not quotas.[21]

After the diversity plan was announced, Rev. Jackson declared that the boycott of Texaco should be ended. During the summer of 1997, with both Lundwall and Ulrich up on obstruction-of-justice charges, Texaco's own experts digitized the tapes and found that the word reportedly said to be "niggers" was in fact "Nicholas," a conclusion that nobody disputes.[22]

As time passes, Texaco's success at implementing and following through on its proposed initiatives will be assessed. By November 1997, all indications pointed toward the company remaining true to its agreements.

Questions

1. How would you rate the effectiveness of Texaco's response to the allegations of racial discrimination?
2. Did Texaco's response address the core problems and issues surrounding racial discrimination and prejudice at the company?
3. If you were Peter Bijur, what would you have done differently?
4. What kinds of company policies can affect long-term change in diversity in a corporate culture such as Texaco?

EXHIBIT 1

Texaco's Initial Press Release Concerning Taped Racial Slurs

TEXACO RESPONDS TO MEDIA INQUIRIES REGARDING ALLEGATIONS IN *NEW YORK TIMES* ARTICLE

FOR RELEASE: MONDAY, NOVEMBER 4, 1996.

WHITE PLAINS, N.Y., Nov. 4 - Texaco was informed last week of new allegations regarding misconduct by certain current and former employees. These allegations relate to a pending employment discrimination lawsuit brought against Texaco and were reported in today's *New York Times*.

The following is a statement from Texaco:

> "If these allegations are true, they represent an outrageous violation of the company's core values and principles. Any such conduct is deplorable and will never be tolerated by Texaco.
> "Texaco has clear and vigorously-enforced policies against discrimination in the workplace. The company is committed to providing a work environment which reflects an understanding of diversity, and is free from all forms of discrimination, intimidation, and harassment. The company also prohibits conduct or language which is unwelcome, hostile, offensive, degrading, or abusive. Such conduct is unacceptable and will not be tolerated.
> "In addition, Texaco enforces strict policies regarding the retention and production of documents. If any documents related to this lawsuit were in fact concealed or destroyed, such conduct would constitute a clear violation of these policies.
> "Immediately upon learning of the allegations of misconduct, Texaco retained outside counsel, Michael Armstrong of Kirkpatrick and Lockhart, to conduct an extensive independent investigation to determine whether these allegations are true.
> "If the company through its investigation determines that the alleged misconduct occurred, it will take appropriate disciplinary action against the employees, which could include termination.
> "Texaco is determined to maintain an environment of respect for the individual and a work environment that allows every employee to develop and advance to the utmost of his or her abilities. We are dedicated to equal opportunity in all aspects of employment and will not allow any violation of law or company policies."

Source: http://www.texaco.com/compinfo/diversity/diversity_main.htm

EXHIBIT 2

STATEMENT BY PETER I BIJUR
Chairman and Chief Executive Officer, Texaco Inc.
November 6, 1996

RE: Allegations of Employee Misconduct

Good afternoon. My name is Peter Bijur, and I am chairman and chief executive officer of Texaco. I have a brief statement for you, after which I will take your questions.

You are all aware of alleged misconduct, first reported by the New York Times on Monday, which referred to statements made by several current and former Texaco employees in 1994. As soon as we heard about these allegations, we immediately hired Michael Armstrong as outside counsel to conduct an independent investigation to determine whether the allegations were true.

At the same time, I spoke and wrote to all of Texaco's employees, denouncing the alleged behavior in the strongest possible terms.

Until this morning, we did not have audible versions of the tapes. I have just today listened to them myself. I can tell you that the statements on the tapes arouse a deep sense of shock and anger among all the members of the Texaco family and decent people everywhere.

They are statements that represent attitudes we hoped and wished had long ago disappeared entirely from the landscape of our country—and certainly from our company.

They are statements that represent a profound contempt not only for the law, not only for Texaco's explicitly clear values and policies, but, even more importantly, for the most fundamental standards of fairness, of mutual respect, and of human decency.

We are now moving quickly to begin righting these wrongs.

The first step in that process is to say, on behalf of all of the people of Texaco, that we believe unequivocally it is utterly reprehensible to deny another human of his or her self-respect and dignity because of race, color, religion or sex.

And it is absolutely deplorable and intolerable to evade the laws of this land.

These beliefs go beyond an understanding of our legal obligations; they are grounded in a recognition of our moral obligations.

Texaco's statement of our core values is very clear. It says, "Each person deserves to be treated with respect and dignity in appropriate work environments without regard to race, religion, sex, national origin, disability or position in the company. Each employee has the responsibility to demonstrate respect for others."

Our corporate conduct guidelines are also clear and state that "it is the obligation of all employees to report known or suspected violations of the law or company policies to their supervisor" or other appropriate corporate officials.

These are not empty words. They enunciate the immutable principles to which we adhere... to which every person in our company has agreed... and which must form the basis of every act and utterance of all Texaco people in the course of our duties. Every employee signs our guidelines each year acknowledging that they have read them, understood them, and are in compliance with them.

Our review of the tapes has made it clear to us that these values and policies have been violated.

With regard to the four individuals involved in the allegations before us, two are active employees. They are both being suspended today pending completion of the investigation, which will be accomplished promptly.

As to the two retired employees, we believe there is sufficient cause to withdraw benefits. Pending the outcome of the independent outside investigation, further financial or other penalties may be imposed.

As I told our employees on Monday, my personal commitment is to intensify our efforts to eliminate forever this kind of behavior from our workplace. To that end, I am also announcing the following steps:

One—senior executives from Texaco will visit every major company location in the U.S. to meet with our people. Their mission will be to apologize to them for the embarrassment and humiliation this has created. We want them to understand both our personal embarrassment and our firm resolve to ensure that nothing like this ever happens again at Texaco.

Two—we will gather employees together immediately to refocus on our core values and on what we each need to do to create a workplace free of intolerance. It will be a time of reflection and a time for taking personal accountability for actions and attitudes.

Three—we are expanding our diversity learning experience to include all employees, in addition to our managers and supervisors. This two-day seminar, in which I have already participated, along with the senior officers of the company, focuses on both the intent and the impact of personal behavior on peers, teams and the organization overall.

Four—we will reemphasize the critical importance of our confidential Ethics Hotline as a vital tool for reporting any behavior—any behavior—that violates our core values, policies or the law. Calls may be made anonymously, 24 hours a day, seven days a week. We are extending this service to a broader list of countries outside of the U.S.

Fifth—I have today asked Judge A. Leon Higgenbotham of the New York law firm of Paul, Weiss, Rifkind, Wharton & Garrison to work side by side with us to assure that the company's human relationship policies and practices are consistent with the highest standards of respect for the individual and to assure that the company treats all its employees with fundamental fairness.

Judge Higgenbotham is Chief Judge Emeritus of the United States Court of Appeals for the Third Circuit and Public Service Professor of Jurisprudence at Harvard University. The Judge is the recipient of numerous honors, including the Presidential Medal of Freedom, the nation's highest civilian honor, and the National Human Relations Award of the National Conference of Christians and Jews. He is the author of IN THE MATTER OF COLOR—Race and the American Legal Process. I am grateful that he will be assisting us.

Sixth—we are also creating a special committee of our Board of Directors, to be headed by John Brademas, President Emeritus of New York University. This committee will be charged with reviewing our company's diversity programs in their entirety—at every level within our company.

Fundamentally, we don't believe the statements and actions on the tapes are representative of Texaco; but we also recognize that we have more to learn—further to go. Our goal is to become a model company in providing opportunities for women and minorities, and in ensuring respect for every individual.

Let me leave you on a personal note, but one in which I know the people of Texaco join me. I want to offer an apology . . . to our fellow employees who were rightly offended by these statements; to men and women of all races, creeds and religions in this country; and to people throughout America and elsewhere around the world: I am sorry for this incident; I pledge to you that we will do everything in our power to heal the painful wounds that the reckless behavior of those involved have inflicted on all of us; and I look forward to the day we are all striving for when the attitudes in question are consigned to a sorrowful chapter of our past— and that we have created for our future, within the very soul of Texaco, a company of limitless opportunity and utmost respect for every man and woman amongst us.

Source: http://www.texaco.com/compinfo/diversity/diversity_main.htm

EXHIBIT 3

TEXACO ANNOUNCES SETTLEMENT IN CLASS ACTION LAWSUIT
Company Moving Ahead Vigorously with Broader Actions to Promote Greater Diversity, Tolerance and Economic Opportunity

FOR IMMEDIATE RELEASE: FRIDAY, NOVEMBER 15, 1996.

WHITE PLAINS, N.Y., Nov. 15 - Texaco Inc. today announced it has reached an Agreement in Principle to settle the Roberts v. Texaco class action lawsuit, brought in 1994 on behalf of a class of approximately 1,400 individuals, comprised of all current and certain former African American employees.
    Under the settlement, which was described to the Court, Texaco agreed to:

    Provide a payment to the plaintiff-class in the amount of $115 million, along with a one-time salary increase of about 11 percent for current employees of the plaintiff-class, effective January 1, 1997;
        Create an Equality and Tolerance Task Force which will be charged with determining potential improvements to Texaco's human resources programs, as well as helping to monitor the progress being made in those programs (three members of the Task Force to be appointed by the plaintiffs, three members by Texaco and a

mutually agreed-upon chairperson); Adopt and implement company-wide diversity and sensitivity, mentoring, and ombuds programs;

Consider nationwide job posting of more senior positions than are currently posted; and Monitor its performance on the programs and initiatives provided for under the settlement agreement.

Commenting on the agreement, Texaco Chairman and Chief Executive Officer Peter I. Bijur said, "With this litigation behind us, we can now move forward on our broader, urgent mission to make Texaco a model of workplace opportunity for all men and women.

"Texaco is committed to developing and instituting specific, effective policies that will ensure that discrimination is wiped out wherever it may be, and that will expand the positive economic impact we can have in the minority community. These policies will be clearly defined and achievable—with measurable goals set out on a specific timetable.

"Today's agreement affords us a renewed opportunity to join in common purpose and unified action to achieve shared goals of greater inclusion and opportunity at Texaco—and in America," Bijur added.

Following the signing of the Agreement in Principle, all relevant legal documents will be finalized.

Source: http://www.texaco.com/compinfo/diversity/diversity_main.htm

EXHIBIT 4

TEXACO ANNOUNCES COMPREHENSIVE PLAN TO ENSURE FAIRNESS AND ECONOMIC OPPORTUNITY FOR EMPLOYEES AND BUSINESS PARTNERS
Company's Initiatives Follow Rigorous Review of Human Resources and Business Partnering Programs

Texaco Outlines Measures to Enhance Company's Performance in Increasingly Competitive and Diverse Marketplace

FOR IMMEDIATE RELEASE: WEDNESDAY, DECEMBER 18, 1996.

WHITE PLAINS, N.Y., Dec. 18 - Texaco Inc. today announced a comprehensive plan to ensure fairness and economic opportunity for its employees and business partners. The company's plan follows a rigorous review by Texaco of its human resources and business partnering programs. The review was undertaken as a result of events over the past six weeks and was conducted as part of Texaco's commitment to ensure that its employment and business partnering practices enhance its ability to compete even more successfully in the complex global market. In its plan, the company outlined detailed programs and initiatives for all employees, including minorities and women, working for and with Texaco.

Texaco Inc. Chairman and CEO Peter I. Bijur said, "Based on our review, we have set forth comprehensive employment and business partnering initiatives that are well-balanced and beneficial to all our employees and bring us a critical competitive advantage in the constantly changing and increasingly diverse environment in which we operate. Our review encompassed every aspect of employee recruitment, hiring, retention and promotion; workplace environment; and business partnering efforts. We sought input from our employees, numerous organizations and individuals, and we looked at the best practices in industry. The result is a broad program that we believe will ensure a fair and open environment in which all employees and business partners can contribute to the full measure of their abilities.

"The goals of our program," Mr. Bijur continued, "were set by determining what the demographics of Texaco's workforce are likely to be in the year 2000. And, to be clear, these are goals—they are not quotas. Goals focus and guide the efforts of a committed organization. Quotas arbitrarily impose rigid results and do not recognize fairness or judgement. We will continue to hire the best qualified candidates for all positions, based on merit and capability.

"And let me underscore another point: this plan was designed specifically to meet Texaco's unique business strategies and, as such, singularly applies to our company. This program is good business for Texaco," Mr. Bijur said.

He added, "This plan builds on a number of strong programs already in place that have yielded progress in recent years. But we are moving ahead quickly with new and enhanced efforts, because we believe that we must continue to expand our perspectives and make full use of resources that generate the creativity and innovation to meet our goals for success in today's competitive marketplace."

Texaco will track the progress of all of the new and enhanced programs outlined in this review and report on these efforts.

REVIEW ADDRESSED RECRUITMENT, HIRING AND DEVELOPMENT, ALONG WITH WORKPLACE ENVIRONMENT

Recruitment And Hiring. Texaco's global competitiveness depends, first and foremost, on its ability to attract and retain a highly capable workforce that reflects the diverse talents of its competitive marketplace throughout its organization. To help achieve this goal, Texaco will in 1997:

> Enhance the interviewing, selection and hiring skills of its managers, in order to better enable them to identify and bring to Texaco the best possible and most capable candidates to help the company reach its operating goals;
>
> Expand its overall college recruitment so that the company can draw upon a broader talent pool;
>
> Use search firms that have a demonstrated record of recruiting from a wide, diverse range of men and women with key competencies for Texaco; and
>
> Undertake, as previously announced, a new, nationwide scholarship and internship program in partnership with INROADS Inc. to develop minority students for management careers in disciplines important to Texaco, such as engineering, the physical sciences, information systems and international business.

Through its previous efforts to improve performance by diversifying its workforce, Texaco increased total minority employment from 16 percent in 1991 to 23 percent today. As part of its effort to enhance its marketplace competitiveness through the implementation of the above programs, the company expects that it will reach a level of 29 percent by the end of the year 2000. Also by that time, Texaco expects that its African-American employment will increase from 9 percent to 13 percent of total employment, and employment of women from 32 percent to 35 percent. These increases will take place in the context of modest overall employment growth during this period.

Retention and Career Development. Texaco believes it can continue to enhance its performance and lower its costs by strengthening career development and promoting the retention of employees. A series of enhanced and new programs will be implemented by mid-1997, under which the company will:

> Develop and implement a new set of core skill and behavior standards required of managers to help ensure that leaders are able to maximize the performance of their teams over the long term;
>
> Establish a mentoring process that will link managers and senior professionals with aspiring employees to provide them with feedback and advice on career success; and Enhance its global succession planning system to improve the identification, selection and development of individuals from all sources using a dynamic, rigorous and disciplined approach.

These programs will provide managers and supervisors with the information and improved skills they need to ensure that promotions are fair and equitable throughout the company.

Workplace Initiatives. Texaco will launch several programs by mid-1997 that will enhance the efficiency of its team-based approach and, as a result, help reduce cycle times and improve productivity. They will do so by creating a more open and inclusive environment, which will promote better understanding, cooperation and teamwork among all employees. The company will seek to:

Implement a redesigned diversity learning experience, launched last year for Texaco managers and supervisors, to encompass all U.S.-based employees. This experience will help all employees evaluate interpersonal skills and behaviors, especially in a more diverse environment, and enable them to communicate and cooperate more effectively;

Ensure that the decisions of Human Resource Committees are aligned as closely as possible with the company's broadened business imperatives by including women and minorities on all such Committees throughout the company;

Introduce a comprehensive, core learning program to support all Texaco managers and supervisors with improved skill and knowledge in change management, selecting and developing a world class team, communicating and coaching; and

Implement an Alternative Dispute Resolution process to include mediation and arbitration, and introduce an ombuds program in which employees may also make use of a confidential outside counselor—both of which should help create a more positive, productive work environment.

Accountability and Oversight. Texaco is committed to achieving its immediate and long-term goals and will continue to hold all employees, especially managers and senior executives, responsible for the success of these programs. The company will establish rigorous reporting structures to increase accountability and also will:

Expand the company's 360-degree feedback process for 1997 to include all managers and supervisors. The employees, peers and supervisor of each manager will complete a confidential questionnaire annually to help evaluate how well that manager demonstrates expected leadership behavior;

Revise further the company's performance evaluation system to ensure alignment between individual and organizational goals, and more closely link managers' compensation to their performance in creating openness and inclusion in the workplace as a means of fostering improved team performance; and

Redesign the company's employee opinion survey, to be conducted annually beginning in 1997, to help managers and teams improve overall performance and monitor the success of Texaco's change efforts.

TEXACO TO EXPAND BUSINESS PARTNERING EFFORTS

Texaco believes that, by broadening its base of vendors and suppliers of services, it will be able to draw upon additional resources that will contribute to the company's competitive position. The company noted that the accelerated and expanded programs being implemented at this point in its review process are consistent with its existing business plans, are expected to help the company achieve or exceed its goals, and will not negatively impact profitability.

The review identified the following areas in which the company will strengthen its business partnering efforts:

Purchasing, Contracting and Services. Texaco's goal is to increase its overall purchasing activities with minority- and women-owned businesses, including providers of professional services, from $135 million in 1996 to a cumulative total of more than $1 billion over the next five years, with the expectation that it will reach at least 6 percent. The program to accelerate purchasing activities is already underway and will encompass the following areas:

Expanding the scope and focus of programs with minority- and women-owned vendors, suppliers, engineering and construction firms, environmental remediation companies and sub-contractors; and

Increasing the amount of work Texaco does with minority- and women-owned professional service firms in the areas of law, advertising, accounting, tax, government and public relations. Texaco also intends to increase its use of women and minority professionals at other firms. In addition, the company has already started to contract with minority-owned advertising agencies, and this program will be expanded in 1997.

Finance. In order to broaden the range of its financial relationships, the company will seek to increase financial activities with minority- and women-owned banks and money managers from $32 million to $200 million.

Texaco is already increasing the number of women and minority banks with which it does business from 21 to 50 and increasing deposits in those banks. Texaco will work to expand its use of other banking services with minority- and women-owned financial firms in key marketplaces.

Texaco will increase the number of women and minority fixed-income and equity managers of its pension fund from 1 to 8, and the funds under management will increase from $31 million to $186 million, or 13 percent of the fund.

Texaco intends to increase its involvement with minority and women businesses by investing $10 million in 1997 in a minority-managed domestic emerging market fund investing in such companies.

Insurance. Texaco will increase insurance coverage from minority- and women-owned insurance companies from $25 million to $200 million. Texaco will seek women- and minority-owned companies to write property and liability coverage for contractors.

IMPROVING RETAIL PERFORMANCE IN A DIVERSE MARKETPLACE

Texaco's wholesale and retail operations must be responsive to the shifting demands of the marketplace. The company will accelerate its program to diversify wholesalers/retailers in key markets. These efforts include:

Wholesalers: Texaco's goal is to double the number of minority- and women-owned wholesaler marketers from 43 to 85 (from 5.5 percent to over 11 percent) within a five-year period. The company also plans to encourage wholesalers to maintain the number of minority and women retail operators at the current level of at least 20 percent of their more than 10,000 retail outlets and to increase the number of under-represented minority retail operators.

Independent/Lessee Retailers: Texaco will work to maintain women and minority independent retail owner and lessee operators at the current level of at least 45 percent of retail outlets in this category. Within five years, it will work to more than triple African-American-owned retail outlets from 35 to 117 (from 2 percent to 6 percent of the total).

Texaco Owned/Operated Outlets: Texaco will work to maintain its current level of at least 70 percent of minority and women managers at company-owned and -operated retail outlets, and will seek to increase its under-represented minority retail and store managers from 67 to 100 (7.4 percent to 12 percent of the total).

Lubricants: Texaco will strive to double the number of minority- and women-owned lubricant distributors from 29 to 58 (from 4.5 percent to 9 percent of the total), and to double the number of lube outlets from 52 to 104 (from 8.7 percent to 17 percent of the total).

Financing: The company will make available financing support for the development and expansion of minority and women wholesale marketers and retailers, as set forth in Texaco's goals. This financing will also support the development of Texaco-owned or Texaco-branded retail outlets in urban core areas. The company will assist minority entrepreneurs in the start up of business operations for branded outlets in these areas, which represent under-developed opportunities for business expansion.

Community Programs: Texaco has long recognized and acted upon the critical importance of local community outreach and support, and has in particular established a strong record of local volunteerism by its employees. Texaco will evaluate in the coming months its level of support for all programs, including women and minority organizations, that complement its business focus and further promote community improvements.

Source: http://www.texaco.com/compinfo/diversity/diversity_main.htm

---

EXHIBIT 5

POLISHING THE STAR

As part of its settlement of a discrimination lawsuit brought by black employees, Texaco has moved on a half-dozen fronts to alter its business practices.

Hiring.   Asked search firms to identify wider arrays of candidates. Expanded recruiting at historically minority colleges. Gave 50 scholarships and paid internships to minority students seeking engineering or technical degrees.

Career Advancement.   Wrote objective standards for promotions. Developing training program for new managers. Developing a mentoring program.

Diversity Initiatives.   Conducted two-day diversity training for more than 8,000 of 20,000 US employees. Tied management bonuses to diversity goals. Developing alternative dispute resolution and ombudsman programs.

Purchasing.   Nearly doubled purchases from minority- or women-owned businesses. Asking suppliers to report their purchases from such companies.

Financial Services.   Substantially increased banking, investment management and insurance business with minority- and women-owned firms. A group of such firms underwrote a $150 million public financing.

Retailing.   Added three black independent retailer, 18 black managers of company-owned service stations, 12 minority or female wholesalers, 13 minority- or women-owned Xpress Lube outlets and 6 minority- or women-owned lubricant distributions.

Source: Adam Bryant *The New York Times, How Much Has Texaco Changed?* November, 1997.*

CASE STUDY: TOSTADAS, TORTILLA CHIPS AND BANK LOANS
Wells Fargo and Salinas Y Salinas

ALBERT'S DECISION

Albert Gomez, a commercial loan officer with Wells Fargo, got back into his crème-colored Lexus after meeting with Raphael and Minerva Salinas, clients with whom he had built a strong relationship over the past three years. It was the year 2000,

This case was prepared by Catharine E. Carrales under the supervision of Assistant Professor Greg Fairchild. It was written as a basis for class discussion rather than to illustrate effective or ineffective handling of an administrative situation.

and the Salinas family wanted funding to expand their tostada and tortilla chip business. They believed that the time was right to pursue a bigger share of the rapidly-expanding Latino market for their premium products. While Gomez believed that market demand justified the expansion and that the Salinas family members were highly competent business owners, he was unsure of the response of Wells Fargo management to this particular loan. Gomez was convinced that the time was right for the Salinases to build a new, state-of-the-art tortilla processing facility. They were requesting an additional $4.25 million loan to fund the construction of a new manufacturing facility. However, there were some things about the Salinas' family that he thought might worry other lenders in the bank. The existing plant would hardly impress his senior managers nor help to build their confidence that the Salinas family were highly capable business owners.

As he navigated through heavy rush hour traffic from the Salinas & Salinas (S&S) facilities in South Gate, California, to his office 20 miles away in Diamond Bar, Gomez reflected on the strengthening of his relationship with the Salinas family since they had met years earlier. He also thought about the risks taken by loan officers in assessing potential clients. Due to the biases of a former Wells Fargo loan officer, the business had almost slipped through Wells Fargo's hands. Since then, the Salinas family had developed a deep trust of Gomez and his partner, John Murillo. They could even be described as family friends.

Between answering calls on his hands-free mobile phone from various clients, returning his colleagues' calls, and weaving through traffic, Gomez began piecing together a game plan for pitching the loan request to his senior credit officer. His key task would be to demonstrate to management that S&S was able to cover its new loan payments. What weighed heavily on his mind, however, was how to overcome the perception of risk that managers within his financial institution might assign to his client. He also wondered whether they would question his objectivity, given his personal closeness to the Salinas family.

BACKGROUND ON SALINAS & SALINAS

Salinas and Salinas (S&S) was a family-owned corn tostada and tortilla chip maker with operations located in South Gate, a community southeast of Los Angeles. Started by Raphael and Minerva Salinas in 1981, the company had grown to include more than 50 employees, working in 24-hour shifts, six days a week (The company did not operate on Sundays, out of respect for the Salinases' beliefs to honor the Sabbath). Annual revenues at the time of the building loan request were approximately $5.1 million, and the Salinas family retained a handsome share of the annual revenues (nearly 25 percent) as compensation. Net income over the past three years had averaged approximately 10 percent of revenues. Not only was their plant running at full capacity, but the corn tostada and tortilla chip market was growing across the country at a rate approximating 3 percent.

Raphael Salinas was first struck by the idea of building his company soon after emigrating from Mexico in 1976 and settling in the Los Angeles metro area. Prior to moving to the United States, Salinas had worked for Pepsico's Mexico subsidiary in a variety of capacities—in sales, marketing, and accounting—but he enjoyed sales most. However, when he first arrived in the United States, Salinas had trouble finding work. This was due, in part, to his lacking the formal education that would confer on an immigrant the legitimacy that employers were seeking. While he did not possess a degree, there were no limits to his drive and ingenuity. Salinas astutely took note of the many neighborhoods in Los Angeles with high concentrations of Mexican immigrants like himself, who were seeking goods that were familiar to them from home. He brokered a relationship with a local wholesaler and began selling tostadas and tortillas door-to-door in these neighborhoods. Raphael knew the product, he understood the consumer, and he had the personal selling skills necessary to leverage the opportunity. Yet he surprised even himself when he began earning $1,000 net profit from just one day's worth (usually a Sunday) of selling products door-to-door. Minerva began assisting him, and they were soon generating the income necessary to support their newly immigrated family of four.

An enterprising and visionary individual, Salinas was not content in his role of middle-man in the tostada and tortilla business. As well as he was doing financially, he also intuitively understood the concept of power in value chains; he recognized that there was a substantial opportunity for profit and decision-making authority as a product manufacturer. Fortunately, the Salinas family had always practiced frugality. They had saved enough money to leverage the opportunity they had discovered, and they decided to start an independent corn tostada and tortilla chip manufacturer. Their first step was the purchase of a small parcel of property in the community of South Gate.

Business began briskly for S&S. Demand exceeded supply for tostada and tortilla chips in the Los Angeles area; in the early 1980s, recently arrived Mexican immigrants had few choices to satisfy their demand for food products that they regularly ate in their home country. The Mexican food craze had just begun to diffuse to the non-Latino population of the United States and Los Angeles, and yet few mainstream supermarkets stocked items that a newly arrived Mexican immigrant would find appealing. Recognizing these opportunities, S&S developed a high-quality and very attractive line of products that was just what the burgeoning Mexican immigrant population had a taste for.

One of the first challenges for the fledgling business was to establish the proper management and culture for the company. An early partner who left the business felt that the brand for the new tostadas should be "Infierno," meaning inferno or hell. However Mr. Salinas felt that the name should reflect his principles and spiritual values, and instead he called the brand El Paraiso (Paradise/Heaven).

THE EARLY YEARS: CHALLENGES TO OVERCOME

Previously unmet demand drove the business's revenues. However, S&S encountered a problem not uncommon to family-run businesses. For the first several years there was no separation between family and business finances, and frequently the family finances were strained to meet the needs of the growing business. Additionally, given their own financial success and frugal ways, it became increasingly difficult to turn away requests from relatives or friends who needed financial assistance. As a result, the Salinases cosigned and paid notes on financial burdens that others created. Typically, these involved personal loans, like automobiles and condominium mortgages. Between the two of them, the Salinas had cosigned $387,000 in loans to relatives. Some of these loans had not been paid on time, tarnishing the Salinases' otherwise spotless credit history.

There were also early competitive challenges. An ongoing consolidation of independent tortilla and tostada chip manufacturers in the Los Angeles market by the Mexican conglomerate Gruma, S.A. de C.V., began in the late 1970s. Gruma entered the United States market in 1976 and shortly thereafter began rolling up the industry here and abroad. Now its brand names included Mission, Maizal, and Guerrero, and its top competitors were major players in the global food market, including Frito-Lay, Bimbo (Mexico's largest commercial baking operation), and Minsa (Mexico's second-largest corn flour producer). At that time Gruma was the world's #1 manufacturer of tortillas, supplying such well-known restaurants as Taco Bell; it maintained its competitive position through the aggressive use of marketing tactics to ensure prime shelf space for its products. For example, the company paid substantial slotting fees demanded by retailers for expanding the product line through the addition of new SKUs.

From the beginning, S&S decided against paying slotting fees. Because S&S products were sold primarily to small grocery stores in predominantly Mexican neighborhoods, where slotting fees were not as common, this tactic did not immediately present as great a threat. Furthermore, the business simply could not afford the added financial burden. As slotting fees became increasingly common and were paid by competitors like Gruma, S&S had to redouble their efforts in retaining the grocery store buyers of their products. Yet even as revenues grew, S&S refused to engage in this practice on the basis of a belief that demand for the products, as opposed to monetary payments, should command shelf space. This strategy relied on consumer demand to drive retailers to stock the Salinas products, without the usual manufacturer's inducements.

Working with suppliers was also a difficult endeavor in the beginning phases of growing the business. Many, if not most, of the tostada and tortilla chip makers did not manufacture their own dough, or *masa,* for their products. Instead, they mainly sourced the masa from Gruma made out of a corn flour called Maseca. Yet the Salinases were not impressed with the Maseca sold by Gruma.

Instead, Mr. and Mrs. Salinas experimented until they developed a formula that provided a taste very similar to the homemade tostadas with which most Mexican immigrants were familiar. Again drawing on their intuitive understanding of value chains, the Salinas family felt that control over the entire manufacturing process was the only way to ensure that consumers would be provided with the highest quality end product. Consequently, they sourced unprocessed corn and boiled it on premises, then mixed the corn with other ingredients to produce the fresh masa used in the product. The corn tortillas were then fried in 100 percent vegetable oil (instead of lard, which is more commonly used in the industry) and were sold in different sizes of crunchy, round corn tostadas (contrary to non-Latino tastes, most Mexican Americans preferred corn over flour tortillas and tostadas). S&S also devised unique packaging that prominently displayed the brand name, El Paraiso, to distinguish it from competitors' products.

Sourcing the corn and other special ingredients carried certain pronounced risks, especially for a small manufacturer such as S&S. For example, supply costs were highly sensitive to the ups and downs of the commodities market for corn; as a relatively small buyer, S&S did not engage in hedging strategies to cover these price fluctuations. Not only that, but as a small buyer, S&S's demand for corn was filled only after the orders from larger buyers, like Gruma, were satisfied.

S&S MANAGEMENT: UNCOMPROMISED VALUE SYSTEM

Apart from the pressures exerted by competitors, buyers, and suppliers, S&S had many issues to address regarding their employees. Typically the employees were quite loyal, staying with S&S through its growth stages. Professional managers were not involved in running the business; instead, Raphael, Minerva and their now-grown daughters chose to maintain their heavy involvement in the day-to-day management of the business even as its scope grew in significant ways. Their very hands-on approach lent a family atmosphere to the business, creating trusting, close, and informal relationships between the workers and the owners.

All employees at S&S were first-generation Hispanic immigrants (mostly Mexican), who lived in the surrounding South Gate community. Most employees lived in small apartments, while the more successful ones were living in small homes. More than one family typically lived in each dwelling. Employees earned minimum and slightly above minimum wages for manual labor, although more technical workers received a slightly higher compensation.

As the business continued to grow, the Salinases imparted more and more of their values and belief system to the company. Having survived the challenges of entrepreneurship, with its accompanying strain on family finances and relationships, the Salinas family continued to infuse the business operations with their spiritual values. They spoke openly of their belief in God and attributed their success first of all to God. As a result of these beliefs, they tended to emphasize a positive mind-set and can-do attitude that was picked up by their workers.

When the business owners sensed the stress caused by the growth of their company, they initiated various practices to ease tensions between workers. For instance, whenever Raphael or Minerva Salinas overheard one employee speaking negatively about another or cursing, they demanded a small ($0.50) payment from the worker on the spot. Similarly, they altered the radios in the manufacturing plant and their fleet of delivery trucks so that drivers could listen only to spiritual music to soothe their nerves as they managed their vehicles through the heavy Los Angeles traffic. They felt that this music had both a calming influence and presented messages in accord with the values of S&S. According to the owners, while at first the employees balked at such treatment, they seemed to accept the demands made on them by management. Productivity went up, and Raphael and Minerva Salinas believed that morale also improved as a result of their maverick approach to management.

AN ENTERPRISING TEAM: ALBERT GOMEZ AND JOHN MURILLO

Albert Gomez, Business Banking Commercial Loan Officer

Albert Gomez was seen by many to be a rising star in the Business Banking Group at Wells Fargo. Within his short tenure, he had distinguished himself by recently being named one of the bank's top 10 commercial loan officers. Ironically, while Gomez had become one of the leading commercial lenders in the entire company, he initially had to wedge his foot in the door to be hired by Wells Fargo.

Ambitious from a young age, he fully applied himself toward academic success. He worked as a paralegal and later as an analyst at a small community bank to put himself through college at the University of Southern California (USC). After graduating from USC, Gomez returned to the same bank in a full-time position as an analyst.

However, Gomez's real dream was to attend law school and become an attorney. While his work at the bank paid the bills (and enabled him to develop some great skills), his dreams remained focused on law school. And having succeeded at everything he had applied himself to, he was surprised when he was rejected from law school not once or twice, but four times.

Deciding that law school was not the path that would lead him to success, Gomez reexamined his goals and decided to fully dedicate himself to a stellar career in banking. He had one problem: his analyst position offered limited career potential. He began applying for other jobs in banking with the goal of becoming a commercial loan officer. Again, he encountered difficulties.

Not one to submit to failure, however, Gomez realized that while his interviews seemed to go well, and he was always invited for second and third round interviews, he never received a positive call-back that resulted in a job offer. He attributed this to his lack of assertiveness. At his next interview, he promised himself he would not let a lack of assertiveness stop him; instead, he would try out his salesmanship skills and demand immediate feedback about the interview and whether he would be offered a job. His next interview for a commercial loan officer position was with Wells Fargo. True to the promise he made himself, Gomez asked for feedback at the end of the interview. The interviewer told him he had done a great job and that if it were up to him, he would hire Gomez. Gomez then demanded to know whether he would be offered the job or not. Taken aback, the interviewer then said he was not in a position to make the hiring decision—he would simply be forwarding his recommendation up the chain.

Gomez was determined to put his sales skills to work. Refusing to take no for an answer, he began suggesting alternatives that would help speed the decision-making. He asked that the hiring manager join them. When that request could not, for scheduling reasons, be fulfilled, he began making offers to his interviewer. He finally hit on one—an offer to join the bank conditionally with a final hiring decision to be made after three months of satisfactory performance—that seemed to resonate with his interviewer. By the time Gomez reached home after the interview, he had a message from Wells Fargo inviting him to join the organization.

He had worked approximately seven years for Wells Fargo when he was first introduced to Salinas & Salinas. By this point Gomez was no newcomer to banking or the Latino community. He had grown up in East Los Angeles speaking Spanish and English. A first-generation immigrant, he had adapted to his new environment and developed an ability to move easily between the Latino and non-Latino communities. He spoke both languages flawlessly and without noticeable accents, and possessed the underlying cultural knowledge that allowed him to recognize economic value where others could not.

John Murillo, Vice President and District Manager, Community Banking

When he was named manager of the South Gate "store" (Wells Fargo terminology for retail branch), one of the first items on John Murillo's to-do list was to pay a visit on all of the businesses that banked at his store. Many of these were small businesses owned and run by local Latino (primarily Mexican) entrepreneurs. His diligence led him to call unannounced at the Salinas & Salinas operations in South Gate. As a Mexican immigrant himself, but more importantly, as a clear expert and enthusiastic banker willing to go the extra mile for his clients, Murillo was warmly received by the family management. Being careful to ensure that Wells Fargo was meeting its clients' needs, he began building a relationship with the Salinas family. His first impressions were that S&S was a healthy and growing business that the bank might be able to assist with different products not currently used by the S&S family, such as working capital lines of credit and treasury management products (e.g., direct deposit capabilities).

Murillo quickly found that the Salinases owned outright their manufacturing plant, along with two small apartment complexes in the South Gate area. The plant had an assessed value of $1.787 million and the apartment complexes were assessed at $287,000 and $217,000. Also the family had a small fleet of seven panel trucks used in deliveries to local stores. In a liquidation sale, he believed that they might be worth approximately $80,000. All of these business expansions had been funded through the cash flow of the firm, and there were no existing loans on these assets.

Shortly after becoming the bank manager for the South Gate store, Murillo met fellow Wells Fargo team member Albert Gomez, when they both attended an informal in-house meeting focused on the issue of growing the bank's presence in the Latino community. They had both been invited to the meeting because of their shared Mexican heritage and their interest in assisting Wells Fargo to reach the untapped Latino market. Learning how to better serve Latino clientele was the main topic of this meeting, convened by senior management within the retail part of the bank, who realized the need to enhance service to this unique and growing community. Gomez, a member of Wells Fargo's Business Banking Group (serving small businesses with annual revenues of less than $20 million), attended the meeting out of personal dedication to the topic and to meet colleagues working in the retail stores with whom he might collaborate.

Murillo's first impressions of Gomez were that he was a very charismatic and determined young banker who appeared bent on success. He noted Gomez's roots in the Latino community and his goal of creating a niche for himself in meeting the financial needs of Latino business owners. He was also impressed with

Gomez's dedication to and passion for building a business to expressly serve the needs of Latino business owners. In his experience, not all the Mexican-Americans Murillo had met shared the passion and drive or the specific skills necessary to meet the financial needs of the Latino segment. Immediately the two decided to pursue their mutual interests and collaborate in targeting client prospects.

Within a week after their initial meeting, Murillo called Gomez and invited him to meet Raphael and Minerva Salinas. The Salinas family had approached Murillo seeking a new loan to buy property adjacent to their plant that would expand their manufacturing capacity. Since this would require a commercial loan, Murillo decided to introduce Gomez to the family in the hopes that the two of them could determine whether Wells Fargo would be able to meet S&S's funding requirements. Mr. and Mrs. Salinas were very receptive toward Gomez, and the first meeting lasted several hours (where Spanish was spoken exclusively, according to the preference of the Salinas family). Mr. Salinas also took the opportunity to remind Murillo and inform Gomez that Murillo's predecessor—also a Mexican-American—had turned down S&S's last business loan request. To add insult to injury, the former store manager stated that he wouldn't lend the Salinas family "a penny" to support their company. Yet because of their culturally-ingrained loyalty, and because Murillo was providing excellent service to the business, S&S continued its banking relationship with Wells Fargo. The meeting was the first in a new chapter in the relationship between the Wells Fargo and the family.

BACKGROUND ON WFC

Wells Fargo (NYSE: WFC) was a diversified financial services company with $370 billion in assets and 134,000 team members. It provided banking, insurance, wealth management and estate planning, investments, mortgage, and consumer finance in 5,800 stores (bank terminology for retail branches) across North America and elsewhere internationally. Wells Fargo was then divided into several business lines: community (retail) banking, credit card services, home mortgage, consumer credit group, private client services, internet services group, ATM banking, business banking group (for businesses with annual revenues up to $20 million), and wholesale banking (encompassing capital markets, middle market and large corporate clients, commercial real estate, asset-based lending, international banking services, and insurance services).

Each local Wells Fargo store was a headquarters for satisfying customers' needs. Many retail (e.g., mortgage) and small business loan decisions were made at the store instead of being forwarded to a regional headquarters for processing; this enabled Wells Fargo to rapidly respond to borrowers who submitted loan applications. The bank's vision was to develop products to satisfy the wide range of customer needs, to help them succeed financially, and to become known as one of America's great companies and the number one financial services provider in each of its markets. With a footprint extending across 23 states, the bank's motto was to "out-local the nationals and out-national the locals."

Executives at Wells Fargo, including Paul Watson, executive vice president in Wholesale Banking, and Todd Hollander, executive vice president in the Business Banking Group (BBG), recognized the need for Wells Fargo to court Latino business-owners more actively. Both men were familiar with the trends in the Latino population, particularly the growth rates that indicated Latinos would become the largest minority group in the United States by the year 2003. They also knew that, to increase Wells Fargo's image as a financial lender of choice among the Latino community, Wells Fargo's team members would need to be able to relate personally to Latino clientele. As a mid-level manager sensitive to these issues, Hollander personally recruited Albert Gomez to BBG and supported Gomez's efforts to increase business with the Latino community in South Gate. These men helped spearhead an effort to increase outreach to Latino retail and commercial clients. See Exhibit 1 for trends in the buying power of minority groups.

Wells Fargo, like all financial institutions, collected data as required by the Community Reinvestment Act. These data specifically captured information such as loans made to low–moderate income borrowers, but the data were not race-related. Despite its compliance with federal requirements, and its efforts to expand its presence within the Latino community, Gomez and Murillo believed that Wells Fargo did not understand how to serve Mexican-Americans, particularly recently-arrived immigrants. Murillo's efforts in this area helped transform the South Gate store, where Mexican-Americans were welcomed with signage in Spanish, background music sourced from a popular Spanish-language radio station, and interior decorating and artwork more consistent with their cultural background (see Exhibit 2). Importantly, all family members, including children, were made welcome in the South Gate store.

DRAMATIC GROWTH OF LATINO INFLUENCE ON U.S. ECONOMY AND CULTURE

One reason for Wells Fargo's interest in the Latino consumer was both the rapid growth and the underserved needs of the market. Census data released from the 2000 U.S. Census Survey attested to the explosion of growth within the U.S. Latino population. Since 1980 the Latino population had more than doubled in size, growing by 53 percent in the 1980s and by 58 percent in the 1990s[23] (for more on Hispanic growth trends, see Exhibit 3). Most Latino firms were concentrated in the southwestern states of Texas, California, and New Mexico, although, many Hispanic-owned businesses were found in New York or Florida, home to many Cuban émigrés (see Exhibits 4 and 5).

Hispanics comprised many distinct groups that shared the Spanish language and certain other cultural similarities. Latinos of Mexican origin were the dominant group numerically in the United States (see Exhibit 6). Like immigrant groups in the past, Latino Americans gradually picked up many of the practices and attitudes common to other Americans. At the same time, their own culture influenced the lives of other Americans. For example, since 1991 salsa had trumped ketchup as the top-selling condiment in the United States, with sales in excess of $640 million in 2002.[24]

Buying power among the fastest-growing ethnic group in the country caught the attention of many corporations. A report sponsored by Spanish-language TV network, Telemundo, forecasted that spending by U.S. Hispanics would grow on average more than 9 percent a year to 2020, outpacing the 6 percent rate for all residents. In turn the Latino share of the U.S. consumer market would climb from 7.3 percent to 13 percent in 2000, according to the report. The report also noted that Hispanic spending would grow well above the nation's average in most consumer sectors, including durable and nondurable goods, housing, and transportation.[25] These figures ensured that all businesses operating in the United States would be paying closer attention to this segment of the population.

MAKING THE CASE: A COMPLICATED FINANCIAL HISTORY

Back in his car, Gomez continued to ponder several issues related to the S&S loan request. While their request for $4.25 million was not extravagant, given the company's annual revenues of approximately $5.1 million, Gomez believed he would face several challenges in persuading his senior credit officer and deputy chief credit officer of the borrower's credit-worthiness (see Exhibit 7 for a note on the commercial bank lending process). Not the least of these worries was his hesitance to bring his managers, particularly Todd Hollander, to the S&S operations to meet the clients. The S&S operations simply lacked a commanding physical presence—people driving by the outside of the facilities would never guess that the company exceeded $4.25 million in annual revenues. The office space likewise lacked an air of formality; Mr. and Mrs. Salinas worked out of a shared 6 × 7 foot space with 1970s wood paneling that was crowded with 5-foot metal file cabinets and papers stacked everywhere.

In addition to the physical layout, Gomez considered other issues that might cause his managers to quickly dismiss the S&S financing request. Loan officers and retail bankers working in heavily Latino areas such as South Gate recognized some key differences between Latino and non-Latino household earnings and savings patterns. For instance, in their home countries, many Latinos carried a legacy of mistrust toward government institutions and therefore toward the large financial institutions controlled by the government. Consequently, when they immigrated to the United States, they were extremely reluctant to open bank accounts or use any additional financial services; they often had built up very little positive credit history.

Credit issues also intertwined with the central role that family played in the Latino population. In fact, the combination of strong family relationships with typically less vigorous financial literacy led Gomez and Murillo to discover an unfortunate trait shared by many in the Latino community: poor credit history. Because familial relationships were so central, older (and particularly more successful) family members often agreed to cosign on home, car, and other merchandise loans for relatives. If the loan recipient missed or was late on the payment, however, embarrassment and pride kept the borrower from telling the person who cosigned on the loan about any problems. When the time arrived for the cosigner to apply for a loan, often (s)he was unhappily surprised when the loan request was denied due to the poor financial management by a family member for whom the person had cosigned. Gomez and Murillo witnessed on several occassions how the unintended consequences and risks of cosigning for family members played out in hampering individuals in otherwise good financial standing from obtaining loans.

Gomez was familiar with the practice of tax minimization that was very common among small business owners. Latino small business owners shared this practice as well, but in the Mexican immigrant community it was also mixed with a deep suspicion and mistrust of the government. Toward this end there was a multitude of accountants and "Enrolled Agents" (persons entitled to represent individuals to the IRS) in Latino neighborhoods who specialized in income minimization techniques. However, by minimizing income, individuals and businesses encountered greater difficulty in securing loans because financial institutions typically approved loans based on the income stream to the business, individual, or family. By reporting little or no income to the IRS, these same individuals and businesses also curtailed their access to capital from financial institutions.

Gomez and Murillo had noticed additional characteristics among Latino families and business owners that had been overlooked by bankers unfamiliar with the Latino community. As indicated, Latinos tended to have larger families than their non-Latino counterparts. Frequently more than one adult income-earner resided at one dwelling. This lifestyle contradicted many bank lending protocols that recognized only the possibility of two income-earners, a mother and father, living under one roof. Household income, as mentioned, was important in qualifying both individuals and even business owners for bank loans. Astute financial institutions had begun the practice of counting the total income from every adult living at the same address to permit the extension of loans that otherwise would not have been approved had only two adults' income been taken into account in the underwriting phase. Accompanying the strong familial relationships prevalent among Latino families, another characteristic identified by Gomez and Murillo was the strong loyalty of Latino clients. For instance, Latino customers tended not only to maintain an account with one bank but to engage more of that same bank's services if the bank earned the family's trust. A bank with a large Latino customer base, therefore, could better maximize the efficiency of its infrastructure by increasing the amount of revenue per customer and thus spend less on the costly enterprise of gaining new customers. If they secured a customer's business, then the bank did not need to worry about Latinos switching to another financial institution due to minimal cost savings. The loyalty trait of Latino clients—provided they felt that they were receiving quality service—would ensure against customer loss due to price-savings gimmicks promoted by competitors.

MAKING THE LOAN: THE SALINAS FAMILY AND WELLS FARGO'S LENDING PRACTICES

The Salinas family exhibited all of the cultural traits Gomez and Murillo had noticed previously. The Salinas family had maintained their relationship with Wells Fargo out of loyalty, even after the Salinases' request for a loan a few years earlier had been breezily dismissed by Murillo's predecessor. Yet the Salinases also created costs, in time and effort spent by Gomez and Murillo, which might have caused less dedicated lending officers to refrain from working with them.

Mr. and Mrs. Salinas had long used an Enrolled Agent, Ms. Guzman, to prepare their business and personal tax returns. Guzman's strategy was to minimize the Salinas family income to the degree that the family would owe almost no taxes. In addition, the Salinas family, as is customary among Latinos, had cosigned loans to family members that had in turn hurt their own credit scores.

Gomez's first priority, after meeting the Salinas family in 1997, had been to help them straighten their books. While Wells Fargo traditionally made available a line of credit equal to 10 percent of the business's annual revenue, it required the business to show sufficient profit after taxes to make the required debt payments. Although the Salinas business should easily have qualified for a $100,000 line of credit based on sales performance, Gomez knew that Wells Fargo would be reluctant to extend this credit because S&S was showing no profit due to Guzman's tax minimization strategies. And the Salinas family, with little awareness of credit and net income and tax issues or the need for audited financial statements, required approximately one year of intense consultation with Gomez before he was able to help qualify S&S for a commercial line of credit (which the bank required to be fully cash-secured).

Gomez knew the family would need persuading before they would agree to part with Guzman's services. After all, she was the next-door neighbor to the S&S operations, and the family had a long relationship with her. After months of patient discussions with the Salinas family and education about how the tax schemes not only limited access to capital for the business but also ensured that the company would remain a mom and pop operation, the Salinases agreed to hire professional accountants recommended by Murillo and Gomez. The accountants helped establish a strong financial foundation and eventually prepared the CPA-reviewed financial statements that were necessary for Gomez to extend an initial commercial loan to S&S. Over time the family also agreed to hire corporate attorneys to create a more sophisticated corporate structure that would limit the family's liabilities and risk, should the company be sued.

Although Guzman's tax minimization strategies had cost the Salinases in previously unforseen ways, they also provided many short-term benefits. The business had funded a lifestyle for the family that was dramatically different from their hardscrabble beginnings. Both of the Salinas daughters owned sizable homes, while many of their twenty-something peers were still renting or living at home. Mr. Salinas had developed a taste for luxury automobiles and owned a small stable of Mercedes that he parked in his multi-car garage. These economic trappings both encouraged and worried Gomez and Murillo.

After another year of close collaboration, S&S was able to apply and qualify for a line of credit that was used to meet working capital requirements and to help fund small capital expansion at their existing operations. The Salinases used this loan to expand their existing plant, purchasing almost all the real estate on the block where they were located. This was a large victory for Murillo, Gomez, and the Salinas family, given that Wells Fargo had required that a smaller $100,000 line of credit be fully cash-secured just a year earlier. Due to the growing demand for their products, S&S began scouting for real estate that would enable them to operate more than five lines of production.

In the interim S&S had increased their fleet of trucks, although the owners, cognizant of their production capacity, refused to deliver outside the Southern California area. S&S allowed independent truck operators to schedule product pickups from their manufacturing site if excess supply was available. Typically, these independent owner–operators would deliver the products to Latino neighborhoods in adjacent states where they would distribute to small- and medium-size grocery chain stores. Because of the frequency with which pickups were scheduled, the Salinas family assumed that demand for their products was strong enough to make the practice lucrative for the operators.

Another year passed before S&S found suitable property that met the needs of the business. Upon locating the property, S&S promptly applied for a loan with Wells Fargo. By this point S&S had secured three loans plus the initial line of credit from Wells Fargo, and both parties valued the relationship very highly.

Gomez listened to the Salinases' well-thought out reasons why the property for which they were requesting a commercial mortgage loan was the best choice. Salinas believed his business had tapped only 5 percent of the total Latino population within the Los Angeles metro area. What most interested Raphael about the property was the opportunity to expand his operations from 5 production lines to 17 (offering the opportunity to more than triple current revenues). This would help the business grow and meet the demands of additional clients such as Vons and Ralph's, mainstream supermarket chains that S&S had not been able to service because their demand exceeded S&S's operating capacity. With inventory turning over on a daily basis at the existing manufacturing facilities, the Salinas family believed continued strong demand would cause the new facility to operate at 100 percent capacity. Furthermore, since the property was located only a few blocks from S&S's existing operations, the company would be able to retain most (if not all) of its employees.

Gomez sketched a back-of-the-envelope analysis to determine whether the Salinases could in fact meet Wells Fargo's debt coverage ratios. He made a few quick assumptions as he prepared a quick analysis of the Salinases' ability to meet their debt obligations:

- First, he assumed an interest on the loan based on the average prime interest rate in 2000 of 9.18 percent (average of the prime interest rate on the first day of each month in 2000; see http://www.nfsn.com/library/prime.htm) and then added a 2 percent spread.
- Second, he assumed that the life of the new building loan would be twenty years.
- Third, he knew that the Salinases had about $1.3 million loans in addition to the commercial mortgage loan they were requesting at the time. He assumed a straight-line amortization of principal over the 20-year lifetime of all loans.
- Fourth, he compounded the interest rate on a quarterly basis; interest charged on outstanding loan balance (of all WF loans) at the beginning of the quarter.
- Fifth, because of their strong loyalty to Wells Fargo, he knew that all loans outstanding were from Wells Fargo.
- Sixth, he assumed depreciation of about $590,000 per year. Finally, he allowed the Salinases a residual personal income of about 75 percent that could be used to service the loan.

Yet Gomez felt there were other risks inherent in the loan request as well. While Gomez witnessed the hustle and bustle of the small S&S operations and had built substantial trust in the Salinases' business acumen, this major expansion program involved a lot of uncertainty. What if the projected demand did not materialize, or worse, Gruma stepped up its efforts to squeeze S&S out of the market?

What if the local authorities stretched out the approval and permit process, causing major delays for the move to the new building and impacting revenues? What if, after all the stress, the Salinases decided to retire and turn over the business to their two daughters to run? Finally, what if his senior credit officers at Wells Fargo simply refused to back this expansion program because they could not see the potential in the company? These and other questions remained at the top of Gomez's mind as he mulled over Raphael Salinas's reminder of the time when the Wells Fargo manager denied his application for a business loan without a second thought. How could Gomez overcome the many challenges to proving that the Salinas company was a risk worth taking, and how should he structure the loan?

Discussion Questions

1. Why was the personal relationship between Murillo and Gomez and the Salinas so important?
2. Why have Murillo and Gomez been so successful in working with the Hispanic community?
3. Why was careful attention to the Latino market a significant aspect of Wells Fargo's strategy?
4. What cultural factors did Gomez fear would undermine the confidence of his managers in the Salinas business?
5. What other examples can you identify of cultural misunderstandings that might hinder a business transaction?

EXHIBIT 1

Trends in Latino and Minority Buying Power

In 2008, the combined buying power of African Americans, Asians, and Native Americans will be more than triple its 1990 level of $456 billion and will exceed $1.5 trillion, a gain of $1.1 trillion, or 231 percent. In 2008, African Americans will account for 61 percent of combined spending, or $921 billion. Over this eighteen-year period, the percentage gains in minority buying power vary considerably by race, from a gain of 345 percent for Asians to 227 percent for American Indians to 189 percent for blacks. All of these target markets will grow much faster than the white market, where buying power will increase by only 128 percent.

The combined buying power of these three groups will account for 14.3 percent of the nation's total buying power in 2008, up from 10.7 percent in 1990. This 3.6 percent gain in combined market share amounts to an additional $381 billion in buying power in 2008. The market share claimed by a targeted group of consumers is important, because the higher their market share, the lower the average cost of reaching a potential buyer in the group.

HISPANIC BUYING POWER

The immense buying power of the nation's Hispanic consumers will energize the U.S. consumer market as never before, and Selig Center projections reveal that this group alone will control about $653 billion in spending power in 2003. In fact, Census 2000 showed that more than one person in eight who lives in the United States is of Hispanic origin. Moreover, the U.S. Hispanic population will continue to grow much more rapidly than the non-Hispanic population over the eighteen-year period, 1990–2008; the nation's Hispanic buying power will grow at a compound annual rate of 8.8 percent. (The comparable rate of growth for non-Hispanics is 4.9 percent.) In sheer dollar power, Hispanics' economic clout will rise from $222 billion in 1990, to $504 billion in 2000, to $653 billion in 2003, and to $1,014.2 billion in 2008. The 2008 value will exceed the 1990 value by 357 percent—a percentage gain that is substantially greater than either the 136 percent increase in non-Hispanic buying power or the 148 percent increase in the buying power of all consumers.

Of the many forces supporting this substantial and continued growth, the most important is favorable demographics, but better employment opportunities also help to increase the group's buying power. Because of both higher rates of natural increase and strong immigration, the Hispanic population is growing more rapidly than the total population, a trend that is projected to continue. Between 1990 and 2008, the Hispanic population will increase by 137 percent compared to 13.7 percent for the non-Hispanic population and the 24.8 percent gain for the total population. The Hispanic population was relatively young, with larger proportions of them entering the workforce for the first time.

U.S. Average Annual Expenditures and Item Share for All Consumers and Hispanic Consumers, 2001

	All Consumers		Hispanic Consumers	
Item	Average Spending Per Consumer Unit (dollars)	Share of Total (percent)	Average Spending Per Consumer Unit (dollars)	Share of Total (percent)
Total Annual Expenditure	39,513	100.0	34,361	100.0
Food at Home	3,086	7.8	3,551	10.3
Food Away from Home	2,235	5.7	2,097	6.1
Alcoholic Beverages	349	0.9	308	0.9
Housing	13,011	32.9	11,747	34.2
Apparel & Services	1,743	4.4	1,857	5.4
Transportation	7,633	19.3	7,083	20.6
Health Care	2,182	5.5	1,343	3.9
Entertainment	1,953	4.9	1,246	3.6
Personal Care Products & Services	485	1.2	467	1.4
Reading	141	0.4	59	0.2
Education	648	1.6	428	1.2
Tobacco Products & Smoking Supplies	308	0.8	177	0.5
Miscellaneous	750	1.9	457	1.3
Cash Contributions	1,258	3.2	727	2.1
Personal Insurance & Pensions	3,737	9.5	2,814	8.2

Note: Estimates for additional sub-cateçories are available only in The Multicultural Economy 2003 package. To order, see page 6.

Source: Shares were calculated by the Selig Center for Economic Growth, based on data obtained from the U.S. Department of Labor, Bureau of Labor Statistics, *Consumer Expenditure Survey,* 2001.

Source: Humphreys, Jeffrey M. "The Multicultural Economy," *Georgia Business and Economic Conditions,* Vol. 63, 2, The University of Georgia, Second Quarter 2003.

EXHIBIT 2

Banking on Change
Aiming at fast-growing Hispanic market

SOUTH GATE—The Wells Fargo Bank branch in this Los Angeles suburb looks like it belongs in Mexico, with an exterior painted the reddish-brown hues of a pueblo and the lobby spiced up with Spanish-language song lyrics and Mexican artwork.

The remodeling is just one of the ways bankers are trying to appeal to the nation's swelling population of Hispanics, a rapidly growing market that traditionally hasn't attracted much special attention from the financial services industry.

"Once you see an emerging opportunity like this, you have to ask yourself what you need to do better," said Carrie Tolstedt who oversees Wells Fargo's retail operations in California.

Banks are introducing new programs to make it easier for Mexican immigrants to open accounts, spending more money on Hispanic ads and overhauling branches in communities like South Gate, where more than 80 percent of the 96,000 residents are Hispanic.

The remodeled branch is "Like a security blanket for our customers. It's much more comfortable for them to come in here now," said Iliana Concepcion, a personal banking officer whose desk sits in front of a painting by the popular Mexican artist Diego Rivera.

In the first year after the renovations, the number of South Gate households with an account at the office increased by 6 percent, Wells said. Before the remodeling, the household growth rate was stuck below 1 percent.

The uptick has translated into longer lines in the branch lobby, but customers waiting up to 30 minutes to see a teller on a recent Friday afternoon didn't seem to mind.

"It's better now," Wells customer Patricia Nava said through an interpreter. "They seem to want to help you more."

If bankers hope to succeed in the Hispanic market, they probably will have to prepare for crowded lobbies and offer more personal services because so much of Latino culture revolves around face-to-face contact, said Andrew Erlich, a minority marketing consultant in Woodland Hills.

The preference for more human interaction runs counter to the banking industry's increasing emphasis on automating services. But with many upscale customers shifting money into mutual funds and brokerage accounts, revenue-hungry bankers are more willing to accommodate Hispanics, particularly the millions of Mexican immigrants who don't have U.S. bank accounts.

The Federal Reserve Bank has estimated that as many as 25 percent of the nation's Hispanics lack bank accounts. Many pay expensive fees to check-cashing services and wire services to transfer money to relatives in Mexico and other Latin American countries.

Bankers believe they can make a decent profit while charging lower fees for similar services.

Having a U.S. banking account can do more than just save Hispanics money. It provides the financial foundation needed to get credit cards, auto loans and home mortgages, said Carlos Santiago, co-chairman of Santiago and Valdes Solutions, a minority consulting firm in San Francisco.

"This has always been a cash rich, credit poor segment of society," Santiago said. "Having a banking relationship can help give them the credibility to change that."

The demographics are a powerful magnet. The U.S. Hispanic population increased by 61 percent between 1990 and 2000, ballooning from 21.9 million to 35.3 million, according to the U.S. Census.

Although many U.S. Hispanics are poor, the group is gaining financial clout. Hispanics' disposable income rose from $530 billion last year to a projected $600 billion this year, according to Santiago and Valdes Solutions.

Most demographers expect such growth to be robust for several decades. California's Hispanic residents, already nearly one-third of the state's population, is projected to outnumber whites sometime in the next 20 to 30 years.

"Any bank that ignores the shift in these demographics is going to be dead in the water," predicted Ken McEldowney, executive director of Consumer Action, a watchdog group specializing in banking issues.

Bankers across the country are courting Mexicans—the biggest piece of the Hispanic market—by letting them open accounts with a form of identification called "matricula consular." These cards, issued by Mexico's U.S. consulates, typically go to immigrants who don't have Social Security numbers or other documents traditionally required.

San Francisco–based Wells became the first U.S. bank to accept matriculas seven months ago and since then has opened more than 25,000 accounts for new customers using that form of identification. Several other major banks also have decided to accept matriculas.

The trend has drawn fire from activists who want illegal immigrants out of the United States and consider matriculas the favored identification of illegals. But the backlash hasn't discouraged the big banks yet.

Bank of America has quadrupled its budget for minority marketing, to $40 million this year. Most of that money is earmarked for the Hispanic market with slogans such as "Creemos en ti"—Spanish for "We believe in you."

Wells is so eager to sign up more Hispanic customers that it is dispatching managers to California farms to talk to immigrant workers about the advantages of having a U.S. banking account.

The success of the remodeled branch in South Gate has encouraged Wells to make similar changes at Southern California branches in two other heavily Hispanic communities—Panorama City and Bell.

"We think there are more risks in not taking these steps, than in taking them," said Robert Byrne, director of Wells' 8-month-old diverse growth segments division.

By Michael Liedtke, Associated Press.

Source: "Banks: Aiming at the Fast-Growing Hispanic Market." *Santa Maria Times* (Los Angeles, California), 5/28/02.

EXHIBIT 3

The Latino Population in the United States:
Facts and Figures

Latinos, or Hispanics, are commonly defined as people with Spanish surnames whose family origins include Mexico, Cuba, Puerto Rico, and other countries of Central and South America. Latinos can be of any race. By 2000, Latinos reached 12.5 percent of the population, nearly twice the proportion of their population compared to 20 years earlier. High levels of immigration and high fertility rates were the main contributors to this growth. Latinos will maintain annual growth rates that exceed 2 percent until the year 2035, greater than any other demographic category within the country.[1]

In Los Angeles County nearly 72 percent of the Latino population is of Mexican origin.[2] Between 1990 and 2000, Los Angeles County had the largest increases in the Hispanic population in California, adding 889,000 people. By 2000, more than 40 percent of the county residents were Hispanic.[3]

[1]Dynamic Diversity: Projected Changes in U.S. Race and Ethnic Composition 1995 to 2050. http://www.mbda.gov/documents/unpubtext.pdf 5-5-2003.

[2]*American Fact Finder,* http://factfinder.census.gov/bf/_lang=en_vt_name=DEC_2000_SF1_U_DPI_geo_id=05 6-10-2003.

[3]"Race/Ethnic Population Estimates: Components of Change for California Counties," April 1990 through April 2000, http://www.dof.ca.gov/html/Demograp/race-eth.htm 6-10-2003.

Yet the terms "Latino" or "Hispanic" are deceptively simple and hide the significant demographic and cultural diversity within the Latino community. Among Latinos in the United States, 66 percent are of Mexican origin; 14 percent Central and South American origin; 9 percent of Puerto Rican heritage; percent are Cuban origin; and the remaining 6 percent are other Latinos. While the Spanish language ties each group together (37.9 percent of Latinos in Los Angeles speak Spanish at home),[4] there remain significant differences in food and culture among the Latino factions.

Culturally, family ties are hugely important to Latinos. Latino family sizes are larger than those of non-Latinos. Among Latino family households, those with Mexican householders were the most likely to have five or more persons (36 percent). Latino family households were larger than their non-Latino white counterparts. A full 31 percent consisted of five or more persons, compared with 12 percent for family households with non-Latino white householders.[5] Thus, when a company or product is adopted by a Latino, it is highly likely that the person's entire family will become loyal as well.

Latino-owned businesses in the United States totaled 1.2 million firms, employed over 1.3 million people and generated $186.3 billion in revenues in 1997. Latino-owned firms made up 6 percent of the 20.8 million nonfarm businesses in the nation and 1 percent of the $18.6 trillion in receipts for all businesses. Four states, California (336,400), Texas (240,400), Florida (193,900) and New York (104,200), accounted for 73 percent of the firms owned by Latinos (see Exhibits 4 and 5). Among Latino groups, Mexicans owned by far the greatest number of Latino-owned firms, 472,000, or 39 percent (see Exhibit 6). Four in 10 Latino businesses had receipts of $10,000 or less. Slightly more than 2 in 10 had receipts between $10,000 and $25,000, while about 2 percent had sales of $1 million or more. Receipts per firm averaged $155,200 for Latino-owned firms, compared with $410,600 for all U.S. firms.[6]

[4] *American Fact Finder.*

[5] "Diversity of the Country's Latinos Highlighted in U.S. Census Bureau Report," http://www.census.gov/Press-Release/www/2001/cb01-41.html. 5-5-2003.

[6] U.S. Businesses Owned by Latinos Top 1 Million; California, Texas, Florida Lead States, Census Bureau Reports. http://www.census.gov/Press-Release/www/2001/cb01-53.html. 5-5-2003.

EXHIBIT 4

States with the Largest Number of Latino-Owned Firms: 1997

	Total	Percent of Total
U.S. total	**1,199,900**	
California	336,400	28.0
Texas	240,400	20.0
Florida	193,900	16.2
New York	104,200	8.7
New Jersey	36,100	3.0
Illinois	31,000	2.6
Arizona	28,900	2.4
New Mexico	28,300	2.4
Colorado	20,900	1.7
Virginia	13,700	1.1

EXHIBIT 5

States with the Largest Percentage of Latino-Owned Firms: 1997

State	Latino-owned Firms (number)	All Firms (number)	Latino-owned as a Percent of All Firms
U.S. Total	**1,199,900**	**20,821,900**	**5.8**
New Mexico	28,300	131,700	21.5
Texas	240,400	1,526,000	15.8
Florida	193,900	1,301,900	14.9
California	336,400	2,565,700	13.1
Arizona	28,900	329,000	8.8
New York	104,200	1,509,800	6.9
New Jersey	36,100	654,200	5.5
Colorado	20,900	410,200	5.1
Nevada	6,600	129,800	5.1
District of Columbia	2,200	45,300	4.8

EXHIBIT 6

Latino-Owned Firms by Ethnic Group: 1997

Ethnic group	Firms	Receipts
Total	**1,199,900**	**186,300**
Mexican	472,000	73,700
Latino—Latin American	287,300	41,000
Other Latino	188,500	20,700
Cuban	125,300	26,500
Puerto Rican	69,700	7,500
Spaniard	57,200	16,900

EXHIBIT 7

How Commercial Banks Make Lending Decisions

COMMERCIAL BANKS TYPICALLY ASSESS FOUR CRITERIA FOR MAKING A LOAN DECISION:

1   **Credit history/FICO scores of the guarantors:** Commercial loan officers research the personal and business credit to ensure that the business applicant and the business's guarantors possess certain criteria reflecting good repayment history. The credit history of the company is researched through Dun & Bradstreet, which produces reports showing lawsuits, bankruptcies, foreclosures, tax liens, judgments, etc. A company with legal issues outstanding and unpaid tax liens may find it difficult to access capital from a commercial bank. Personal credit is measured by a FICO score of 680 or more as reported by TRW, Experian, or other personal credit reporting agency.

2 **Primary source of repayment:** This is an interest coverage ratio that is used to determine the extent to which recurring profits are sufficiently available to service the applicant's existing and proposed debt. This ratio is measured using the following formula: (Profits + Depreciation + Interest + Owner's Residual Income)/(Annual Debt Service Requirements on all Business Debt). Owner's residual income is the cash the owner(s) could elect to keep in the company if they had/wanted to. Bankers estimate the percentage of the owner's take-home income from the business they believe could have been left in the business to service the proposed new debt.

3 **Secondary source of repayment (collateral):** If the primary source or repayment is not sufficient to meet the loan payments, but the company and its guarantors are otherwise creditworthy, banks research other avenues to help them approve a loan for the applicant. Generally, this involves examining other liquid company assets including accounts receivable, inventory, equipment, or real estate that can be used as collateral and sold.

4 **Tertiary source of repayment:** The owner's net worth outside of the business, that is, what the guarantors can add to the deal, including personal liquid assets or real estate.

In addition, most banks require that a company's leverage not exceed a predetermined level. Importantly, in considering whether to extend loans to small businesses, banks are particularly concerned that the business can demonstrate a history of success. Because 80 percent of new businesses fail in the first 2 years, banks generally insist that a company have 3 years of financial information or audited financial statements before they will extend capital to the company.

Notes

1. Eichenwald, Kurt. *The New York Times,* "Texaco Executives, On Tape, Discussed Impeding a Bias Suit," November 4, 1996, Section A, Page 1, Column 1.

2. *Business Week,* "Texaco: Lessons from A Crisis-in-Progress," News: Analysis & Commentary, December 2, 1996.

3. Eichenwald, Kurt. *The New York Times,* "Investigation Finds No Evidence of Slur on Texaco Tapes," November 11, 1996, http://www.dorsai.org/~jdadd/texaco2.html.

4. Texaco, Inc., Home Page, "A Brief History of Texaco," http://www.texaco.com/compinfo/history_d.html.

5. Bijur, Peter, I. Statement of Chairman and CEO, Texaco, Inc. to Company Employees, Friday, November 15, 1996, http://www.texaco.com/compinfo/pr/pr11_15b.html.

6. Texaco, Inc., Home Page, "A Brief History of Texaco," http://www.texaco.com/compinfo/history_d.html.

7. Jenkins, Holman, W., Jr., " History of a $20 Million Lie, Business World," *Wall Street Journal.* Tuesday, August 12, 1997, p. A15.

8. Fritsch, Peter, " Texaco's New Chairman Navigates PR Crisis," *The Wall Street Journal,* Friday, November 8, 1996, pp. B1, B5.

9. *The Economist,* "Black Hole: Race in the Workplace," November 16, 1996, v341, n7992, p27.

10. Court TV Library Home Page, Report from Independent Investigator, http://205.181.114.35/library/business/texaco/report.html

11. Eichenwald, Kurt, "Investigation Finds No Evidence of Slur on Texaco Tapes," *The New York Times,* November 11, 1996.

12. Court TV Library Home Page, Report from Independent Investigator, http://205.181.114.35/library/business/texaco/report.html

13. Texaco, Inc., Home Page, http://www.texaco.com/compinfo/diversity_main.htm.

14. *The Economist,* "Black Hole: Race in the Workplace," November 16, 1996, v341, n7992, p27.

15. Texaco, Inc., Home Page, http://www.texaco.com/compinfo/diversity/diversity_main.htm.

16. *Business Week,* "Texaco: Lessons from a Crisis-in-Progress," December 2, 1996, p. 44.

17. Culbertson, Katherine, *The Oil Daily,* Independent retailers brace for boycott of Texaco stations, November 13, 1996, v46, n216, p. 1.

18. Texaco, Inc., Home Page, http://www.texaco.com/compinfo/diversity/diversity_main.ht.

19. *Business Week,* "Texaco: Lessons From a Crisis-in-Progress," December 2, 1996, p. 44.

20. *The Oil Daily,* "Texaco Hires Race Adviser," December 2, 1996 v46, n227 p. 5.

21. *The Oil Daily,* "Texaco Calms Dispute, Setting Out Minority Employment Goals," December 19, 1996 v46, n240 p. 3.

22. Holman, W. Jenkins, Jr., *The Wall Street Journal,* "History of a $20 Million Lie," August 12, 1997, p. A15.

23. Demographic Trends in the 20th Century: Census 2000 Special Reports, http://www.census.gov/prod/2002pubs/censr-4.pdf, 5 May 2003.

24. Liz Rogers, "Spicy Sauce a Versatile Condiment that Can Complement Any Dish," *Observer-Reporter,* 8 September, 2002. http://www.observer-reporter.com/356907727396363.bsp 6-24-03.

25. Eduardo Porter, "Hispanic Buying Power to Soar, Outpacing the National Average," *Wall Street Journal,* 18 April 2003.

5 AGE

The focus of this chapter is the age group protected by the Age Discrimination in Employment Act of 1967 (ADEA): workers age 40 and over. Although the focus of this chapter is older workers, it is important to recognize that other people of a variety of ages may be discriminated against because of their age, for example, younger workers or women in their childbearing years.

Objectives

- To examine the relationship between older workers and the workplace.

- To examine the impact of the baby-boomer generation on the workplace.

- To examine flexible organizational models that help keep talented older workers working productively for longer periods of time.

- To examine how age discrimination can emerge as the result of a highly aggressive diversity plan that prioritizes other primary dimensions of diversity.

Preview Questions

- Does society need to rethink the traditional notion of retirement?

- What strategies can managers implement in an effort to manage effectively their older employees?

- Can employing older workers provide a competitive advantage? Why or why not?

Some Important Dates

1903 The state of Colorado passes legislation specifying that no employer may discharge anyone between the ages of 18 and 60 because of his or her age.

1958 Age is added to the New York State statute barring discrimination in employment.

1967   Congress passes the Age Discrimination in Employment Act of 1967 (ADEA) protecting individuals who are between 40 and 65 years of age from discrimination in employment.

1989   Congress eliminates mandatory retirement at age 70 or any other age.

1990   Older Workers Benefit Protection Act becomes law. It bans employers from denying benefits to older employees because of age, unless the cost of providing the benefits can be shown to increase with age.

1996   In *O'Connor v. Consolidated Coin Caterers Corp.*, the U.S. Supreme Court rules that ADEA does not require a fired worker to show that he or she was replaced by someone under 40 to prove age discrimination.

2000   In *Kimel v. State of Florida Board of Regents*, the high court rules that state government agencies are protected by the Constitution from being sued for money damages under the ADEA.

AS LAYOFFS RISE, SO DO AGE-DISCRIMINATION CHARGES

ONE thing has gone up since the economy has gone down: charges of age discrimination.

Over the last two fiscal years, age-discrimination complaints filed with the Equal Employment Opportunity Commission have risen more than 24 percent, reaching levels not seen since the early 1990's.

The sharp increase, labor experts say, is largely attributable to the convergence of a weak economy and an aging work force—nearly 50 percent of the labor pool is made up of baby boomers, and the percentage of workers over 65 has increased from the last decade. There are now more older workers for employers to discriminate against, and more economic incentives to do so.

"The knee-jerk reaction of employers is often that they need to cut costs, and since older workers are perceived as costing more, they become targets of layoffs," said Laurie McCann, a senior lawyer at AARP.

When companies are forced to reorganize, older employees are often perceived as being unable to keep up with new technologies. And because federal courts are often persuaded by arguments that reductions based on economic needs and business strategies do not constitute age discrimination, employers are emboldened to use such rationales as a cover to purge older workers, said John Clifford, a labor lawyer in Washington.

Such tendencies are compounded in sectors of the economy that say youth is essential to innovation and progress, like technology. Because technology has been hit particularly hard in the downturn, Ms. McCann said, the stereotypes about the inability of older workers to keep pace and adapt, or that they represent higher costs, have an especially pernicious effect.

William S. Payson can speak personally about the industry's suspicious attitude toward older people. When he moved to Northern California in 1987 as a retired chief executive of a business-to-business marketing firm, he had such difficulty finding employment that he

---

organized a brigade of his similarly challenged peers to wear buttons that read "hire the retired" around Silicon Valley. Today, Mr. Payson, now 79, is the chief executive of SeniorTechs.com, an employment database for older information technology workers.

He said that the relentless quest for youth had always permeated the culture of technology, and that the dot-com boom made matters worse. These days, the "senior" tech workers that Mr. Payson's Web site serves are 35 and older. "It's amazing to think that in the technology industry today, 35 is over the hill," Mr. Payson said.

Frederic Clancy, 71, and James Hurd, 60, would agree. They filed age-bias charges with the E.E.O.C. and a suit in federal court after being laid off from their sales jobs with Tektronix in 2000, an electronic equipment company.

According to the complaint, they and a co-worker were abruptly transferred out of their telephone and cable sales group to form a new unit to sell an older, less desirable line. The three men were the oldest members of the sales force. (The third was planning on retiring in a year, and did.) Mr. Clancy and Mr. Hurd, each with about two decades at Tektronix, were told that their sales experience was needed in the new unit, Mr. Clancy said.

What they say in the complaint is that, unbeknown to them, Tektronix was planning to sell their new unit. Four months after they were transferred, it was sold and Mr. Clancy and Mr. Hurd were notified that they would be terminated. "Prior to being transferred to the new unit, I was the top sales producer in my group and made the most money for the group that year," said Mr. Clancy, who had received dozens of sales awards. "It was inconceivable to me that I would be let go."

For Mr. Hurd, the disbelief was compounded when he tried to find another position within the company, something he said that was promised to him. When a sales position previously held by Mr. Hurd opened up, he saw it as a stroke of luck. "I had trained the guy leaving," Mr. Hurd said, "so there was no question of being qualified."

Instead, he was told that he was not right for the position. Upon being terminated, Mr. Hurd spent more than a year looking for work.

Mr. Clancy and Mr. Hurd ultimately settled their case. Tektronix officials declined to comment, citing a confidentiality clause in the settlement agreement.

Ms. McCann of AARP says that problems of proof hamper age-bias cases, especially when the question is failure to hire. "A lot of the discrimination in the technology industry is at the hiring end, and since you're not usually given a reason why you're not hired, it is difficult to prove," she said.

D. Jan Duffy, a San Francisco employment practices consultant and lawyer, said that many older employees were reluctant to litigate. "Plaintiffs' lawyers used to lament three years ago that they could not get clients to bring suits challenging egregious discrimination because the clients could so easily find other work, so it wasn't worth it to litigate," she said. "Today, while the effects of discrimination are so much worse, since it is so hard to find work, many of the people over 50 I have seen are just giving up and leaving the industry altogether, rather than asserting their claims."

Mr. Payson argues that older workers need to take an entrepreneurial approach to seeking employment. He points to the demands for contract work in older computer languages, which mostly older technology workers are skilled to program.

(continued)

But for 58-year-old Marilyn Langenberg, such contract work was not a salvation. As a contract software programmer in Silicon Valley, she has been out of that line of work for 22 months and is now employed as a flower arrangement designer.

Ms. Langenberg said that contract work was a last resort that she turned to when she could no longer avoid the age problem. She said she was repeatedly told she was overqualified.

Ms. Langenberg has not had health insurance for three years. Still, she said, the thought of filing an age-discrimination suit has never crossed her mind. "I have always been far more interested in finding a job," she said.

ESSAY: IT'S TIME TO RETIRE RETIREMENT

In the past few years, companies have been so focused on downsizing to contain costs that they've largely neglected a looming threat to their competitiveness, the likes of which they have never before experienced: a severe shortage of talented workers. The general population is aging and, with it, the labor pool. People are living longer, healthier lives, and the birthrate is at a historic low. While the ranks of the youngest workers (ages 16 to 24, according to Bureau of Labor Statistics groupings) are growing 15 percent this decade as baby boomers' children enter the workforce, the 25- to 34-year-old segment is growing at just half that rate, and the workforce population between the ages of 35 and 44—the prime executive-development years—is actually declining.

In the United States, the overall rate of workforce growth faces a sharp drop. After peaking at nearly 30 percent in the 1970s (as the baby boomers as well as unprecedented numbers of women entered the workforce), and holding relatively steady at 12 percent during the 1990s and again in the present decade, the rate is projected to drop and level off at 2 percent to 3 percent per decade thereafter. That translates into an annual growth rate of less than 1 percent today and an anemic 0.2 percent by 2020. Meanwhile, age distributions are shifting dramatically. The proportion of workers over 55 declined from 18 percent in the 1970s to under 11 percent in 2000—but it's projected to rebound to 20 percent by 2015.

Ken Dychtwald is the founding president and CEO of Age Wave, a San Francisco–based think tank and consulting firm focused on the maturing marketplace and workforce. A psychologist, gerontologist, and adviser to business and government, he is the author of 10 books, including Age Wave (J. P. Tarcher, 1989) and his latest book, Age Power (J. P. Tarcher, 1999). Tamara Erickson is an executive officer and member of the board of directors for the Concours Group, a management consulting, research, and education firm based in Kingwood, Texas. Bob Morison is an executive vice president and the director of research of the Concours Group. Dychtwald, Erickson, and Morison are coauthors of a forthcoming book about the impact of demographic shifts on the workplace (Harvard Business School Press, 2005). They can be reached at kdychtwald@agewave.com, tjerickson@concoursgroup.com, and rfmorison@concoursgroup.com.

About the Research

Our year long research project, "Demography is Destiny," concluded in the fall of 2003 and was conducted by the Concours Group in partnership with Ken Dychtwald and Age Wave. Sponsored by 30 major public and private organizations in North America and Europe, the project explored the emerging business challenges presented by workforce aging and other profound shifts in workforce demographics. On the basis of our findings, we developed a series of management actions and pragmatic techniques for anticipating, coping with, and capitalizing on those changes. Member organizations shaped the focus and direction of the project, shared their experiences as part of the field research, and participated in a series of workshops. (For a management summary of our research findings, see http://www.concoursgroup.com/Demography/DD_MgmtSumm.pdf.)

In other words, we've recently passed what will prove to be a historic low in the concentration of older workers. Just when we've gotten accustomed to having relatively few mature workers around, we have to start learning how to attract and retain far more of them.

During the next 15 years, 80 percent of the native-born workforce growth in North America—and even more so in much of Western Europe—is going to be in the over-50 cohort. In the next decade or so, when baby boomers—the 76 million people born between 1946 and 1964, more than one-quarter of all Americans—start hitting their sixties and contemplating retirement, there won't be nearly enough young people entering the workforce to compensate for the exodus. The Bureau of Labor Statistics projects a shortfall of 10 million workers in the United States in 2010, and in countries where the birthrate is well below the population replacement level (particularly in Western Europe), the shortage will hit sooner, be more severe, and remain chronic.

The problem won't just be a lack of bodies. Skills, knowledge, experience, and relationships walk out the door every time somebody retires—and they take time and money to replace. Given the inevitable time lag between the demand for skills and the ability of the educational system to provide them, we'll see a particularly pronounced skill shortage in fast-growing technical fields such as health care. What's more, employees are your face to the marketplace. It's good business to have employees who reflect the ethnic, gender, and, yes, age composition of your customer base—especially when those customers are well off. Baby boomers will be the most financially powerful generation of mature consumers ever; today's mature adults control more than $7 trillion in wealth in the United States—70 percent of the total. As the population at large ages, and ever-more spending power is concentrated in the hands of older customers, companies will want to show a mature face to their clientele—and yet those faces will be in high demand.

The problem is pretty clear. Workers will be harder to come by. Tacit knowledge will melt steadily away from your organization. And the most dramatic shortage of workers will hit the age group associated with leadership and key customer-facing positions. The good news is that a solution is at hand: Just as companies are learning to market to an aging population, so they can also learn to attract and employ older workers.

And yet, despite irrefutable evidence of workforce aging, many managers may be marching their companies straight off a demographic cliff. According to a recent survey from the Society for Human Resource Management, two-thirds of U.S. employers don't actively recruit older workers. Furthermore, more than half do not actively attempt to retain key ones; 80 percent do not offer any special provisions (such as flexible work arrangements) to appeal to the concerns of mature workers; and 60 percent of CEOs say their companies don't account for workforce aging in their long-term business plans. Instead, relying on the mistaken assumption that the future will be populated by a growing pool of talented and loyal young workers, companies are systemically offering older workers the "package" and skimming people out of the labor force from the top age brackets down.

Little wonder that baby boomers and "mature" workers (those 55 and above) are feeling little loyalty to their current employers. These employees are bottlenecked, with too many people competing for too few leadership positions. They're distrustful, fearful, and defensive, knowing that they're "too old" to easily find work elsewhere and likely to be pushed out before the "official" retirement age. They're struggling to update their skills, and they're feeling burned out after 30-plus years on the job. Meanwhile, they stand back and watch as recruiting, training, and leadership development dollars, as well as promotion opportunities, are overwhelmingly directed at younger employees, with little thought to the skills and experience that the over-55 crowd can bring to bear on almost any business problem.

In short, most baby boomers want to continue working—and they may need to, for financial reasons—but they may not want to work for you. Twenty percent of those collecting employer pensions are still working in some capacity, and among people under 60 who are already collecting pensions, more than 50 percent are working. Among those age 55 and older who accepted early retirement offers, one-third have gone back to work. But these working retirees are more likely to be working part-time or be self-employed than their not-yet-retired counterparts—in other words, they're working on their own terms. That's increasingly where you'll need to meet these older workers if you want to gain access to their skills. As the labor market tightens, they will have more choices, and the most capable and accomplished among them are likely to be the most mobile and financially independent; they're the ones who are most likely to move on. The challenge is to find a way to reconnect with these employees before they're ready to take a retirement package and run—perhaps to a competitor.

We recently conducted a yearlong research project in which we looked at the implications for businesses of an aging workforce. Broadly speaking, our findings suggest an urgent need to find ways to attract and retain employees of all ages. But of most concern is the potentially debilitating mass retirement that threatens to starve many businesses of key talent in the next 10 to 15 years. On the basis of our research, we've concluded that the concept of retirement is outdated and should be put out to pasture in favor of a more flexible approach to ongoing work, one that serves both employer and employee. In this article, we'll describe how companies can retain the skills of employees well past the traditional age of retirement by moving from a rigid model where work ceases at a certain age to a more flexible one where employees can become lifelong contributors.

CREATE A CULTURE THAT HONORS EXPERIENCE

If companies are to win back the hearts and minds of baby boomers and other generations of mature workers, they need to start with the work environment itself, which has become increasingly alienating to anyone over the age of 50. Human resource practices are often explicitly or implicitly biased against older workers, and these biases can seep into the culture in a manner that makes them feel unwelcome.

It starts with recruiting, in subtle ways such as the choice of words in a job advertisement. Even high-energy, young-in-spirit older workers, for example, may interpret an ad stressing "energy," "fast pace," and "fresh thinking" as implicitly targeting younger workers and dismiss the opportunity out of hand. Mature workers are more likely to be attracted to ads emphasizing "experience," "knowledge," and "expertise."

Traditional recruiting channels such as want ads or help wanted signs may not attract older workers either. Twelve years ago, pharmacy chain CVS looked at national demographic trends and concluded that the company needed to employ a much greater number of older workers. But managers didn't know how to find them—older people shopped in the stores but didn't apply for openings, perhaps believing they wouldn't be hired. Now the company works through the National Council on Aging, city agencies, and community organizations to find and hire productive new employees.

Interviewing techniques can be unintentionally off-putting as well. Being left alone for half an hour to build something with Legos or being asked to perform the type of verbal gymnastics Microsoft became famous for in job interviews (example: how are

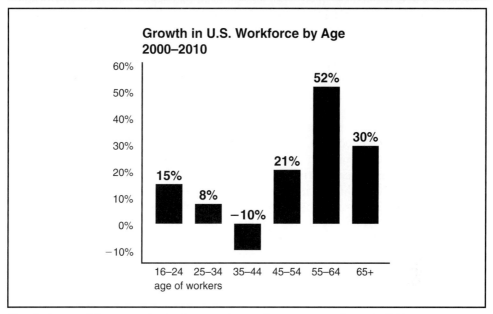

FIGURE 5-1   Who Will Run Your Company?

Growth in U.S. Workforce by Age 2000–2010

If we look at workforce growth rates by age segment, the patterns are dramatic. In the current decade, the ranks of youngest workers (ages 16 to 24, according to Bureau of Labor Statistics groupings) are growing by 15%, thanks to the "echo boom" as baby boomers' children enter the workforce. The 25- to 34-year-old segment is growing at just half that rate, and the workforce population between 35 and 44 years old is actually declining. With the baby boom generation moving into middle age and its vanguard nearing retirement age, the fastest workforce growth rates are in the three oldest age segments.

M&Ms made?) may be daunting to candidates accustomed to a more traditional approach to demonstrating their skills. One major British bank realized that its psychometric and verbal-reasoning tests were intimidating to older candidates and replaced these tests with role-playing exercises to gauge candidates' ability to handle customers. And Nationwide, Britain's largest building society, has begun short-listing job candidates by telephone to reduce the number of applicants who are rejected because they look older.

Training and development activities also tend to favor younger employees. According to the Bureau of Labor Statistics, older workers (age 55 plus) receive on average less than half the amount of training that any of their younger cohorts receive, including workers in the 45 to 54 age range. One reason may be that they're reluctant to ask: As people well established in their careers and very busy on the job, they may not feel or want to admit the need for training and development. And yet many midcareer and older employees require refresher training in areas from information technology to functional disciplines to nonhierarchical management methods. The challenge is to make them feel as though it's not a sign of weakness to ask. At Dow Chemical, the companywide expectation is that employees at all levels will continue to learn and grow; as a result, employees regularly seek training and development opportunities, readying themselves for their next career moves.

Most important, mature workers will be attracted to a culture that values their experience and capabilities—an environment that can take some time and effort to build. The Aerospace Corporation is a company that has, over the years, built a reputation for valuing experience and knowledge. Nearly half of its 3,400 regular, full-time employees are over age 50—a clear signal to job candidates that experience is appreciated. CVS has made great strides in creating a company that is more welcoming to older employees, having more than doubled the percentage of employees over age 50 in the past 12 years. It has no mandatory retirement age, making it easy to join the company at an advanced age and stay indefinitely (six employees are in their nineties). The company boosts its age-friendly image through internal and external publications. Company and HR department newsletters highlight the productivity and effectiveness of older workers, and the company coproduces with a cosmetics company a senior-focused magazine that's called *In Step with Healthy Living*.

Older workers can see that CVS honors experience. A year ago, after taking a buyout package from his management job in a major drugstore chain, 59-year-old Jim Wing joined CVS as the pharmacy supervisor for the company's southern Ohio stores. What influenced his decision? "I'm too young to retire. [CVS] is willing to hire older people. They don't look at your age but your experience." Pharmacy technician Jean Penn, age 80, has worked in the business since 1942. She sold her own small pharmacy to CVS five years ago and began working in another CVS store the next day. She was recently given a 50-year pin. ("Turns out they don't make 60-year pins," she says.) By giving Penn credit for time served before she joined the company, CVS once again sent a strong signal about the value attached to experience.

OFFER FLEXIBLE WORK

While older employees won't sign on or stick around if the HR processes and culture aren't welcoming, the substance and arrangement of work are even more important. Companies need to design jobs such that staying on is more attractive than leaving. Many mature workers want to keep working but in a less time-consuming and pressured capacity so that they may pursue other interests. And many baby boomers have a direct and compelling need for flexibility to accommodate multiple commitments, such as caring for children and elderly parents at the same time. Flex work—flexible in both where and when work is performed, as well as flexibility in the traditional career path—can offer many attractions and rewards and appeal to employees' changing needs.

The concept of flexible work is not new, of course, and many companies offer it in some form—job sharing, telecommuting, compressed workweeks, and part-time schedules. But such programs are usually small in scale and, in practice, are often taken up by new mothers and others with consuming family commitments. What's more, the implicit bargain is often that employees who participate will see their careers suffer for it. Companies that have successful flex programs not only make these programs easily accessible to older workers but also structure them so that people who participate don't feel that they're being sidelined or overlooked for promotions—and so that participation leads to a win-win for employer and employee.

Look at ARO Incorporated, a business process outsourcer based in Kansas City, Missouri. Six years ago, its staff turnover was at 25 percent, which limited its productivity as an operator of contract call centers, back-office and forms processing, outbound customer interaction, and more. Kansas City hosts some 90 call centers, so employees had numerous other options, and the applicant pool was shallow.

Michael Amigoni, the company's chief operating officer, soon found a way to cut costs and improve service by upgrading the company's technology to allow some 100 teleworkers to remain off-site. He then actively recruited baby boomers, who were attracted to the flexibility, to fill these jobs. Employees were not permitted to do the work simultaneously with child care, elder care, or pet care, and company managers visited people's homes to make sure they had an appropriate working environment. While some younger workers signed on initially, the company found that these employees missed having an office community and largely dropped out.

Meanwhile, ARO gained access to a large pool of mature, experienced employees, who, on the whole, have stayed with the company longer than younger employees have. Turns out, they're also a much better match for the company's customer demographics. "ARO has clients in the insurance and financial services sectors, and a lot of the people we talk to are older," says Amigoni. "It helps that the people making the calls are older, because they are in similar circumstances to customers." For insurance companies, a lot of ARO's work is underwriting, which involves asking questions about health, among other things. It's useful to have workers who are facing some of the same health concerns—their own or perhaps their parents'—that their customers are. ARO has found that younger, entry-level workers cannot make these connections as easily. Turnover is now down to 7 percent, and productivity is up 15 percent, partly because the company now has more seasoned staff. To boot, the company was able to expand without having to move into a larger facility, which it didn't want to pay for.

Other companies offer flexibility in work assignments to reignite older employees who have come to find their jobs a bit stale—an approach that can be of particular value in appealing to highly paid managerial talent. For example, four years ago, Deloitte Consulting looked at the firm's demographics and realized that by 2003, 40 percent of its then 850 partners would be 50 or older and eligible to retire at 55. The firm didn't want to lose this talented group of men and women en masse, so it created what it called a Senior Leaders program, which enabled partners in their early fifties to redesign their career paths. (The program, along with a similar program at Deloitte's sister company, Deloitte & Touche, is currently on hold as the two companies reintegrate operations following last year's decision not to separate as planned.)

Here's how the Senior Leaders program worked: Each year, a 10-member global selection committee assessed candidates who had made a unique contribution to the firm and would continue to add significant value. The committee then sat down with each nominated employee to customize a second career with the firm, including flexible hours and work location, special projects, and the opportunity to engage in mentoring, research, training and development, company promotions, or global expansion. Deloitte still has about a dozen active senior leaders, most of whom opted for full-time work in their rejuvenated roles. The partner who launched the program told us: "The biggest surprise was the prestige the program gained. Being a senior leader became extremely prestigious both to the firm and to the clients."

Still other companies appeal to older workers' desire for flexibility by reducing hours in the years leading up to retirement. The reduced hours are an attractive option because it gives workers opportunities to pursue outside interests. At Varian, a leading provider of radiotherapy systems, employees age 55 and over who have a minimum of five years of service and who plan to retire within three years can negotiate a reduced work schedule. The typical arrangement is four days per week the first year and three days a week thereafter. Half-time is the minimum, and two half-timers can job share. Participants retain full medical and dental benefits and can request a return to full-time work if the new schedule results in economic hardship.

We are strong advocates of flexible work, in all the varieties described here, not only because it's a way to entice older workers to continue working but also because it forms the foundation of a flexible new approach to retirement, one that assumes people can continue to contribute in some way well into their "retirement" years.

INTRODUCE FLEXIBLE RETIREMENT

Flexible retirement is flexible work in the extreme—a logical extension of the flexible work models just described, where the work may continue indefinitely.

Retirement, as it's currently understood, is a recent phenomenon. For almost all of history, people worked until they dropped. It was only during the Great Depression that, desperate to make room in the workforce for young workers, governments, unions, and employers institutionalized retirement programs as we know them today, complete with social security and pension plans. When the modern notion of retirement was first articulated near the end of the nineteenth century, the designated retirement age of 65 was longer than the life expectancy at the time. Over the last 50 years, the average retirement age declined steadily, in the United States, Great Britain, and Canada, the average retirement age is currently around 62. Meanwhile, life expectancies have increased, leaving more years for leisure.

But in fact, many people don't want a life of pure leisure; half of today's retirees say they're bored and restless. A recent AARP/Roper Report survey found that 80 percent of baby boomers plan to work at least part-time during their retirement; just 16 percent say that they won't work at all. They're looking for different blends—three days a week, for example, or maybe six months a year. Many want or need the income, but that's not the only motivator. People tend to identify strongly with their work, their disciplines, and their careers. Many wish to learn, grow, try new things, and be productive indefinitely, through a combination of commercial, volunteer, and personal pursuits. They enjoy the sense of self-worth that comes with contributing to a business or other institution, and they enjoy the society of their peers. For some people, the workplace is their primary social affiliation.

For all these reasons, the notion of retirement as it is traditionally practiced—a one-time event that permanently divides work life from leisure—no longer makes sense. In its place, companies are starting to design models in which employees can continue to contribute in some fashion, to their own satisfaction and to the company's benefit. Some regulations currently restrict our vision of workers moving seamlessly in and out of flexible work arrangements without ever actually retiring. The IRS prohibits defined benefits plans from making distributions until employment ends or an employee reaches "normal" retirement age. And pension calculations often discourage people even from reducing their hours with a current employer prior to retirement because payouts are often determined by the rate of pay in the last few years of work. But a growing number of companies have found ways to call on the skills of retired employees for special purposes.

From the standpoint of the employee, these flex programs offer opportunities to mix work and other pursuits. They also offer personal fulfillment and growth, ongoing financial rewards, and continued enjoyment of the society of colleagues. For employers, the programs provide an elastic pool of staff on demand and an on-call cadre of experienced people who can work part-time as the business needs them. Recruiting and placement costs are close to zero because the business is already in contact with these workers, and training costs are minimal. They know the organization and the organization knows them; they fit in right away and are productive without ramp-up time. And they bring scarce skills and organizational knowledge that can't be matched by contractors unconnected with the organization.

Retirees can also act as leaders on demand. Corporations periodically face waves of executive retirements, and many have done a poor job of maintaining the leadership pipeline. A group of experienced executives who can step in at a moment's notice can both fill gaps and help bring the next generation of leaders up to speed.

Typically, these programs allow an employee to take regular retirement and then, sometimes after a specified break in service (typically six months), return to the employer as an independent contractor, usually for a maximum of 1,000 hours a year. (The IRS imposes the hourly restriction to discourage companies from substituting full-time employees with retirees and thus avoiding expenses such as benefits and FICA. Employees who work more than 1,000 hours per year usually need to be contracted through an agency and make their services available to other employers as well.)

While most such programs today lack sufficient scale to make a difference in a company's overall staffing, serving instead as a safety valve and a source of specific skills and experience, large corporations would do well to bring these programs up to scale as labor markets tighten. An example of a program at a scale proportional to the overall employee population is that of the Aerospace Corporation, which provides R&D and systems-engineering services to the air force. The personnel needs of this California-based company vary from year to year and contract to contract, and its Retiree Casual program helps level the staffing load.

Long-term employees can generally retire with full benefits at age 55 or older. As part of the Retiree Casual program, they can then work on a project-consulting basis for up to 1,000 hours per year at their old base salaries, sometimes less, depending on roles and responsibilities. Eighty percent of retirees sign up, and some start back the day after they retire. About 500 retiree casuals are available at any given time, while 200 are working. They work various patterns—most work two days per week, but some work six months on, six months off (the 1,000-hour limit is approximately the equivalent of half-time). A few (three to four a year) are so indispensable that they have to be dropped from the program and contracted via an agency after they hit the 1,000-hour limit. Most participate into their midsixties, some beyond 80.

The program assures the company a degree of "corporate memory," according to George Paulikas, who retired in 1998 at age 62 as an EVP after spending his entire post-PhD career with the company. He was off only a couple of weeks before being asked back to help on a project and has worked part-time ever since—about one-quarter time last year. "You don't want people with enormous experience to just walk out the door. The Retiree Casual program keeps expertise around and helps transfer it to others. People often remark that we don't have many consultants around here. Actually, we do, but they're called retirees, and they already know the business inside out." Paulikas sticks with the program because it allows him to keep his association with the organization but on his own terms. "This program is a pleasant way to keep associated with a great organization, great people, great work. I get to work less often and with less intensity." And because he's not working full-time, Paulikas has been able to pursue other professional interests; he works as a consultant to the Institute for Defense Analyses and is a member of the National Academy of Sciences Space Studies Board.

Monsanto has a similar program, which it calls the Resource Re-Entry Center. It's open to all employees who leave the company in good standing and want to return to a part-time position, though departing employees have to wait six months after leaving a full-time job. Managers are directed to use retirees for job sharing, for cyclical spikes, and for temporary positions in the case of unplanned leaves. They're told not to attempt a reduction in benefit costs by hiring retirees for long-term work. Participants are eligible for company savings and investment plans as well as spot bonuses (though not the normal bonus structure). Originally, participants were limited to 1,000 hours of work per year to ensure the program wouldn't interfere with pension payouts, but Monsanto recently relaxed the requirement for those people whose pensions wouldn't be affected, such as retirees who had received a lump-sum payout.

Jim Fornango, who retired from Monsanto in 1996 at the age of 53, has returned to work on a variety of projects since 1998. He likes the flexibility: "I spend the amount of time I want doing things I want. I'm not locked into a structure." And, like Paulikas, he's been able to explore other interests at the same time; he serves as a substitute teacher and as a counselor to other teachers.

· · ·

It's fashionable to invest heavily in high-potential employees, creating programs that give these select (and historically young) people the leadership experiences they'll need to ascend quickly through an organization. Why not, then, develop a similar type of program aimed at older and midcareer workers with the skills, abilities, and experiences that your organization most needs? A lifelong-contributor or high-retention program could call on a variety of techniques to reengage these valuable players. Such a program might include fresh assignments or career switches, mentoring or knowledge-sharing roles, training and development, and sabbaticals—all of which have the potential to rejuvenate careers while engendering fresh accomplishments and renewed loyalty.

And yet in our research, we didn't find a single company that explicitly created such high-retention pools among over-55 workers. Some businesses are taking the first step: Sears, for example, has expanded its talent-management and retention focus to include not just highly promotable people but also solid contributors and pros with specific, tough-to-replace skills. Dow Chemical has oriented its human resource management systems toward "continuous rerecruitment" of its workforce, in part by encouraging people to move into different roles throughout their careers. And companies like Aerospace and Monsanto are using their retiree programs to retain employees with valuable skills. But by and large, in most companies, the over-55 crowd continues to get very little attention from management.

That's going to have to change. Sixty-five isn't what it used to be. In 2001, Bob Lutz, then 69, was recruited to join General Motors as vice chairman of product development, charged with rejuvenating the product line as he had done at Chrysler with the Dodge Viper, Chrysler PT Cruiser, and Dodge Ram truck line. In last fall's World Series, the winning Florida Marlins were led by 72-year-old Jack McKeon, called out of retirement early in the season to turn around the fortunes of a youthful but underperforming club. Collecting Grammy Awards in 2000 were Tony Bennett, Tito Puente, and B. B. King—combined age around 220. Al Hirschfeld's caricatures graced the print media for more than 75 years, and he was still drawing when he passed away last year, his 100th. And then there's the litany of business executives called out of already active retirement to inject stability, direction, confidence, and sometimes legitimacy into major corporations in need of leadership. Examples include 67-year-old Harry Stonecipher, who recently succeeded Phil Condit as Boeing's CEO; John Reed, named interim chairman and CEO of the New York Stock Exchange; Allan Gilmour, vice chairman of Ford, who rejoined the company after retirement; and Joseph Lelyveld, who stepped in temporarily at the *New York Times* last year.

But then, maybe 65 was never what we thought. Lee Iacocca once told *Wired,* "I've always been against automated chronological dates to farm people out. The union would always say, 'Make room for the new blood; there aren't enough jobs to go around.' Well, that's a hell of a policy to have. I had people at Chrysler who were 40 but acted 80, and I had 80-year-olds who could do everything a 40-year-old can. You have to take a different view of age now. People are living longer. Age just gives experience. Besides, it takes you until about 50 to know what the hell is going on in the world."

What Iacocca understood was that people don't suddenly lose the talent and experience gained over a lifetime at the flip of a switch. It's not good business to push people out the door just because your policies say it's time. Smart companies will find ways to persuade mature workers to delay retirement or even eschew it entirely as long as they remain productive and healthy.

Discussion Questions

1. What differences are there in what attracts older and younger workers?
2. Older workers are one group who might help companies keep their workforces at full strength; what other groups might contribute to this effort?
3. What attitudes and policies inhibit the effectiveness of companies' strategies for hiring older workers?
4. Why might older workers be particularly interested in flexible work schedules and assignments?
5. What advantages do firms obtain by creating flexible work schedules and assignments for older workers?

CASE STUDY: ASLEEP AT THE WHEEL: FORD MOTOR COMPANY'S EXCLUSION OF THE OLDER WORKER

Ford Motor Company—founded by Henry Ford in 1903 with 11 associates, $28,000, and the slogan "I will build a motorcar for the great multitude"—was sued for age discrimination in 2001 and again in 2003.

Jacques Nasser, who became chief executive officer of the multibillion dollar automaker in January 1999, quickly began an aggressive crusade to infuse diversity into the tradition-based Ford. Two years later, Nasser was ousted and replaced by Henry Ford's great-grandson, Chairman William Clay Ford, Jr. One

Authors: Dr. Kathryn A. Cañas and Dr. Harris Sondak, The University of Utah of the primary reasons for Nasser's fall from power was his well-intentioned diversity initiative that ironically became a method of exclusion of and discrimination against older workers.

In a 2000 address to top executives, Nasser complained: "I do not like the sea of white faces in the audience and Ford Motor Co. must ensure that in the future the company reflects the broad spectrum of Ford's customers."[1] These words reflected his seemingly aggressive position on workplace diversity—Ford must diversify to maintain its competitive edge. Taking the conventional Ford company on an unconventional journey, Nasser pushed his employees full speed ahead: "While we honor our traditions, we are not bound by them. The energy and ambition of the Ford team to create new ways is almost limitless. As long as they keep their eyes on the road and their hands on the wheel."[2]

Despite his efforts to increase diversity at Ford, Nasser found his company facing two class-action age discrimination lawsuits in addition to a number of individual discrimination lawsuits. The story of how a revolutionary crusade for diversity lead to serious charges of age discrimination begins with an understanding of the dynamic yet polarizing leadership style of former Ford CEO Jacques Nasser.

JACQUES NASSER

Nasser's impressive career with Ford began in 1968 when, at age 20, he accepted a job as a financial analyst with Ford of Australia. Accepting international assignments—that some may have found unappealing—enabled Nasser to move up in the company as he found himself working in Thailand, Venezuela, Argentina, and the Philippines. Nasser had a reputation for being a "rising star" and "ahead of his time," for example, when he encouraged "suppliers to cooperate and piece parts together into modules before shipping them to Ford assembly plants."[3] Just as Nasser was known for his creative problem-solving skills, he was also known for his toughness. While working in Argentina in 1985, Nasser was held hostage for three days when a Ford plant was seized during a political uprising; he eventually collapsed from exhaustion.[4]

In 1990, Nasser returned to his homeland to help salvage the deteriorating Ford of Australia by cutting the 15,000-person workforce in half and improving productivity by 40 percent. In 1996 he became Ford's head of automotive operations in Detroit; he helped Ford reduce costs by $3 billion, in part by eliminating weak vehicles like the Aspire, Aerostar, and Thunderbird.[5] In 1999, when he became Ford's CEO, he was viewed as a unique leader known for his involvement with employees and direct, immediate feedback on issues ranging from employee presentation skills to car design.

Although Nasser was described by many as pioneering and charming, he was also perceived, by others, as polarizing. And while his fearless leadership style won him prestigious honors such as the 1999 Automobile Industries Man of the Year, this same quality led to the creation of his nickname, "Jac the Knife," which reflected his reputation as a "bare-knuckle" cost cutter, unafraid to eliminate superfluous workers.[6] According to David E. Cole, director of the University of Michigan's Office for the Study of Automotive Transportation, "He is a very polarizing figure . . . People have strong emotions about him one way or the other. He's a compelling guy."[7]

Nasser never tried to hide his unique style or his four-tier plan for Ford's transformation: to improve Ford's customer focus, to develop leaders at every level, to embrace the digital consumer age, and to diversify his workforce. While Ford executives and employees embraced Nasser's goals, they slowly began to question his methods for achieving them. The main concern ultimately became his aggressive campaign—what was often described as a revolution—to diversify Ford's workforce.

NASSER'S DIVERSITY CRUSADE

Passion was, perhaps, Nasser's most captivating quality. It was this passion—stemming from his personal experience: being born in Lebanon and then emigrating with his parents to Australia—that functioned as the catalyst behind his diversity initiative. Nasser's history, which he openly shared with his employees, illuminated the source of his desire to make diversity thrive on a systemic level within Ford.

Telling his personal story to Wharton Business School students, Nasser said: "I didn't look Australian, and when I went to school, I was different than the kids in my class. I spoke Arabic, not English. My lunch was tabouli and flat bread, and kids would laugh at me. But I stayed with my food. The lesson I learned was, it's okay to be different. Be yourself. Be your own brand. Stand up for what you believe in."[8]

One would assume that Nasser's philosophy would not conflict with a company that has identified diversity as "one of our founding principles" since early in its history. In 1913, for example, Henry Ford's offer to pay $5 a day attracted thousands of immigrants and African Americans drawn to the prospect of earning twice the typical daily wage—a wage proudly claimed by Ford as being "credited with helping to create the black middle class."[9] By 1916, Ford employed people who represented 62 nationalities and more than 900 people with disabilities.[10] Additionally, Ford hired many disabled veterans returning from World War I in 1919, thus "making the automaker one of the first companies to hire people with disabilities and to adapt work environments to their specific needs."[11]

Nasser viewed excellence in diversity management not only as a continuation of and respect for Ford's long-standing traditions but also as a competitive advantage. Specifically, he desired the best possible reputation for diversity management so that Ford could recruit and retain the best minority employees. The value of a diverse workforce was, for Nasser, obvious: "Greater inclusion of minorities is a priority for two reasons. It's the right thing to do. It's also good business."[12] Impressively, in 1999, Ford made 30 percent of its new hires minorities and raised the percentage of minority managers to 15 percent. In its July 2000 issue, *Fortune* magazine rated Ford the country's 30th best company for minorities—no other automaker made the top 50.[13]

Ford's diversity numbers are indeed notable. According to the company's annual report, the number of women and minorities working for Ford was 47.5 percent of its workforce in 2001. African Americans accounted for 19 percent of Ford employees, and the percentage of Latinos working for Ford was 3.1. The percentage of women and people of color in management positions at Ford was 34.9 in 2001.[14]

In an effort to tap into African American, Hispanic, and Asian markets, Ford actively recruited and trained minority dealers. Under the program, the candidates completed two years of business classes, and as a way to reciprocate, Ford helped finance their dealerships.[15]

THE PERFORMANCE MANAGEMENT PROCESS (PMP)

As Nasser pushed Ford in ambitious new directions—embracing diversity, urging employees to get closer to customers, hiring outsiders to shake up Ford's culture, expanding Ford's luxury-car portfolio, and overhauling management pay and performance practices—Ford's bottom line was taking a hit. Net losses in 2001 totaled $5.5 billion, down from earnings of $3.5 billion the previous year.[16] Of course, although it is impossible to ignore external forces such as September 11th and the Firestone tire debacle, some observers charged that Nasser simply ignored the basics, citing for example, "quality gaffes" found in vehicles such as the 2002 Explorer[17] and the misuse of the performance evaluation system he initiated.

Nasser's evaluation system was called the Performance Management Process (PMP) and was modeled after systems used by such companies as General Electric and Microsoft. Used specifically to rank Ford's 18,000 top managers, the PMP was a type of grading system that evaluated employees on a curve. More specifically, 10 percent of the employees were rated by management as "A"; 80 percent as "B"; and 10 percent as "C." "B" employees were divided into two categories, "B-1" and "B-2," with "B-2" employees considered less productive. All "A" and "B" performers were eligible for bonuses and pay increases, although lower-level "B" employees received fewer benefits than higher-rated employees and were in jeopardy of being downgraded to "C" performer status. Those who did not improve after two years could be demoted or fired.[18]

Under Nasser, part of top managers' bonuses hinged on how well they accomplished their diversity goals. Ford set specific goals for hiring and promoting minorities and women and tied executive compensation to meeting those objectives. This tie-in to promotions was one of Nasser's diversity initiatives that ultimately helped employees—mostly older white men—successfully sue Ford for age discrimination.

OLDER WORKERS SUE

At the same time that Ford was attempting to recruit, train, and retain diverse employees, it faced two class-action discrimination lawsuits: *Siegel vs. Ford Motor Co.* and *Streeter vs. Ford Motor Co.* Both lawsuits accused the company of age discrimination, but whereas Siegel was brought by older workers of both sexes and several ethnicities, the Streeter plaintiffs were all white men.[19] Interestingly, the Streeter plaintiffs at first claimed "reverse discrimination" but ultimately dropped the race and gender discrimination charges, thereby focusing only on age discrimination.

The Siegel suit gained national recognition because the AARP—formerly known as the American Association of Retired Persons—supported the lawsuit both financially and with staff time.[20] In the Siegel lawsuit, the plaintiffs charged that the PMP "was part of senior management's plan to eliminate older employees from Ford Motor Company's salaried workforce" in violation of the Michigan Civil Rights Act.[21] According to the lawsuit, a preliminary review of the statistics demonstrated that older workers disproportionately received "C" ratings. Plaintiffs alleged that the performance criteria were "rooted, in part, on the negative stereotypical assumptions about older employees."[22]

Further, the plaintiffs charged that Ford managers had worked aggressively to promote minorities and women while eliminating white male employees because their "compensation and upward mobility" were "contingent upon meeting diversity goals."[23] More specifically, the complaint explained how 10 percent of executives' bonuses were contingent on their reaching diversity goals, in other words, certain percentages of minorities and females at the various levels of Ford management.[24]

Fueling the discrimination lawsuit fire was the damaging testimony, as described in the complaint, from Ford executives. For example, David Murphy, Ford's former human resources vice president, said: "We are in the middle of transforming one of the biggest companies in the world. You aren't going to do that by pleasing everybody, by having some kind of consensus. We know we are going to upset some people. Maybe they shouldn't be a part of Ford Motor Co."[25]

As noted in the complaint, Richard Parry-Jones, vice president of product development and quality, said: "We are trapped in a mono-cultural environment that is dominated by old white males. We need to change. We need more employees who are more reflective of our consumer base."[26] Echoing similar sentiments was head of Ford Credit, Don Winkler, who said: "We went to headhunters who didn't find us 51-year-old white males." Regarding the replacement of white males by minorities and women, he said, "Some people had to take packages and go."[27] The combination of the Nasser-initiated PMP and bold testimony from Ford executives worked together to shape the image of Ford as a company guilty of age discrimination.

THE AGE DISCRIMINATION IN EMPLOYMENT ACT

The main argument in the lawsuits was that Ford violated the Age Discrimination in Employment Act (ADEA)—signed into law in 1967 by President Lyndon B. Johnson—which required Americans to refrain from the adverse treatment of older workers those over 40. The ADEA made it unlawful for an employer to refuse to hire, to fire, or to take any other adverse action against a worker because of his or her age.[28]

The language Congress used in the ADEA to define unlawful age discrimination is as follows:

It shall be unlawful for an employer:

1. to fail to hire or to discharge any individual or otherwise discriminate against any individual with respect to his compensation, terms, conditions, or privileges of employment, because of such individual's age;
2. to limit, segregate, or classify its employees in any way which would deprive or tend to deprive any individual of employment opportunities or otherwise adversely affect his status as an employee, because of such individual's age; or
3. to reduce the wage rate of any employee in order to comply with this Act.[29]

Age discrimination is gaining increased attention because of the influential baby-boomer generation. According to Raymond F. Gregory, author of *Age Discrimination in the American Workplace: Old at a Young Age,* the baby boomers account for more than 70 million workers in the U.S. workplace—just under 50 percent of the entire workforce. In 2006, the entire baby-boomer generation fell within the protections of the federal laws against acts of age discrimination. As Gregory explains: "[A] vast army of workers"—known for its education, independence, and work savvy—"stands ready to contest employer acts of age discrimination."[30]

The baby-boomer generation will be forced to confront the pervasive, damaging stereotypes of the older worker. Glen Lenhoff, a lawyer who represented the Ford plaintiffs, spoke to the issue of stereotypes: "I think there is a significant increase in the perception within many large corporations that people over 45 lack energy and aren't receptive to new ideas . . . I think some corporations feel that such a person is not consistent with a dynamic and evolving company."[31]

According to Gregory, "the sources of age discrimination are inaccurate, stereotypical conceptions of the abilities of older workers in general."[32] Older workers are often stereotyped as stubborn, inflexible, resistant to change, unproductive, slow learners, more expensive, and eager to retire at the earliest opportunity.[33] The result of such stereotyping is how the "[u]njustified views of the diminished abilities of older workers coalesce or merge into stereotypical beliefs that form the basis for employer decisions affecting older workers."[34]

Such damaging stereotypes negatively affected both men and women in the Ford workplace. Making it clear that the discrimination lawsuits were not just about men was 54-year-old Dr. Sanaa Taraman, an Egyptian-born advanced program engineer, who maintained that she was targeted primarily because of her age. "I'm only 54 and I planned to work another 10 years . . . now they are forcing us to leave."[35]

James Brazin, 55, a mechanical engineer at Ford's Livonia transmission technical center and plant, had a streak of 32 positive annual performance reviews in a row oddly broken by a "C" grade for 2000. Brazin expressed his frustration: "My work had always been exceptional and now all of a sudden I'm at the bottom." Brazin described how his supervisor explained his "C" rating by saying "you're an old guy just like me."[36]

Angelo Guido, 52, formerly a chief engineer with Ford, said the policy played a role in his decision to retire from the company after 31 years. "I didn't like it but it was a method they were going to use. It didn't seem right. Everybody felt lousy about it."[37]

FORD SETTLES AND LOOKS TOWARD THE FUTURE

In December 2001, Ford Motor Co. agreed to pay $10.5 million, including $2.6 million in attorneys' fees, to settle two class-action lawsuits alleging that Ford's performance evaluation policy discriminated against older employees;[38] the settlement benefited more than 425 managers.[39] Had the lawsuits gone to trial, plaintiffs' lawyers planned to present studies that illustrated how older Ford managers were far more likely to receive poor job evaluations in 2000 than their younger counterparts.[40]

According to AARP CEO Bill Novelli: "This is a major victory not only for the employees but for all those who are fighting against workplace age discrimination in any form, whether it involves direct layoffs or, as in this case, sham job ratings."[41] Laurie McCann, senior attorney with AARP foundation litigation, maintained: "The message here is that age discrimination will not be tolerated. Employers shouldn't balance their books on the backs of older employees and they can't try to force out older workers and get away with it."[42]

In response to the suits, Ford made changes to its evaluation policy. Spokesperson Anne Gattari backtracked from Ford's original assertions about the PMP policy. She said that Ford would now rank its employees as "top achievers," "achievers," or "improvement required" responding to the fact that "some managers expressed concern that the system has been having an adverse effect on teamwork and morale."[43] Further, Ford has abandoned forcing supervisors to rank a certain percentage of employees in the lowest tier and has initiated giving supervisors more discretion in awarding bonuses or merit raises.[44]

Joe Laymon, the new vice president of corporate human resources, said: "The new program will drop the PMP moniker and focus more on building bonds between supervisors and workers." Laymon continued: "We have a system that has objectives built in it. We have a system that has periodical reviews. We have a system that has very strong coaching and counseling features built in. We have a performance system that has a final appraisal."[45] In short, the company claims that it is making progress at diversifying the automaker's workforce but not at the expense of older employees.

Having been sued for age discrimination in 2001 and then again in 2003,[46] Ford has seemingly still not found a solution to managing its older workforce. Despite Ford's troublesome past, *DiversityInc's* June/July 2004 issue ranked Ford the number three U.S. company for diversity; the year prior Ford was number one. *DiversityInc.* hailed Ford as "a supplier-diversity champion, using vendors of color and women and building wealth in their communities."[47] Again praising Ford, the magazine highlighted how Ford "spent 6 percent of its total procurement budget, $3.2 billion, with first-tier diverse suppliers, while the company spent $1.3 billion with second-tier diverse suppliers."[48]

In addition to achieving this coveted spot in *DiversityInc's,* 2003 and 2004 rankings, Ford has earned positive recognition from other minority organizations. The Michigan Minority Business Development Council named Ford its corporation of the year for 2002,[49] and the Gay & Lesbian Alliance Against Defamation awarded Ford the "Fairness Award."[50] Responding to the need to educate its employees about diversity, Ford developed the Multicultural Alliance. According to Director of Diversity and Worklife Planning and Peer Review Rosalind Cox, the Alliance's mission is "to educate Ford's departments on the benefit multicultural markets bring the company."[51] And impressively, Ford leads all other automakers with the largest percentage of minority-owned or-operated dealerships in the United States.[52]

Ford's diversity initiatives are both innovative and laudable; however, weaknesses remain. Although DiversityInc has ranked Ford in the top 10 of its Top 50 Companies for Diversity in the past, Ford fell to 37th in the 2006 ranking. In addition, Ford failed to make it into the magazine's top 10 companies for "Recruitment and Retention," "Supplier Diversity," "African Americans," "Latinos," "Asian Americans," "GLBT Employees," and "Executive Women." Also in 2006, Ford lost one of the auto industry's most influential women leaders, Anne Stevens, who was executive vice president and COO of the Americas. Further, in the Ford Motor Company *2005 Annual Report,* there is no mention of domestic diversity as an organizational value or as a competitive advantage in the chairman's message from William Clay Ford. And finally, with Ford's new CEO, Alan Mulally, former executive vice president of Boeing, who replaced William Clay Ford in September 2006, it is yet to be determined whether Ford will remain as dedicated to diversity initiatives as it has been in the past.

Ford Motor Co. maintains that diversity is a "distinct advantage" and that diversity is one of their "top corporate priorities."[54] With such serious claims of diversity commitment—in light of the company's historical tie to diversity and its future plans to manage diversity—comes the responsibility of valuing the knowledge and experience of the older worker.

Discussion Questions

1. Why did Nasser's progressive goal—to diversify Ford's workforce—backfire?
2. How did Nasser's personal story and work background affect his approach and philosophy on managing diversity?
3. Why was Ford's evaluation system, the PMP, the source of contention for Ford employees who felt discriminated against? In moving away from the PMP, what did Ford do to improve this evaluation system? Did these changes create a more accurate system of evaluation?
4. The number of older workers in the workforce is increasing—many people now work into their late 60s and 70s. How can businesses adapt to and benefit from this trend?

Notes

1. Mark Truby, "Age-bias Claims Jolt Ford Culture Change," *Detroit News,* April 29, 2001, http://www.detnews.com/2001/ autos/0104/29/a01-218162.htm; Julie Foster, "Ford's Controversial Diversity Campaign: Automaker Faces Suit over Discrimination

against Older White Males," May 16, 2001, http://www.worldnetdaily.com/news/printer-friendly.asp?ARTICLE_ID=22838.

2. Jacques Nasser live Web cast July 27, 2000, http://www.npr.org/programs/npc/2000/000727.jnasser.html.

3. Mark Truby and Bill Vlasic, "Bold Ford CEO Leads a Cultural Revolution: Nasser's Hard-driving Style Draws Praise, Criticism," *Detroit News,* August 20, 2000, http://www.detnews.com/specialreports/2000/nasser/leadlead.htm.

4. Ibid.

5. Ibid.

6. Mark Truby, "Nasser's Outgoing Style Makes Him Target of Rumors," *Detroit News,* August 20, 2000, http://www.detnews.com/specialreports/2000/nasser/rumors/rumors.htm.

7. Ibid.

8. Jacques Nasser, speech delivered at Wharton Business School, October 1999, http://webi.wharton.upenn.edu/researchDocDetail.asp?intDocID=142 and http://leadership.wharton.upenn.edu/digest/10-99.shtml.

9. "Ford Centennial Marks History of Diversity," news release, http://media.ford.com/newsroomrelease_display_new.cfm?release=15657.

10. Ibid.

11. Ibid.

12. "Ford News Briefs Weekly News Digest: Nasser Urges More Effort to Attract Minorities as Customers," *Detroit News,* January 12, 1998, http://www.mdcbowen.org/p2/bh/ford/ford_charged.htm.

13. "New Ford Evaluation System Focuses on Coaching, Counseling," *DiversityInc,* April 23, 2002, http://www.diversityinc.com/members/2783print.cfm.

14. Ibid.

15. Mark Truby, "Diversity Gives Ford a New Look: Aggressive Recruiting of Minorities and Women Is Sweeping Away Old Guard," *Detroit News,* August, 20, 2000, http://www.detnews.com/specialreports/2000/nasser/diversity/diversity.htm.

16. Ford's Financial Health for 2003, http://www.ford.com/en/company/about/corporateCitizenship/principlesProgressPerformance/our-performance/fin-health-data.htm.

17. Joanne Muller, "Commentary: Ford: Jacques Nasser Can't Do It All," *BusinessWeek Online,* June 18, 2001, http://www.businessweek.com:/print/magazine/content/01_25/b3737047.htm?mz.

18. Julie Foster, "Ford's Controversial Diversity Campaign: Automaker Faces Suit over Discrimination against Older White Males," WorldNetDaily.com, May 16, 2001, www.worldnetdaily.com/news/article.asp?ARTICLE_ID=22838

19. Linda Bean, "Ford Settles 'White Male' Lawsuit, Second Class-Action for $10.5 Million," *DiversityInc,* 18 December, 2001, http://www.diversityinc.com/public/1992print.cfm.

20. Linda Bean, "Ford's 'Older Worker' Lawsuits May Be Nearing Settlement," *DiversityInc,* November 5, 2001, http://www.diversityinc.com/members/1649print.cfm.

21. "AARP Foundation Litigation Attorneys Represent Older Workers Harmed by Discriminatory Performance Appraisal System," AARP Foundation, September 26, 2001, http://www.aarp.org/litigation/releases/2001/siegelann.html.

22. Ibid.

23. Foster, "Ford's Controversial Diversity Campaign."

24. Ibid.

25. Ibid.

26. Ibid.

27. Ibid.

28. Raymond F. Gregory, *Age Discrimination in the American Workplace: Old at a Young Age* (New Jersey: Rutgers University Press, 2001); 29 U.S.C. Sections 621–34. For more on the issue of age discrimination, see AARP, *Employment Discrimination against Midlife and Older Women: An Analysis of Discrimination Charges Filed with the EEOC,* vol. 1 (Washington, D.C. AARP Women's Initiative, 1997); AARP, *Valuing Older Workers: A Study of Costs and Productivity* (Washington, D.C.: AARP, n.d.); Robert Coulson, *Empowered at Forty* (New York: Harper Collins, 1990); Daniel P. O'Meara, *Protecting the Growing Number of Older Workers: The Age Discrimination in Employment Act* (Philadelphia: University of Pennsylvania, Wharton School, Industrial

Research Unit, 1989); Richard A. Posner, *Aging and Old Age* (Chicago: University of Chicago Press, 1995); Sara E. Rix, ed., *Older Workers: How Do They Measure Up? An Overview of Age Differences in Employee Costs and Performance* (Washington D. C.: Public Policy Institute of the AARP, 1994); For a complete historical account of age discrimination, see Kerry Segrave, *Age Discrimination by Employers* (North Carolina: McFarland, 2001).

29. Statistical Abstract of the United States 1998 (Washington, DC: U.S. Department of Commerce, 1998), 15, 21.

30. Gregory, *Age Discrimination in the American workplace,* 2.

31. Alejandro Bodipo-Memba, "Ford Sued on Diversity," *Detroit Free Press,* February 17, 2001, http://www.freep.com/money/business/age17.

32. Gregory, *Age Discrimination in the American workplace,* 21–22.

33. Ibid., 24.

34. Ibid., 22.

35. Truby, "Age-bias Claims Jolt Ford Culture Change."

36. Ibid.

37. Ibid.

38. Bean, "Ford Settles 'White Male' Lawsuit.

39. "Court OKs $10.6 Million Settlement of Ford Age Bias Case," *U.S. newswire,* March 14, 2002, www.highbeam.com/doc/161=83770764.html.

40. Mark Truby, "Ford Settles Key Bias Suits," December 19, 2001, http://www.detnews.com/2001/autoinsider/0112/19/c01=370389.htm.

41. "Court OKs $10.6 Million Settlement.

42. Bean, "Ford Settles 'White Male' Lawsuit.

43. Linda Bean, "Ford Puts the Brakes on Controversial Evaluation System," *DiversityInc,* July 10, 2001, http://www.diversityinc.com/public/1169print.cfm.

44. Bean, "Ford Puts the Brakes on Controversial Evaluation System."

45. "New Ford Evaluation System Focuses on Coaching, Counseling," *DiversityInc,* April 23, 2002.

46. Mark Truby, "New Bias Lawsuits Hits Ford, Visteon: Older Workers without College Degrees Claim They Get Passed Up for Promotions," *Detroit News,* April 14, 2003, http://www.detnews.com/2003.autoinsider/0304/14/a01=136079.htm.

47. Yoji Cole, "Top 10 Companies for Diversity: What Makes Them Exemplary," *DiversityInc,* June/July 2004: 64.

48. Ibid.

49. Michelle Krebs. "Ford Continues to Promote Diversity," *Automotive News,* June 16, 2003, http://proquest.umi.com.

50. The Center for Corporate Citizenship at Boston College. "Ford Holds Diversity Summit," December 5, 2003, http://www.imakenews.com/cccbc/e_article000208048.cfm.

51. Cole, "Top 10 Companies for Diversity," 64.

52. Ford Motor Company, "Minority Dealer Operations," http://www.dd.ford.com/mada/about_mada.html.

53. Ford Motor Company, *2002 Annual Report: Starting Our Second Century,* http://www.ford.com.

54. Ford Motor Company, diversity statement, "On the Team," http://www.mycareer.ford.com/ONTHETEAM.ASP?CID=15.

6 | RELIGION AND SPIRITUALITY

Religion, as a federally protected class, includes all aspects of religious observance and practice as well as belief. Thus, the employer must accommodate an employee's observance of his or her religious beliefs when reasonable—that is, when the accommodation does not cause undue hardship on the employer's business.

Objectives

■ To examine the relationship between religion and/or spirituality and the workplace.

■ To examine why employees are increasingly attempting to bring their religious beliefs into the workplace, thereby putting pressure on organizations to manage the role of religion in the workplace.

■ To examine how and why an organizational leader, Tom Chappell of Tom's of Maine, makes his spiritual framework the foundation of the organizational culture.

Preview Questions

■ How should management accommodate a variety of conflicting spiritual perspectives in the workplace?

■ What are the potential advantages and disadvantages of an organizational leader's making his or her religious perspective the philosophical framework of the organization?

■ How can a manager turn the accommodation of employees' religious and/or spiritual perspectives into a competitive business advantage?

Some Important Dates

1791   The Bill of Rights of the U.S. Constitution guarantees free exercise of religion, assuring citizens that no one religious institution or perspective holds a legally preferred status.

1963   Supreme Court prohibits mandatory prayer in public schools.

1964   The Civil Rights Act, signed by President Johnson, prohibits discrimination on the basis of race, religion, ethnicity, national origin, and creed (gender was added later).

1972   Congress amends Title VII of the Civil Rights Act to make clear that it protects *all* aspects of religious observance and practice, so that employers will not pick and choose among religions or aspects of religious practice.

1976   Election of Jimmy Carter, the first U.S. president to be openly evangelical Christian.

1987   Supreme Court holds that Title VII of the Civil Rights Act of 1964 does not prohibit religious organizations from discriminating in hiring policies in favor of members of the religion.

2003   Eleventh Circuit Court of Appeals rules that Chief Justice Roy Moore of the Alabama Supreme Court must remove the monument of the Ten Commandments from the rotunda of the Alabama Supreme Court building that he had installed there.

THE MANY DELICATE ISSUES OF SPIRITUALITY IN THE OFFICE

Every three weeks or so, Buddy Brandt, a partner at the Manhattan law firm of Brandt, Steinberg & Lewis, closes the door to his office, turns off the phone and sits down to study a facet of Judaism.

Mr. Brandt said this kind of study—it might be a book in the Old Testament, the history of Zionism or an aspect of Jewish law—brings "peace and relief" in the middle of a hectic day. On a deeper level, he said, "It fills an important spiritual niche in my life. And it helps put life's difficulties in proper perspective."

With Americans spending so much time on the job, some of them are finding ways to bring spirituality to the office, rather than relegating it to weekend religious services. This can mean simply trying to treat others well, saying a prayer to start the day, or thinking about the sermon heard on Sunday.

This phenomenon is virtually impossible to quantify, but studies by the Tanenbaum Center for Interreligious Understanding, as well as the Harris Poll and the Pew Forum on Religion and Public Life, suggest that religion is increasingly important to Americans, both in private life and in public. "We know the percentage of Americans that identify themselves as religious and God-believing is probably the highest in the developed world: 90 percent," said Georgette F. Bennett, a sociologist and the founder of the Tanenbaum Center. "And we know from our surveys that as people get older, religion becomes more important to them." The work force is aging, so it would not be surprising to find religion playing a larger role in the workplace, she said.

Several organizations exist to help make that mixing of faith and work easier, like Spirit at Work in East Haven, Conn., an information clearinghouse for people and organizations interested in spirituality in the workplace. In addition, groups like Forum for Faith in the Workplace in Columbus, Ohio, and Marketplace Network in Boston aim to motivate and equip Christians to apply biblical principles in their work.

Christopher Scott, executive director of Forum for Faith in the Workplace, said interest in spirituality has grown

Eilene Zimmerman, *New York Times,* August 15, 2004, http://select.nytimes.com/search/restricted/article?res=F60C15F93E5B0C768DDDA10894DC404482.

tremendously. "It's a very uncertain world, and people are looking for an anchor to hold onto," he said. "We find people increasingly feel they can't live two lives: doing one thing on Sunday and something else the rest of the week."

The organization, which serves Central Ohio, holds an annual dinner honoring those in the secular workplace who exemplify "living out their faith," and attendance has risen in the last four years to just under 300 from 50, Mr. Scott said.

Many experts on religion and culture say the desire to incorporate personal religious faith into work has been rising for at least a decade, but some also say there was a burst of interest after the terrorist attacks of Sept. 11, 2001.

David W. Miller, executive director of the Yale Center for Faith and Culture, whose research specializes in ethics and spirituality in the workplace, helped edit a list of groups like Spirit at Work or Forum for Faith in the Workplace well before Sept. 11. "After the attacks, the growth of these groups was simply exponential," he said.

Ken Blanchard, co-founder and chief spiritual officer of the Ken Blanchard Companies, a management consulting firm based in Escondido, Calif., exemplifies the intertwining of religion and work. He says he is a devout Christian and uses Jesus as his leadership model.

Each morning, Mr. Blanchard sends an inspirational voice mail to all 250 employees. The message includes prayer requests from employees but no actual praying. "I also praise people for a job well done," he said. "I quote from the New and Old Testaments, Buddha, Moses, Martin Luther King. I talk about movies I've seen, books I've read."

Mr. Blanchard said employees who are not religiously or spiritually inclined are not treated differently from those who are. "Everyone here knows I think they

should have something in their life that is bigger than themselves, but that's it."

There can be a fine line, however, between religious self-expression and proselytizing. Christy Munger, an associate publicist at Ruder Finn in Manhattan, recalled a conversation that began when a colleague asked about Ms. Munger's occasional use of alcohol. Ms. Munger, who describes herself as an evangelical Christian, said she answered with an explanation about using the Bible as a guide in life. Ms. Munger told her colleague that the Bible "teaches us not to rely on things, but to rely on God for strength and joy."

Ms. Munger said she considered her explanation "standing up for truth," not proselytizing. "I haven't made anyone uncomfortable—I think maybe angry—and I hope, perhaps, have caused some questioning," she said.

In general however, complaints about proselytizing and other forms of religious discrimination have risen substantially over the last decade. The Equal Employment Opportunity Commission received 2,532 complaints of religious discrimination in 2003, an increase of 75 percent from 1993, said Dianna Johnston, assistant legal counsel for the agency. Those complaints run the gamut from proselytizing to failing to accommodate someone's religious beliefs.

Employees who are uncomfortable in a workplace where faith is frequently discussed can simply steer clear of those discussions. But that can mean missing out on office gossip and networking opportunities.

"It's hard to have a pot-luck Bible study with fellow employees and not talk about work; if you aren't there, you will wind up missing out on important information," said Myrna Marofsky, president of ProGroup, a diversity consulting firm in Minneapolis and author of "Religion in the Workplace: A Guide to Navigating the Complex Landscape."

ESSAY: TAKING RELIGION TO WORK

Just a decade ago, there were only 25 religious employee-resource groups. Today, there are more than 900, according to the International Coalition of Workplace Ministries (ICWM). The faith-at-work movement is a corporate experiment that has no precedent. Just as a new medication may take years to reveal its side effects, it will take years before we know if people of different faiths, atheists and agnostics, gays and evangelical Christians, can practice their brands of morality in the workplace and work cohesively and successfully together.

This faith-at-work experiment is taking place inside many notable large corporations, including American Express, AOL, American Airlines, Continental Airlines, Texas Instruments and Ford Motor Co., all of which have religious or spiritual employee-resource groups. And the list of companies is growing.

What is happening in society and the personal lives of employees that has compelled them to reveal their faith and religion at work? And just as importantly, why are some companies complying with this trend, even embracing it, while others shy away from religion at work?

There certainly are cultural, social, economic and political developments that have fueled the faith-at-work movement. For one, we are in the midst of a heightened consciousness of faith and religion, much of which can be attributed to the election of self-described born-again-Christian President George W. Bush.

The residual effects of the terrorist attacks of Sept. 11, 2001, also brought Americans closer to their respective faiths and made them more vocal about professing those faiths while bringing Islam and other eastern religions more into the mainstream consciousness.

"Most of the media after Bush's election got a wake-up call about this when they discovered that the real turning point for Bush that put him over the edge was the Christian vote," says Os Hillman, director of ICWM and author of *The 9 to 5 Window: How Faith Can Transform the Workplace.* "What Bush has shown is that all Americans should be free to express religious beliefs, including at work," says Hillman.

"Sept. 11 heightened the sense of the need for faith and something higher, to try and understand what happened," says Douglas Hicks, associate professor of leadership and religious studies at the University of Richmond and author of *Religion and the Workplace.* "It also raised an awareness of Islam in America, both in terms of hostility toward a misperception of Islam or Islamic extremist."

Although these events and political trends have influenced the faith-at-work movement, they were fueled by an era in which Americans collectively sought answers to the economic realities taking place in their lives. Indeed, how Americans view work and the role it plays in their lives has undergone a transformation in the last two decades.

There was a time when employment was one of the most stabilizing forces in our lives, says Martin Rutte, coauthor of *Chicken Soup for the Soul at Work* and a national lecturer who has addressed the Harvard Business School. "People began to say, 'If the company isn't the source of security, then what is?' And for some of these people it became the spiritual, God, religion."

The faith-at-work movement also reflects the life stage of the dominant generation in today's work force—baby boomers, born between 1946 and 1964. They are represented

C. Stone Brown, *DiversityInc*, Magazine, November/December 2005.

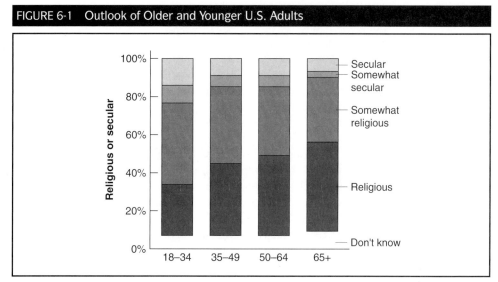

FIGURE 6-1   Outlook of Older and Younger U.S. Adults

Source: American Religious Identification Survey (ARIS) 2001. The Graduate Center, City University of New York.

by 73.2 million workers, 25 percent of the U.S. population. "Because the baby-boomer generation is so large, the spiritual issues it's facing have a major impact on what the world thinks is appropriate conversation [at work]," says Rutte.

In addressing religious diversity as a workplace issue, there are palpable differences with other "diverse" groups. For example, traditional employee-resource groups were created for mentoring and as support networks for people who face similar challenges in a white-male-dominated corporate community. So then, what's the justification for forming a Christian employee-resource group, when Christianity is the country's dominant religion? However, for many companies that have ventured into the faith-at-work experiment, there is a business case in the faith-at-work movement.

DRIVING THE BUSINESS CASE

Ford Motor Co., No. 11 on The DiversityInc Top 50 Companies for Diversity list 2005, started Ford Interfaith Network (FIN) after Sept. 11, 2001, at the request of a group of Christian employees. The company required the employees to come up with a business case, as well as to show how the group would be inclusive.

Ultimately, after weeks of talks, the group came back to management with representatives from eight different religions in the company, forming FIN.

FIN is a structured network that was created to avoid many of the tensions and conflicts that might arise by mixing religion and work.

"We felt that by indicating to people that this was something that our company stands behind, it would help to increase morale, employee engagement," says Rosalind Cox, manager of Diversity and Worklife Planning. "When your company gets behind you with something you value personally ... it keeps you engaged. You want to stay and work for that employer."

Under FIN, each religion has a representative on the network's executive committee. The chairperson is voted in by members of the executive council. There is a formal way to address questions about another member's faith when they meet.

For example, if a Mormon has a question about the Quran, or a Muslim about the Torah, the individuals write questions down and present them to the other religion's representative before their meetings. The questions might be answered by the representative or by an invited religious scholar.

Dan Dunnigan, chair of FIN, is empowered by learning about the religious differences in the network.

"What I love is interacting with others with diverse doctrinal views to my own," says Dunnigan, adding that there are common bonds he finds in different religions. "Like hard work, the overall concept of things like virtuous living and high morals, importance of family, integrity ... values that are important to me, I can find are important to people of other faiths."

FIN, though, didn't get off to a smooth start, he recalls, declining to go into specifics. "There are some places in the world where people kill each other over religious differences and nothing like that was ever threatened. But when you get together and you've got so much diversity, it takes a while to get to those common touch points," he says.

Those touch points can start with participating in each others' events, says Jordan born Kamal Shenaq, a Ford engineer who came to the United States in 1983. "For example, celebrating Christmas, celebrating the new year for Jews, celebrating the new year for Hindus ... Ramadan for Islam ... we always invite each of them to attend these celebrations and we share with each other."

Shenaq, who is Muslim, represents what many would view as the business case for religious employee networks because it affords him time to pray and have a place to wash his feet. "This helps us at the work environment to be very productive because when I feel I'm at work and I'm respected and I can talk about my religion ... I will work even more and be more loyal to Ford Motor Co," he says.

The request for a religious network came at a time when Ford was trying to find ways to be more inclusive, says Cox. "One of the things we were really focusing on, particularly that year, was this whole concept of accepting people as 'whole' people and that your faith and your religion is a very vital part of who you are ... we can't expect people to leave [religion] at the door of the company when they come to work," Cox says.

The verdict still is out on whether companies should expect people to leave their faith at the door. However, if it's going to be embraced, Ford's interfaith approach seems to have merit.

A strong advocate for the interfaith approach to religious understanding is the Council on American-Islamic Relations (CAIR), an Islamic civil-rights and advocacy group, based in Washington, D.C.

"Interfaith dialogue is something that we promote and encourage at the grassroots level with all of our chapters. It is the best way to get to know one another and break down these stereotypes that people have," says Rabiah Ahmed, CAIR spokesperson. "It's been our experience that when people know Muslims on a personal level, whether that be at work or school ... they tend to have more positive attitudes toward Islam."

FIGURE 6-2   Self-Described Religious Identification of U.S. Adult Population (Weighted Estimate With Rounded Figures)

Classification	Population	Percentage
Christianity	160,000,000	77%
Denominations With More Than 1 Million Adherents		
Catholic	50,873,000	
Baptist	33,830,000	
Christian (No Denomination Supplied)	14,190,000	
Methodist	14,140,000	
Lutheran	9,580,000	
Presbyterian	5,596,000	
Pentecostal	4,467,000	
Episcopalian/Anglican	4,407,000	
Mormon	2,831,000	
Churches of Christ	2,787,000	
Non-Denominational	2,503,000	
Congregational/UCC	2,489,000	
Jehovah's Witness	1,378,000	
Assemblies of God	1,105,000	
Evangelical	1,032,000	
No Religion	29,000,000	14%
Other Religions	8,000,000	4%
Denominations With More Than 1 Million Adherents		
Judaism	3,451,000	
Islam	1,104,000	
Buddhism	1,082,000	
No Answer	11,000,000	5%
Total U.S. Adult Population	208,000,000	

Source: American Religious Identification Survey (ARIS) 2001. The Graduate Center, City University of New York.

The U.S. Census Bureau cannot legally ask questions regarding religion. Consequently, there are only a few surveys on a national level that collect such data. The 2000 Religious Congregations Membership Study (RCMS) and the 2001 American Religious Identification Survey (ARIS) are the most comprehensive.

Conducted every 10 years to parallel the U.S. census, the RCMS provides a county-by-county listing of religious congregations, memberships and total adherents. The RCMS data is collected by the Association of Statisticians of American Religious Bodies and published jointly by the American Religion Data Archive and the Glenmary Research Center.

For statistical reasons, the RCMS data does not include millions of adherents from denominations largely associated with blacks. As a result, the data used for the charts and tables in this article is from the ARIS.

First conducted in 1990 by The Graduate Center of the City University of New York, the ARIS compiled a follow-up study in 2001 of religious identification among U.S. adults. The survey also assessed about 20 other personal characteristics to develop more inclusive profiles of religious groups.

FIGURE 6-3 Outlook of Racial/Ethnic Groups in U.S.

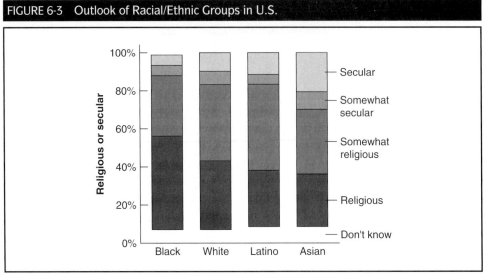

Source: American Religious Identification Survey (ARIS) 2001. The Graduate Center, City University of New York.

Texas Instruments (TI) started its Christian employee-resource group about five years ago, which was followed by the formation of the Muslim group after Sept. 11.

It might surprise some people that there haven't been any problems, says Terry Howard, global diversity director. "Here it is, five years later, and no problems at all," says Howard, who notes that there have been business benefits that TI didn't even anticipate.

He tells the story of one of the founding members of the Christian employee-resource group, who later became chair of the TI diversity network and led TI's market-penetration initiatives in Latin America and China. "I sit back and say to myself, 'Look at what we would have lost out on had we said no,'" says Howard.

TI honored its employees' requests to express their faith at work because it made good business sense, he says. "We don't want people coming to work and masking or hiding something that is near and dear to them. We don't want someone coming to TI saying, 'I've got to hide the fact that I'm a person of faith,'" says Howard. "It's wasted time and energy—we want you to spend your time and energy focusing on helping TI get business results."

Companies can say it's all about being inclusive and building morale, which may be true. However, they have little legal recourse in putting the brakes on the faith-at-work movement, especially after opening the floodgates to nonreligious groups to form networks. Ironically, religious groups were one of the last to form, yet they have the most legal protections—an amendment to Title VII of the Civil Rights Act of 1964 prohibits workplace discrimination based on religion.

Companies really have to accommodate all groups, even the extremes of gays and lesbians to evangelical Christians, says Hicks. "They are legal and are part of the American workplace today ... and let me add, Christian resource groups are legal, including the ones that have an evangelical bent, and are part of the American workplace."

They may be part of the American workplace, but for how long? And will companies backpedal on religious diversity when conflicts arise?

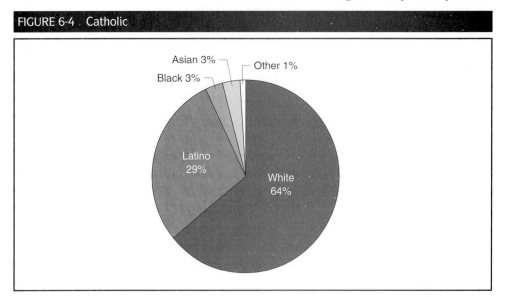

FIGURE 6-4 . Catholic

Source: American Religious Identification Survey (ARIS) 2001. The Graduate Center, City University of New York.

WORKPLACE CONFLICTS

The most obvious opponents of the faith-at-work movement are agnostics, people who question the existence of a higher being, and atheists, who do not believe in any God. For many of them, companies are stepping out of bounds by sanctioning religious employee networks and they say the damage ultimately will affect everyone.

Bobbie Kirkhart, president of the Atheist International Alliance, argues that religious diversity isn't the same as race, gender and ethnic diversity and, therefore, shouldn't be afforded the same status.

"All of these groups [blacks, women, gays] are groups that don't traditionally have power and they are binding together, for protection, for comfort. I think an employer would be very upset if there were a white-male networking group. And for the same reason, the religious networking group has no place, no rationale," says Kirkhart, a former self-described Christian Protestant who grew up in the Bible Belt.

If companies were consistent with the criteria to form networking groups, minority faiths, such as Muslims, Jews, Buddhists and Sikhs, would be permitted to form groups, but not a Christian group, adds Kirkhart. "I wouldn't be concerned about a Muslim group, because they are a group that doesn't have power."

Some companies, such as Wells Fargo, No. 40 on The DiversityInc Top 50 companies for Diversity list 2005, have very strict guidelines on the creation of employee-resource groups, and religion doesn't meet the criteria, says Melissa Morey, assistant vice president, corporate communications.

"What we base this on is 'primary dimensions of 'diversity,' so it's things about ourselves that we can't change ... your color or ethnicity," says Morey. "The primary reason we don't have religious groups is there are just so many different religions that we simply can't accommodate all of them."

FIGURE 6-5   Muslim

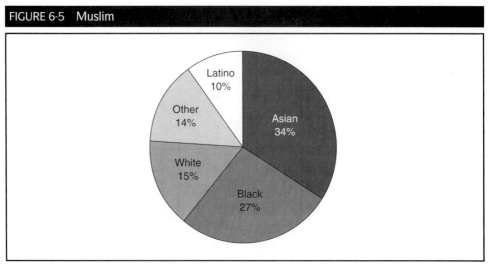

Source: American Religious Identification Survey (ARIS) 2001. The Graduate Center, City University of New York.

Wells Fargo, however, does permit informal religious gatherings on site. "If there is a group of people who want to get together in a conference room to have prayer service ... we are accommodating to that," Morey says.

Kirkhart, who says she was fired from a teaching job when her boss objected to her atheist beliefs, says everyone should fear the faith-at-work movement, not just nonbelievers. "Once the power grab starts, it's not just atheists ... in today's climate, Muslims, then certainly Wiccans, and Hindus, and pretty soon it's going to be the wrong kind of Christian."

Hicks does agree that bringing different world views together has the potential to be very divisive. Although proselytizing isn't permissible in almost all workplaces, employees should be comfortable about inviting coworkers to off-work religious activities. But employees who do this also must be willing to accept "no" from their coworkers, Hicks says. "As soon as a coworker shows a non-interest in being invited, they have to respect that ... just as their own views are respected."

Kirkhart, who now teaches in the Los Angeles school system, says proselytizing happens all the time, even with atheists. But it's the bullies she fears, whom she describes as people who don't care about your level of discomfort. "Then you have to go to the employer. There are laws, and atheists [and non-believers] have the same legal protections under the law as religions do. You should take action," she says.

EVANGELICALS VS. GLBTs

What might become a more explosive conflict than atheists conflicting with religious coworkers are the potential conflicts between Christian employee-resource groups and gay-and-lesbian groups.

Evangelical Christians, the religious group that has been right of center on issues including school prayer and anti-gay-rights legislation, are estimated to number 70 million people, according to a "CBS News" report.

FIGURE 6-6   Evangelical

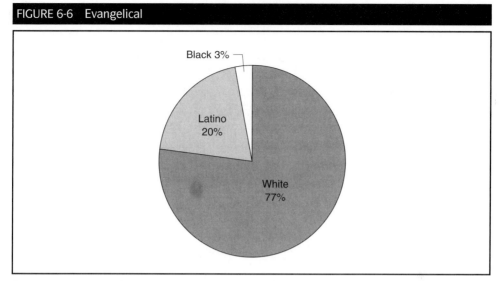

Black 3%

Latino
20%

White
77%

Source: American Religious Identification Survey (ARIS) 2001. The Graduate Center, City University of New York.

Companies certainly are aware of the potential clash between the two groups as the faith-at-work movement continues to grow. Hicks, though, warns there shouldn't be an assumption that there always is going to be conflict or a clash between the two groups. "It's not true that 'all' evangelicals are against homosexuality or are intolerant of it. Because it's portrayed that way, it sometimes misses the quiet understanding that is happening in workplaces," he says.

Hicks prefers to see the networks as a vehicle for tolerance rather than conflict.

"Talking about [conflicts] and bringing them to light in the workplace through employee-resource groups on any side isn't necessarily a bad thing. It can be a way to mitigate conflict."

That was exactly the approach taken at TI, when the gay-and-lesbian network group had concerns about the formation of the Christian network. Instead of allowing a potential problem to get its footing, the company was proactive, bringing both groups together in meetings.

"It was a non-issue for us because we made it a non-issue. We got people in the room talking and it didn't take a lot of facilitation and all of that. And all of a sudden the groups came together and worked together," says Howard.

It's not always as simple as making this conflict a non-issue. All evangelical Christians may not be intolerant of GLBTs in the workplace, but it would be naive for companies not to prepare for this conflict given the track record of evangelicals' public stance against gay marriages, gay rights and active and threatened boycotts against companies that don't hold their viewpoint.

This year, Microsoft Corp. made headlines when it initially supported House Bill 1515, a Washington initiative to protect gay rights in the workplace. That made the long-time gay-friendly company a boycott target of evangelicals in Seattle. The boycott threat forced the company to change its position from public support to neutral. Although the company ultimately changed its position back to public support, the bill was defeated by one vote in the Washington Senate.

FIGURE 6-7 · Religious Discrimination in the Workplace ·

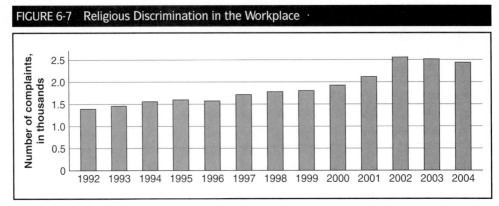

Source: Equal Employment Opportunity Commission.

Hillman, an evangelical Christian, opposes companies bringing fundamentally different employee-networking groups together. "The whole purpose of what corporations are trying to do is say, 'We acknowledge that your group exists and we are allowing this group to operate within the framework of this company.'"

Hillman, who has advised companies such as The Coca-Cola Co. and Toyota on faith-at-work issues, says companies should promote fairness for each group and leave it at that. "I don't think the corporation would want to get into a kind of a mix of how one group should mix with another as much as having fair rules for each group as they meet within the context of the corporation."

FAITH EMBRACE OR BACKLASH?

Even though more companies are embracing religious expression in the workplace, after the terrorist attacks of Sept. 11, not all groups have been accepted equally.

Since 2001, the Equal Employment Opportunity Commission reports that workplace-discrimination complaints against people of Muslim, Jewish, and "other" faiths have been on the rise.

Muslim backlash has been the most pronounced, but other groups that are perceived to have origins in the Middle East also have faced a high degree of discrimination in the workplace.

The first steps involve educating people about Islam and the Muslim community, says Ahmed of CAIR, whose organization consults with companies about understanding of the Muslim religion. "Truly, we feel that a lot of ignorance that people have about Islam is based on miseducation or lack of information."

That ignorance carries over to the hostility toward Sikhs in the United States. Sikhs, who wear beards and turbans, often are thought to be Muslims, causing them added discrimination in this post–Sept. 11 climate.

One of the major problems of workplace discrimination facing Sikhs, who predominantly come from Northern India and now are the world's fifth-largest religion, is the prohibition against wearing beards and turbans. "Sometimes, the food industry has discriminated against Sikhs even though they were willing to put a hair net on their beard," says Rajwant Singh, president of Sikh Council on Religion and Education.

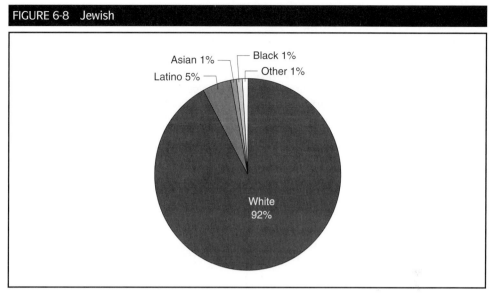

FIGURE 6-8   Jewish

Source: American Religious Identification Survey (ARIS) 2001. The Graduate Center, City University of New York.

One 1988 high-profile case involved a Domino's Pizza new hire—Prabhjot Singh Kohli, who filed a complaint with the Maryland Human Relations Commission because the company dress code required him to shave his beard. Ultimately, Domino's settled out of court and changed its dress code to permit beards. "We don't cut our hair in any part of the body. So we have long hair, which is tucked in under a turban or hair covering," says Singh, adding that hair for Sikhs is a symbol of spirituality and connection with humanity.

The Sikh religion also collided with the automobile industry's health and safety requirements because certain jobs require employees to wear hard hats, which would restrict the wearing of turbans.

"OSHA [Occupational Safety and Health Administration] has given an exception, and that provided an opportunity for Sikhs to be in the car industry with Chevrolet and GM, and they are doing very well ... I would say at least 50 to 100 [Sikh] employees at each of these companies," says Singh.

THE FUTURE

Religious diversity appears to have a future in corporate America, in part because companies want to be competitive and attract the best talent available. But also, companies are recognizing that faith and religion are an important part of an employee's identity, and accommodation is no longer an option. Perhaps this marks a shift in diversity management where recognition of one's "inner self" is as important as external features, such as race, ethnicity, gender, disability, and sexual orientation.

"Companies are starting to really understand that to really affirm an employee means you should affirm them in all aspects of their lives," says Hillman. "If it's in a way that is equal to everyone, they are learning it makes a better employee and it provides a better place to work."

Discussion Questions

1. Should employees create religious employee-resource groups in the workplace? What are the pros and cons for the organization of allowing this practice?
2. Does encouraging interfaith organizations among employees provide a competitive advantage for business? If so, how?
3. What potential conflicts may arise in the workplace as a result of the formation of religious employee-resource groups and/or interfaith organizations?
4. If tolerance for and education about different religions seem to be the trend in today's workplace, why has the number of complaints filed with the EEOC risen steadily over the past 10 years?

CASE STUDY: PURITY OF SPIRIT: TOM'S OF MAINE

Tom's of Maine is a living, breathing—and profiting—proof that a business enterprise can be good for the earth, good for society, good for its employees, and good for its shareholders

Tom Chappell[1]

Tom's of Maine, located in Kennebunk, Maine, is a manufacturer and marketer of all-natural personal care products. The family-owned company was founded by the husband and wife team of Tom and Kate Chappell. The couple started the company because they were unable to find natural personal care products for their family to use and consequently believed that there must be a market for such products.

All company products are made from natural ingredients, so they are free of artificial colors, sweeteners such as saccharin, synthetic preservatives, flavors, and fragrances. Additionally, they contain no animal by-products and are not tested on animals.[2]

Sales of company products are strongest on the East and West Coasts. Target customers are active, health-conscious adults who read labels, are involved in their communities, and value education. Company sales were approximately $35 million in 2001. The company's flagship product is toothpaste, which historically has accounted for 60 percent of its revenues, with a national market share of about 1 percent. The U.S. toothpaste industry is a $1.7 billion per year business. Current market leaders are Procter and Gamble's Crest and Colgate-Palmolive's Colgate brands.[3]

At the beginning of 2000, Tom's had 120 employees but found itself in a self-imposed hiring freeze because of its heavy investment in a new line of alcohol-free cough, cold, and wellness products. With the introduction of the new line, the company was marketing about 150 products. In addition to toothpaste and wellness products, the company also produces deodorant, flossing ribbon, mouthwash, soap, shampoo, and shaving cream.

This case has been adapted by Dr. Kathryn A. Cañas and Dr. Harris Sondak from a case written by Dr. Edmund R. Gray, Department of Management, Loyola Marymount University, and Kimberly S. Petropoulos.

HISTORY

In 1968, Tom and Kate Chappell left Philadelphia and their positions in the corporate world for Kennebunk, Maine, where they "moved back to the land" and experimented with natural food and personal care items and other environmentally friendly products. Two years later, with a $5,000 loan from a friend and a single product named Clearlake, they started Tom's of Maine. Clearlake was the first nonphosphate liquid laundry detergent offered for sale in the United States. In addition to being less polluting, Clearlake came in refillable containers that were labeled with postage-paid mailers to facilitate customers returning them for reuse.[4]

The company inaugurated its signature all-natural personal care product line in 1973 with soap, shampoo, and skin lotion. Natural toothpaste was introduced in 1975. Other products followed, first baby shampoo, then deodorant, mouthwash, and shaving cream. Early on, Tom's products were distributed principally through health food stores. Moreover, from the very beginning, the company shunned the conventional practice of testing products on animals.

By 1981, sales had risen to $1.5 million. Having achieved this level, Chappell wanted to take his products into the mainstream market. To accomplish this goal, he knew that he needed to add professional talent to manage the growth of new accounts, more complex distribution channels, and a burgeoning advertising budget. Hence, he added a few new board members with business acumen and then hired several experienced marketing executives along with some young MBAs. As a result, Tom's of Maine implemented a strategy of aggressive growth by expanding beyond health food stores to big supermarkets and drugstore chains. This strategy resulted in an increase of sales to approximately $2 million in 1983.

The rapid growth strategy, however, exposed a germinating conflict between Chappell and the new professionals. For instance, the new MBAs tried to convince Chappell to add saccharin to his toothpaste to sweeten it, thus making it more palatable to the mainstream market. As Chappell perceived it, they were promoting decisions based on the numbers rather than adhering to his vision of commitment to natural products. Recalling this time in company history, Chappell noted that "our values were pushed to the margin, growth and profit dominated business planning."[5] As a consequence of these tensions, Tom Chappell found time spent at his company less and less fulfilling and began to search for inspiration elsewhere. He remembers confiding to two old friends that he was considering going to theological seminary and becoming an Episcopal minister. But one of the friends suggested that perhaps Tom's of Maine was his ministry.[6]

In 1988, Chappell enrolled on a part-time basis at Harvard Divinity School. For the next three years, he spent two and a half days a week in Kennebunk running the company and the remainder of the work week in Cambridge. At Harvard, he studied the writings of the great moral and religious philosophers, such as Immanuel Kant, Martin Buber, and Jonathan Edwards, and tried to relate their ideas to business in general and to Tom's of Maine in particular. On returning to Tom's full-time, Chappell's first priority was to codify the company's mission and values. Over an intense period of three months, first with the participation of the board of directors and later the entire company staff, two key documents—"Statement of Beliefs" and "Mission Statement"—were developed and approved (see Appendix A).[7]

Nineteen ninety-three and 1994 were trying years for Tom's of Maine. The company's newly reformulated deodorant did not perform consistently and was disliked by customers. On discovering these problems, Chappell ordered a recall at a cost of $400,000 to the company (to help cover the cost, the advertising budget was slashed 25 percent) and apologized to the company's customers. The incident came to be known throughout the company as the "deodorant debacle" and led to a significant revision of its product development process.[8]

The product recall, along with stiffer competition from the major brands (e.g., Crest and Colgate), which had introduced their own healthy baking soda toothpastes, led to the company's first loss—$400,000 in fiscal 1994. In response, Chappell hired additional salespeople with major brand experience, added a former PepsiCo executive to the board, and introduced new toothpaste flavors along with an entire line of fruity-flavored children's toothpaste. Earnings recovered to $650,000 in 1995.

Representing a sizable investment for the company, Tom's introduced a major new line of wellness products in 1999. The new line included natural echinacea tonics, nasal decongestants, Cough & Cold Rub, Natural Muscle Balm, and liquid herbal extracts. These products were developed by an interdisciplinary team of pharmacognosists (natural-medicine specialists), herbalists, and chemists put together by the company. To assure the quantity and quality of botanicals needed, the company purchased its own farm in Saxton Rivers, Vermont. Additionally, the company contracted with other organic growers for the required ingredients not produced on its farm. The new line was distributed through health food stores in the United States, Canada, and the United Kingdom.[9]

Tom and Kate Chappell seriously considered selling the company in the mid-1990s to achieve financial freedom and to pursue other interests. Working with their investment banker, they established specific criteria for the acquisition based on their company's beliefs and mission. They insisted that price not be the controlling factor in the decision but rather the dedication of the acquiring firm to the company's stated values. Six potential purchasers were identified but all found the acquisition criteria too restrictive and dropped out of the bidding. The Chappells found at that time that they could not sell their business without compromising their own values, which they were unwilling to do.[10] However, the Chappells sold an 86 percent interest in their company to Colgate-Palmolive in March 2006 for $100 million dollars. Under the purchase agreement, the Chappells retain day-to-day management control as CEO and vice president for three years. Colgate has agreed to keep the business located in Maine and to maintain the Chappell's socially conscious management principles; in particular, Colgate has agreed to donate $125,000 annually to charity, exceeding the company's previous yearly contributions.[11]

A SPIRITUALITY-INSPIRED BUSINESS PHILOSOPHY

Tom Chappell grew up in western Massachusetts surrounded by farms and fields, and his family enjoyed frequent vacations in Maine. Early in life he developed a love of the land and a sensitivity to the natural environment that eventually became a vital part of his business philosophy. The fact that he was raised in the

Episcopal Church and that his father was a successful entrepreneur also played a large role in the development of his personal values. Chappell has said, "When you have a family business, it becomes the DNA of every member of the family."[12]

Although Tom Chappell expressed his strongly held personal values of respect for both people and nature from the founding of the company, he was also a highly competitive businessman who wanted to grow a large and successful company. The conflicts between the company's emerging professionalism as it grew and Tom's personal values eventually led to his enrollment at Harvard Divinity School. While at Harvard he came to the conclusion, as his friend had suggested several years earlier, that the company was his true ministry, and there he developed a language that would allow him to "debate his bean-counters."[13]

Early in his academic program Chappell studied the work of Martin Buber, the twentieth-century Jewish philosopher who argued that people can have two opposite attitudes toward others, leading to two distinct types of relationships. In one, the "I-It" relationship, people treat other people as objects and expect something back from each relationship. In the other, the "I-Thou" relationship, the individual relates to others out of respect, friendship, and love. In other words, people see others either as objects to use for their own selfish purposes or honor them for their own sake. Chappell concluded that he and Kate instinctively had been doing business using the I-Thou relationship, and his professional managers were behaving in terms of the I-It model.

Chappell was also deeply influenced by the writings of the eighteenth-century American philosopher Jonathan Edwards. Edwards believed that an individual's identity comes not from being separate but from being connected or in relationship to others. Chappell began thinking of Tom's in this light, perceiving it not simply as a private entity but in relation to other entities including employees, customers, suppliers, financial partners, governments, the community, and even the earth itself. He concluded that the company had obligations to each of these that could be defined in terms of time, money, and priorities.

The ideas of Buber, Edwards, and other philosophers became the ideological underpinnings for the development of Tom's of Maine's purpose, mission, and belief statements. Once this moral foundation was in place, Chappell's next challenge was to manage the company in accordance with its stated values.

Two events illustrate the trade-offs presented by the new decision criteria. The first centered on the company's application, in the early 1990s, to the American Dental Association (ADA) to receive its Seal of Acceptance for three fluoride toothpaste flavors. The ADA required a standard efficacy protocol that is lethal to rats. Rather than compromise its values, the company worked with the ADA to develop an acceptable test that could be conducted on human subjects and in 1995 received the association's coveted seal. Because of the cumbersome process of developing a new protocol, the firm's application for acceptance took several years longer and cost approximately 10 times as much as it would have otherwise.

Interestingly, a year later the Food and Drug Administration (FDA) suggested a set of new rules for fluoride toothpaste that required testing on animals. Tom's strenuously lobbied the FDA to modify these rules and eventually identified a nonanimal protocol that was acceptable to the agency.[14]

The second event occurred during the formulation of plans for the new wellness line. It was determined that the company could save $250,000 if it located the entire production and packaging operation for the product line in Vermont as opposed to the original plan of extracting the herbs in Vermont and shipping them back to Maine for packaging. Rather than make the financially optimal decision, Chappell, adhering to the company's commitment to the Kennebunk community, split the work between the two locales.

VALUES-CENTERED LEADERSHIP

In 1999, Tom Chappell summed up his philosophy of business decision making in his book *Managing Upside Down: The Seven Intentions of Values-Centered Leadership.*[15] Here he rejects the concept of managing for maximum financial gain and instead argues for reversing the values of American business by placing social and ethical responsibilities at the apex of the business goal hierarchy. He further asserts that if a company makes people and other entities the central focus of its decision making, it will be rewarded through the marketplace with growth and profits. He underscores this assertion in the book's introduction: "I have been running our company according to a mission of respecting customers, employees, community, and the environment, and we are creating more products and making more money than I ever dreamed."

The book's title, *Managing Upside Down,* also refers to flattening the organizational hierarchy and empowering people and teams at the lower end of the structure. Indeed, Chappell credits the large expansion of the company's product line during the last three years of the 1990s to the creativity and follow-through of his newly empowered product-development teams (known in the company as Acorns).

Chappell devotes a major portion of the book to what he calls the seven intentions of values-centered leadership (see Appendix B). The intentions are guidelines that managers who desire to run profitable businesses that are also socially and morally responsible can apply. After the publication of the book, Chappell established a nonprofit educational foundation, The Salt Water Institute, founded in Boulder, Colorado, and now located in Portland, Maine, to teach these "intentions" and his overall philosophy of managing through moral values.[16]

ORGANIZATIONAL DESIGN AND DIVERSITY

Tom Chappell describes the organizational structure at Tom's of Maine as a triangle inside a circle. The circle represents the team, which is the basic unit of organization. Teams meet in circles (there are no elongated conference tables at Tom's) to emphasize equality and to encourage everyone to contribute ideas. Chappell credits the circle concept with the creation of many of the innovative ideas and solutions that have helped the company grow and prosper in recent years. He asserts, "the power of the circle is in its openness; it is the place where you are willing to open up and listen."[17] He also credits the circle with improving employee morale.

The triangle symbolizes the company's authority structure. As Chappell sees it, Tom's is not a consensus organization. There is a leader on each team who is accountable to a higher manager, and there is a clear chain of command. Ideally, the two systems—circle and triangle—work in harmony: The circle encourages participation and creativity, and the triangle provides an apparatus for decision making and accountability.

Tom Chappell also sees intentional diversity as a critical element of the company's organizational design. After returning from divinity school, he came to the conclusion that diversity in hiring is not simply a moral responsibility but also can lead to marketplace advantage for the firm. He explained his thinking this way:

> It was not long before I realized that the more sensitive my executives and I could become to the differences of the people we were trying to serve, and the more perspectives we could plug into our discussions about product design, business strategy, and customer service, the more broadly the company could range to meet its financial objectives. We had to listen to as many different sources as possible, both inside and outside the company."[18]

Because Tom's was a male-dominated company through most of its history, Chappell made bringing more women into the company a priority. By 1993, 40 percent of the workforce was female, and two key department managers were women. But Chappell also sees diversity as much more than simply hiring and promoting women and people of color. For Chappell, diversity encompasses factors such as age, education, experience, and background; a diversity of perspectives combined with the openness of a circle results in more innovative and effective business decisions. In support of its diversity goal, the company has a policy of open hiring for all jobs. In other words, when a job becomes open, all candidates, inside and outside, are given equal consideration. The thinking is that hiring only from within the company leads to greater homogeneity, the very opposite of what the company hopes to achieve.[19]

EMPOWERING EMPLOYEES AND THE COMMUNITY

Chappell, since returning to the company full-time, has devoted much of his time to formulating the company's mission and beliefs and to molding a corporate culture that embodies these tenets. Commenting on one of the bigger mistakes he made, Chappell noted that simply handing down the company's mission and beliefs is not enough, that it is important for the staff to see the company mission in action and that "you have to do the training."[20] In practice this includes setting the example through his own behavior and decisions, encouraging and rewarding the people who "live the mission," and holding workshops and seminars on topics of company values and behavior.

Tom's policy on volunteerism is one prominent way the company is trying to live its mission. Under this policy, employees are encouraged to spend 5 percent of their paid work time (two hours per week or two and a half weeks per year) doing volunteer work for nonprofit organizations of their choosing. This policy was instituted in 1989 and has proved popular with employees as well as helpful to the beneficiaries. Volunteer chores have been as varied as the interests of Tom's diverse workforce.

Many company employees take advantage of this opportunity by volunteering at local food shelters, The Animal Welfare Society, Big Brothers–Big Sisters, and at the their children's schools. In one unique example, an employee brought her dog once a week to a nursing home to provide comfort and companionship for the residents.

In addition to promoting individual volunteerism, the company occasionally organizes day-long projects that may include as much as one third of its work-force. In one instance, 14 employees, including Tom Chappell, drove to Rhode Island and spent the day helping clean up an oil spill. One of the participating employees commented afterward that the venture not only was helpful to the people of Rhode Island but also was a bonding and team-building experience for the participating employees.[21]

The company provides a generous benefit package to its employees, includ-ing 4 weeks of parental leave for both mothers and fathers, as well as offers flexi-ble work schedules, job sharing, and work-at-home programs. Child-care and elder-care referral service is provided, and child care is partially reimbursed for employees earning less than $32,500 annually. Largely as a result of these family-friendly policies, Tom's was named in 1998, for the sixth year in a row, by *Working Mother* as one of the 100 best companies for working moms.[22]

RESPECTING THE INDIVIDUAL AND THE ENVIRONMENT

Tom Chappell perceives his company as a social and moral entity as well as a busi-ness organization and has fashioned a body of policies and programs to help real-ize this goal. These initiatives include policies in the areas of the environment, ani-mal rights, and consumer issues as well as community- and environmentally based giving programs.

Giving Programs

Tom's of Maine has committed to donating 10 percent of its pretax profits to non-profit organizations. In the early years when profits were lean, the company con-fined most of its giving to community organizations and environmental groups in Maine and Massachusetts. As profits grew and more money became available, donations to charities widened in scope and dollar amount. The company's grant program is divided into four general areas: education, the arts, the environment, and indigenous peoples.[23]

Approximately 40 to 50 grants per year are awarded either in the form of one-time grants or multiyear pledges. Most are in the $500 to $5,000 range, with larger amounts reserved for the multiyear pledges. Recent beneficiaries include Harvard Divinity School's Center for the Study of Values in Public Affairs, the Maine Audubon Society, and elementary education programs in Maine for teach-ing about the environment. An early grant from the company began the curbside recycling program in Kennebunk. Other donations have gone to the Rainforest Alliance, Maine Women's Fund, Maine Business for Social Responsibility, the National Parks and Conservation Fund, and a project in Portland, Oregon, to protect its regional watersheds.

In 1999, Tom's of Maine was the sole corporate sponsor of "Reason for Hope," a PBS documentary about the scientist/conservationist Jane Goodall. The company views this sponsorship as a natural fit because it shares common values with Dr. Goodall. Prior to sponsoring the television special, the company for two years had been contributing to the Jane Goodall Institute and the related "Roots and Shoots," an international environmental and humanitarian teaching program. In support of this program, the company included coupon inserts with its products that encouraged customers to mail back the coupons; in return, Tom's promised to donate $1 for each coupon returned. Additionally, the company offered to pay the $25 initiation fee for any school or community wishing to establish a Roots and Shoots program.

Tom's sponsors the national environmental radio program *E-Town*. The company has also made product donations to needy causes. For instance, in April 1999 it sent 50,000 bars of soap to the American Red Cross for families in war-ravaged Kosovo.

Environmental Policies

In addition to giving to environmental causes, Tom's has introduced numerous proenvironmental practices in its operations. Toothpaste is packaged in aluminum tubes that can be recycled when empty rather than in the less expensive, nonrecyclable plastic laminates used by most other manufacturers. Moreover, its toothpaste as well as some of its other products are packaged in 100 percent recycled paperboard cartons, of which 65 percent is postconsumer content.

Mouthwash and glycerin soap are packaged in natural-color HDPE (type 2) plastic bottles, which are considered better for recycling than other options. Shampoo is bottled in containers made from recycled milk jugs, and these bottles are, in turn, recyclable. All leaflets that are enclosed in the packaging are printed on dioxin-free paper using soy-based inks. All outgoing products are shipped in boxes made from 95 percent post-consumer cardboard. Also, because Tom's products are made from all-natural ingredients, they are biodegradable.

In the mid-1990s, the company installed an ecologically improved system for filtering the factory's wastewater. With this system, by the time water reaches the leaching bed in a field near the manufacturing facility, it has run through a tank containing layers of peat moss, stone, gravel, and sand that remove the majority of its pollutants.[24] Additionally, the company's farm in Vermont, where the botanical ingredients for its wellness line are grown, practices sustainable harvesting of herbs and is certified organic.

Respect for animals is an important value at Tom's. Consequently, the company does not use any animal ingredients in its products. Moreover, in 1991 the company extended its prohibition on animal testing to its suppliers, requiring them to sign a written guarantee that the ingredients supplied have not been tested on animals.[25]

Consumer Policies

Tom's of Maine's mission emphasizes full disclosure of product information and open dialogue with its customers. From the beginning, the Chappells have always listed all ingredients contained in their products on the packaging along with the source of the ingredients and an explanation of their purpose. They believe that this policy builds customer confidence and loyalty. A related trust-building measure is the signature of Kate and Tom Chappell on all company products.

Another trust-building company policy is to answer every letter from its customers with a personalized return letter. Organizationally, this is the responsibility of the company's Consumer Dialogue Team. This is no small task, since the firm receives some 10,000 letters per year (the team estimates that about 80 percent of them represent positive consumer feedback).

As another means of communicating with its customers, Tom's includes inserts with many of its products. Recently, the company teamed up with Leave No Trace, Inc. (LNT), an organization that promotes responsible outdoor skills, for an insert campaign. The inserts stressed the six principles of Leave No Trace and provided additional environmentally responsible tips for campers.

SPIRITUALITY IN THE WORKPLACE

Tom's of Maine is only one example of the corporate trend in spiritually informed leadership.[26] It is indeed a difficult task for leaders who want to instill their values in the workplace to "create a complex, multivocal conversation among managers and employees about what values the company should uphold" rather than to use their power to impose their beliefs by declaring that "his or her values should apply to the company."[27] In other words, there is a difference between requiring a workforce to embrace one's religious beliefs and empowering all employees through a spiritual framework.

Associate Professor of Leadership Studies and Religion at the University of Richmond's Jepson School Dr. Douglas A. Hicks, who is an ordained minister in the Presbyterian Church and author of two books, *Inequality and Christian Ethics* and *Religion and the Workplace: Pluralism, Spirituality, and Leadership,* maintains that an important goal for leaders is to create a framework of "respectful pluralism." Respectful pluralism reflects an organization that is not "aligned with any explicitly religious, spiritual, or other comprehensive worldview" and where "organizations should allow for significant employee expression of various aspects of their identity on an equal basis."[28] He explains that when such expression occurs there is a shift from a workplace that is simply described as "diverse" to one that represents "pluralism"—"a term that reflects a positive quality of relationships among diverse people."[29]

Tom's of Maine is, perhaps, one of the few companies that reflects pluralism insofar as its spiritual philosophy is based on the interconnection among its founders, employees, management, shareholders, community, environment, and the earth.

Discussion Questions

1. How should management accommodate a variety of conflicting spiritual perspectives in the workplace?
2. Tom Chappell created a spiritual framework for Tom's of Maine, a family-owned business. Can such a framework be created for a publicly traded company? What differences might there be in its effects?

3. To what extent is Tom Chappell's spiritual perspective responsible for the company's organizational culture and the company's successes and/or failures?
4. What risks might a company encounter when encouraging the expression of spiritual values in the workplace? What advantages does it gain?

Notes

1. Tom Chappell, *The Soul of a Business: Managing for Profit and the Common Good* (New York: Bantam Books, 1993), 215.
2. Tom's of Maine Information Sheets, undated.
3. Bette Popovich, "Focus Report: Cosmetics/ Personal Care 2000: Multi-Benefit Products Top Dental Care Market," *Chemical Market Reporter.*
4. Tom's of Maine Information Sheet, undated.
5. Chappell, *The Soul of a Business,* 25.
6. Ibid.
7. Ibid., 20–31.
8. J. C. McCune, "Making Lemonade: Companies Must Try and (Sometimes Fail) in Order to Succeed," *Management Review* 86 (1997): 49–54.
9. Chappell, "Letters to the Editor," *Harvard Business Review* 75 (1997): 194–95.
10. Tom's of Maine Information Sheet, "Tom's Takes a Natural Step to Wellness."
11. Seth Harkness, "Colgate to Buy Tom's of Maine," *Portland Press Herald,* March 22, 2006, A1.
12. Thomas Garvey May, "You Get What You Give," *Natural Foods Merchandiser's New Product Review,* Spring 2000, 1.
13. "Interview with Tom Chappell, Minister of Commerce," *Business Ethics* 8, no. 1 (1994): 16.
14. "Respect for Animals," www.tomsofmaine. com/mission.
15. Tom Chappell, *Managing Upside Down: The Seven Intentions of Values-Centered Leadership* (New York: William Morrow, 1999).
16. May, "You Get What You Give," 1, 6, 8; "New Book by Tom's of Maine CEO Proves that Doing Good Is Good for Business," Jane Wesman Public Relations, news release, 2000.
17. Chappell, *Managing Upside Down,* 119.
18. Ibid., 134.
19. Ibid., 128–51.
20. C. Adams, "Breakaway (Special Report): The Entrepreneurial Life—Upfront: Brushing Up on Values," *Wall Street Journal* 27 (1999) 6.
21. J. C. McCune, "The Corporation in the Community," *HR Focus* 74 (1997): 12–14, "Corporate Volunteerism at Tom's," www.tomsofmaine.com.
22. "Tom's Named One of 100 Best Companies for Working Mothers," www.tomsofmaine.com.
23. The Tom's of Maine Grant Program, www.tomsofmaine.com.
24. Elissa Wolfson, "Brushing Up on Business," *E: The Environmental Magazine,* July/ August 1995, 10.
25. "Respect for Animals."
26. Other examples of spiritual leadership include the following: C. W. Pollard of ServiceMaster, Max De Pree of Herman Miller, and S Truett Cathy of Chick-Fil-A.
27. Douglas A. Hicks, *Religion and the Workplace: Pluralism, Spirituality, Leadership* (New York: Cambridge University Press, 2003), 191.
28. Ibid., 184.
29. Ibid.

Appendix A

THE TOM'S OF MAINE MISSION

To serve our customers by providing safe, effective, innovative natural products of high quality.

To build relationships with our customers that extend beyond product usage to include full and honest dialogue, responsiveness to feedback, and the exchange of information about products and issues.

To respect, value, and serve not only our customers but also our coworkers, owners, agents, suppliers, and community; to be concerned about and contribute to their well-being; and to operate with integrity so as to be deserving of their trust.

To provide meaningful work, fair compensation, and a safe, healthy work environment that encourages openness, creativity, self-discipline, and growth.

To contribute to and affirm a high level of commitment, skill, and effectiveness in the work community.

To recognize, encourage, and seek a diversity of gifts and perspectives in our worklife.

To acknowledge the value of each person's contribution to our goals and to foster teamwork in our tasks.

To be distinctive in products and policies which honor and sustain our natural world.

To address community concerns, in Maine and around the globe, by devoting a portion of our time, talents, and resources to the environment, human needs, the arts, and education.

To work together to contribute to the long-term value and sustainability of our company.

To be a profitable and successful company while acting in a socially and environmentally responsible manner.

To create and manage a system of accountability which holds each person in the Company's employment or governance responsible for individual behavior and personal performance consistent with the Company's Beliefs, Mission, Destiny, Performance Goals, and Individual Work Plans.

Statement of Beliefs

We believe that both human beings and nature have inherent worth and deserve our respect.

We believe in products that are safe, effective, and made of natural ingredients.

We believe that our company and our products are unique and worthwhile, and that we can sustain these genuine qualities with an ongoing commitment to innovation and creativity.

We believe that we have a responsibility to cultivate the best relationships possible with our coworkers, customers, owners, agents, suppliers, and community.

We believe that different people bring different gifts and perspectives to the team and that a strong team is founded on a variety of gifts.

We believe in providing employees with a safe and fulfilling work environment and an opportunity to grow and learn.

We believe that competence is an essential means of sustaining our values in a competitive marketplace.

We believe our company can be financially successful while behaving in a socially responsible and environmentally sensitive manner.

We believe that we have an individual and collective accountability to the Company's beliefs, mission, destiny, and performance goals.

Appendix B

1. **Intention #1: Connect.** Set aside your own ego, open up, and connect to an outside universal force that is bigger than you and available to everyone, the power of goodness.
2. **Intention #2: Know Thyself, Be Thyself.** Explore who you are, your gifts, and what you care most about in life; these are the clues to finding meaning in your work.
3. **Intention #3: Envision Your Destiny.** Envision your future with your head and your heart: Your values in today's world call you to serve. How? The answer is your destiny, and as soon as you hear it, this destiny makes total sense.
4. **Intention #4: Seek Advice.** Every leader makes mistakes, which is why the values-centered manager never makes a decision without using the secret weapon of Managing Upside Down—a diverse group of expert advisors.
5. **Intention #5: Venture Out.** Build a creative strategy for every dimension of your new business, make sure it is aligned with your values, and go for it—even if there is nothing like it in the world.
6. **Intention #6: Assess.** No matter how creative we might choose to be or how unique we are in the marketplace, we are still accountable to our values, visions, and goals. Managing Upside Down is a trial-and-error process, and assessment requires constant affirmation and editing.
7. **Intention #7: Pass It On.** It is our responsibility to fellow humans to be in a state of constant donation. When we receive gifts, knowledge, goodness, extra time, and profits, we are obliged to pass them along to others. In the process, we set up an exchange or experiences and a trial-and-error process that can help us all improve.

7 | SEXUAL ORIENTATION

There is no federal law protecting gay men and lesbians in the workplace; the decision to protect gays and lesbians is made by each state. Currently, 13 states have laws protecting gays and lesbians in the workplace, namely, California, Connecticut, Hawaii, Maryland, Massachusetts, Minnesota, Nevada, New Hampshire, New Jersey, New York, Rhode Island, Vermont, and Wisconsin. The District of Columbia also prohibits discrimination against gays and lesbians because of their sexual orientation. In addition, 253 Fortune 500 companies offer domestic partner health insurance benefits, and 430 include sexual orientation in their nondiscrimination policies.

Objectives

- To examine the relationship between members of the gay lesbian bisexual transgender (GLBT) community and the workplace.

- To examine the changing societal views of the GLBT community and the current legislation supporting GLBT rights in the workplace.

- To examine how a public organization blatantly discriminated against gays and lesbians in the workplace.

Preview Questions

- How can managers most effectively accommodate people who have conflicting opinions about homosexuality in the workplace?

- How should managers handle a situation in which disparaging remarks are made to a gay coworker?

- Can a public company openly discriminate against gays and lesbians in the workplace? What influence do shareholders have in such decisions?

Some Important Dates

1924 The Society for Human Rights in Chicago becomes the country's earliest known gay rights organization.

1962 Illinois becomes the first U.S. state to decriminalize homosexual acts between consenting adults.

1973   The American Psychiatric Association removes homosexuality from its official list of mental disorders.

1982   The *Village Voice*, a New York City weekly newspaper, becomes the first employer to offer domestic partner benefits to its lesbian and gay employees.

1982   Wisconsin becomes the first state to outlaw discrimination on the basis of sexual orientation.

1993   The "Don't Ask, Don't Tell" policy is instituted for the U.S. military, permitting gays to serve in the military but banning homosexual self-identification and activity.

1996   The city of San Francisco passes the nation's first equal benefits ordinance, which requires employers that contract with the city government to offer the same benefits to employees' domestic partners as they offer to their legal spouses.

2000   Vermont becomes the first state in the country to recognize legal civil unions between gay or lesbian couples. The law states that these "couples would be entitled to the same benefits, privileges, and responsibilities as spouses." It stops short of referring to same-sex unions as marriage, which the state continues to define as pertaining only to heterosexual couples.

2004   On May 17, same-sex marriages become legal in Massachusetts.

2005   Wal-Mart Stores, the nation's largest private employer, adopts a new definition of family that includes same-sex partners recognized under state law.

WAL-MART SETS A NEW POLICY THAT PROTECTS GAY WORKERS

Wal-Mart Stores, the nation's largest private employer, has expanded its antidiscrimination policy to protect gay and lesbian employees, company officials said today.

The decision to include gay employees under rules that prohibit workplace discrimination was hailed by gay rights groups, already buoyed by a Supreme Court ruling last week that struck down a Texas sodomy law, as a sign of how far corporate America has come in accepting gay employees.

The decision was first disclosed today by a Seattle gay rights foundation that had invested in Wal-Mart and then lobbied the company for two years to change its policy. The group, Pride Foundation, which along with several investment management firms holding stock in Wal-Mart had met as shareholders with company officials to discuss the policy, received a letter last week from Wal-Mart outlining the new employee protections. Wal-Mart officials confirmed the policy change today.

"It's the right thing to do for our employees," Mona Williams, Wal-Mart's vice president for communications, said in a telephone interview. "We want all of our associates to feel they are valued and treated with respect—no exceptions. And it's the right thing to do for our business."

Ms. Williams said the company was sending out a letter today to its 3,500 stores and that store managers would then convey the policy change to the company's more than 1 million employees. She said that while investors like Pride Foundation had a role in the decision, the most important factor was a letter to senior management officials about

(continued)

six weeks ago from several gay Wal-Mart employees, saying that unless the company changed its policy the employees would "continue to feel excluded."

Wal-Mart has been careful not to alienate its customers who might hold conservative views. In recent months, the company has decided to stop selling three men's magazines it said were too racy and to partially obscure the covers of four women's magazines on sale in checkout lines. The company said customers felt the magazine cover headlines were too provocative and planned to use U-shaped blinders to cover them.

Wal-Mart has also refused to sell CD's with labels warning of explicit lyrics.

Ms. Williams said she saw no conflict between the decision to limit the distribution of entertainment products based on content and the decision to protect gay employees.

"In each case, we sit down and think through the individual decisions," she said. "Putting in the blinders was the right thing to do. In this case, once again, we talked about it and decided it was the right thing to do."

With Wal-Mart making the policy change, 9 of the 10 largest Fortune 500 companies now have rules barring discrimination against gay employees, according to the Human Rights Campaign, a gay rights group in Washington, D.C., that monitors discrimination policies and laws.

The exception is the Exxon Mobil Corporation, which was created in 1999 after Exxon acquired Mobil, and then revoked a Mobil policy that provided medical benefits to partners of gay employees, as well as a policy that included sexual orientation as a category of prohibited discrimination.

Wal-Mart said it had no plans to extend medical benefits to unmarried couples, but gay rights groups that have pressed for coverage for domestic part-

ners said they would continue to lobby the company to do so.

Among the Fortune 500 companies, 197 provide domestic partners with medical coverage, including several of the major airlines and the Big Three automakers, and 318 have antidiscrimination policies that extend protection to gay employees, according to the Human Rights Campaign.

With Wal-Mart now joining the ranks of companies with protections for gay employees, and in light of last week's Supreme Court ruling, gay rights groups said they expected many corporations, and possibly state governments, to follow suit.

"A major argument against equal benefits, against fair treatment of employees, has been taken away," said Kevin Cathcart, executive director of the Lambda Legal Defense and Education Fund, referring to the Supreme Court ruling on Lawrence v. Texas. "And so even within corporations it's a very different dialogue today, a very different dialogue."

There is no federal law prohibiting discrimination in the workplace on the basis of sexual orientation, but 13 states, the District of Columbia and several hundred towns, cities or counties have such legal protections in place for public and private employees, according to the latest information from the Human Rights Campaign.

As outlined in the letter to Pride Foundation, Wal-Mart's new policy states, "We affirm our commitment and pledge our support to equal opportunity employment for all qualified persons, regardless of race, color, religion, gender, national origin, age, disability or status as a veteran or sexual orientation."

It goes on to say that managers and supervisors "shall recruit, hire, train and promote in all job positions" based on those principles and "ensure that all personnel actions" are taken based on those principles.

The company said that it also revised its policy on harassment and inappropriate conduct to include sexual orientation and that the new written policy would encourage employees to report discriminatory behavior to management.

As the nation's largest private employer and one whose stores are not unionized, Wal-Mart has long been the target of organized labor, and some of its labor practices have been challenged in lawsuits. One lawsuit, filed in San Francisco, accused the company of favoring men over women in promotions and pay.

In addition, the company faces more than 40 lawsuits accusing the company of pressuring or forcing employees to work unpaid hours.

While Wal-Mart attributed the discrimination policy change to the letter from its gay employees, it had been under pressure from several investors, including the Seattle group and three other management investment firms with stock in the company.

They are all members of the Equality Project, a nonprofit group in New York that monitors corporate policies on sexual orientation and lobbies for protections for gay employees.

Under Securities and Exchange Commission regulations, any stockholder with $2,000 or more in shares can introduce a "shareholder resolution" on an array of company policy issues, including antidiscrimination rules. The resolutions are not binding, and the shareholders have no influence over "ordinary business," including benefits and wages, according to S.E.C. officials.

The Seattle group and the other investors began discussions with Wal-Mart in August 2001, when several members of the groups went to the company headquarters in Bentonville, Ark., to try and persuade officials to change the policy, several group members said. As investors in General Electric and McDonald's, the Seattle group had already pressured the companies, through shareholder resolutions, and both companies have since extended workplace protections to gay employees.

Wal-Mart initially said it would study the issue, said Zan McColloch-Lussier, campaign director for Pride Foundation. But in a conference call in the spring of 2002, Mr. McColloch-Lussier recalled, company officials told the group, "Thanks, you've educated us, but we're not going to change our policies, we'll do management training."

More letters and telephone calls were exchanged, and then last Friday a letter came announcing the policy change.

Arthur D. Ally, president of the Timothy Plan, a religious-based investment group that had pressured the company about the magazines, said today that he would not sell Wal-Mart stock because of the revised antidiscrimination policy but would object to certain sensitivity training programs like "taking every employee in an organization and indoctrinating them in the homosexual agenda."

It was unclear today exactly how Wal-Mart planned to train employees, but Ms. Williams said that a computer-based training program would include discussion of sexual orientation.

Sarah Kershaw, *New York Times.* (Late Edition (East Coast)). New York, N.Y.: Jul 2, 2003. pg. A.1. *Copyright New York Times Company Jul 2, 2003.*

ESSAY: SELECTIONS FROM *STRAIGHT TALK ABOUT GAYS IN THE WORKPLACE:* CREATING AN INCLUSIVE, PRODUCTIVE ENVIRONMENT FOR EVERYONE IN YOUR ORGANIZATION

Liz Winfeld, a nationally recognized expert in workplace diversity specific to sexual orientation, gender identity, and domestic partner benefits, discusses a wide range of topics in her book. *Straight Talk about Gays in the Workplace: Creating an Inclusive, Productive Environment for Everyone in Your Organization*, 3rd ed. The following essay is excerpted from that book. The goal of the various selections is to provide a basic understanding of the situation facing GLBTs in the workplace.

THE CHANGING LANDSCAPE[1]

Beyond the increase in the number of states or commonwealths that have laws inclusive of sexual orientation and gender identity for the purposes of employment, housing, public accommodations, and credit, there are other very significant changes in our society on issues that involve sexual orientation and gender identity.[2]

- The 2000 U.S. Census found 15 million self-identified gay/lesbian people and almost a million who self-identified as being part of a same-sex household, with or without children.[3]
- Sixty-three percent of registered voters are in favor of civil unions for same-sex couples in the United States.[4]
- A plurality, or about 47 percent of Americans, favor full legal marriage for same-sex couples. In the group of people aged 18 to 35, this percentage jumps to more than 65 percent.[5]
- Eleven states bar, by executive order, discrimination against gay people in state employment. Only eight years ago, there were none.
- Gallup reported in December 2003[6] that 79 percent of all Americans believe that gay people should be allowed to openly serve in the military.
- Six out of ten (62 percent) heterosexual adults say that employees with same-sex partners should be equally eligible for key workplace benefits available to spouses of married employees in general.[7]
- More than 7,000 organizations in the public, private, nonprofit, and university sectors offer domestic partner benefits to either same-sex only or same- and opposite-sex couples and their families. There were exactly 100 such organizations on January 1, 1992.
- The percentage of organizations that include the words "sexual orientation" in their nondiscrimination policies has increased 7 to 10 percent every year for the past 10 years. Currently, 157 organizations (all sectors) also include "gender identity" or "gender identity/expression" in their nondiscrimination policies. Three years ago, there were less than 20. Now this number comprises 25 of the Fortune 500 alone.[8]
- At least 30 states have adoption laws on the books or have a preponderance of legal decisions to support second-parent/step-parent adoption by same-sex couples.
- Forty-six states have adoption laws that allow people, regardless of sexual orientation, to adopt children if they are otherwise qualified to do so.

- Sodomy laws have been declared unconstitutional, signaling a growing aware-ness that sexual orientation is part of who you are, and not entirely what you do. Also, perhaps, that whatever it is you "do" is private, as long as it's between con-senting adults.

What is behind the trend toward expanding the classifications of people who can take advantage of the civil and workplace rights that all Americans are otherwise enti-tled to? I think it's this: In 1990, only about 25 percent of Americans reported having a gay friend or acquaintance. In 2000, that percentage was over 50 percent.[9] According to the Gill Foundation in 2003, the percentage of straight people who say they know at least one gay person is 90 percent.[10] And findings from the Human Rights Campaign (HRC) Public Report from February 2004 show that more than 60 percent of gay/les-bian people are out to even their casual acquaintances and co-workers.[11]

The data support the conclusion that seizing every opportunity to be as inclusive as possible is not only good for the individual and the collective psyche; it's also arguably good for the bottom line. To this point, Professor Richard Florida, of Carnegie Mellon University, and Gary Gates, a demographer at the Urban Institute, released data from a study they did in May 2003.[12] Some of their conclusions follow:

- New ideas and cutting-edge industries that lead to sustained prosperity are more likely to exist where gay people feel welcome.
- Most centers of tech-based business growth also have the highest concentration of gay couples. Conversely, major metropolitan areas with few gay couples tend to be slow- or no-growth places.
- Innovation and economic vitality are closely associated with the presence of gay people and other overt indicators of acceptance and diversity such as a high per-centage of immigrants and the level of racial and ethnic integration.
- Creative, innovative, and entrepreneurial activities tend to flourish in the same kinds of places that attract gays and others outside the norm.

According to Florida, more than a few heterosexuals look for a "visible gay community as a signal of a place that's likely to be both exciting and comfortable. . . . They are looking for signs that nonstandard people, and ideas, are welcome."

This is an incredibly powerful quote and set of data because it reinforces what many believe about people and how they like to be treated. We want to see signs that the places where we reside and work acknowledge us. Furthermore, people want to know that if they exhibit creativity, innovation, or thinking outside of the box then they aren't going to get slapped down for it. Places that exhibit an acceptance of diversity are more likely to also be places that will accept innovations of thought and action. This frees people and allows them to put forth their best effort.

STRATEGIES FOR INCLUSION IN THE NEW WORLD[13]

The strategies at managers' disposal to deal effectively with sexual orientation and gender identity in the workplace are

- endorsing the nondiscrimation policies such as the proposed Employment Non-Discrimination Act (ENDA),
- domestic partner benefits,

- employee networks/alliances—mentoring,
- marketing to the LGBT community,
- internal and external outreach, and
- knowledgeable internal resources and reference libraries.[14]

Nondiscrimination Policies and the ENDA

In 2000, 42 percent of Americans thought that sexual orientation was protected in a federal statue. I don't know what the percentage is now, but I would guess that still more than one third of all Americans believe this. The fact is that neither sexual orientation nor gender identity is part of any federal statute, code, or law. Fourteen states have laws that extend workplace protections, and a couple hundred local jurisdictions (including states, cities, towns, counties) have executive orders or ordinances that refer to these matters. Only four states and about 50 other jurisdictions provide protections to people on the basis of gender identity.

What this means is that LGBT people in 36 states and the majority of all jurisdictions have no protections under the law in terms of whether they can be fired or not hired in the first place just for being gay or straight, or can be denied credit or service in a hotel or a restaurant based on real or perceived sexual orientation.

When an organization includes the words *sexual orientation* and/or *gender identity* in its nondiscrimination policies, it is not just blowing smoke. These policies matter as statements of intent by the organization. They say, "This is who we are, and this is how we intend to treat people who work here or with whom we become affiliated." Absent any other protections, people outside the mainstream look for these policies because more often than not these days, they're all they're going to get.

As of March 2004, 2,632 organizations included sexual-orientation language in their nondiscrimination policies. Seventy-five percent of the Fortune 500 were included in that number. Of these 2,632, one hundred-sixty-two also included gender identity or gender identity/expression.[15]

An example of a nondiscrimination policy is the ENDA. This policy, largely unknown to many, has been floating around Congress for about five years now. It would

- extend to sexual orientation federal employment discrimination protections currently provided based on race, religion, sex, national origin, age, and disability;
- block public and private employers, employment agencies, and labor unions from using an individual's sexual orientation as the basis for employment decisions, such as hiring, firing, promotion, or compensation;
- allow for the same procedures and similar, but somewhat more limited, remedies as permitted under Title VII and the Americans with Disabilities Act; and
- apply to Congress, with the same procedures as provided by the Congressional Accountability Act of 1995, and presidential employees, with the same procedures as provided under the Presidential and Executive Office Accountability Act of 1996.

Domestic Partner Benefits

As of the beginning of 2005, about 7,000 organizations had domestic partner benefits (DPBs) in place for same-sex couples, and about two thirds of those had DPBs for heterosexual couples. These companies were of all kinds, of all sizes, and in all market segments, which is to say, public entities, including cities and states; private companies, including a majority of the Fortune 100; colleges and universities, including those beholden to state legislatures for funding; and private, nonprofit organizations, unions, and associations.

Why the explosion in DPBs? It is for two simple reasons. First, the population of people, gay or straight, living in families of their making absent marriage has been steadily increasing for more than 15 years. The 2000 and 2002 U.S. Census studies gave us counts of how many gay Americans there are (about 15 million self-reported on the 2000 census and that was probably low by about 10 million or so) and 600,000 gay, self-reported heads of or partners in households with or without children (again, probably low by several millions), and the U.S. Census in 1994 and 1998 had already reported that the number of Americans living in unmarried-partner households had increased at five times the rate of married households. In 1998, 5.9 million people in the United States were living with a partner. Of these, approximately 28 percent, or 1.7 million people, were in same-sex relationships.

The second reason is that almost two decades of data firmly support the notion that DPBs are a low-cost, high-return way to demonstrate inclusion that results in little or no backlash. The plain fact is that study after study unequivocally bears out that upward of 90 percent of Americans believe that if you have a family and you work to support them, you deserve the benefits of that labor. There is also this: The Employee Benefits Research Group found in a survey of 279 HR professionals representing 19 industries in the United States that DPBs are the number-one recruitment tool for executives and the third-ranked recruitment tool for management and line workers.[16] DPBs were found to be a more effective hiring incentive than telecommuting options, hiring bonuses, stock options, and 401(k) plans, among other things.

Employee Networks/Alliances—Mentoring

Employee networks of any kind allow people with similar interests or characteristics to interact with others who are like them. In the case of a group formed around sexual orientation, the existence of such a group may serve to help individuals who are gay or transgender know that they are not alone. Feeling like "the only one" is a depressing condition common to many gay workers.

The following structure for successful employee networks has been implemented at a number of organizations, large and small.

1. Identify a leadership team for the employee network. There people will likely, at first, be the ones who led the charge for the employee network to be formed and probably have also done a lot of "underground outreach" to others in the organization. The network's leadership team will typically have four to six people on it and, thanks to technology, they don't have to be located in the same place.

2. The leadership team organizes subcommittees and appoints a person who is not on the leadership team to head up each one. These subcommittees can be in as many areas as are deemed necessary or desired. They can be for budget, for community outreach, for internal education, for internal and external policy, for cooperation with other employee groups, for marketing and assisting revenue generation, for liaison with HR, for communications, for Pride events, for growing membership activities.

There can be, in short, a committee for everything the network thinks it would like to get into.

3.   Each member of the leadership team is also the primary liaison between a committee (or, if necessary, more than one) and the leadership team. It's this person's job to know what the committee is doing, what it would like to do, what it needs, and so on so that he or she can present those things to the leadership team.

4.   A member of senior management is appointed as a liaison or mentor for each person on the leadership team and, therefore, to a committee. The communication that the leadership team member shares with the team in general is also shared with his or her management liaison. In this way, an effective and orderly communication channel is created between all the committees and the organization as a whole.

What's really good about this structure is that is allows for maximum participation across the enterprise while also providing for maximum oversight of all activities of the network, communication of those activities, and control over who is doing what without it appearing as if "big brother" is watching.

Marketing to the LGBT Community

The gay market segment is, according to Mulryan/Nash and the Simmons Market Research Bureau, one of the fastest, if not the fastest, growing demographics for products and services in the United States.[17] That statement was true when first written in 1998, and it's still true today. Since 1997, which was the first year that ad revenues in LGBT media topped $100 million, they have continued to grow in that market at a rate of more than 25 percent per year.

Witeck-Combs and Harris Interactive reported that there are 15 million self-identified gay and lesbian people as of the 2000 U.S. Census and surveys done in 2002.[18] According to their report, focused strictly on the market implications of these population numbers, buying power for the LGBT community was $451 billion in 2002 and is projected to reach $608 billion by 2007, a cumulative increase of more than 34 percent from 2002 figures. By comparison, African American spending power is projected to reach $852.8 billion by 2007; Latino spending power projected to reach $927.1 billion; and Asian American spending power to be at $454.9 billion.[19]

If you want to leverage the LGBT market, you have to first know what's important to it. The research shows that the LGBT market is among the most attention-starved, loyal, and easy mark for marketers to build early dominance in if they take the plunge. There is great truth in the theory that the gay market is open to organizations that take its requirements into consideration, both as employees and as patrons.

What follows is a description of what matters to the LGBT market, and I think that this information is significant not only in and of itself, but also because it can now be gathered with a great deal more reliability than just targeting people who subscribe to magazines.[20]

- LGBT consumers have a deeper trust for products and brands that target gay consumers, but even more for products offered by companies that have progressive policies toward all employees, including but not limited to LGBT employees.
- Fifty-six percent of all LGBT people sampled agreed that they more often trust brands from progressive companies, with 41 percent reporting that they strongly agree.

- The most important public policy issues to LGBT consumers are
  - Protection for LGBT people from workplace discrimination
  - Passing laws that discourage antigay bias crimes
  - The right of gays to parent, including adoption
  - The right to civil marriage for same-sex couples
  - Securing federal benefits such as social security, pensions, and family and medical leave
  - HIV/AIDS funding, care, treatment, and prevention
  - Specifically including gender identity in all public and private protection policies
  - Ending the military's "Don't Ask, Don't Tell" policy
  - Research for women's health issues, including breast and cervical cancer
  - Equal treatment of binational couples
  - Securing benefits administered at the state level
- By a ratio of 47 percent (LGBT) to 18 percent (heterosexual), gay consumers are more likely to make a purchasing decision based on their awareness of a company's diversity policies.
- With all other factor being equal (such as price, quality, value, and function) LGBT consumers were more likely to favor one organization's products and services over another if they knew that the salesperson or representative was also LGBT. This was 56 percent of the total for financial services; 51 percent for health care; 49 percent for large purchases such as cars and houses; 42 percent for everyday purchases such as groceries; and 42 percent for computers or home entertainment products.
- Eighty percent of LGBT respondents to an August 2001 poll said they would be willing to recommend a particular company or vendor to others based on favorable inclusion policies. This was compared to 26 percent of heterosexual respondents to the same question.
- Fifty-six percent of LGBT respondents in the August 2001 poll said they "shop at stores that advertise to people like me."
- Ninety-four percent of LGBT people said they shop at stores that make them feel welcome as compared to 88 percent of heterosexual people.

What should leap out from these various statistics is that the growing atmosphere of awareness and visibility encourages people who were once considered to be very much on the fringes to be willing and able to make spending decisions based on information about a particular organization's policies toward people—in most cases, toward all people.

Internal and External Outreach Strategies

Internal outreach means ensuring that all communication uses inclusive language and that all people, regardless of background, are made to feel welcome.[21]

In this day and age, it's also very important that all employee groups have equitable use of and access to internal electronic bulletin boards or intranets as a way of publicizing events or engendering communication among members. Again, if some groups have full access to these systems and some groups don't, this doesn't send the right message.

Internal outreach also means doing everything possible to encourage participation by all types of people in the organization and going out of the way, perhaps far out of the way, to work to provide a safe environment where closeted gay people can come out or participate in any way that feels safe to them.

Community outreach means getting involved in some of what is going on in the communities in which you operate. It means supporting local organizations such as Parents, Families and Friends of Lesbians and Gays (PFLAG)[22] or endorsing ENDA to Congress. It also means allowing your employees to participate in community speaking programs and/or to work on behalf of your company in support of Meals on Wheels programs or the fight against breast and ovarian cancer. Put more than your money out there; give people the opportunity to represent you in these causes in their community. The PR you'll get from this will be well worth the negligible expense.

Knowledgeable Internal Resources

Make sure there is a resource room, kiosk, or person who is up to speed on all of what is going on relative to sexual orientation in every single facility that you maintain. Other strategies that the organization may want to consider spearheading include the following:

- A hotline to report all forms of harassment and discrimination including, but not necessarily limited to, sexual orientation;
- A system of accountability for a nonhostile work environment by division, work group, business unit, geography, or other criteria;
- Expansion of existing reward/award programs to include recognition of superior efforts to engender a safer, better working environment for all—with an emphasis, perhaps, on sexual orientation; and
- Encouragement of gay employees to bring their partners to appropriate enterprise-wide events, or to display items from their personal lives.

If the organization and individuals therein adopt some or all of these strategies for inclusion, benefits will be reaped in terms of greater productivity that is the direct result of almost universal increased job satisfaction.

TOOLS AND TECHNIQUES[23]

What follows is a summary list of tools and techniques that a manager can implement as a way to become a more effective manager and leader within his or her organization.

1. Educate yourself about sexual orientation in order to formulate, and where necessary express, a position that balances one's own opinion with the change-agent behavior encouraged by the organization.
2. Try to avoid making heterosexist assumptions; that is, don't assume that everyone you work with or come into contact with is heterosexual.
3. Share anything you've learned about human sexuality and homophobia that might encourage others to adopt productive behaviors.
4. Use inclusive language whenever possible in all communications.
5. Encourage gay and transgender co-workers to be part of the social groups you form at work, including bringing their partners to functions when appropriate.
6. Take time to understand the local laws and ordinances that relate to sexual orientation and gender identity, and especially your organization's nondiscrimination policies. If you have questions about these policies, ask.
7. If you have questions about orientation, use organizational resources or resources on the Internet to try to get answers.

8. Display items in your workspace, such as books, magnets, and posters, that demonstrate your awareness of inclusiveness.
9. If someone asks you a question or confronts you with an opinion about sexual orientation in the workplace that you feel unprepared for, feel free to say that you don't know how to respond, but that you will get back to her or him. Then reach out to the organizational resources available to you so that you can respond in a meaningful and helpful way.
10. Refuse to laugh at antigay humor.
11. Cite company policy about nondiscrimination, or simply walk away from a group that is indulging in verbal discrimination. If you feel comfortable doing so, personalize the issue by saying, for example, "What you just did/said offends me."
12. Encourage other people to read books or attend education sessions on sexual orientation in order to avail themselves of other points of view if they seem particularly troubled by the issue.

Discussion Questions

1. Why, do you think, is the number of gay residents in a community associated with the innovation and economic growth of the area?
2. Is it a good idea for businesses to offer domestic partner benefits? Who should be eligible for these benefits—just gay couples or unmarried heterosexual couples too?
3. What is the most inclusive way to invite employees to come to company-sponsored social events?
4. How can managers accommodate people who have conflicting opinions about homosexuality? In particular, what should they do when some employees are uncomfortable with others?
5. What alternative responses can you use when coworkers are making disparaging remarks about gays?

CASE STUDY: THE CRACKER BARREL RESTAURANTS

Discrimination against lesbians and gays is common in the workplace. Sole proprietors, managing partners, and corporate personnel officers can and often do make hiring, promoting, and firing decisions based on an individual's real or perceived sexual orientation. Lesbian and gay job applicants are turned down, and lesbian and gay employees are passed over for promotion or even fired by employers who view homosexuality as somehow detrimental to job performance or harmful to the company's public profile. Such discrimination frequently results from the personal biases of individual decision makers. It is rarely written into company policy and thus is difficult to trace. However, in January 1991, Cracker Barrel Old Country Store, Inc., a chain of family restaurants, became the first and only major American

John Howard, University of York, United Kingdom, in Carol P. Harvey and M. June Ailard, *Understanding and Managing Diversity: Readings, Cases, and Exercises,* 3rd ed. (Englewood Cliffs, NJ: Prentice Hall, 2005), pp. 302–310.

John Howard is lecturer in American history and associate faculty in women's studies at the University of York, United Kingdom. A native of Brandon, Mississippi, he is the author of "Men Like That: A Southern Queer History," 1999, University of Chicago Press and the editor of "Carryin' On in the Lesbian and Gay South," 1997, New York University Press.

corporation in recent memory to expressly prohibit the employment of lesbians and gays in its operating units. A nationally publicized boycott followed, with demonstrations in dozens of cities and towns.

THE COMPANY: A BRIEF HISTORY OF CRACKER BARREL

Cracker Barrel was founded in 1969 by Dan Evins in his hometown of Lebanon, Tennessee, 40 miles east of Nashville. Evins, a 34-year-old ex-Marine sergeant and oil jobber, decided to take advantage of the traffic on the nearby interstate highway and open a gas station with a restaurant and gift shop. Specializing in down-home cooking at low prices, the restaurant was immediately profitable.

Evins began building Cracker Barrel stores throughout the region, gradually phasing out gasoline sales. By 1974, he owned a dozen restaurants. Within five years of going public in 1981, Cracker Barrel doubled its number of stores and quadrupled its revenues: In 1986, there were 47 Cracker Barrel restaurants with net sales of $81 million. Continuing to expand aggressively, the chain again grew to twice its size and nearly quadrupled its revenues during the next five years.

By the end of the fiscal year, August 2, 1991, Cracker Barrel operated over 100 stores, almost all located along the interstate highways of the Southeast and, increasingly, the Midwest. Revenues exceeded $300 million. Employing roughly 10,000 nonunionized workers, Cracker Barrel ranked well behind such mammoth family chains as Denny's and Big Boy in total sales, but led all U.S. family chains in sales per operating unit for both 1990 and 1991.

As of 1991, Cracker Barrel was a well-recognized corporate success story, known for its effective, centralized, but authoritarian leadership. From its headquarters, Cracker Barrel maintained uniformity in its store designs, menu offerings, and operating procedures. Travelers and local customers dining at any Cracker Barrel restaurant knew to expect a spacious, homey atmosphere; an inexpensive, country-style meal; and a friendly, efficient staff. All were guaranteed by Dan Evins, who remained as president, chief executive officer, and chairman of the board.

THE POLICY: NO LESBIAN OR GAY EMPLOYEES

In early January 1991, managers in the roughly 100 Cracker Barrel operating units received a communique from the home office in Lebanon. The personnel policy memorandum from William Bridges, vice president of human resources, declared that Cracker Barrel was "founded upon a concept of traditional American values." As such, it was deemed "inconsistent with our concept and values and . . . with those of our customer base, to continue to employ individuals . . . whose sexual preferences fail to demonstrate normal heterosexual values, which have been the foundation of families in our society."

Throughout the chain, individual store managers, acting on orders of corporate officials, began conducting brief, one-on-one interviews with their employees to see if any were in violation of the new policy. Cheryl Summerville, a cook in the Douglasville, Georgia, store for 3½ years, asked if she were a lesbian, knew she had to answer truthfully. She felt she owed that to her partner of 10 years. Despite a history of consistently high performance evaluations, Summerville was fired on the spot, without warning and without severance pay. Her official separation notice, filled out by the manager and filed with the state department of labor, clearly indicated the reason for her dismissal: "This employee is being terminated due to violation of company policy. The employee is gay." Cracker Barrel fired as many as 16 other employees across several states in the following months. These workers, mostly waiters, were left without any legal recourse. Lesbian and gay antidiscrimination statutes were in effect in Massachusetts and Wisconsin and in roughly 80 U.S. cities and counties, but none of the firings occurred in those jurisdictions. Federal civil rights laws, the employees learned, did not cover discrimination based upon sexual orientation.

Under pressure from a variety of groups, the company issued a statement in late February 1991. In it, Cracker Barrel management said, "We have revisited our thinking on the subject and feel it only makes good business sense to continue to employ those folks who will provide the quality service our customers have come to expect." The recent personnel policy had been a "well-intentioned overreaction." Cracker Barrel pledged to deal with any future disruptions in its units "on a store-by-store basis." Activists charged that the statement did not represent a retraction of the policy, as some company officials claimed. None of the fired employees had been rehired, activists noted, and none had been offered severance pay. Moreover, on February 27, just days after the statement, Dan Evins reiterated the company's antagonism toward nonheterosexual employees in a rare interview with a Nashville newspaper. Lesbians and gays, he said, would not be employed in more rural Cracker Barrel locations if their presence was viewed to cause problems in those communities.

THE BOYCOTT: QUEER NATIONALS VERSUS GOOD OL' BOYS

The next day, when news of Cracker Barrel employment policies appeared in the *The Wall Street Journal, New York Times,* and *Los Angeles Times,* investment analysts expressed surprise. "I look on [Cracker Barrel executives] as pretty prudent businesspeople," said one market watcher. "These guys are not fire-breathing good ol' boys." Unconvinced, lesbian and gay activists called for a nationwide boycott of Cracker Barrel restaurants and began a series of demonstrations that attracted extensive media coverage.

The protest movement was coordinated by the Atlanta chapter of Queer Nation, which Cheryl Summerville joined as cochair with fellow cochair Lynn Cothren, an official with the Martin Luther King, Jr., Center for Non-Violent Social Change in Atlanta. Committed to nonviolent civil disobedience, lesbian and gay activists and supporters staged pickets and sit-ins at various Cracker Barrel locations, often occupying an entire restaurant during peak lunch hours, ordering only coffee.

Protesters were further angered and spurred on by news in June from Mobile, Alabama. A 16-year-old Cracker Barrel employee had been fired for effeminate mannerisms and subsequently was thrown out of his home by his father. Demonstrations continued throughout the summer of 1991, spreading from the Southeast to the Midwest stores. Arrests were made at demonstrations in the Detroit area; Cothren and Summerville were among several people arrested for criminal trespass at both the Lithonia and Union City, Georgia, stores. Reporters and politicians dubbed Summerville the "Rosa Parks of the movement," after the woman whose arrest sparked the Montgomery, Alabama, Bus Boycott of 1955–1956.

Support for the Cracker Barrel boycott grew, as organizers further charged the company with racism and sexism. Restaurant gift shops, they pointed out, sold Confederate flags, black mammy dolls, and other offensive items. The Cracker Barrel board of directors, they said, was indeed a good ol' boy network, made up exclusively of middle-aged and older white men. In addition, there was only one female in the ranks of upper management.

THE RESOLUTION: NEW YORK ATTEMPTS TO FORCE CHANGE

Meanwhile, New York City comptroller, Elizabeth Holtzman, and finance commissioner, Carol O'Cleiracain, at the urging of the National Gay and Lesbian Task Force, wrote a letter to Dan Evins, dated March 12, 1991. As trustees of various city pension funds, which owned about $3 million in Cracker Barrel stock, they were "concerned about the potential negative impact on the company's sales and earnings, which could result from adverse public reaction." They asked for a "clear statement" of the company's policy regarding employment and sexual orientation, as well as a description of "what remedial steps, if any, [had] been taken by the company respecting the employees dismissed."

Evins replied in a letter of March 19 that the policy had been rescinded and that there had been "no negative impact on the company's sales." Unsatisfied, the city of New York officials wrote back, again inquiring as to the status of the fired workers. They also asked that the company put forth a policy that "would provide unequivocally" that discrimination based on sexual orientation was prohibited. Evins never responded.

Shortly thereafter, Queer Nation launched a "buy one" campaign. Hoping to gain additional leverage in company decision making, activists became stockholders by purchasing single shares of Cracker Barrel common stock. At the least, they reasoned, the company would suffer from the relative expense of mailing and processing numerous one-cent quarterly dividend checks. More importantly, they could attend the annual stockholders meeting in Lebanon, Tennessee.

In November 1991, company, officials successfully prevented the new shareholders from participating in the annual meeting, and they used a court injunction to block protests at the corporate complex. Nonetheless, demonstrators lined the street, while inside, a representative of the New York City comptroller's office announced the submission of a resolution "banning employment discrimination against gay and lesbian men and women," to be voted on at the next year's meeting. The resolution was endorsed by the Philadelphia Municipal Retirement System, another major stockholder. Cracker Barrel refused any further public comment on the issue.

THE EFFECT: NO DECLINE IN CORPORATE GROWTH

The impact of the boycott on the corporate bottom line was negligible. Trade magazines reiterated the company's claim that neither sales nor stock price had been negatively affected. Indeed, net sales remained strong, up 33 percent at fiscal yearend 1992 to $400 million, owing in good part to continued expansion: There were now 127 restaurants in the chain. Though the increase in same-store sales was not as great as the previous year, Cracker Barrel at least could boast growth, while other chains blamed flat sales on the recession. Cracker Barrel stock, trading on the NASDAQ exchange, appreciated 18 percent during the first month after news of the scandal broke, and the stock remained strong throughout the next fiscal year, splitting three-for-two in the third quarter.

Dan Evins had good reason to believe that the firings and the boycott had not adversely impacted profitability. One market analyst said that "the feedback they get from their customers might be in favor of not hiring homosexuals." Another even ventured that "it's plausible . . . the majority of Cracker Barrel's local users support an explicit discriminatory policy." Such speculation was bolstered by social science surveys indicating that respondents from the South and from rural areas in particular tended to be less tolerant of homosexuality than were other Americans.

Queer Nationals looked to other measures of success, claiming at least partial victory in the battle. Many customers they met at picket lines and inside restaurants vowed to eat elsewhere. Coalitions were formed with a variety of civil rights, women's, labor, and peace and justice organizations. Most importantly, the media attention greatly heightened national awareness of the lack of protections for lesbians and gays on the job. As the boycott continued, increasing numbers of states, counties, and municipalities passed legislation designed to prevent employment discrimination based on sexual orientation.

THE OUTCOME: STAND-OFF CONTINUES

As the November 1992 annual meeting approached, Cracker Barrel requested that the Securities and Exchange Commission make a ruling on the resolution offered by the New York pension fund administrators. The resolution, according to Cracker Barrel, amounted to shareholder intrusion into the company's ordinary business operations. As such, it should be excluded from consideration at the annual meeting and excluded from proxy ballots sent out before the meeting. The SEC agreed, despite previous rulings in which it had allowed stockholder resolutions regarding race or gender based employment bias.

Acknowledging that frivolous stockholder inquiries had to be curtailed, the dissenting SEC commissioner nonetheless expressed great dismay: "To claim that the shareholders, as owners of the corporation, do not have a legitimate interest in management-sanctioned discrimination against employees defies logic." A noted legal scholar warned of the dangerous precedent that had been set: "Ruling an entire area of corporate activity (here, employee relations) off limits to moral debate effectively disenfranchises shareholders."

Thus, the stand-off continued. Queer Nation and its supporters persisted in the boycott. The Cracker Barrel board of directors and, with one exception, upper management remained all-white, all-male bastions. Lynn Cothren, Cheryl Summerville, and the other protestors arrested in Lithonia, Georgia, were acquitted on charges of criminal trespass. Jurors ruled that the protestors' legitimate reasons for peaceably demonstrating superseded the company's rights to deny access or refuse service. Charges stemming from the Union City, Georgia, demonstrations were subsequently dropped. Meanwhile, within weeks of the original policy against lesbian and gay employees, Cracker Barrel vice president for human resources William Bridges had left the company. Cracker Barrel declined comment on the reasons for his departure.

By 1996, Cracker Barrel annual net sales reached a billion dollars. The company still had not issued a complete retraction of its employment policy, and those employees fired were never offered their old jobs back. In contrast, for a year's work, chairman Dan Evins pulled in over a million dollars in salary, bonus, awards, and stock options; president Ronald Magruder, over four million.

As of Cracker Barrel's fiscal year-end, July 30, 1999, a total of 11 states and the District of Columbia offered protections for lesbians and gays on the job, both in the public and private sectors. With a total of 396 restaurants and 58 Logan's Roadhouse affiliates in 36 states, Cracker Barrel now operated in six of those states with protections: California, Connecticut, Massachusetts, Minnesota, New Jersey, and Wisconsin. (The other states with antidiscrimination statutes are Hawaii, Nevada, New Hampshire, Rhode Island, and Vermont.) Moreover, plans for expansion seemed destined to take the company into areas even less receptive to employment discrimination. As one business editor had correctly predicted, "Cracker Barrel isn't going to be in the South and Midwest forever. Eventually they will have to face the issue—like it or not."

THE PROPOSAL: FEDERAL LEGISLATION

In 39 states it is perfectly legal to fire workers because they are gay—or straight. For example, a Florida bar owner recently decided to target a lesbian and gay clientele and so fired the entire heterosexual staff. Queer activists boycotted, and the bar eventually was forced out of business. Still, for the vast majority of Americans, employment discrimination based on sexual orientation remains a constant threat.

The vast majority of Americans, 80 percent, tell pollsters that lesbians and gays should have equal rights in terms of job opportunities. In every region including the South, among both Democrats and Republicans, solid majorities support-federal legislation to remedy the situation. Nonetheless, despite several close votes in Congress, the Employment Non-Discrimination Act, or ENDA, has yet to be passed into law.

Although there are no federal laws to prevent discrimination based on sexual orientation, protections do exist for workers on the basis of religion, gender, national origin, age, disability, and race. Citing these civil rights statutes, the NAACP is supporting a group of employees and former employees in a class-action lawsuit against Cracker Barrel. The suit alleges that the company repeatedly discriminated against African-Americans in hiring, promotions, and firing practices. Further, African-American workers are said to have received less pay, to have been given inferior terms and conditions of employment, and to have been subjected to racial epithets and racist jokes, including one told by Dan Evins.

Discussion Questions

1. How could Cracker Barrel's policy statement have been well-intentioned?
2. What benefits did Cracker Barrel achieve by ridding itself of lesbian and gay employees? What were the disadvantages?
3. How should the perceived values of a customer base affect companies' personnel policies? In a large national corporation, should personnel policies be uniform across all operating units or should they be tailored by region according to local mores?

References

1. *Atlanta Journal-Constitution,* 6, 11 July 1993; 2, 3 April 1992; 29 March 1992; 4, 18, 20 January 1992; 9 June 1991; 3, 4, 5 March 1991.
2. Carlino, Bill. "Cracker Barrel Profits Surge Despite Recession." *Nation's Restaurant News,* 16 December 1991, 14.
3. — — —. "Cracker Barrel Stocks, Sales Weather Gay-Rights Dispute." *Nation's Restaurant News,* 1 April 1991, 14.
4. Cheney, Karen. "Old-Fashioned Ideas Fuel Cracker Barrel's Out-of-Sight Sales Growth and Profit Increases." *Restaurants & Institutions,* 22 July 1992, 108.
5. Cracker Barrel Old Country Store, Inc. *Annual Report,* 1999.
6. — — —. *Annual Report,* 1996.
7. — — —. Notice of Annual Meeting of Shareholders to Be Held on Tuesday, November 26, 1996; 25 October 1996.
8. — — —. *Third Quarter Report,* 30 April 1993.
9. — — —. *Second Quarter Report,* 29 January 1993.
10. — — —. *First Quarter Report,* 30 October 1992.
11. — — —. *Annual Report,* 1992.
12. — — —. Securities and Exchange Commission Form 10-K, 1992.
13. — — —. *Annual Report,* 1991.
14. — — —. Securities and Exchange Commission Form 10-K, 1991.
15. — — —. *Annual Report,* 1990.
16. "Cracker Barrel Hit by Anti-Bias Protests." *Nation's Restaurant News,* 13 April 1992, 2.
17. "Cracker Barrel Sued for Rampant Racial Discrimination in Employment." NAACP Press Release, 5 October 1999.
18. "Cracker Barrel's Emphasis on Quality a Hit with Travelers." *Restaurants and Institutions,* 3 April 1991, 24.
19. Dahir, Mubarak S. "Coming Out at the Barrel." *The Progressive,* June 1992, 14.
20. "Documented Cases of Job Discrimination Based on Sexual Orientation." Washington, DC: Human Rights Campaign, 1995.
21. Farkas, David. "Kings of the Road." *Restaurant Hospitality,* August 1991, 118–22.
22. Galst, Liz. "Southern Activists Rise Up." *The Advocate,* 19 May 1992, 54–57.
23. Greenberg, David. *The Construction of Homosexuality.* Chicago: University of Chicago Press, 1988.
24. Gutner, Toddi. "Nostalgia Sells." *Forbes,* 27 April 1993, 102–3.
25. Harding, Rick. "Nashville NAACP Head Stung by Backlash from Boycott Support." *The Advocate,* 16 July 1991, 27.
26. — — —. "Activists Still Press Tennessee Eatery Firm on Anti-Gay Job Bias." *The Advocate,* 9 April 1991, 17.
27. Hayes, Jack. "Cracker Barrel Protesters Don't Shake Loyal Patrons." *Nation's Restaurant News,* 26 August 1991, 3, 57.
28. — — —. "Cracker Barrel Comes Under Fire for Ousting Gays." *Nation's Restaurant News,* 4 March 1991, 1, 79.
29. "Investors Protest Cracker Barrel Proxy Plan." *Nation's Restaurant News,* 2 November 1992, 14.
30. *Larry King Live.* CNN television, aired 2 December 1991.
31. *Oprah Winfrey Show.* Syndicated television, aired January 1992.
32. Queer Nation. Documents on the Cracker Barrel Boycott. N.p., n.d.
33. "SEC Upholds Proxy Ruling." *Pensions and Investments,* 8 February 1993, 28.
34. Star, Marlene Givant. "SEC Policy Reversal Riles Activist Groups." *Pensions and Investments,* 26 October 1992, 33.
35. *The* (Nashville) *Tennesseean,* 27 February 1991.
36. *20/20.* ABC television, aired 29 November 1991.
37. Walkup, Carolyn. "Family Chains Beat Recession Blues with Value, Service." *Nation's Restaurant News,* 5 August 1991, 100, 104.
38. *The Wall Street Journal,* 9 March 1993; 2 February 1993; 26 January 1993; 28 February 1991.
39. Wildmoon, KC. "QN Members Allowed to Attend Cracker Barrel Stockholder's Meeting." *Southern Voice,* 10 December 1992, 3.
40. — — —. "Securities and Exchange Commission Side with Cracker Barrel on Employment Discrimination." *Southern Voice,* 22 October 1992, 1.
41. — — —. "DeKalb Drops Most Charges Against Queer Nation." *Southern Voice,* 9 July 1992, 3.

Notes

1. The material in this section is excerpted from chapter 1, "The Changing Landscape," in *Straight Talk about Gays in the Workplace: Creating an Inclusive, Productive Environment for Everyone in Your Organization, 3rd ed.* (Brighamton, NY: Harrington Park Press, 2005)

2. Not all the laws cover the same things in the same ways in each of the 14 states, but what they have in common is that they are all laws as opposed to executive orders, ordinances, or regulations and so carry the weight of litigation. I have chosen not to publish the names because it is likely that one or two more will be added to the list by the time this books appears, and just publishing numbers and percentages is difficult in this rapidly changing environment.

3. Witeck-Combs/Harris Interactive, "HRC Public Report," February 2004. Available online at www.witckcombs.com.

4. Witeck-Combs/Harris Interactive, "HRC Public Report."

5. Human Rights Campaign, "Gay Families Deserve Nothing Less Than Equality under the Law," January 22, 2004. Available online at www.hrc.org.

6. Frank Newport, "Iraq, Economy Remain Most Important Problems," Gallup News Service, Gallup Polls, December 13, 2004. Available online at www.gallup.com/polls.

7. Witeck-Combs/Harris Interactive, "6 of 10 Heterosexuals Say," 2003.

8. Human Rights Campaign, "Workplace." Available online at www.hrc.org/workplace.

9. Harris Interactive/Witeck-Combs, "New Harris Interactive/Witeck-Combs Internet Survey Confirms Gays and Lesbians Are among Heaviest Internet Users," April 2000. Available online at www.witeckcombs.com.

10. Statistics available online from the Gill Foundation at www.gillfoundation.com

11. Witeck-Combs/Harris Interactive, "HRC Public Report," 2004.

12. Richard Florida, "Gay-tolerant Societies Prosper Economically," *USA Today,* May 1, 2003, p. 13A.

13. The material in this section is excerpted from chapters 2, 6, 7, and 8 in Winfeld, *Straight Talk about Gays in the Workplace.*

14. Winfeld also includes education in this list; however, it is too expansive to cover in this essay. For more on this topic, please refer to chapters 4 and 5 in Winfeld, *Straight Talk about Gays in the Workplace.*

15. Alistair D. Williamson, "Is This Time Right to Come Out? *Harvard Business Review,* July 1, 1993, p. 43.

16. Society of Human Resources Management, "Human Resources Management Issues and Trends" (June 16) (Alexandria, VA: Society of Human Resources Management, 1999).

17. Overlooked Opinions Inc., "Mulryan/Nash-Simmons Market Research Report—Sexual Orientation and the Market," 1998.

18. Witeck-Combs/Harris Interactive, "The Gay and Lesbian Market: New Trends, New Opportunities," 2004. Available online at www.witeckcombs.com.

19. These figures are from the Selig Center for Economic Growth at the University of Georgia.

20. Unless otherwise noted, all research bulleted here comes from Witeck-Combs/Harris Interactive between 2001 and March 2004. Available online at www.witeckcombs.com.

21. A note about inclusive language: When I refer to this, I don't mean that organizations should stop using words such as husband or wife. There's nothing wrong with those words. A simple insertion of *partner* or, if you prefer, *significant other* signals to everyone that the organization is aware that, as of right now, not everyone has a husband or wife or even spouse as those terms are commonly understood today.

22. Parents, Families and Friends of Lesbians and Gays, available online at www.pflag.org.

23. The material in this section is excerpted from chapter 2, "Strategies for Inclusion in the New World," in Winfeld, *Straight Talk about Gays in the Workplace.*

8 DISABILITIES

The Americans with Disabilities Act of 1990 (ADA) includes protection from discrimination based on a disability as well as requirements regarding access and accommodations for disabled employees, vendors, and patrons. The ADA defines a disability as a physical or mental impairment that substantially limits one or more major life activities, which include walking, talking, breathing, seeing, hearing, learning, sitting, standing, lifting, sleeping, working, and caring for oneself.

Objectives

- To examine the relationship between people with disabilities and the workplace.

- To examine how to work most effectively with people with disabilities.

- To examine why people with disabilities are at a "critical disadvantage" when compared with people without disabilities.

- To examine successful programs and organizations creating accessibility for people with disabilities.

Preview Questions

- Why are people with disabilities at a critical disadvantage when compared with people without disabilities?

- How can organizations most effectively create accessibility within their companies for people with disabilities?

- Why might people with disabilities be unmotivated to apply for a job, and what disincentive might discourage employers from hiring a person with a disability?

- How can negative cultural assumptions and stereotypes of people with disabilities be managed at work?

Some Important Dates

1829   Louis Braille invents the raised-point alphabet that has come to be known as Braille.

1864   Institution for the Deaf and Dumb and Blind is authorized by the U.S. Congress to grant college degrees. It is the first college in the world established for people with disabilities.

1869   The first wheelchair patent is registered with the U.S. Patent Office.

1890–1920   Progressive activists push for the creation of state worker's compensation programs. By 1913, twenty-one states have established some form of worker's compensation; the figure rises to 43 by 1919.

1916   British Braille becomes the English language standard (although New York Point and American Braille are both being used in the United States) because of the wealth of code already available in the British Empire.

1921   The American Foundation for the Blind (AFB), a nonprofit organization recognized as Helen Keller's cause in the United States, is founded.

1927   The *Buck v. Bell* Supreme Court decision rules that forced sterilization of people with disabilities is not a violation of their constitutional rights. By the 1970s, over 60,000 disabled people are sterilized without their consent. Nationally, 27 states begin wholesale sterilization of "undesirables."

1935   The Social Security Act is passed. This law establishes federally funded old-age benefits and funds to states to assist blind individuals and disabled children. The act extends existing vocational rehabilitation programs.

1947   The President's Committee on National Employ the Physically Handicapped Week is held in Washington, DC. Publicity campaigns, coordinated by state and local committees, emphasize the competence of people with disabilities.

1960   Social Security amendments of 1960 eliminate the restriction that disabled workers receiving Social Security Disability Insurance (SSDI) benefits must be 50 or older.

1961   The American National Standards Institute, Inc. (ANSI) publishes American standard specifications for making buildings accessible to, and usable by, people with physical limitations.

1971   The National Center for Law and the Handicapped is founded at the University of Notre Dame, Indiana. It becomes the first legal advocacy center for people with disabilities in the United States.

1975   The Education of All Handicapped Children Act (PL 94-142) requires free, appropriate public education in the least restrictive setting. This act is later renamed The Individuals with Disabilities Education Act (IDEA).

1990   The Americans with Disabilities Act is signed into law.

BY TELECOMMUTING; THE DISABLED GET A KEY TO THE OFFICE, AND A JOB

About two years ago, NBC gave Ms. Pearce the option of working at home when she needed to, and today she splits her time, spending three days a week at the office and two at home. After 36 years at NBC, Ms. Pearce said she could not imagine leaving her job, even when she found herself overwhelmed by her disease, her medical appointments, the physical therapy, and the adjustment to a wheelchair.

"I never want to let work go," said Ms. Pearce, who climbed her way up from researcher to senior producer. "I was always very focused on work, very driven. I loved it since the day I started."

The American workplace has had to adapt to the passage of the Americans With Disabilities Act, which was signed into law in 1990. Offices and factories now contain accomodations like large-letter computer screens, elevators, wider doorways for wheelchairs, accessible work stations, and special parking spaces. But these improvements and modifications are useless if a disabled employee cannot get to work.

Telecommuting, either full time, part time, or over short periods when the need arises, is an important aid to disabled workers who struggle with a commute, and labor experts say the practice is on the rise among the disabled.

Douglas Kruse, a professor of human resource management at Rutgers University, estimates that 7 percent of employed people with disabilities currently work 20 hours or more a week from home, compared with 4.1 percent in 1997. He estimates that in 10 years, at least 10 percent of workers with disabilities will be telecommuting. The figure could rise as high as 20 percent, he said, "depending on technological developments and the success of efforts to increase the employment of people with disabilities, since many of those who are not currently employed will find this type of work attractive."

Many disabled workers say they consider telecommuting to be the single most important factor enabling them to work. Robert O'Byrne, a senior applications specialist for New York Life and a quadriplegic, said he would be on public assistance if his employer had not allowed him to work from home. Mr. O'Byrne was injured at 19 when he slipped on a swimming pool deck and hit his head. He was unable to hold any jobs because of his disability until New York Life gave him the telecommuting option.

Mr. O'Byrne, 41, who taught himself programming, goes to the office for occasional meetings, driven there by his father in a specially equipped van. But, he said, the hour-and-a-half commute from his home in Wyckoff, N.J., to the company's offices in Manhattan, would be too exhausting.

The job at New York Life "gave me a sense of purpose," he said. "Instead of being a ward of the state, I now pay taxes."

Many employers who have been offered telecommuting are happy with the arrangement. Bill Wheatley, a vice president for NBC News, said Ms. Pearce's telecommuting schedule, which was unusual for the network when it was put in place, is working out well for all concerned.

Mr. O'Byrne's employer, New York Life, offers telecommuting to all employees. Fe Azores, New York Life's director of recruiting, said she thought that telecommuting had contributed to the productivity of the company's disabled workers.

Christine McMahon, chief operating officer of Easter Seals in New York, New Hampshire and Vermont, said: "We haven't even begun to see the bubble on telecommuting among the disabled. It's going to be more and more available."

Earlier this year, the United States Equal Employment Opportunity Commission published a fact sheet (available online at www.eeoc.gov/facts/telework.html) describing situations where allowing

(continued)

disabled workers to work from home could be considered a reasonable accommodation under the Americans With Disabilities Act.

Sharon Rennert, senior attorney adviser of the A.D.A. division at the commission, said her office was getting a lot of questions from employers and from people with disabilities about when it was appropriate or necessary for companies to offer telecommuting options.

The key for each company, Ms. Rennert said, is whether the employee would clearly be unable to handle the job without telecommuting and whether the job was conducive to a work-at-home environment. Ms. Rennert stressed that decisions should be made on an individual basis between employer and employee.

Assuming the work can be done from home, the commission recommended that the companies allow disabled individuals to work at home, whether there is a formal program or not.

While Ms. Rennert said telecommuting was not a clear-cut requirement under the disabilities act, she said the fact sheet "puts it on the radar screen for employers."

Mark Cheskin, an employment lawyer in Miami with the firm of Morgan, Lewis & Bockius, said that in many employment cases, courts have been wary of the idea that telecommuting might be required under the disabilities act. But, he added, with the commission's recently published fact sheet and improvements in technology, "I believe we're going to see more courts go in favor of employees."

Advocates for disabled people say that telecommuting could help lower the jobless rate among this population. Only 3 out of 10 disabled people aged 18 to 64 are employed either full time or part time, compared with 8 out of 10 people without a disability, according to a 2000 survey by the National Organization on Disability and Harris Interactive.

"Telecommuting is a promising trend for the disabled and one way to get the unemployment rate down," said Professor Kruse of Rutgers. But he warned that it may not be appropriate for every disabled worker.

Many have no problem getting to the office, he said. Another concern is "that the disabled won't be in the mainstream of office life," he said. Telecommuters sometimes feel they are passed over for promotions or special projects because they lack face-to-face time with supervisors.

Still, for some disabled workers, telecommuting is the only option, said Donna Walters Kozberg, president of Lift, a job placement and training group for the disabled that helped Mr. O'Byrne find his job at New York Life.

She says she is happy to see employers becoming more accepting of the practice even in a tough economy. "This is a way firms can cut down on their overhead by reducing office space," she said. In addition, she said, high-speed Internet connections and improved computer security are making employers feel more comfortable with workers tapping into company networks from home.

Correction: July 24, 2003, Thursday An article on the front page of the Job Market section on Sunday about the use of telecommuting by disabled workers misstated the name of the disease that has caused Janet Pearce, a producer at NBC News, to split her time between home and office. It is multiple sclerosis, not muscular sclerosis.

ESSAY: SELECTIONS FROM *THE INCLUSIVE CORPORATION: A DISABILITY HANDBOOK FOR BUSINESS PROFESSIONALS*

Although most disabled people want no special treatment and greatly appreciate being treated the same as everyone else, there are occasions when it is helpful to know commonly accepted manners that promote inclusion.

The following suggestions are distilled from years of experience, many published treatments of the topic, and the suggestions of many individuals who are disabled. Please keep in mind that there are no hard and fast rules of disability etiquette, like other types of etiquette and people frequently disagree on optimal practices. For example, one authority cautions those meeting someone with a disability: "A handshake is NOT a standard greeting for everyone." Another source lists as one of its first precepts of communicating with people who have disabilities: "Offer to shake hands when introduced." When dining some people who are blind appreciate it when sighted companions describe the location of the food they are served ("The salmon is at 'six o'clock' on your plate; mashed potatoes are at nine.") Others consider such help to be a disability cliché. People can and do disagree on these practices. There are no universal rules.

The following are some useful tips, by no means all one could know on the subject, but some helpful information with which to start.

GENERAL CONSIDERATIONS

- Begin by imagining how you would like to be treated if you were the person with whom you are interacting.
- Interact with a person, not a disability. Do not pay more attention to the disability than is warranted.
- Do not assume anything. If you do not know, ask.
- Always speak to a disabled person directly, even if he or she is using an interpreter.
- Be patient and willing to learn. Be prepared to take a little extra time or exert a little extra effort.
- Offer assistance if it seems to be needed, and wait for your offer to be accepted before acting.
- Make effective communication a priority. Studies repeatedly show that social acceptance is the single most important factor in job success and employee satisfaction.
- Relax. A sincere commitment to including people with disabilities will compensate for most mistakes. A sense of humor should cover much of the rest.

Excerpted from *The Inclusive Corporation: A Disability Handbook for Business Professionals* by Griff Hogan. Reprinted with the permission of Swallow Press, Ohio University Press, Athens, Ohio.

INTERACTING WITH PEOPLE WHO HAVE MENTAL HEALTH–RELATED DISABILITIES

Considerations

- There are many types of mental and emotional illnesses. Some are severe, and others are relatively mild and more easily managed.
- Mental illness can be chronic or short-term. A large proportion of the population experiences some sort of mental illness at some time.
- Mental illness can be caused by biochemical, emotional, or environmental factors.
- There are many types of medication available to assist in the treatment of mental illness.
- The presence of mental illness or the fact that a person takes a psychoactive drug does not automatically preclude his or her being able to work.
- Some medications used to treat mental illness have side effects.
- Some individuals are uncomfortable talking about their illness.
- Mental illness is an example of an "invisible disability." For this reason, it is particularly important that the confidentiality of the individual involved be preserved.
- Mental illness is the disability most frequently encountered and dealt with in employment situations.

Suggestions for Interacting with People Who Have Mental Health–Related Disabilities

- Always discuss issues related to mental illness in private. A quiet location with no distractions is generally best.
- The dignity and autonomy of people with mental illness are sometimes undermined. Treat the individual with respect, and involve him or her in problem solving.
- Do not attempt to counsel the individual or provide therapy.
- In the workplace, behavioral policies must always apply to all. If training on mental illness is provided to employees, it should be provided to all and without reference to any specific person or incident. Make sure both trainers and training participants understand the importance of confidentiality and respect for coworkers.

INTERACTING WITH PEOPLE WHO HAVE PHYSICAL DISABILITIES AND MOBILITY LIMITATIONS

Considerations

- There are many reasons for a person to use a wheelchair, walker, crutches, brace, or other device. People with physical limitations have a wide range of capabilities, and may need assistance or assistive devices only at particular times, or not at all.

- Wheelchairs, walkers, canes, and other devices come in all shapes and sizes. Some wheelchairs are sleek and lightweight, others are quite heavy and cumbersome.
- Do not consider any space for which you are responsible (office, interview location, recreational area, etc.) to be physically accessible unless you know it to be the case.

Suggestions for Interacting with People Who Have Physical Disabilities and Mobility Limitations

- If you are unsure whether a person would like to shake hands, ask.
- Regard a wheelchair, cane, walker, or similar device as an extension of the person's body. Never lean on a person's wheelchair, or touch it without permission.
- If you are conversing with someone in a wheelchair for more than a few moments, use a chair so your face will be at eye level. If a chair is not available, kneel or crouch facing the person.
- When expecting someone who uses a wheelchair, see that a reasonably wide path is clear. Move aside a chair, or otherwise prepare a place for him or her to sit.
- Many people find standing for extended periods uncomfortable. When possible, provide places to sit and rest.

INTERACTING WITH PEOPLE WHO HAVE LEARNING DISABILITIES

Considerations

- Learning problems are a common disability.
- Learning disabilities affect how people process information, and may influence how they think, speak, write, read, listen, spell, or perform mathematical computations.
- There are a great number of types of learning disabilities. The stereotype of someone with a learning disability "reversing" the letters in a word is accurate for only a small minority of people.

Suggestions for Interacting with People Who Have Learning Disabilities

- If you need to know how a person with a learning disability best learns or works, begin by asking him or her.
- Be prepared to communicate in multiple formats: notes, written instructions, tape recordings, verbal directions, etc.
- Be prepared to allow a person with a learning disability to practice a new skill, or otherwise physically experience an action, rather than assuming he or she will understand just by reading or hearing about it.
- Say literally what you mean. Using subtleties such as intonation, humor, irony, or suggestion to communicate your message may be counterproductive.

- Encourage someone with a learning disability to work creatively and to develop productive nontraditional methods of working.

INTERACTING WITH PEOPLE WHO HAVE DEVELOPMENTAL DISABILITIES

Considerations

- There are many levels or intellectual deficiency, and intelligence is multi-faceted. Be willing to take time to understand how a person learns and prefers to communicate.
- All too often, adults with intellectual deficiencies are treated condescendingly or as children.
- Many people with developmental disabilities are extremely reluctant to discuss their learning problems. Some go to great lengths to "pass" as a person without a disability.
- Because of their previous experience, many people with intellectual limitations are particularly sensitive to signs of approval or disapproval. Your smile and undivided attention can pay great dividends.

Suggestions for Interacting with People Who Have Developmental Disabilities

- Avoid condescension and childish treatment.
- Keep your conversation simple.
- Avoid busy, noisy, or confusing environments in which to work and communicate.
- Do not hurry conversations or interactions.
- Be prepared to repeat or paraphrase, or to ask politely that a comment be repeated.
- When giving instructions, break them down into component steps.
- Encourage the use of aids that promote learning or remembering: charts, lists, colored folders, pictures, labels, etc.

INTERACTING WITH PEOPLE WHO HAVE HEARING IMPAIRMENTS

Considerations

- Some people, especially people born deaf, do not consider themselves to have a disability in the traditional sense. They regard deafness as a culture, and describe themselves as "Deaf" with a capital D.
- There are many different levels of hearing loss. Most people with hearing impairments have some hearing.
- Not all people who are deaf use sign language. Not all people who are deaf or hearing impaired can read lips or speak.
- Not all people with hearing impairments use hearing aids or augmentative devices. Those who do use them may not do so all the time.

- While many deaf and hearing-impaired people can read lips, the best lip readers can make out only about 35 percent of spoken words.
- Sign language has its own rules, customs, grammar, and idioms. It is not a simple translation of English.
- While a slight increase in volume may enhance your communication with some people who have hearing impairments, excessive volume is inappropriate and may cause feedback in hearing aids.

Suggestions for Interacting with People Who Have Hearing Impairments

- Find out the way in which the person prefers to communicate.
- To get a person's attention, tap him or her politely on the shoulder.
- Be prepared to use notes, or to communicate through an interpreter.
- Always look at the person with whom you are speaking, not the interpreter.
- If a person uses a hearing aid, avoid conversations in noisy, open areas. Do not shout. Speak clearly in a normal tone of voice.
- If a person reads lips, keep obstructions (smoking materials, hands, food, etc.) away from your face. Speak deliberately in short, simple sentences. Some simple gestures (nodding, shrugging shoulders) and facial expressions (furrowed brow, surprised look) may be helpful.
- Be patient and willing to repeat your message.

INTERACTING WITH PEOPLE WHO HAVE SPEECH IMPAIRMENTS

Considerations

- Many things can cause speech impairments, such as hearing loss, stroke, cerebral palsy, or traumatic head injury.
- People with speech impairments are frequently misperceived as intoxicated or mentally disabled.
- A person with a speech impairment may be easier to understand at particular times, and his or her speech may deteriorate with fatigue or in stressful situations.
- Successful communication can be a function of time: allowing time for a person to express himself or herself, allowing yourself time to understand. Eventually, you may be able to improve your receptive ability, and the speaker may be able to adjust to your listening style.

Suggestions for Interacting with People Who Have Speech Impairments

- If you do not understand what a person has said, ask politely for a repetition. Do not pretend you have understood when you haven't.
- An area with background noise or distractions may make communication more difficult. Consider moving to a quieter location.
- In meetings or group discussions, people with speech disabilities can have difficulty being heard. Help them by assuring that the group allows them an opportunity to speak.

- Do not attempt to speak for another person or finish his or her sentences.
- When necessary ask short, simple questions to confirm your understanding.
- If necessary, consider using written or some other form of communication.

INTERACTING WITH PEOPLE WHO HAVE VISUAL DISABILITIES

Considerations

- Levels of visual impairments range continuously from mild myopia to total blindness.
- Legal blindness is defined as 20/200 vision to the best correction.
- Many people who are considered blind do have some sight.
- Many people who are blind consider it to be more of an inconvenience than a disability.
- Although many blind people use Braille, most do not. Many use adaptive equipment such as text magnifiers and computers equipped with voice synthesis.

Suggestions for Interacting with People Who Have Visual Disabilities

- When you encounter a person with a visual impairment, introduce yourself or announce your presence and the names of those with you. Excuse yourself before you leave.
- Offer to describe the physical layout of a room, the position of food on a plate, and the names of other people present in a room.
- When guiding someone with a visual disability, do not grab him or her. Offer to be a "sighted guide." Let them take your arm; they will probably allow you to walk half a step ahead of them. Point out doors, curbs, stairs, and possible obstructions as you approach them.
- Don't pet or interact with a guide dog. The dog is working, and a vital part of its owner's safety and independence.
- Be aware that changing a physical environment (moving furniture, adding or deleting items, painting) can cause problems for someone with a visual disability. Inform the person of any alterations about which they should know.

GETTING STARTED

Anyone who has ever traveled in a foreign country knows that the natives tend to appreciate any effort by a visitor to understand their culture and speak their language. People who have disabilities also appreciate those who sincerely try to understand and communicate with them. That might involve something as simple as offering someone who is tired a place to sit down, or it could be as complex as taking lessons in sign language. The important thing is to make the effort.

Discussion Questions

1. Why are there no hard and fast rules about how to interact politely with people with disabilities?
2. When might it be rude rather than helpful to move someone in a wheelchair?
3. How can you avoid the common tendency to treat adults with developmental disability as if they were children?
4. Is sign language universal, or are their many sign languages like spoken language? Does sign language have slang?
5. What can you do to make sure that a person with a speech impairment contributes his or her ideas in a group meeting?
6. Is it inconsiderate to use expressions like "I see what you mean" or "see you later" to someone with vision impairment?
7. How might experience traveling in a foreign country help you interact with people with disabilities?

CASE STUDY: IN THE EYE OF THE PERFECT STORM: ORGANIZATIONS CREATING ACCESSIBILITY—BOOST, IBM, AND GM

At a BOOST, Inc. graduation we meet Darryl.

An exciting buzz of anticipation drifted through the audience as Darryl maneuvered his wheelchair into position near the front row of chairs. With a coordinated thrust from those muscular arms, he strained to lift his body to an upright position. The room grew quiet. As one foot was placed ahead of the other, beads of perspiration began to appear on Darryl's forehead . . . until he triumphantly arrived at the podium a few steps away. He stretched his arms wide in celebration. The gigantic smile on his face electrified his cheering peers.[1]

BOOST, the Business Organization and Occupation Service Training Program, trains people with disabilities for specific jobs within sponsoring organizations. Darryl's graduation from BOOST was indeed an accomplishment, not only because he was experiencing the advancing effects of polio but because in completing the BOOST training program, he was about to attain one of his lifelong goals: a long-term career at an established organization. In Darryl's case, the organization was Discover Card—a BOOST sponsor—where he has now worked for seven years.

Darryl's experience is an exception to the difficult situation facing people with disabilities who want to obtain and retain a long-term career. Why do so few organizations choose to work hand-in-hand with organizations—like BOOST—that have the simple yet significant goal of helping qualified people with disabilities get good jobs? Why are internal models of accessibility so rare in established organizations? The answer to these questions is that people with disabilities must face a seemingly unyielding obstacle: "the perfect storm."

The perfect storm is, in this case, the intersection of three systems of discrimination for people with disabilities: an inadequate social structure; relentless, negative

Authors: Dr. Kathryn A. Cañas and Dr. Harris Sondak, The University of Utah stereotypes; and a two-sided disincentive to enter the workforce. The strength of the perfect storm creates a situation in which people with disabilities are, in many instances, at a disadvantage when compared with people without disabilities.

A "CRITICAL DISADVANTAGE"

Americans with disabilities constitute an estimated 49 million people, or 20 percent of the population. In other words, one in every five people has a disability, and as some experts estimate, there is an 80 percent chance that an average person will experience some kind of disability in the course of his or her lifetime. Even with the likelihood that so many people will be in this group, Americans with disabilities are, according to the 2004 National Organization on Disability/Harris Survey, still at a "critical disadvantage" when compared with nondisabled Americans.[2] The following statistics reflect this disadvantage:

- Thirty-five percent of people with disabilities report being employed full or part time, compared with 78 percent of those who do not have disabilities.
- People with disabilities are three times as likely to live in poverty with annual household incomes below $15,000 (26 percent versus 9 percent).
- People with disabilities remain twice as likely to drop out of high school compared with people without disabilities (21 percent versus 10 percent).
- People with disabilities are twice as likely to have inadequate transportation (31 percent versus 13 percent), and a much higher percentage go without needed health care (18 percent versus 7 percent).
- People with disabilities are less likely to socialize, eat out, or attend religious services than their nondisabled counterparts.
- Life satisfaction for people with disabilities trails, with only 34 percent saying they are very satisfied compared with 61 percent of those without disabilities.
- People with disabilities are much more worried about their future health and well-being. Half are worried about not being able to care for themselves or being a burden to their families, compared with a quarter of other Americans.[3]

Alan A. Reich, National Organization on Disability president, expresses his concern about these findings: "Progress is too slow" and the "gaps are still too large." These statistics are important, Reich explains, because "everyone knows people with disabilities; and anyone can acquire a disability at any time. Everyone has a stake in these findings."[4]

Also contributing to this critical disadvantage is that emergency planning is insufficient for people with disabilities. According to a recent nationwide Harris Interactive survey of emergency managers in states and cities throughout the nation, 69 percent of emergency managers said that they had incorporated the needs of people with disabilities into their emergency plans. Although this percentage may seem adequate, other findings proved more troublesome: Only 54 percent of the emergency managers had plans for dealing with schools for students with disabilities; 59 percent said they did not have plans for pediatric populations with disabilities; and 76 percent said that they did not have a paid expert to deal with emergency preparedness for people with disabilities.[5]

The critical disadvantage is thus based on a number of elements: employment, transportation, health insurance, concerns about the future, general life satisfaction, and emergency planning. When people with disabilities constitute such a high percentage and when other minority groups are making significant strides toward equality, why are people with disabilities at such a critical disadvantage? One possible answer—the perfect storm.

THE PERFECT STORM

The perfect storm gains its strength from three interconnecting systems of discrimination. The first is the inadequate social structure for people with disabilities; the second is a set of pervasive cultural assumptions about hiring people with disabilities; and the third is a two-sided disincentive for both employee and employer. The power of this triple threat and the damage it leaves behind is reflected in the many lives that are diminished by it.

Inadequate Social Structure

Activism on behalf of the disabled is relatively new, and this movement's lack of historical roots contributes to its relatively weak institutional structure. Women and African Americans, by contrast, have developed protective social structures formalized by laws such as Title VII of the Civil Rights Act, affirmative action, and the Pregnancy Discrimination Act. Further, organizations such as the National Association for the Advancement of Colored People (NAACP) and the National Organization for Women (NOW) represent legitimate and powerful vehicles for social change.

People with disabilities are just beginning to experience some workplace equality since the passage of the Americans with Disabilities Act (ADA) in 1990, and educational equality with the Individuals with Disabilities Education Act Amendments of 1997 (IDEA). Without long-standing laws and experienced organizations to protect the rights of people with disabilities, the disability rights movement remains less influential than other civil rights efforts, thus making the crusade for social justice a more difficult process.

Contributing to the challenge of creating a strong social structure for people with disabilities is the extensive diversity represented among members of the disabled community. The life experiences of people with spinal cord injuries or muscular dystrophy, for example, are different from those of people with learning disabilities or who are HIV-positive. Furthermore, people who are deaf, a condition that is classified by the ADA as a disability, often do not consider themselves to be disabled.

Further complicating the situation is the confusion about what conditions are considered disabilities protected by the ADA. The ADA makes it clear that when determining whether or not a specific condition is a disability, the question is always the same: Does the diagnosable condition substantially limit one or more major life activities (i.e., walking, seeing, hearing, speaking, breathing, learning, sitting, standing, etc.)? Even with this legal standard in place, there is still debate surrounding the ADA: Do people with cancer or severe diabetes qualify under the ADA? At what point during an individual's condition do people who are addicted to alcohol or drugs, severely depressed, or HIV-positive qualify under the ADA?

Understanding and managing these issues may help people with disabilities strengthen their movement's social and institutional structure and, as a result, gain more access to and influence within the public arena. Because the disability rights movement represents a youthful, fluid, and diverse effort, gaining a legitimate voice and communicating a unified message will, of course, be difficult. Compounding the inadequate social structure for people with disabilities is a cultural mythology based on a trio of damaging assumptions about the disabled.

Cultural Assumptions about Hiring People with Disabilities

Stereotypes, attitudes that make assumptions about whole groups of people, often distort reality and disempower individuals in their daily lives. American culture and attitudes make assumptions that lead managers not to hire people with disabilities. Although each of the following assumptions—people with disabilities are unreliable, expensive, and likely to sue their company—is indeed damaging on its own, together the assumptions constitute a pervasive cultural mythology that erects barriers to employment that are likely to harm both people with disabilities and their potential employers.

Assumption 1: People with Disabilities are Unreliable

Unsurprisingly, virtually all people with disabilities want to live as fulfilling a life as possible; for them, like for most people, a positive experience in the workplace typically translates to a more optimistic outlook on life. As Dr. Norma Carr-Ruffino, a leading expert in workplace diversity, explains: Most people with disabilities "want to work, regardless of the extent of their impairment, and see work as a major route to self-fulfillment. They want to find work that draws on their skills and talents and helps them live a more abundant life."[6] Challenging the perception that employees with disabilities are frequently sick is the fact that people who are disabled tend to have better-than-average attendance and turnover records.[7] Fraser Nelson, Executive Director of the Disability Law Center of Salt Lake City, reminds us that "being disabled is not an illness, it is a condition; understanding this distinction is important to discrediting the assumption that being disabled translates to taking more sick days."[8]

Workers with disabilities are often cast—albeit incorrectly—as less productive than their coworkers without disabilities. According to studies, employers have not only expressed more favorable attitudes toward employing persons with severe disabilities in the workplace but also viewed workers with severe disabilities as dependable, productive workers who can interact socially and foster positive attitudes on the part of their coworkers.[9] In addition, 50 percent of managers rate their employees with disabilities higher than those who are not disabled on the following dimensions: willingness to work hard, reliability, punctuality, and attendance.[10] Although the reality is that workers with disabilities are just as dependable as their coworkers, the stereotype of being unreliable is insidious and persists deep within American attitudes. This stereotype makes it easy for managers to make the next assumption—that workers with disabilities are costly—without carefully evaluating the reality.

Assumption 2: Accommodating People with Disabilities in the Workplace Is Costly

Evaluating whether accommodating people with disabilities is expensive is difficult and complex. There is some evidence that accommodating those with disabilities has made them more expensive to hire, but the reliability of the data showing this trend is disputed. Moreover, there is also evidence that suggests that hiring people with disabilities not only costs relatively little but can be a savvy business decision.

According to the National Organization on Disability, a study that surveyed companies employing people with disabilities found that only 24 percent reported that any accommodations were needed. In addition, among companies that did indeed provide accommodations, "for 34 percent of businesses the average cost was $100 or less, and for 71 percent of businesses it was $500 or less. Forty-six percent of accommodations were simple things like providing a ramp or adapting a desk to fit a wheelchair." In a separate survey of employers who used the U.S. Department of Labor's Job Accommodation Network, 71 percent reported that "the cost of accommodation was $500 or less on average." This study also reflected the fact that "[a] dollar spent on accommodations leads to an estimated $35 dollars in benefits."[11]

Echoing these results is evidence reported by National Public Radio science correspondent Joseph Shapiro which indicated that 51 percent of all accommodations cost nothing; and for the other 49 percent, the average cost of an accommodation was $300. Interestingly, the study also highlighted that less than 1 percent of accommodations cost $5,000 or more.[12] To help buttress substantial costs that organizations may have to absorb, tax incentives are often available.

However, some researchers argue that employment rates among people with disabilities declined after the passage of the ADA, despite its prohibitions against discrimination in hiring, suggesting that employers are reluctant to spend even the relatively small amounts required to accommodate these potential workers.[13] Whether this decline is real or merely apparent is a controversial issue and depends on how researchers define such complicated concepts as "disability" and "employment" and how they account for the effects of disability insurance and Social Security. In any case, it may be that because many accommodations are fixed costs, the expenses associated with accommodating disabled people will decline in years to come. For example, constructing a ramp for the use of its first employee who uses a wheelchair is a cost that a firm will not have to duplicate for subsequent hires.

In light of the ambiguity about whether accommodating disabled employees is in fact costly, it is premature to assume that this is true. The negative impact of this assumption is further compounded by another, that employees with disabilities are likely to sue their employer.

Assumption 3: People with Disabilities Are Likely to Sue their Employer

When employers believe that they may be sued if they decide to fire an employee with a disability, it is not surprising that qualified, disabled job candidates do not get hired. The employers' rationale is simple: Why take the unnecessary risk of being sued? But this perceived risk begs the question whether there is in fact excessive litigation against companies for discriminating against employees with disabilities.

According to DiversityInc.com, over the past decade, employees and potential employees have "brought charges against companies citing discrimination based on disabilities associated with conditions ranging from alcoholism and epilepsy to multiple sclerosis and the HIV virus."[14] More specifically, more than $436 million has been paid in settlements to more than 31,000 people, and another $28.1 million was paid in court-ordered fines through 491 ADA cases brought by the Equal Employment Opportunity Commission (EEOC) from 1993 through 2002.[15] What are the issues underlying this litigation, and is the fear of being sued a legitimate concern for employers?

According to Supreme Court Justice Sandra Day O'Connor, the high court's heavy load of disability-rights cases is the result of holes in the ADA. Although the original goal of the ADA was to help introduce qualified people with disabilities into the workplace, it is so complex and ambiguous that it creates uncertainty among employers about how to comply with a law with continually changing interpretation and enforcement. O'Connor explains that the ADA was written and passed hurriedly by Congress: "It's an example of what happens when . . . the sponsors are so eager to get something passed that what passes hasn't been as carefully written as a group of law professors might put together." And as a result, "it leaves lots of ambiguities and gaps and things for courts to figure out."[16]

Lawsuits brought by employees against their employers are indeed expensive for firms, but the portion of these costs attributable to the ADA is very difficult to determine. It is possible that fear of being sued for wrongful termination leads to decreased hiring of people with disabilities.[17] Research suggests, however, that even if there has been a decline in employment rates of people with disabilities since the passage of the ADA, its likely explanation is not primarily fear of litigation but rather the costs of accommodation.[18]

It is important for employers to understand that although the ADA protects people with disabilities from workplace discrimination, it also protects the employer who hires people with disabilities. First, employers do not have to hire individuals with disabilities who are not qualified for the job, nor do they have to give preference to persons with disabilities over other applicants. Second, employers are not required to make accommodations that would cause them undue hardship, in other words, when the accommodations are excessively expensive or interfere with a business imperative. Third, if a person does not identify himself or herself as having a disability, employers generally do not have to make any accommodation unless the disability is obvious. Finally, the ADA provides some subsidies for hiring disabled workers.

Disincentives

The third source of discrimination is the complexity of the American health care and insurance systems as they relate to people with disabilities. Why would a firm seek an employee whose participation in its health insurance plan will raise its costs? Conversely, why would a person with a disability assume a position in a company that may not provide affordable or adequate health insurance, or risk losing disability benefits because the salary surpasses the amount sanctioned by the federal government?

Social Security Disability Insurance (SSDI) and Supplemental Security Income (SSI) are the two options through which people with disabilities may obtain public insurance. People with general disabilities who make more than $830 per month, or $1380 per month if they are blind, are not eligible for these public programs.[19] Employer-provided insurance is an alternative to SSDI and SSI, so in deciding whether to be employed a person with disabilities must consider the costs of health care and insurance against the benefits of working.

Furthermore, rising health care costs make it especially expensive for employers to employ people with disabilities. To contain their costs, most companies have passed on an increasing share of the costs for health insurance to employees and have selected plans with many use restrictions.[20] This situation has thus created a two-sided disincentive: First, employers may be more reluctant to hire people with high-cost medical conditions; and second, people with disabilities may not be as interested in entering the workforce if they risk losing their benefits without an adequate substitute provided by their employers.

According to Diane D. Russell, Director of the Governor's Committee on Employment of People with Disabilities in the state of Utah, deciding how to navigate these economic issues "can become so complicated that there are programs specifically for people who are receiving Social Security Disability Benefits and would like information on how work may affect their benefits."[21] She explains that in such a program, a benefits planner will meet people with disabilities and review their situations to help determine if and how they can go to work and not lose benefits, particularly health benefits.

The perfect storm, as discussed here, consists of three systems of discrimination that combine to create a situation that positions people with disabilities at a critical disadvantage. To help guide both employers and people with disabilities through this seemingly insurmountable storm is the mission of BOOST, Inc.

CREATING ACCESSIBILITY AS AN INTERMEDIARY: BOOST, INC.

The perfect storm has created a situation in which people with disabilities who are looking to attain meaningful employment face a unique problem. Some view this problem as essentially a disconnect between the qualified potential employee with a disability and the employer who is fearful of hiring someone with a disability.

Unafraid to tackle this disconnect, and act as intermediaries, are a number of organizations led by individuals dedicated to bridging this gap and improving lives.[22] An example of such an individual is Debbie Inkley, the inspired founder and president of BOOST, Inc. Motivated by past personal experiences, Inkley is directly responsible for the incredible success of the 8-week BOOST Program, which boasts more than 3,500 graduates internationally, with 65 percent now employed by established organizations worldwide. BOOST's growth is impressive, as it has spread quickly across the country—from Utah and Arizona to Ohio, Illinois, Delaware—and even internationally, to Scotland.

The BOOST Program defines itself as "a business, community, and volunteer-based program that provides opportunity for employment through customer service and other skills training to people with physical, emotional, financial, and domestic challenges."[23] The BOOST goal is simple: to provide people with disabilities the opportunity to obtain "[r]eal jobs with competitive pay and the opportunity for advancement."[24]

Inkley emphasizes that the participants are certified in a "customer-focused curriculum which will foster and improve employment potential."[25] The BOOST curriculum teaches the following: computer skills such as MS Word, Excel, and PowerPoint; communication skills such as business writing, problem solving, public speaking, and interpersonal communication; customer service and sales skills; and career development skills such as résumé writing, mock interviews, and goal setting. Also included in the BOOST curriculum are business math and basic financial literacy, and just as important, sessions in self-confidence and self-worth.

Participants discover the BOOST Program through a variety of sources; they are often referred by employees from the sponsoring company or are recommended by community organizations such as churches, schools, and local and state government agencies. Prior to enrolling in the program, all applicants are prescreened and interviewed by the BOOST administrative team. To gain entrance into the program, participants must commit to attending every session, supply their own transportation to the classes, and have obtained or be currently working on a high school diploma or GED. Between 8 to 12 students are accepted into each class, and the program fills up quickly. At the end of each course, a job fair is held where business partners, along with the sponsoring company, have the opportunity to hire the graduates.

Although participants are from varying backgrounds with a wide range of challenges, Inkley claims that a "synergy" that "transcends differences" develops in which participants "learn from each other" and "support each other" with the end result being "unique friendships" that are cultivated from the experience. And as the participants become more independent through the program, they develop "a vast increase in self-esteem and self-confidence."[26]

In sum, BOOST is an across-the-board "win" for participants, community, and employer.[27] First, participants gain marketable skills as well as confidence and self-respect. Second, community and government agencies are more successful through participant training and job placement with help from the private sector. There is no cost to referring agencies; BOOST is funded totally by the sponsoring company. Third, the employer receives a pool of qualified prospective employees from a previously untapped source, thereby gaining insight into diversity as a competitive advantage as well as creating a more inclusive workforce.

CREATING ACCESSIBILITY FROM WITHIN: IBM AND GM

Utilizing an organization that acts as a bridge between employer and employee, like BOOST, Inc., is one way to help people with disabilities navigate the perfect storm. A second is for organizations to embrace accessibility through an in-house or internal approach. Although very few companies do this effectively, two examples of innovative, impressive models of recruiting, hiring, and retaining employees with disabilities are International Business Machines Corporation (IBM) and General Motors (GM).

IBM

IBM's history of employing people with disabilities dates to 1914, when IBM hired its first employee with a disability, 76 years before the ADA was enacted.[28] At IBM today, people with disabilities make up approximately 2 to 3 percent of the company's staff of more than 355,000. Nearly half of these employees with disabilities are working in technology positions such as electrical engineer, IT architect, or software programmer.[29]

Because IBM's model of accessibility is uniquely comprehensive, it could become a model for other companies to emulate. IBM's progressive philosophy on accessibility is to create and maintain

> a holistic, end-to-end approach to accessibility. Accessibility . . . means going beyond product compliance with regulations to include a better user experience and the vision to ultimately improve a person's total quality of life. We see this as a global journey to gain business advantage. A journey that begins with accessible technology infrastructure and ends with business transformation.[30]

On a philosophical level, IBM's mission is poignant. And when the mission is translated to a practical level—specifically in terms of internships, recruitment, accommodations, and the IBM Accessibility Center—we see that IBM is indeed enacting its vision.

An IBM internship program called Entry Point provides an opportunity for students with disabilities to get on-the-job experience in their majors and learn about the myriad of careers IBM offers nationwide. Project View and Project Able are two recruiting programs that reach outstanding college candidates of diverse backgrounds including people with disabilities. As a direct result of Project Able, which was launched in 1999, 84 college students and 139 professionals with disabilities have been hired at IBM.[31]

Internally, IBM provides a range of accommodations and assistive devices for employees who have disabilities. IBM has

- constructed ramps, power doors, parking facilities, and other accommodations to provide access for people with impaired mobility;
- captioned videotapes and provided sign language interpreters and note takers for classes and meetings for employees who are deaf or hard of hearing;
- recorded company publications on audiocassettes for employees and retirees who are visually impaired;
- provided adaptive services or modifications to enable people with disabilities to use work-related equipment (e.g., screen readers and display-screen magnifiers; keyboard guards and special switches; real-time captioning of meetings and Webcasts; telecommunications devices and telephone amplifiers);
- provided travel assistance for employees with mobility impairments.[32]

In addition to assisting their employees, 5 years ago IBM merged existing accessibility groups to form a worldwide Accessibility Center with locations in the United States, Europe, Japan, and Australia. The Center "fosters product accessibility, works toward the harmonization of worldwide standards, applies research technologies to solve problems experienced by people with disabilities, creates industry-focused solutions, and generates accessibility awareness."[33]

IBM's Director of Diversity Communications Jim Sinocchi states: "We consider diversity strategic to our organization. We don't hire people who are disabled just because it's a nice thing to do. We do it because it's the right thing to do from a business standpoint."[34] Sinocchi, who broke his neck while surfing on a vacation 20 years ago, speaks freely about his experiences as a paraplegic, "The problem is that people equate disability with stupidity. When I go out to dinner, the waiter won't ask me what I want. He'll ask the people I'm with what I want to have. This pervasive attitude must be broken for disabled workers to make a full contribution to society."[35] With its serious commitment to accessibility, IBM works daily to break this prejudice.

General Motors

Like IBM, GM understands the value of hiring people with disabilities. The GMability philosophy maintains that

> GM has long been committed throughout its global operations to hiring people with varied backgrounds. This hiring practice is the right thing to do, but just as important, it creates a competitive advantage for GM. Having a workforce that reflects the marketplace helps GM more effectively reach customers and provide products and services they want.[36]

Gary Talbot, a member of the U.S. Access Board, works as a vehicle systems engineer at the GM headquarters. According to Talbot, "With GM, if they decide that they want you as an employee, there isn't anything they won't do to help you succeed."[37] Reflecting its respect for its employees and their value to the company, GM responds expeditiously to requests and concerns and goes well beyond what is legally required or typically provided. For example, when Talbot suggested that the company replace the newly installed refrigerators in the 38 break rooms with side-by-side models so employees using wheelchairs could reach their food, GM quickly made the necessary improvements. In a second example, when Talbot's office did not fit his wheelchair, the company remodeled it twice before they reached the correct configuration.[38]

One of GM's strengths is its open communication between employer and employee. As Talbot explains: "Workplaces need to provide cultures in which employees feel they can be honest about their needs."[39]

Many of the improvements for GM employees with disabilities came through suggestions from the company's Affinity Group for People with Disabilities. This Affinity Group—which consist of GM employees and retirees who meet once a month to discuss accessibility issues in the workplace—acts as a link between diverse employee groups and management and is formed around "employee initiatives" and is "employee-driven." The primary goal of these groups is "to create professional development opportunities for their members and to serve as an information resource to the Corporation on issues that affect that constituency."[40]

In addition, GM is reinforcing its commitment to provide transportation solutions for people with disabilities. GM's Sit-N-Lift seat—a fully motorized, rotating lift-and-lower passenger seat that makes it easier for people with disabilities to enter and exit the vehicle—is being expanded beyond the Chevrolet Venture and Pontiac Montana vehicle lines to include the new Chevrolet Uplander, Pontiac Montana SV6, Buick Terraza and Saturn RELAY crossover sport vans.[41]

As illustrated here, there are two approaches to embracing accessibility in the workplace: the first is to work in tandem with an outside program to bring qualified, motivated employees with disabilities into the workplace; the second is to work from within to create innovative models of recruiting and retaining employees with disabilities. Both of these approaches offer people with disabilities the opportunity not only to navigate the perfect storm but to conquer it by moving forward with an organization that creates real opportunities and an inclusive environment.

DARRYL AND THE BOOST PROGRAM

Earlier, we met BOOST graduate Darryl, who is an example of someone who was empowered by a training program and a sponsoring organization that embraced accessibility. Although the BOOST graduation was indeed one of Darryl's proudest moments, his life had not always been so uplifting.

Finding the BOOST Program symbolized not only Darryl's final attempt at finding meaningful work but his final attempt to create a meaningful life for himself. "Darryl was searching for something to hang onto while surrounded by intense bigotry, out of control diabetes, the advancing effects of polio, and the increasing bouts of depression."[42] After entering the BOOST Program:

> Darryl quickly moved from a feeling of isolation and depression to a sense of being appreciated and respected. He became very popular with his BOOST classmates and Discover Card employees as his charismatic personality blossomed in the work environment. 'You actually feel you can accomplish something,' Darryl believes. 'It's extremely meaningful. I didn't see people looking or staring; I just got a kick out of that. So, it relaxes you enough to where you feel that you can accomplish something without having to second-guess yourself and you can just go ahead and do it.'[43]

Discussion Questions

1. According to the HOD/Harris survey, people with disabilities are at a "critical disadvantage" when compared with people without disabilities. Why, do you think, is this the case, when legislation such as the ADA was passed in 1990 in an attempt to improve the lives of people with disabilities?

2. What are the various provisions of the two most significant pieces of legislation for people with disabilities: the ADA and the IDEA?

3. What can society in general and people with disabilities in particular do to change the cultural assumptions that cast people with disabilities as unreliable, expensive, and likely to sue their employer?
4. Why haven't other companies followed the lead of those organizations, like IBM, that have effectively embraced disabilities as a significant component of diversity—viewing the recruitment and the retention of people with disabilities as a competitive advantage?

Notes

1. Debbie Inkley and Dale Inkley, *Dignity* (Denver, CO: Paros Press, 2003), 13.
2. "Landmark Disability Survey Finds Pervasive Disadvantage: 2004 N.O.D./Harris Survey Documents Trends Impacting 54 Million Americans," June 25, 2005, http://www.nod.org/content.cfm?id=1537. Other Web sites that provide insight into the situation facing Americans with disabilities are http://www.adaportal.org; http://www.ilr.cornell.edu/ped/DisabilityStatistics/; http://www.dsc.ucsf.edu/main.php; and http://www.worksupport.com/Main/factsres.asp.
3. "Landmark Disability Survey Finds Pervasive Disadvantage."
4. Ibid.
5. "Survey on Emergency Preparedness for People with Disabilities: Survey Reveals Gaps in Emergency Preparedness for People with Disabilities," November 10, 2004, http://www.nod.org; Final report, http://www.nod.org/content.cfm?id=1586#episurvey.
6. Norma Carr-Ruffino, *Diversity Success Strategies* (Boston: Butterworth-Heinemann, 1999), 241. See also Norma Carr-Ruffino, *Managing Diversity: People Skills for a Multicultural Workplace* (New Jersey: Pearson Custom Publishing, 2003).
7. R. Greenwood and V. A. Johnson. "Employer Perspectives on Workers with Disabilities," *Journal of Rehabilitation* 53 (1987): 37–46 as quoted in Taylor Cox, *Cultural Diversity in Organizations* (San Francisco: Berrett-Koehler, 1993), 90.
8. Fraser Nelson, Executive Director of the Salt Lake City Disability Law Center, personal interview, October 13, 2004.
9. J. M . Levy, D. J. Jessop, A. Rimmerman, F. Francis, and F. & P. H. Levy. "Determinants of Attitudes of New York State Employers towards the Employment of Persons with Severe Handicaps," *Journal of Rehabilitation* 59, no. 1 (1993): 49–54, in Darlene D. Unger, "Employers' Attitudes toward Persons with Disabilities in the Workforce: Myths or Realities?" *Focus on Autism and Other Developmental Disabilities* 17, no. 1 (2002), http://www.worksupport.com/Main/proed17.asp.
10. Carr-Ruffino, *Diversity Success Strategies,* 242.
11. Seth Egert, "EEOC Forum Addresses Disability in the Workplace," March 16, 2004, http://www.nod.org/content.cfm?id=1501.
12. Joseph Shapiro, *No Pity: People with Disabilities Forging a New Civil Rights Movement* (New York: Times Books, 1993), as quoted in Carr-Ruffino, *Diversity Success Strategies,* 254.
13. Thomas DeLeire, "The Americans with Disabilities Act and the Employment of People with Disabilities," in David C. Stapleton and Richard V. Burkhauser, eds., *The Decline in Employment of People with Disabilities: A Policy Puzzle* (Kalamazoo, Michigan: W. E. Upjohn Institute for Employment Research, 2003), 259–77.
14. Angela D. Johnson, "Americans with Disabilities Act: Is Your Company Compliant?" DiversityInc.com, July 28, 2003, http://diversityinc.com/public/5343.cfm.
15. Ibid.
16. "Justice Sandra Day O'Connor Pokes Holes in Americans with Disabilities Act," DiversityInc.com, March 14, 2002, www.diversityinc.com/members/2575.com. For more information on the ADA, see http://www.eeoc.gov/facts/adaqa1.html.
17. Burkhauser and Stapleton, "A Review of the Evidence and Its Implications for Policy Change," in *The Decline in Employment of People with Disabilities,* 369–405.

18. Daron Acemoglu and Joshua Angrist, "Consequences of Employment Protection: The Case of the Americans with Disabilities Act." *Journal of Political Economy* 109, no. 5 (2001): 915–56.

19. The Work Site—Social Security Online, http://www.socialsecurity.gov/work/Resources Toolkit/redbook_page.html.

20. Burkhauser and Stapleton, "Introduction," in *The Decline in Employment of People with Disabilities,* 12–13. See also Nanette Goodman and Timothy Waidmann, "Social Security Disability Insurance and the Recent Decline in the Employment Rate of People with Disabilities," in *The Decline in Employment of People with Disabilities.*

21. Diane D. Russell, Director of the Governor's Committee on Employment of People with Disabilities in the State of Utah, personal interview, December 22, 2004.

22. Additional examples of organizations that provide a variety of services and information for individuals with disabilities include AbilityNet, Access Hall County, Advocacy and Resource Center, American Association of People with Disabilities, Black Hills Workshop and Training Center, Council for Disability Rights, Disabled Businesspersons Association, Disabled Living Foundation (DLF), Easter Seals, Elwyn, Inc., Goodwill Industries, Job Accommodations Network, LifeStream, Inc., New Horizons Un-Limited, Over the Rainbow Association, People First, People with Disabilities Foundation, Triangle Inc., Whole Access, WORK Inc., and Work Ability.

23. BOOST, Inc. "BOOST Informational Packet: The Premier Source for Companies Helping People Help Themselves," 2004. For more on BOOST, Inc. see the BOOST, Inc. Web site: http://www.boostinc.com; Joan Leotta, "Discover: Giving Ability a Boost," Solutions Marketing Group, April 12, 2004, http://www.disability-marketing.com/profiles/boost.php4;

Kelly J. P. Lindberg, "Ready, Disabled and Willing: Providing Business with a Stable Non-Traditional Workforce, *Utah Business,* April 2004, 52–53.

24. "BOOST Informational Packet," 2004.

25. Ibid.

26. Debbie Inkley, personal interview, October 15, 2004.

27. Ibid.

28. "Accessibility at IBM: An Integrated Approach; Evolving from Philanthropy to Business Transformation," http://www-306.ibm.com/able/access_ibm/execbrief.html#evolving.

29. Joe Mullich, "Hiring without Limits," *Workforce Management,* June 2004, http://www.workforce.com/section/09/feature/23/74/24/.

30. "Accessibility at IBM."

31. Mullich, "Hiring without Limits."

32. "Accessibility at IBM."

33. Ibid.

34. Mullich, "Hiring without Limits."

35. Ibid.

36. "Gmability Philosophy," http://www.gm.com/company/gmability/workplace/400_diversity/index.html.

37. Jennifer Gatewood, "Above and Beyond," *Human Resource Executive Magazine,* September 2004, http://www.hreonline.com/HRE/storylink.jsp?storyId=4222745.

38. Ibid.

39. Ibid.

40. Life@GM./Benefits. "Affinity Groups," http://www.gm.com/company/careers/life/lif_benefits_affinity.html.

41. "OnStar Improves Accessibility for People with Disabilities," *Road and Travel.* July 26, 2004, http://www.roadandtravel.com/oempages/onstar/hardofhearing.htm.

42. Inkley and Inkley, *Dignity,* 9.

43. Ibid., 11.

9 | EXEMPLARY ORGANIZATIONS

A number of organizations have been praised in their efforts to manage diversity and have been identified as exemplary organizations in terms of diversity management. Although there are a number of diversity rankings, we have chosen to focus on DiversityInc's 2006 "The Top 50 Companies for Diversity"[1] for a few reasons: first, DiversityInc's methodology for determining the ranking is public knowledge,[2] second, the results of the ranking were recognized by credible media outlets such as the *Wall Street Journal, BusinessWeek,* MSNBC, and CNN; and third, the ranking examines four important areas of diversity: human capital, CEO commitment, corporate communications, and supplier diversity.

Objectives

■ To identify and examine some exemplary organizations in diversity management.

■ To examine in depth one particular organization known for having a cutting-edge diversity management policy.

■ To examine the effects top leadership can have on an organization's diversity management policy.

Preview Questions

■ How does a diversity policy become systemic throughout an organization?

■ What role does organizational leadership have in the success of a diversity policy?

■ How does an organization go about creating a culture of change in an effort to manage diversity?

■ What is the role of diversity task forces? How can they be implemented effectively?

The following list of the top-ranking companies briefly outlines their strategic attempts to implement diversity initiatives systemically throughout their organization.

#1: Verizon Communications/Wireless

• There is strong CEO leadership in terms of diversity management; specifically, CEO Ivan Seidenberg "signs off on executive compensation tied to successful completion of diversity benchmarks"; Seidenberg also is the chair of Verizon's diversity council.[3]

- Reflecting an organizational culture that values diversity, "[f]ive percent of the annual bonus for directors and above is tied to diversity goals."[4]
- In terms of supplier diversity, 2,505 of the businesses are owned by women and people of color; certifications of authenticity are required to ensure that diverse suppliers are owned by people of color and/or women.
- Additional DiversityInc rankings: #1: "Top 10 Companies for Recruitment & Retention"; #8: "Top 10 Companies for African Americans"; #9: "Top 10 Companies for Latinos."

#2: Consolidated Edison Co. of New York

- Leadership is directly involved with diversity management; Kevin Burke, who is chairman, president, and CEO "personally reviews and signs off on diversity metrics and progress, including those for supplier diversity."[5]
- A high value is placed on mentoring programs, which are used to "facilitate employee development." In particular, Con Ed of New York "developed an executive-mentoring program that matches senior executives with candidates who are women and/or people of color."[6]
- Additional DiversityInc rankings: #5: "Top 10 Companies for Recruitment & Retention"; #5: "Top 10 Companies for African Americans,"; #3: "Top 10 Companies for Latinos"; #2: "Top 10 Companies for Supplier Diversity."

#3: The Coca-Cola Company

- The fact that Coca-Cola settled a class-action lawsuit filed by its black employees for $192.5 million 6 years ago and now ranks in the Top 10 for diversity management shows its dedication to diversity management.
- According to Director of Diversity and Workplace Fairness Steve Bucherati: "Now, you have women and people of color attracted to opportunities to work with Coca-Cola despite . . . that lawsuit, which speaks to what we're doing."[7]
- In terms of access to promotions, "The company rule is that all candidate slates must feature at least one person of color and/or woman to ensure that groups of people who are represented less in the company's upper echelons are given the opportunity to advance up the company ladder."[8]
- According to Don Knauss, president of the Atlanta-based company's North American operations, diversity is one of the four "strategic planks" of his business plan.[9]
- Additional DiversityInc rankings: #2: "Top 10 Companies for Recruitment & Retention."

#4: Health Care Service Corp. (HCSC)

- Four out of the six direct reports of president and CEO Ray McCaskey's are women. In fact, "of HCSC's senior management, 46 percent are women."[10]
- Other diversity statistics are as follows: Blacks account for 19 percent of the company's employees and 19 percent of its board of directors. Latinos account for 8 percent of senior management.

- One of HCSC's strengths, according to McCaskey, is providing relevant medical plans for its employees. In particular, it provides "coverage for single parents and domestic partners of gay, lesbian, and heterosexual employees."[11]
- Diversity exists systemically in HCSC because each business unit is required to create its own diversity plan with a focus on four diversity areas: mandatory diversity training, hire/selection and development, diversity principles, and diversity week.

#5: HBO

- In terms of salaries, "of HBO's 10 percent highest-paid employees, 45 percent are women, who comprise 54 percent of the company's employee pool."[12]
- Further, 51 percent of HBO's managers are women, 17 percent of whom are black, 8 percent Asian, and 5.75 percent Latina.
- HBO actively recruits women, people of color, people with disabilities, and gays and lesbians.
- Additional DiversityInc rankings: #6: "Top 10 Companies for Recruitment & Retention"; #9: "Top 10 Companies for Asian Americans"; #8: "Top 10 Companies for Executive Women."

The rest of the "Top 50 Companies for Diversity" include:

#6: PricewaterhouseCoopers
#7: Turner Broadcasting
#8: Abbott
#9: BellSouth
#10: Blue Cross and Blue Shield of Florida
#11: JPMorgan Chase
#12: Comerica
#13: HSBC
#14: Sodexho
#15: Cingular Wireless
#16: Colgate-Palmolive
#17: Wells Fargo
#18: PepsiCo
#19: Sempra Energy
#20: Macy's/Bloomingdale's
#21: Wachovia
#22: Marriott International
#23: Allstate
#24: Ernst & Young
#25: Bank of America
#26: IKON Office Solutions
#27: Citigroup
#28: SunTrust Banks
#29: Toyota North America
#30: American Express
#31: Hewlett-Packard

#32: Cox Communications
#33: Starwood Hotels
#34: Merck & Co.
#35: Bausch & Lomb
#36: Kaiser Permanente
#37: Ford Motor Co.
#38: Kraft Foods
#39: Sprint Nextel
#40: MGM Mirage
#41: Harris
#42: Novartis Pharmaceutical Corporation
#43: DaimlerChrysler
#44: Merrill Lynch & Co.
#45: Starbucks Coffee Co.
#46: SC Johnson
#47: WellPoint
#48: Prudential Financial
#49: Compuware
#50: Darden

CASE STUDY: DIVERSITY AS STRATEGY

When most of us think of Lou Gerstner and the turnaround of IBM, we see a great business story. A less-told but integral part of that success is a people story—one that has dramatically altered the composition of an already diverse corporation and created millions of dollars in new business.

By the time Gerstner took the helm in 1993, IBM already had a long history of progressive management when it came to civil rights and equal employment. Indeed, few of the company's executives would have identified workforce diversity as an area of strategic focus. But when Gerstner took a look at his senior executive team, he felt it didn't reflect the diversity of the market for talent or IBM's customers and employees. To rectify the imbalance, in 1995 Gerstner launched a diversity task-force initiative that became a cornerstone of IBM's HR strategy. The effort continued through Gerstner's tenure and remains today under current CEO Sam Palmisano. Rather than attempt to eliminate discrimination by deliberately ignoring differences among employees, IBM created eight task forces, each focused on a different group such as Asians, gays and lesbians, and women. The goal of the initiative was to uncover and understand differences among the groups and find ways to appeal to a broader set of employees and customers.

The initiative required a lot of work, and it didn't happen overnight—the first task force convened almost two years after Gerstner's arrival. But the IBM of today looks very different from the IBM of 1995. The number of female executives worldwide has increased by 370 percent. The number of ethnic minority executives born

David Thomas, *Harvard Business Review* 82, no. 9 (September 2004).
David A. Thomas (dthomas@hbs.edu) is a professor of organizational behavior and human resource management at Harvard Business School in Boston.

in the United States has increased by 233 percent. Fifty-two percent of IBM's Worldwide Management Council (WMC), the top 52 executives who determine corporate strategy, is composed of women, ethnic minorities born in the United States, and non-U.S. citizens. The organization has seen the number of self-identified gay, lesbian, bisexual, and transgender executives increase by 733 percent and the number of executives with disabilities more than triple.

But diversity at IBM is about more than expanding the talent pool. When I asked Gerstner what had driven the success of the task forces, he said, "We made diversity a market-based issue . . . . It's about understanding our markets, which are diverse and multicultural." By deliberately seeking ways to more effectively reach a broader range of customers, IBM has seen significant bottom-line results. For example, the work of the women's task force and other constituencies led IBM to establish its Market Development organization, a group focused on growing the market of multicultural and women-owned businesses in the United States. One tactic: partnering with vendors to provide much-needed sales and service support to small and midsize businesses, a niche well populated with minority and female buyers. In 2001, the organization's activities accounted for more than $300 million in revenue compared with $10 million in 1998. Based on a recommendation from the people with disabilities task force, in October 2001 IBM launched an initiative focused on making all of its products more broadly accessible to take advantage of new legislation—an amendment to the federal Rehabilitation Act requiring that government agencies make accessibility a criterion for awarding federal contracts. IBM executives estimate this effort will produce more than a billion dollars in revenue during the next 5 to 10 years.

Over the past two years, I have interviewed more than 50 IBM employees—ranging from midlevel managers all the way up to Gerstner and Palmisano—about the task force effort and spent a great deal of time with Ted Childs, IBM's vice president of Global Workforce Diversity and Gerstner's primary partner in guiding this change process. What they described was a significant philosophical shift—from a long tradition of minimizing differences to amplifying them and to seizing on the business opportunities they present.

CONSTRUCTIVE DISRUPTION

Gerstner knew he needed to signal that diversity was a strategic goal, and he knew that establishing task forces would make a powerful impression on employees. Early in his tenure, Gerstner had convened various task forces to resolve a range of strategic choices and issues. He used the same structure to refine and achieve IBM's diversity-related objectives.

Gerstner and Childs wanted people to understand that this was truly something new. IBM had a long practice of being blind to differences and gathering demographic information only to ensure that hiring and promotion decisions didn't favor any particular group. So this new approach of calling attention to differences, with the hope of learning from them and making improvements to the business, was a radical departure. To effectively deliver the message and signal dramatic change, IBM kicked off the task forces on Bastille Day, July 14, 1995.

"We chose Bastille Day...because it's considered to be a historic day of social disruption," Childs told me. "We were looking for some constructive disruption."

Each task force comprised 15 to 20 senior managers, cutting across the company's business units, from one of the following demographic employee constituencies: Asians; blacks (African-American and of African decent); gays/lesbians/bisexuals/transgender individuals (GLBT); Hispanics; white men; Native Americans; people with disabilities; and women. To be eligible, members had to meet two criteria: executive rank and member of the constituency. (Three of the groups—people with disabilities, Native Americans, and GLBT—didn't have enough representation in the executive ranks to fill the task forces, so membership also included midlevel managers.) Members were chosen by Ted Childs and Tom Bouchard, then senior vice president of human resources, based on their knowledge of and experiences with the top executive team. In particular, Childs sought executives who had spoken to him or to a colleague in his office about their own experiences and perceptions that diversity was an untapped business resource; he persuaded those individuals to participate by describing the effort as a chance to make a difference and eliminate some of the roadblocks they may have faced in their careers.

Each task force also had two or more executive cochairs who were members of the constituency. For these roles, Childs and Bouchard recruited high-performing, well-respected senior managers and junior executives who were at least at the director level. Each task force was also assigned an executive sponsor from the WMC, who was charged with learning about the relevant constituency's concerns, opportunities, and strategies and with serving as a liaison to top management. The executive sponsors were senior vice presidents, and most reported directly to Gerstner. They were selected by Bouchard and Childs based on their willingness to support the change process and on the potential for synergies within their given business areas.

The first sponsor of the women's task force, for instance, was the senior vice president of sales and marketing worldwide. Childs knew that the company's senior executives believed that potential buyers in many countries outside of the United States wouldn't work with female executives and that this could interfere with women's success in international assignments. By connecting this SVP with the women's task force, Bouchard and Childs hoped these barriers could be better understood—and that opportunities for women to advance in the sales organization might improve. Similarly, the SVP for research and development was asked to sponsor the people with disabilities task force, with the expectation that if he could get closer to the day-to-day experiences of people with disabilities in his own organization, he would gain new insights into the development of accessible products.

Sponsors were not necessarily constituents of their groups. The sponsor for the white men's task force was a woman; the sponsor for the women's task force, a man. Indeed, there was a certain advantage to having sponsors who didn't come from the groups they represented. It meant that they and the task force members would have to learn from their differences. A sponsor would have to dig deep into the issues of the task force to represent its views and interests to other WMC members.

In addition to having a sponsor, cochairs, and members, each task force was assigned one or two HR employees and a senior HR executive for administrative support, as well as a lawyer for legal guidance. The groups also received logistical and research support from Childs's Global Workforce Diversity organization, which was responsible for all of IBM's equal employment and work/life balance programs.

Once the task forces had been set up and launched, Bouchard sent an e-mail to every U.S. employee detailing the task forces and their missions and underscoring how important the initiative was to the company. In his message, he acknowledged IBM's heritage of respecting diversity and defined the new effort in business terms. Here's an excerpt from the e-mail:

> To sustain [IBM's recognition for diversity leadership] and strengthen our competitive edge, we have launched eight executive-led task forces representing the following IBM employee constituencies . . . . We selected these communities because collectively they are IBM, and they reflect the diversity of our marketplace.

He also encouraged employees to respond with specific suggestions for how to make IBM a more inclusive environment. Childs then compiled more than 2,000 responses to the e-mail and channeled them to the appropriate task forces. As a result of these suggestions, the task forces focused on the following areas for evaluation and improvement: communications, staffing, employee benefits, workplace flexibility, training and education, advertising and marketplace opportunities, and external relations.

The initial charge of the task forces was to take six months to research and report back to the CEO and the WMC on four questions: What is necessary for your constituency to feel welcome and valued at IBM? What can the corporation do, in partnership with your group, to maximize your constituency's productivity? What can the corporation do to influence your constituency's buying decisions, so that IBM is seen as a preferred solution provider? And which external organizations should IBM form relationships with to better understand the needs of your constituency?

At first, skepticism prevailed. Here's what one white male executive told me:

> This whole idea of bringing together people in the workplace and letting them form these groups was really repugnant on its face to a lot of people, and of course IBM had been a nonunion company in the United States for a long, long time. I mean, having groups was like letting them into your living room.

And from a black executive:

> I was somewhat skeptical, and there was a level of reluctance in terms of how successful this would ultimately become in IBM, given some of the complex issues around the topic of diversity.

The groups faced other challenges as well. When the women's task force met for the first time, many members were relieved to hear that some of their colleagues were sharing similar struggles to balance work and family; at the same time, some of IBM's women believed strongly that female executives should choose between having children and having a career. The dissenting opinions made it more difficult to present a united front to the rest of senior management and secure support for the group's initiatives.

Task force members also disagreed on tactics. Some within the black task force, for instance, advocated for a conservative approach, fearing that putting a spotlight on the group would be perceived as asking for unearned preferences, and, even worse, might encourage the stereotype that blacks are less capable. But most in the group felt that more aggressive action would be needed to break down the barriers facing blacks at IBM.

In both cases, members engaged in lengthy dialogue to understand various points of view, and, in light of very real deadlines for reporting back, were forced to agree on concrete proposals for accomplishing sometimes competing goals. The women's group concluded that IBM needed to partner with its female employees in making work and family life more compatible. The black group decided it needed to clarify the link between its concerns and those of the company—making it clear that the members were raising business issues and that the task force effort was not intended to favor any group.

During the six months of the initial phase, Childs checked in with each group periodically and held monthly meetings to ensure that each was staying focused. The check-ins were also meant to facilitate information sharing across groups, especially if several were grappling with similar issues. The task forces' work involved collecting data from their constituencies, examining internal archival data to identify personnel trends, and reviewing external data to understand IBM's labor and customer markets. Their most critical task was to interpret the data as a means of identifying solutions and opportunities for IBM. Task forces met several times a month, in subcommittees or in their entirety, and at the end of the research period, Childs met with each group to determine its top issues—or the "vital few." These were defined as the issues and concerns that were of greatest importance to the group and would have the most impact if addressed. Childs and the task force cochairs also realized that not addressing these issues would hamper the credibility of the initiative with front-line employees.

On December 1, 1995, the task forces met to share their initial findings. Again, the date was chosen with the idea of sending a message to employees: It was the 40th anniversary of Rosa Parks's refusal to give up her seat on a bus in Birmingham, Alabama, to a white passenger. That act, of course, led to her arrest and ignited the Birmingham bus boycotts that ushered in the modern U.S. civil rights movement. Just as the Bastille Day launch signaled a release from old ways of thinking, the timing of this meeting indicated a desire for a radically new approach to diversity.

Several of the task forces shared many of the same issues, such as development and promotion, senior management's communication of its commitment to diversity, and the need to focus on recruiting a diverse pool of employees, especially in engineering and science-related positions. Other concerns were specific to particular groups, including domestic partner benefits (identified by the GLBT task force) and issues of access to buildings and technology (raised by the people with disabilities task force). Overall, the findings made it clear that workforce diversity was the bridge between the workplace and the marketplace—in other words, greater diversity in the workplace could help IBM attract a more diverse customer set. A focus on diversity was, in short, a major business opportunity.

All eight task forces recommended that the company create diversity groups beyond those at the executive level. In response, IBM in 1997 formed employee network groups as a way for others in the company to participate. The network groups today run across constituencies, offering a variety of perspectives on issues that are local or unique to particular units. They offer a forum for employees to interact electronically and in person to discuss issues specific to their constituencies.

Another recommendation, this time put forth by the women's group, aimed to rectify a shortage in the talent pipeline of women in technology, identifying young girls' tendency to opt out of science and math in school as one of the causes. To encourage girls' interest in these disciplines, in 1999 a group of women engineers and scientists in Endicott, New York, ran a pilot "EXITE" (Exploring Interests in Technology and Engineering) camp. The program brought together 30 middle-school girls for a week that summer to learn about science and math in a fun, interactive way from female IBM employees. In 2000, the women's task force replicated the program in five other locations throughout the United States, reaching 400 girls, and in 2001 the program expanded internationally. In 2004, IBM will have a total of 37 EXITE camps worldwide—15 in the United States, one in Canada, eight in Asia-Pacific, six in Europe, and seven in Latin America. After the girls attend camp, they are assigned an IBM female scientist or engineer as a mentor for one year.

Since 1999, IBM has reached 3,000 girls through EXITE camps. In 2003 alone, 900 girls attended, and in 2004, 1,100 will have gone through the program. In collaboration with IBM's technology group, the women's task force also created a steering committee focused on retaining women in technology currently at IBM and attracting female scientists from universities.

As for external initiatives that arose from the task forces, IBM's Market Development (MD) unit came directly out of the groups' responses to the third question: What can IBM do to influence your constituency's buying decisions, so that the company is seen as a preferred solution provider? It became clear that IBM wasn't well positioned in relation to the market's fastest growing entrepreneurial segments—female- and minority-owned businesses. The MD was formed as a unit of the Small and Medium-Sized Business Sales and Marketing organization. Initially, the group helped IBM revamp its communications strategy for reaching female- and minority-owned companies. Its role has since evolved into identifying and supporting sales and marketing strategies aimed at these important segments.

The MD's efforts have directly translated into hundreds of millions of dollars in new revenue. More important to IBM's senior executives, the MD is elevating the company's overall level of cultural competence as it responds to the needs of IBM's diverse customer base. A case in point is advertising, where the MD convened teams from the task forces and the advertising department to create constituency casting guidelines and other communications. These changes have helped ensure appropriate representation of constituencies in all aspects of the company's marketing, with the guidelines forming the basis for ongoing discussions about how to reach and relate effectively to IBM's diverse customer base.

The people with disabilities task force (PWD), which initially focused on compliance with accessibility laws, began in 2001 to think about making the leap from compliance to market initiatives. That same year, Ted Childs arranged for each task force to meet with senior management, including Sam Palmisano, then IBM's president. The PWD task force leaders took the opportunity to point out the tremendous market potential in government contracts if IBM made its products more accessible. Palmisano agreed, and PWD received the green light it needed to advance its projects.

One reason for the increased focus on accessible technology was that in June 2001, the U.S. Congress implemented legislation mandating that all new IT equipment and services purchased by federal agencies must be accessible. This legislation—known as Section 508—makes accessibility a more important decision criterion than price in many bid situations, thus creating an opportunity for accessibility IT leaders to gain market share, charge a price premium, or both, from federal buyers. In addition to legislation, other indicators made it clear that the demand for accessibility was growing: a World Health Organization estimate of more than 750 million disabled people across the globe, with a collective buying power of $461 billion, and an increase in the number of aging baby boomers in need of accessible technology.

IBM believes that business opportunities will grow as countries around the world implement similar legislation. Furthermore, the private-sector opportunity for accessible technology could be far greater than that of the government as companies address a growing aging population. IBM's worldwide Accessibility Centers comprise special teams that evaluate existing or future IBM technologies for their possible use in making products accessible. There are now a total of six IBM Accessibility Centers, in the United States, Europe, and Japan.

PILLARS OF CHANGE

Any major corporate change will succeed only if a few key factors are in place: strong support from company leaders, an employee base that is fully engaged with the initiative, management practices that are integrated and aligned with the effort, and a strong and well-articulated business case for action. IBM's diversity task forces benefited from all four.

Demonstrate Leadership Support

It's become a cliché to say that leadership matters, but the issue merits discussion here because diversity is one of the areas in which executive leadership is often ineffectual. Executives' espoused beliefs are frequently inconsistent with their behavior, and they typically underestimate how much the corporation really needs to change to achieve its diversity goals. That's because diversity strategies tend to lay out lofty goals without providing the structures to educate senior executives in the specific challenges faced by various constituencies. In addition, these strategies often don't provide models that teach or encourage new behaviors.

IBM has taken several approaches to helping executives deepen their aware-ness and understanding. To begin with, the structure of the task forces—how they operate and who is on them—immerses executive sponsors in the specific chal-lenges faced by the employee constituency groups. The groups are a formal mech-anism for learning, endorsed at the highest levels of the company.

Second, the chief diversity officer, Ted Childs, acts as a partner with the CEO as well as coach and adviser to other executives. In addition to educating them on specific issues, as he did when the company decided to offer domestic partner benefits, Childs also works to ensure that they behave in ways that are consistent with the company's diversity strategy. A senior executive described Childs's role as a coach and teacher:

> I know that he's had a number of conversations with very senior people in the company where he's just sat down with them and said, "Listen, you don't get it, and you need to get it. And I care about you, and I care about this company. I care about the people who are affected by the way you're behaving, and so I owe it to you to tell you that. And here's how you don't get it. Here's what you need to do to change."

And third, Gerstner and later Palmisano not only sanctioned the task force process but actively sought to be role models themselves. A number of the execu-tives I interviewed were struck by Gerstner's interest and active involvement in the development of high-potential minority and female senior managers and junior executives; he took a personal interest in how they were being mentored and what their next jobs would be. He also challenged assumptions about when people could be ready for general management assignments. In one case, Gerstner and his team were discussing the next job for a high-potential female executive. Most felt that she needed a bigger job in her functional area, but Gerstner felt that the proposed job, while involving more responsibility, would add little to the candidate's development. Instead she was given a general management assignment—and the team got a signal from the CEO about his commitment to diversity. His behavior communicated a sense of appreciation and accountability for people development. Indeed, account-ability for results became as critical in this domain as it was for all business goals.

Gerstner also modeled desired behaviors in his interactions with his direct reports. One of them told me this story:

> During a board of directors dinner, I had to go to [my daughter's] "back-to-school night," the one night a year when you meet the teachers. I had been at the board meeting that day. I was going to be at the board meet-ing the next day. But it was the dinner that posed a problem, and I said, "Lou, I'll do whatever you want, but this is the position I am in," and . . . he didn't even blink. He said, "Go to back-to-school night. That is more important." And then . . . he told the board at dinner why I wasn't there and why it was so important . . . to make it possible for working parents to have very big jobs but still be involved parents. He never told me that he told the board. But the board told me the next day. They . . . said, "You

should know that Lou not only said where you were but gave a couple minute talk about how important it was for IBM to act in this way."

CEO leadership and modeling didn't stop when Gerstner left. One senior executive who is a more recent arrival to the WMC described how Palmisano communicates the importance of the diversity initiative:

> Executive involvement and buy-in are critical. Sam has played a personal and very important role. He personally asked each task force to come and report its progress and agenda to him. He spent time with the [task force that I sponsor] and had a detailed review of what we are doing on the customer set. What are we focused on internally? How can he help in his role as CEO? He's really made it clear to the senior-level executives that being good at [leading the diversity initiative] is part of our job.

Engage Employees as Partners

While the six-month task force effort was consistent with IBM's history of promoting equal opportunity, the use of the task force structure to address issues of diversity represented a significant culture shift. IBM was an organization that had discouraged employees from organizing around any interest not specifically defined by the requirements of their jobs. The idea of employees organizing to advocate was anathema. One white male executive said, "Does this mean that we can have a communist cell here? Are we going to have hundreds and hundreds of these?" The skepticism reached up to the highest levels: When Childs first proposed the task force strategy, Gerstner asked him one question: "Why?"

But in the end, IBM's task force structure paved the way for employee buy-in because executives then had to invite constituent groups to partner with them in addressing the diversity challenge. The partnerships worked because three essential components were in place: mutual expectations, mutual influence, and trust.

When the task forces were commissioned, Childs and Gerstner set expectations and made sure that roles and responsibilities were unambiguous. Initially, the task forces' charters were short, only six months (the groups are still active today), and their mission was clear: to explore the issues, opportunities, and strategies affecting their constituencies and customers. Once this work was done, it fell to the corporation's senior executives to respond and to report on the task forces' progress at various junctures to the WMC. Gerstner and Childs followed up with the task force sponsors to ensure that the groups were gathering meaningful information and connecting it to the business.

The task forces' work has evolved to focus on more tactical issues, and the organization has demonstrated its willingness to be influenced, committing significant resources to efforts suggested by the groups. Trust was also built as the task force structure allowed employees more face time with executives—executives they would likely not have had a chance to meet—and provided new opportunities for mentoring. According to one task force participant:

> What got me to trust that this was a real commitment by the WMC was when I saw them ask for our advice, engage us in dialogue, and then

take action. They didn't just do whatever we said, but the rationale for actions was always shared. It made me feel like our opinions were respected as businesspeople who bring a particular perspective to business challenges.

The task force structure has been copied on a smaller scale within specific business units. Even without a mandate from corporate brass, most units have created their own diversity councils, offering local support for achieving each unit's specific diversity goals. Here, too, the employee partnership model prevails.

Integrate Diversity with Management Practices

Sustaining change requires that diversity become an integrated part of the company's management practices. This was a priority for Gerstner, who told me:

If you were to go back and look at 10 years' worth of executive committee discussions, you would find two subjects, and only two, that appeared on every one of the agendas. One was the financial performance, led by our CFO. The second was a discussion of management changes, promotions, moves, and so on, led by our HR person.

In my interviews, among the most frequently mentioned diversity-related HR practice was the 5-minute drill, which began with Gerstner's top team and has cascaded down from the chairman to two levels down from CEO. The 5-minute drill takes place during the discussion of management talent at the corporate and business unit levels. During meetings of the senior team, executives are expected at any moment to be able to discuss any high-potential manager. According to interviewees, an explicit effort is made to ensure that minorities and females are discussed along with white males. The result has been to make the executives more accountable for spotting and grooming high-potential minority managers both in their own areas and across the business. Now that it's been made explicit that IBM executives need to watch for female and minority talent, they are more open to considering and promoting these individuals when looking to fill executive jobs.

Managing diversity is also one of the core competencies used to assess managers' performance, and it's included in the mandatory training and orientation of new managers. As one executive responsible for designing parts of this leadership curriculum commented, "We want people to understand that effectively managing and developing a diverse workforce is an integral part of what it means to manage at IBM."

Both Gerstner and Palmisano have been clear that holding managers accountable for diversity-related results is key. Gerstner noted, "We did not set quotas, but we did set goals and made people aware of the people in their units who they needed to be accountable for developing." And Palmisano said, "I reinforce to our executives that this is not HR's responsibility; it is up to us to make sure that we are developing our talent. There is a problem if, at the end of the day, that pool of talent is not diverse."

Link Diversity Goals to Business Goals

From the beginning, Gerstner and Childs insisted that the task force effort create a link between IBM's diversity goals and its business goals—that this would be good business, not good philanthropy. The task force efforts have led to a series of significant accomplishments.

For instance, IBM's efforts to develop the client base among women-owned businesses have quickly expanded to include a focus on Asian, black, Hispanic, mature (senior citizens), and Native American markets. The Market Development organization has grown revenue in the company's Small and Medium-Sized Business Sales and Marketing organization from $10 million in 1998 to hundreds of millions of dollars in 2003.

Another result of the task forces' work has been to create executive partner programs targeting demographic customer segments. In 2001, IBM began assigning executives to develop relationships with the largest women- and minority-owned businesses in the United States. This was important not only because these business sectors are growing fast but because their leaders are often highly visible role models, and their IT needs will grow and become increasingly more sophisticated. Already, these assignments have yielded impressive revenue streams with several of these companies.

The task force effort has also affected IBM's approach to supplier diversity. While the company has for decades fostered relationships with minority-owned businesses as well as businesses owned by the disabled, the work of the task forces has expanded the focus of IBM's supplier diversity program to a broader set of constituencies and provided new insights on the particular challenges each faced. The purpose of the supplier diversity program is to create a level playing field. It's important to note, though, that procurement contracts are awarded on the merits of the bid—including price and quality—not on the diversity of the vendor. In 2003, IBM did business worth more than $1.5 billion with over 500 diverse suppliers, up from $370 million in 1998.

The cynics have come around. One black executive said, "Yes, I think [the initiative] has been extremely effective if you look at where we started back in the mid-nineties. I can tell you that I was somewhat skeptical [at first]." Another commented on the growing acceptance of the effort across IBM: "You can see that support actually changed over time from 'I'm not sure what this is about' to . . . a complete understanding that diversity and the focus on diversity make good business sense."

Perhaps the best evidence of the task forces' success is that the initiative not only continues but has spread and has had lasting impact. In more than one instance, after an executive became a task force sponsor, his or her division or business unit made significant progress on its own diversity goals. Leaders of some of the task forces described seeing their sponsors grow in their ability to understand, articulate, and take action on the issues identified by their groups. One executive described how the task force sponsor experience had been important for him as a business leader and personally, as well as for IBM:

There is no doubt that this is critical for how we manage the research organization, because of the need for diverse thought. It has affected me substantially because . . . I became involved with diverse populations outside of IBM that I may well not have been connected with if it hadn't been for my involvement with the task force. I'm on the Gallaudet University [school for the deaf] board. Without the task force, I would have never thought of it. And so this has been a terrific awakening, a personal awakening . . . . Since it's focusing particularly on accessibility, we can help in a lot of ways with technology for accessibility, and Gallaudet turns out to be, for the subset of people who are hearing impaired, a terrific place to prototype solutions in this space.

Such comments were not atypical. In many instances, the sponsorship experience was developmental in important and unexpected ways. Having eight task forces means that in a group of 52 top leaders, there is always a critical mass strategically connected to the issues. Today, more than half of the WMC members have been engaged with the task forces in the role of sponsor or task force leader prior to being promoted to the senior executive level.

For IBM, that makes good business sense. The entire effort was designed to help the company develop deeper insights into its major markets, with a direct tie to two of Gerstner's central dictates. One: IBM needed to get closer to its customers and become more externally focused. Two: It needed to focus on talent—attracting, retaining, developing, and promoting the best people. On both measures, the company has come a long way.

Discussion Questions

1. IBM created eight task forces to enhance diversity within the organization. Which constituencies do these task forces represent? What was the purpose of the task forces? Did they help IBM manage diversity? How?
2. Lou Gerstner said: "We made diversity a market-based issue . . . . It's about understanding our markets, which are diverse and multicultural." What implications does this statement have for IBM's marketing strategy?
3. Describe how IBM has focused extensively on people with disabilities both internally with their own employees and externally with their products and customers. What impact has this approach had on IBM?
4. Describe IBM's four "pillars of change." How have these pillars affected IBM and its diverse employees?

Notes

1. For more details on DiversityInc's "Top 50 Companies for Diversity," see *DiversityInc Magazine,* June 2006.
2. For more details on DiversityInc's Top 50 2006 methodology, see Barbara Frankel, "Top 50 2006 Methodology," *DiversityInc Magazine,* June 2006, 38.
3. Yoji Cole, "Verizon Communications/ Wireless," *DiversityInc Magazine,* June 2006, 42.
4. Ibid.
5. Ibid., 44.
6. Ibid.
7. Ibid., 46.
8. Ibid.
9. Ibid.
10. Ibid., 48.
11. Ibid.
12. Yoji Cole, "HBO," *DiversityInc Magazine,* June 2006, 50.

PART III

EXERCISES: DEVELOPING THREE ESSENTIAL SKILLS

In this third part, "Exercises: Developing Three Essential Skills," we include 19 exercises that encourage our readers to expand their understanding of diversity as individuals and members of organizations. The purpose of the first group of exercises is to encourage self-awareness and self-assessment of one's knowledge of diversity and one's personal stereotypes and biases. The second group of exercises aims to help individuals better understand how diversity pertains to themselves, their society, and their organization. The third group of exercises provides tools that can be used to examine how diversity is understood and managed within organizations.

CHAPTER

10 ANALYZING SELF

EXERCISE: YOUR PIE CHART

Purpose
The purpose of this exercise is three-tiered: to compare your own cultural background with that of others; to raise awareness of the importance of self-identity based on affiliations with groups; and to consider the influence of self-identity on individuals' experiences in organizational settings.

Introduction
Personal characteristics (some changeable, others not), which may influence an individual's basic self-image and sense of identity, may also influence experiences in the workplace. *Primary dimensions* of diversity are essentially unchangeable personal characteristics (e.g., gender, race, ethnicity, age, sexual orientation, and physical and mental abilities).

Secondary dimensions of diversity, however, are changeable personal characteristics that are acquired and may be modified or abandoned throughout life (e.g., education, income, marital and parental status, religion, political affiliation, and work experience). Of course, secondary characteristics are not completely self-determined; educational background, work experience, income, and marital status are affected by others' decisions. However, people generally have more control over secondary dimensions of diversity than over primary dimensions.[1]

Guidelines
1. Working individually, create a pie chart identifying group affiliations that have some importance in your self-concept. These affiliations may be based on any of the primary and secondary dimensions of diversity mentioned or on some other personal characteristic that is particularly important to you. Indicate the approximate importance of each group by the size of the slice of pie that you assign it.
2. Participate in a discussion based on the following questions:
   - What did you learn about yourself?
   - What surprised you the most?
   - What group affiliations were mentioned the most?
   - What did you learn about others that surprised you?
   - How does your self-identity influence your experiences in organizational settings?

Source: Taylor Cox and Ruby L. Beale, *Developing Competency to Manage Diversity: Readings, Cases and Activities* (San Francisco: Berrett-Koehler, 1997).

EXERCISE: AWARENESS OF CULTURAL IDENTITY

Purpose:

The purpose of this exercise is to shed light on personal dimensions of diversity and their meaning to you.

Guidelines

Answer the following questions to understand better who you are.

1. What are the various cultures that I belong to? (Include your race/ethnicity, culture, nation of origin, gender, sexual orientation, age, physical abilities, class, and religion.) With which ones do I most strongly or closely identify? Which seem the least important to my cultural identity?
2. During what critical incident or time period did I initially become aware of each of my various cultural identities?
3. Being my (race/ethnicity/culture/nationality) means:
4. Being male/female means:
5. Being my age means:
6. Being my religion means:
7. Having my physical (dis)abilities means:
8. Being my sexual orientation means:
9. Growing up poor/working class/middle class/upper class means:
10. Some of the things I see as benefits from my background are:
11. Some liabilities (things I need to watch out for personally and in relationship to others) are:
12. What are some of the names used in referring to the cultural groups of which I am a member? Which ones are acceptable and unacceptable to me? How does hearing the unacceptable ones make me feel?

Source: Marquita Byrd, *The Intracultural Communication Book* (New York: McGraw-Hill, 1993).

EXERCISE: SOCIALIZATION AND THE "ISM" PRISM

Purpose

According to William Sonnenschein, a lecturer at the Haas School of Business of the University of California at Berkeley, we all have biases, or "isms," in our belief system. The "ism" prism allows us to explore and understand our biases and their sources. The prism uses questions about how we have been socialized to show us the origins of our beliefs, attitudes, and values. The subject areas include the following:

- Family influences
- Personal experiences
- Educational experiences
- Peer influences
- Media influences
- Critical incidents

Guidelines

In the following example, the question, How do I feel about Native Americans? is put into the prism. You could also use other questions such as, Does my social status affect the way I communicate? How do I feel about older workers? or How do I feel about people with disabilities? Putting such questions into the prism allows you to look at your life's influences. What comes out the other side of the prism is how these influences have affected you.

Example question: How Do I Feel about Native Americans?

FAMILY INFLUENCES
- What were my parents' attitudes toward Native Americans?
- What were the attitudes of my other relatives?

PERSONAL EXPERIENCES
- Did I know any Native Americans?
- Did I see reservations as I traveled?
- Did I have other personal experiences with Native Americans?

EDUCATIONAL EXPERIENCES
- What did I learn in history at school about Native Americans?

PEER INFLUENCES
- Did I play the game "Cowboys and Indians" as a child? How did playing or not playing affect me?
- What were my friends' attitudes about Native Americans?

MEDIA INFLUENCES
- What did TV tell me about Native Americans? Movies?
- What did I read in newspapers? Books? Other media?

CRITICAL INCIDENTS
- What critical incidents happened during my life that might have affected or changed my view?

Source: William Sonnenschein, *The Diversity Toolkit: How You Can Build and Benefit from a Diverse Workforce* (Chicago: Contemporary Books, 1997), 32.

EXERCISE: DIVERSITY QUESTIONNAIRE

Purpose

The purpose of this exercise is to help you gauge your openness to and awareness of diversity, as measured by your behavior and communication patterns.

Guidelines

Next to each question place the number that best describes your own actions and beliefs.

1 = almost always
2 = frequently
3 = sometimes
4 = seldom
5 = almost never

_____ **1.** Do you recognize and challenge the perceptions, assumptions, and biases that affect your thinking?

_____ **2.** Do you think about the impact of what you say or how you act before you speak or act?

_____ **3.** Do you do everything you can to prevent the reinforcement of prejudices, including avoiding using negative stereotypes when you speak?

_____ **4.** Do you encourage people who are not from the dominant culture to speak out on their concerns, and do you respect those issues?

_____ **5.** Do you speak up when someone is making racial, sexual, or other derogatory remarks, or is humiliating another person?

_____ **6.** Do you apologize when you realize you may have offended someone with inappropriate behavior or comments?

_____ **7.** Do you try to know people as individuals, not as representatives of specific groups, and welcome different types of people in your peer group?

_____ **8.** Do you do everything that you can to understand your own background and try to educate yourself about other backgrounds, including different communication styles?

Scoring: The lower your score, the better you communicate and improve the climate in your diverse organization and the community at large. To improve your communication, increase your use of the behaviors listed.

Source: William Sonnenschein, *The Diversity Toolkit: How You Can Build and Benefit from a Diverse Workforce* (Chicago: Contemporary Books, 1997), 47.

EXERCISE: FIRST THOUGHTS

Purpose

The purpose of this activity is to help you recognize that stereotyping is unfair and becomes a barrier to good communication and accepting people as individuals. This exercise encourages you to examine the stereotypes of the groups of people with whom you interact.

Introduction

Before you begin this exercise, you need to understand two important concepts: stereotype and prejudice.

A *stereotype* is an exaggerated belief or fixed idea about a person or group that is held by people and sustained by selective perception and selective forgetting. Stereotypes come from two sources: (1) incomplete, distorted information and limited personal experience and (2) outside sources such as others' interpretations of cultural behavior. Stereotypes are natural but often destructive because they are unfair, do not allow for individuality, and interfere with communication.

A *prejudice* is a preconceived idea or negative attitude formed before the facts are known. It is a bias without reason, resistant to all evidence. Prejudice implies inferiority, leads to suspicion, and is detrimental to communication and interpersonal relations.

Guidelines

1. Write the first two or three adjectives that come to your mind for each of the groups listed:

Persons with disabilities	Whites
New Yorkers	Asians
Californians	African Americans
Teachers	Gays and lesbians
Latinos	Managers
Women	Men

2. Working in groups of three, discuss your reactions to the exercise and to stereotyping in general. (Discuss the words used in each category, the categories that were easy and difficult, and the reasons for regarding them as such).

3. Discuss other stereotyped groups to which members of your group may belong: blondes, farm boys, intellectuals, jocks, and the like.

4. Discuss the importance of overcoming labels and stereotypes, and offer specific ways to counteract stereotypes. For example, recognize stereotypes for what they are and where they come from; look at each person as an individual; give examples of individuals who do not fit the stereotype; remain open-minded and not influenced by opinions of others.

Source: Jonamay Lambert and Selma Myers, *50 Activities for Diversity Training* (Amherst, MA: Human Resource Development Press, 1994), 59–63.

EXERCISE: MASCULINE AND FEMININE SPEAKING STYLES

Purpose

The purpose of this exercise is to create self-awareness of how gender affects your communication style.

Introduction

According to Julia T. Woods, "Researchers report that masculine socialization teaches most men to see talk as a means of accomplishing instrumental goals. They talk when there is a problem or when there is a need to explain something, or inform or advise others. Research also indicates that masculine socialization encourages men to be assertive . . . they learn to initiate topics when they wish." Feminine talk, on the other hand, is "expressive—a means of communicating thoughts and a way to establish and sustain connections with others." And, "the content of communication doesn't need to be significant for conversation to be valuable. Talking is relating. Communication is an end in itself, regardless of what is being communicated."[2]

It is important to note, however, that these styles are not exclusive to the specific gender. In other words, some women communicate in a more "masculine" style, and some men communicate in a more "feminine" style. All of us use both types of communication at least some of the time.

Guidelines

1. With the understanding that "masculine talk" and "feminine talk" are on two ends of a continuum, locate where your own communication style fits on the continuum.
2. In what situations do you use characteristics of "masculine talk" and when do you use characteristics of "feminine talk"?
3. Is it useful to describe communication styles as "masculine" and "feminine," or is there a more representative way to describe communication styles?

MASCULINE TALK

1. You use talk to assert yourself and your ideas.
2. You find that personal disclosures can make you vulnerable.
3. You use talk to establish your status and power.
4. You match your experiences with those related by others as a competitive strategy to command attention.
5. To support others, you do something helpful—give advice or solve a problem for them.
6. You don't share the talk stage with others, and you interrupt them to make your point.
7. You believe that each person is on his or her own in conversations, responsible for being heard.
8. You use responses to make your own points and sometimes try to outshine others.
9. You are assertive so that others will perceive you as confident and in command.
10. You think that talking should convey information and accomplish goals; extraneous details get in the way of achieving something.

FEMININE TALK

1. You use talk to build and sustain rapport with others.
2. You like to share yourself and learn about others by disclosing through communication.
3. You use talk to create symmetry/equality between people.
4. You match your experiences with those related by others to show understanding and empathy.
5. To support others, you express understanding of their feelings.
6. You include others in conversation by asking questions and encouraging them to elaborate.
7. You try to keep the conversation going by asking questions and expressing interest in others' ideas.
8. You want to be responsive to let others know you care about what they say.
9. You are reserved in a conversation so that others feel free to add their ideas.
10. You believe that talking enhances relationships; details and interesting side comments increase the depth of connection.

Source: This exercise was prepared by Kathryn A. Cañas and Harris Sondak.

Notes

1. Marilyn Loden and Judy B. Rosener, "Dimensions of Diversity," *Workforce America: Managing Employee Diversity as a Vital Resource* (Homewood, IL: Business One Irwin, 1991), 17–35.
2. Julia T. Wood, "Gender, Communication, and Culture," in Larry Samovar and Richard Porter, *Intercultural Communication: A Reader, 7th ed.* (New York: Wadsworth, 1994), 155–164; William Sonnenschein, *The Diversity Toolkit: How You Can Build and Benefit from a Diverse Workforce* (Chicago: Contemporary Books, 1997), 71.

C H A P T E R

11

UNDERSTANDING DIFFERENCE

EXERCISE: WHAT CONSTITUTES SEXUAL HARASSMENT?

Purpose

The purpose of this exercise is to help you understand what constitutes sexual harassment.

Introduction

According to the EEOC, sexual harassment is a form of sex discrimination that violates Title VII of the Civil Rights Act of 1964. Unwelcome sexual advances, requests for sexual favors, and other verbal or physical conduct of a sexual nature constitutes sexual harassment when submission to or rejection of this conduct explicitly or implicitly affects an individual's employment, unreasonably interferes with an individual's work performance, or creates an intimidating, hostile, or offensive work environment.

There are two types of sexual harassment: quid pro quo and hostile work environment. *Quid pro quo,* which means "this for that," involves a person with power over someone else who uses that power to either benefit or harm a person based on their willingness to participate in or tolerate some form of sexual behavior. A *hostile work environment* exists when an individual is exposed to conduct that is: sexual in nature, severe and/or pervasive, and unwelcome or unwanted; a power imbalance may or may not exist.

Guidelines

Discuss each scenario and determine whether it constitutes sexual harassment.

Scenario One

Mary and Bill work in the same department. Mary and Bill are friendly, but nothing romantic has occurred between them. Mary asks Bill if he would like to go out after work.

Scenario Two

Charles is attracted to his coworker, Shelly. He tells her one morning, "you look really nice today."

Scenario Three

At a company party, employees are called up individually to receive year-end bonuses. Susan is shocked to discover that whereas the men in her department receive cash, she and her female coworkers receive flowers.

Source: This exercise was prepared by Kathryn A. Cañas, P. Corper James, and Harris Sondak.

Scenario Four

Adam and a coworker are looking at a sexually explicit Web site. Someone walks in and sees the Web site. That person is offended and reports the incident to Adam's supervisor, who never tells Adam about the complaint. The person walks into Adam's office three more times in the next several months and again sees sexually explicit material on Adam's screen. The person never tells Adam that he is offended.

EXERCISE: THE OLDER EMPLOYEE

Purpose

The purpose of this exercise is to help you examine workplace biases faced by older individuals and to consider how organizations can make the work environment both fair and comfortable for workers of all ages.

Introduction

Older workers are much more common now than ever before. The employment rate of workers who are more than 55 years old has been rising dramatically in many countries. Further, in the United States, 15 percent of the labor force consists of older workers, a proportion that has been gradually increasing owing to longer life expectancies, financial needs, and the desire to continue working. Finally, the many baby boomers, people born between 1946 and 1964, are presently entering the ranks of older workers.[1]

Older workers, however, are at a disadvantage in obtaining new jobs or holding onto their present jobs during corporate downsizings and restructurings. Managers tend to judge them as weak on flexibility, acceptance of new technology, and ability to learn new skills, all valuable traits in the rapidly changing global economy. Although older workers today are more ready to embrace new technologies than their counterparts in prior generations, the myth persists that "you cannot teach an old dog new tricks." If investing in older workers is seen as yielding little in return, corporations will not give older workers the chance to learn the skills they need to stay current in their jobs.[2]

Guidelines

1. Form teams of four to six members. Select one person from each team to play the role of an older employee, Fran Bello, who will be joining the team after it has begun work on a new project. The individuals playing the role of Fran gather outside the classroom to await further instruction. The instructor distributes a background sheet on the team and its new project to all members except Fran; the team should review the project and then begin work on it.
2. As a team, work on the project.
3. The instructor distributes an interoffice memo about the new employee. After team members have read the memo, Fran joins the team.
4. Continue to work on the project as a team.
5. Participate in a discussion based on the following questions:

QUESTIONS FOR TEAM MEMBERS OTHER THAN FRAN BELLO:
- What assumptions, if any, did you make after reading the memo announcing Fran's arrival?
- What was your first impression of Fran?
- How did Fran affect your team's effectiveness?

QUESTIONS FOR INDIVIDUALS PLAYING THE ROLE OF FRAN BELLO:
- How did you disclose your skills or lack of skills relevant to the project to the team members?

- Did the team respect what you had to offer?
- Did you feel fully included as a member of the team?

GENERAL QUESTIONS:
- How did the team dynamics change after Fran's arrival?
- What similar real-life situations have you experienced?
- How can employers ensure that older employees are fully included in the teams to which they are assigned?

Source: Kathleen R. Butterworth, Christopher R. Corcoran, and Gary N. Powell, in Gary N. Powell, *Managing a Diverse Workforce: Learning Activities* (Thousand Oaks, CA: Sage, 2004), 79.

EXERCISE: RELIGION AND SPIRITUALITY: WHAT COULD BE HAPPENING HERE?

Purpose
The purpose of this exercise is to help you understand better the intersection of religion and the workplace.

Introduction
There is a strong movement toward bringing religion and spirituality into the workplace. Because so much time is spent at work, some people no longer want to separate work and religion. It is critical for business leaders to understand the role of religion in today's workforce.

Guidelines
In small groups, use the following questions as a guide to discuss each scenario:

- What are the possible explanations for this person's behavior?
- How should management respond to this situation?
- How should the employee respond to this situation?
- How should the employee's coworkers respond to this situation?
- Do you have personal knowledge about certain religions? If so, share this knowledge with your group.

Scenario One
Sonia, who was recently hired, started to wear loose-fitting clothes and a headscarf to work. Behind her back, some coworkers responded with comments such as "Sonia is going to scare off potential clients with her crazy outfits" and "I wonder if Sonia is a part of a radical religious group." Sensing negative sentiments from her coworkers, Sonia becomes more self-conscious and less communicative.

Scenario Two
Harte Consulting, LLC was thrilled to hire Jonathan onto their team. Jonathan's résumé was of the highest quality—he graduated from a top business school with honors. His coworkers are confused, however, when Jonathan seems resistant to working on Saturdays. He claims to have prior engagements and responsibilities. His coworkers begin to question his dedication to his team in particular and the company in general.

Scenario Three
Maya—who has just declared, "I'm really hungry"—is at a business lunch where she is served chicken, green beans, and garlic potatoes. She eats the beans, seems uninterested in the rest of her food, and then orders dessert. Her coworkers look at her strangely, and after lunch, they discuss her odd behavior.

Scenario Four
The department's coed softball team has always been considered a big deal since it began 10 years ago. The softball games are played on Sunday mornings and afternoons. Jenny, who was an all-star softball pitcher in high school and college, has just been transferred into the department, and her new coworkers are thrilled that their team has just become more competitive. Jenny, however, declines to be part of the team. Jenny is now tagged as "not a team player" throughout the office.

Source: This exercise was prepared by Kathryn A. Cañas and Harris Sondak.

EXERCISE: DISCRIMINATION BASED ON SEXUAL ORIENTATION: COUNTING THE COSTS

Purpose

The purpose of this exercise is to help you gain insight into the personal and organizational costs of discrimination based on sexual orientation.

Introduction

The disapproval of homosexuality causes both heterosexual and gay people to react in complex and sometimes counterproductive ways. It can force gay people into the "corporate closet"—that is, they go to great lengths to hide their sexual orientation at work. It can separate people who could work together productively and enjoy one another's company. It may cause them to avoid each other or to sabotage one another's efforts. In extreme cases, homophobia results in harassment, violence, or expensive litigation that can destroy the lives of the individuals involved and drain the organization's resources.

Guidelines

The following are examples of situations in which the costs of discrimination based on sexual orientation add up. In the space beneath each example, list what you believe would be one personal cost to the people involved and one cost to the organization to which the individuals belong. Here is an example:

Sarah is a model employee except that she never talks about herself when the others are discussing their husbands and wives. She knows that they think she is cold and reserved, but she is afraid to tell them about her life with her woman partner for fear of being rejected or even fired.

Personal cost

There may be damaged relationships among coworkers; the job becomes uncomfortable for Sarah and those around her.

Organizational cost

Sarah always feels on guard; she may quit for a more comfortable job; the company must spend time and money to replace her.

Now you try it. What do you think the costs are in each of the following situations?

1. When the other managers—all men—go to lunch, they gradually stop inviting Wilson, who is rumored to be gay.

Personal cost

_____

_____

_____

Organizational cost

_____

_____

_____

2. Mae Linn gives preferential treatment to gay men when hiring applicants. She believes that they are more creative and sensitive and will treat women better than straight men will.

Personal cost

_____
_____
_____

Organizational cost

_____
_____
_____

3. Since telling others that she is a lesbian, Jayne has noticed that David, a coworker, has begun to make passes at her. She has heard via the grapevine that he has told his buddies she will be a "real challenge."

Personal cost

_____
_____
_____

Organizational cost

_____
_____
_____

4. Stephen has felt depressed for several weeks and has given people around the office different explanations. When his coworkers discover that he and a long-term male partner just broke up, they wonder what else Stephen is hiding.

Personal cost

_____
_____
_____

Organizational cost

_____
_____
_____

Source: Amy J. Zuckerman and George F. Simons, *Sexual Orientation in the Workplace: Gay Men, Lesbians, Bisexuals, and Heterosexuals Working Together* (Thousand Oaks, CA: Sage, 1996), 16–19.

EXERCISE: THE TEN COMMANDMENTS OF INTERACTING WITH PEOPLE WITH DISABILITIES

Purpose

The purpose of this exercise is to help foster more effective communication and collaboration with people with disabilities.

Introduction

The goal of the AXIS Center for Public Awareness of People with Disabilities is to create a positive public awareness of people with disabilities and to strengthen the voices of people with disabilities through advocacy. AXIS has issued a list of guidelines that offer insight into what to do when communicating with people who have disabilities.[3]

Guidelines

In groups of four or five, discuss the following questions after reading the "commandments":

- Do you work with people with disabilities? If yes, what has been your experience?
- Do you follow the "commandments" when speaking with people with disabilities?
- Which "commandments" are most difficult to follow?
- Do you have friends with disabilities? If so, what is their advice on effective communication?

TEN COMMANDMENTS FOR COMMUNICATING WITH PERSONS WITH DISABILITIES

1. When talking with a person with a disability, speak directly to that person rather than through a companion or sign language interpreter who may be present.
2. When introduced to a person with a disability, it is appropriate to offer to shake hands. People with limited hand use or who wear an artificial limb can usually shake hands. (Shaking hands with the left hand is an acceptable greeting.)
3. When meeting a person with a visual impairment, always identify yourself and others who may be with you. When conversing in a group, remember to identify the person to whom you are speaking.
4. If you offer assistance, wait until the offer is accepted. Then listen to or ask for instructions.
5. Treat adults as adults. Address people who have disabilities by their first names only when extending that same familiarity to all others present. (Never patronize people who use a wheelchair by patting them on the head or shoulders.)
6. Leaning or hanging on a person's wheelchair is similar to leaning or hanging on a person and is generally considered annoying. The chair is part of the personal body space of the person who uses it.
7. Listen attentively when you are talking with a person who has difficulty speaking. Be patient and wait for the person to finish, rather than correcting or

speaking for the person. If necessary, ask short questions that require short answers, a nod, or a shake of the head. Never pretend to understand if you are having difficulty doing so. Instead, repeat what you have understood and allow the person to respond. The response will clue you in and guide your understanding.

8. When speaking with a person in a wheelchair or a person who uses crutches, place yourself at eye level in front of the person to facilitate the conversation.

9. To get the attention of a person who is hearing-impaired, tap the person on the shoulder or wave your hand. Look directly at the person and speak clearly, slowly, and expressively to establish if the person can read your lips. Not all people with a hearing impairment can lip-read. For those who do lip-read, be sensitive to their needs by placing yourself facing the light source and keeping hands, cigarettes, and food away from your mouth when speaking.

10. Relax. Don't be embarrassed if you happen to use accepted, common expressions that seem to relate to the person's disability, such as "see you later" or "did you hear about this?"

Source: This exercise was developed by Kathryn A. Cañas and Harris Sondak.

EXERCISE: CULTURAL DIVERSITY

Purpose

The purpose of this exercise is to help you discuss culture clashes and to promote good intercultural communication practices.

Guidelines

1. Divide participants into groups of four or five. Give each group one case study.
2. Allow a few minutes for everyone to read the cases.
3. Have each group discuss what was happening in its case, how culture played a part, how the situation could have been handled, and whether the conflict could have been avoided.
4. Have each group report and discuss the different responses.

Case 1: Ethnic Joke

You are in a meeting and before the boss comes in, there's a general feeling of camaraderie, with many jokes. You suddenly realize that an ethnic joke has been told, and as you look up and see the face of the person whose group has been slandered, you realize he's been hurt. There is an awkward silence for a moment, and then general sports banter takes over and the subject is changed.

QUESTIONS

- How do you feel?
- What should you do?

Case 2: Anticipation of a New Colleague

One of your white male coworkers has been told he will be getting a new black colleague as his officemate. Before the white man has even met his new office mate, he is heard grumbling and groaning about all the trouble he will have and how he doesn't have time to offer the new man all the help he knows he will need. You are standing nearby when he vents his feelings.

QUESTIONS

- Why is the white employee so concerned?
- What can you do to help the situation?

Case 3: Performance Evaluation Giggles

The "mainstream" supervisor calls in the Laotian employee for a semiannual evaluation. After the supervisor offers some positive aspects of the evaluation, she begins to discuss areas for improvement. Since the Laotian employee looks down at the floor during the entire feedback session, the supervisor concludes that the employee is hiding something. When the supervisor tries to draw it out of him, the employee begins to giggle.

QUESTIONS

- How might this behavior be explained? What do you think is taking place?
- How should the manager address this situation? What procedure should she set up?

Source: Jonamay Lambert and Selma Myers, *50 Activities for Diversity Training* (Human Resource Development Press, 1994), 81–83.

Case 4: The Invisible Woman

Ben is a successful purchasing manager with a reputation for being hard working and fair. In his regular Monday morning buyers' meeting, the participants are Harry, Charlie, Jim, and Sally; Ben gets along with them all. After the latest meeting, Ben is surprised when Sally approaches him almost in tears, and complains, "Ben, first thing in today's meeting, I suggested we consolidate the commodity purchasing into one section. Before I was halfway through, you cut in to let Jim speak. By the end of the meeting, you agreed with my idea, but gave Jim all the credit." Sally is thinking, Nobody listens to me; is there something wrong with me? Ben doesn't know what to think, and besides, he can't even remember Sally's bringing up the idea in the first place. Is something wrong with Sally today? he wonders; Why is she making a federal case out of this? He makes a joke to minimize the situation.

QUESTIONS

- What is happening here?
- If you were Ben, would you have been able to understand what was going on and avoided it?
- If you put yourself in Sally's shoes, how would you have handled the situation?

Notes

1. U.S. Department of Labor, Bureau of Labor Statistics. (2003). Employment and Earnings (Table 3). Retrieved October 14, 2003, from http://www.bls.gov/cps.
2. Imel, S. (1996). Older workers: Myths and realities. Retrieved January 28, 2004, from http://www.cete.org/acve/docgen. asp?tbl= archive&ID=A029; Myths about aging: Helping seniors improve with age. (2003). Retrieved October 3, 2003, from http://www.go60.com/myths.htm
3. Reference: AXIS Center for Public Awareness of People with Disabilities, www.axiscenter.org/index.html.

CHAPTER 12 | ASSESSING ORGANIZATIONS

EXERCISE: EXAMINING EXEMPLARY LEADERS IN MANAGING DIVERSITY

Purpose
Your task is to locate and examine organizational leaders who embrace diversity and who manage diversity effectively.

Guidelines
First, research any of the following organizational leaders on your own and then, in small groups, pool all your information. As groups, report your findings to the class. Here are a few topic areas and questions to guide your research:

- *Background* What is the professional background of this leader? Is there any personal information or experience that led to his or her passion for managing diversity?
- *Status of Diversity Within Organization* What role did diversity play before the leader became a part of the organization?
- *Philosophy* What is the leader's philosophy on diversity management?
- *Strategies* What strategies did the leader implement to transform the way in which the organization managed diversity?
- *Goals* What were the diversity-related goals implemented by the leader? What are his or her future goals related to diversity?
- *Current Status* What is the current status of the organization in terms of diversity in particular and overall success in general

EXAMPLES OF ORGANIZATIONAL LEADERS FROM WHOM YOU MAY CHOOSE:
- Sharon L. Allen, Deloitte and Touche
- Kenneth Chenault, American Express
- Johnnetta B. Cole, The United Way
- Louis V. Gerstner, Jr., IBM
- Andrea Jung, Avon Products, Inc.
- Dick Parsons, Time Warner
- Antonio Perez, Eastman Kodak
- David M. Ratcliffe, Southern Company
- Steve Reinemund, PepsiCo
- Johnathan Rodgers, TV One
- Jeff Valdez, SiTV

Source: This exercise was developed by Kathryn A. Cañas and Harris Sondak.

EXERCISE: ANALYSIS OF CONSULTING COMPANIES

Purpose

The purpose of this exercise is to develop your knowledge of what consulting companies are offering as diversity training. The specific objective is to get a more detailed understanding of the strategies and procedures employed by high-profile diversity consulting companies in their effort to help organizations manage diversity.

Introduction

Consulting firms can be very helpful to organizations in improving their diversity management and diversity training has become a multi-billion dollar industry. It is important, therefore, to be knowledgeable about what consulting companies are offering in their attempt to help organizations understand and manage diversity as a competitive advantage.

Guidelines

Research the listed companies and answer the following questions:

- How do these consulting companies define diversity? What is their philosophy on managing diversity?
- How do they help companies manage their diverse workforce? What are their areas of specialization?
- How do these consulting companies ensure that diversity is managed systemically (on all levels) within the organization?
- How do they measure the impact of their recommendations and training?
- Where do these consulting companies fall short?

Consulting Company	**Web site**
1. Aequus Group LLC	http://www.aequusgroup.com
2. Berkshire Associates	http://www.berkshire-aap.com/ services/diversity.aspx
3. Cook Ross	http://www.cookross.com
4. Diversity Training Group	http://www.diversitydtg.com
5. Elsie Y. Cross Associates	http://www.eyca.com/home.html
6. Global Lead	http://www.globallead.com
7. J. Howard A. Associates	http://www.jhoward.com
8. The Kaleel Jamison Consulting Group	http://www.kjcg.com
9. Lambert & Associates	http://www.lambert-diversity.com
10. Lee Gardenswartz and Anita Rowe	http://www.gardenswartzrowe.com/ home.html
11. NVC Consulting	http://nvcconsulting.net
12. PRISM International, Inc.	http://prismdiversity.com
13. Tulin Diversiteam Associates	http://www.diversiteam.com
14. The Winters Group, Inc.	http://www.wintersgroup.com

Source: This exercise was prepared by Kathryn A. Cañas and Harris Sondak.

EXERCISE: OPENING THE SPORTS PAGE

Purpose

The purpose of this exercise is to help you examine diversity in professional sports.

Guidelines

1. Every time you open the sports page, it seems that diversity is a topic of interest. Read the following current-event snapshots of sports and diversity, use the internet to research how far these organizations have come in terms of diversity, and then, in groups, discuss the following questions:

   - Is NASCAR embracing diversity as a way to change its image as a white male sport? Why or why not?

   - Why is the NBA getting high marks in diversity management while other sports organizations struggle?

   - Is the NFL's "Rooney Rule" too simple to be effective and create real change?

   - What are the challenges facing the PGA in terms of diversity? How many American-born minorities, international players, and women play on the tour?

NASCAR

On May 20, 2004, it was announced that Earvin "Magic" Johnson will assist NASCAR with its diversity management. In particular, he will (1) help complete selection of the Executive Steering Committee for Diversity; (2) assist NASCAR with creating grassroots programs such as Drive for Diversity that identify and develop African Americans, Hispanic, and women drivers and crew members; (3) help NASCAR develop marketing programs that will increase the sport's visibility in urban communities and raise awareness of career and competitive opportunities in motorsports; (4) serve as an advisor to NASCAR Chief Operating Officer George Pyne who has day-to-day operational responsibilities for all aspects of diversity in NASCAR.[1]

NBA

According to the National Basketball Association News Wire, "The NBA was given an A for racial diversity by a university study released Wednesday that examined employees from the front offices to the hardwood. The NBA also is tied with Major League Soccer for tops in providing opportunities for women. . . . Most of the study focused on the 2003–04 season. In the NBA league offices, 43 percent of the professionals were women and 29 percent were minorities."[2]

NFL

According to Jarrett Bell, "With a record six black head coaches set to patrol the sidelines for NFL teams this season [2004–05], the league's efforts to level the playing field of opportunity for those jobs apparently is working. In the 27 months since NFL owners adopted the so-called Rooney Rule, which penalizes teams for not interviewing minorities for head coaching jobs, 4 of the 15 such openings were filled by black candidates. It is a stark contrast to the climate in recent years, such as in 1997 when black candidates were bypassed for all 11 available coaching jobs. Yet despite progress on the coaching front, leaders of the Fritz Pollard Alliance (FPA), an affinity group that monitors and promotes opportunities for minorities, are calling for an expansion of the rule to apply to executive and front office positions."[3]

PGA

Minorities and women are the fastest growing segments of the golf population. "For Professional Golf Association (PGA) tour commissioner Tim Finchem, recruiting minorities and women to the sport is a key to reaching his goal of 'a billion rounds played each year by more than 55 million people.'"[4] The PGA has developed the PGA Tour Diversity Internship Program with the goal of seeking and identifying diverse prospects for future employment within the golf industry, and Tiger Woods' Foundation offers clinics across the U.S. that reach out to minority children.

Source: This exercise was developed by Kathryn A. Cañas and Harris Sondak.

PROJECT: THE DIVERSITY CONSULTING TEAM

The final team project is a diversity analysis of a local organization. Following the project description are tools that will help your team craft effective survey and interview questions, thereby allowing you to examine the role of diversity in your specific organization.

General Description

Your task is to write a team paper that takes the form of a "business proposal." In this paper you will examine a specific, local organization. In your teams of approximately five students, you will need to do the following:

1.   **Locate an organization that will allow you to perform a diversity analysis.** At the beginning of the semester, teams should brainstorm possible organizations to examine for their final project. Typically, communication between students and organizational members is facilitated in an organization in which one of the team members has a connection—either a team member or perhaps a close friend or relative works there. The teams may choose an organization that currently has a clear and comprehensive diversity plan in place, or they may choose an organization that does not have any diversity policy. Although the organization must be local—so the students can easily make observations, perform surveys and interviews, and so forth—the organization may also be a division of a large national company, a medium-sized company, or even a small company. It is suggested, however, that the company have at least 15 employees. The team's approach when examining a larger organization with an established diversity policy is to find the diversity strengths and areas of opportunity within that organization and to improve their policy through recommendations. The team's approach when examining a smaller organization that has little—if any—policy on diversity is to build a long-term plan from the bottom up.

2.   **Conduct primary and secondary research.** Primary research, your own assessment of the situation, is helpful when determining the organization's philosophy and approach to diversity management. After receiving permission to distribute a survey and request interviews, teams should take sufficient time to craft both. Successful surveys typically include both questions measured by a Likert scale and a few open-ended questions. Students may also want to begin their survey with a clear definition of diversity, because diversity is often defined narrowly (e.g., only the color of one's skin) instead of using more inclusive characteristics such as race, gender, religion, disabilities, sexual orientation, age, family status, etc. Students may also want the person answering the survey to record his or her gender, age, organizational status, and the like. In terms of interviews, the students should try to interview people in leadership and supervisory positions, especially any one person in charge of diversity management within the company. In addition to the primary research gathered by the students, secondary research, either about the organization or the context in general, is also important: Web sites; written policies; mission, vision, value statements; diversity pamphlets or manuals; magazine or newspaper articles; and so forth.

3.   **Examine the research.** Take sufficient time to examine the findings from both the surveys and interviews. After examining the surveys, students might contemplate questions including the following: Are there any trends in the findings? Are there distinct differences in how men and women responded to the questions? Do the answers to the questions reveal any diversity management strengths and weaknesses within the organization?

After examining responses to the interview questions, students might contemplate questions including the following: Do lower and middle management view diversity in the same way as upper management? Do the organizational leaders view diversity as a competitive advantage? Do the organizational leaders have an inclusive understanding of diversity? Is there a disconnect between how the organizational leaders view diversity and how other members of the organization view diversity?

4.   **Make organizational recommendations.**   After examining all the primary and secondary information, the students should choose either one main problem or various problems on which to focus their recommendations. The students may craft their recommendations in terms of phases (e.g., a four-phase plan to manage one serious diversity problem) or in terms of years (e.g., a 5-year plan to manage three main problems). It is important, to explain each recommendation in detail. For example, if a team decides that diversity training is one of the recommendations, it must also articulate details about the training—what type of training, material to be covered, and so forth. Or, if the team decides to recommend a diversity mentoring program, it must include details about the design of this program.

Specifics on Paper
In this paper, the team is to:

1. *Briefly describe the organization you researched.*
- What is the organization's history/background?
- How does the organization's history affect the way it perceives and manages diversity?

2. *Articulate your research method.*
- How did you gather your primary and secondary information?
- In terms of primary information, incorporate a discussion of your survey and interview results. You may include copies of the survey and interview questions in accompanying appendixes.
- In terms of secondary information, be sure to reference all Web sites, material from the organization (e.g., annual report, pamphlets, etc.), books, magazine articles, newspaper articles, journal articles, and the like.

3. *Explain what type of diversity policy the organization currently has in place.*
- What are the policy's strengths and weaknesses?
- Are the employees knowledgeable about this policy? If so, how do the employees respond to this policy?
- Is the diversity managed sporadically or systemically within the organization?
- If the organization does not have any diversity management policy, discuss the organization's general strengths and weaknesses in light of diversity's potential role within the organization.

4. *Focus on one or several of the organization's problems in regard to managing diversity.*
- Explicate the problem or problems in detail. For example, after examining your research, you may see problems emerging such as lack of

effective training, ineffective recruitment efforts, few women in upper management positions, lack of family-friendly policies, no clear understanding of diversity as a competitive advantage, or a lack of vision for diversity.

5. ***Explain what type of diversity policy the organization needs to be successful when managing diversity.***

(In your plan, you may focus on making recommendations for what you perceive as the most serious problem, or you may focus on making recommendations for a number of problems. There are a number of models of effective diversity management that have been implemented by organizations. If you borrow such strategies, be sure to clearly reference the source.)

- Does the organization need both short-term and long-term recommendations? Both internal (employees, policies) and external (marketing, reaching new customers) recommendations?
- Would this organization benefit from a 5-year plan in which the diversity plan is implemented slowly over a number of years?
- If appropriate, delineate the steps that the organization should follow to be successful in managing diversity.
- Explain how and why your recommendations would improve the organization's current situation.

Specifics on Presentation
1. Combined with this paper is a 20- to 25-minute team presentation.
2. In the presentation you should describe the organization, your research, your research methods, and your diversity plan for this company.
3. In addition to being graded on the content, you will be graded on the following:

OPENING
- Effective attention-getting strategy
- Articulation of purpose and significance
- Brief discussion of team's credibility (if necessary)
- Preview of main points

PRESENTATION STYLE
- Used eye contact and gestures to engage audience
- Matched voice volume/inflection and facial expressions to reinforce the spoken message
- Avoided distracting mannerisms
- Used movement and varied location to reinforce key elements of the message
- Used a natural conversational delivery style—extemporaneous not memorized
- Engaged audience interaction appropriately and made modifications based on audience reaction

VERBAL PRESENTATION
- Used logical, easy-to-follow structure
- Incorporated smooth transitions between topics
- Included a combination of evidence types (facts, statistics, examples, stories, testimony)

- Referenced sources clearly
- Spoke to audience's needs and values
- Covered company history, strengths/weaknesses, recommendations

GRAPHIC PRESENTATION
- Used appropriate visuals for the situation
- Visuals were simple, readable, and professional
- Visuals were presented in a skillful, nondistracting manner

CLOSING
- Summarized main points
- Ended with an effective concluding device that created a sense of closure
- Message was memorable (it was unique or compelling enough to cause action)
- Handled questions and challenges effectively

Source: This exercise was developed by Kathryn A. Cañas and Harris Sondak.

TOOL TO ASSIST DIVERSITY CONSULTING TEAM PROJECT: NINE SYMPTOMS THAT MAY INDICATE A NEED FOR DIVERSITY TRAINING

Purpose

The purpose of this exercise is to help you develop your skills in identifying potential diversity-related concerns and/or problems within organizations.

Guidelines

1. Organizational members respond to the checklist, checking off any symptoms they observe in the organization.
2. Checklists are then collected and results are tabulated for use by the requesting individual or group.

_____ 1. Insensitive comments or jokes told in the work unit regarding age, gender, ethnicity sexual orientation, or physical ability

_____ 2. Inability to retain members of diverse groups

_____ 3. Open conflict between groups or between people from different groups

_____ 4. Lack of diversity throughout all levels of the organization

_____ 5. Cultural faux pas committed out of ignorance rather than malice

_____ 6. Diversity-related blocks in communication that impede work flow

_____ 7. Formal EEOC complaints

_____ 8. Expressions of isolation from the work group

_____ 9. Incidents that reveal that individuals are not valued for the unique contributions they can make

Source: Lee Gardenswartz and Anita Rowe, *The Managing Diversity Survival Guide: A Complete Collection of Checklists, Activities, and Tips* (Boston: McGraw-Hill, 1994), 4–5.

TOOL TO ASSIST DIVERSITY CONSULTING TEAM PROJECT: MANAGING DIVERSITY QUESTIONNAIRE

Purpose

The purpose of this exercise is to provide a method for you to assess three levels of an organization's effectiveness in managing a diverse workforce: individual attitudes, organizational values, and management practices.

Guidelines

1. Individuals respond to the questionnaire based on their perception of the organization and how it functions.
2. Questionnaires are collected and scored both for total and for individual attitudes, organizational values, and management practices separately (see scoring guide that follows). The higher the scores, the more effective the organization.

In this organization:	Very true	Somewhat true	Not true
1. I am at ease with people of diverse backgrounds.	_____	_____	_____
2. There is diverse staff at all levels.	_____	_____	_____
3. Managers have a track record of hiring and promoting diverse employees.	_____	_____	_____
4. In general, I find change stimulating, exciting, and challenging.	_____	_____	_____
5. Racial, ethnic, and gender jokes are not tolerated in the informal environment.	_____	_____	_____
6. Managers hold all people equally accountable.	_____	_____	_____
7. I know about the cultural norms of different groups.	_____	_____	_____
8. The formation of ethnic and gender support groups is encouraged.	_____	_____	_____
9. Managers are flexible, structuring benefits and rules that work for everyone.	_____	_____	_____
10. I feel free to disagree with members of other groups without fear of being called prejudiced.	_____	_____	_____
11. There is a mentoring program that identifies and prepares women and people of color for promotion.	_____	_____	_____
12. Appreciation of differences can be seen in the rewards managers give.	_____	_____	_____

	Very true	Somewhat true	Not true
13. I feel there is more than one right way to do things.	_____	_____	_____
14. Members of the nondominant group feel they belong.	_____	_____	_____
15. One criterion of a manager's performance review is developing the diversity of his/her staff.	_____	_____	_____
16. I think that diverse viewpoints make for creativity.	_____	_____	_____
17. Turnover rates among women and people of color are similar to those among other groups.	_____	_____	_____
18. Managers give feedback and evaluate performance so employees don't "lose face."	_____	_____	_____
19. I am aware of my own assumptions and stereotypes.	_____	_____	_____
20. Policies are flexible enough to accommodate everyone.	_____	_____	_____
21. Managers get active participation from all employees in meetings.	_____	_____	_____
22. I think there is enough common ground to hold staff together.	_____	_____	_____
23. The speaking of other languages is welcomed.	_____	_____	_____
24. Multicultural work teams function harmoniously.	_____	_____	_____
25. Staff members spend their lunch hour and breaks in mixed groups.	_____	_____	_____
26. Money and time are spent on diversity development activities.	_____	_____	_____
27. Managers effectively use problem-solving skills to deal with language differences or other culture clashes.	_____	_____	_____
28. I feel that working in a diverse staff enriches me.	_____	_____	_____
29. Top management backs up its value on diversity with action.	_____	_____	_____
30. Managers have effective strategies to use when one group refuses to work with another.	_____	_____	_____

SCORING:

Very true = 2 points; Somewhat true = 1 point; Not true = 0 points

_____ Individual attitudes and beliefs: Items 1, 4, 7, 10, 13, 16, 19, 22, 25, 28

_____ Organizational values and norms: Items 2, 5, 8, 11, 14, 17, 20, 23, 26, 29

_____ Management practices and policies: Items 3, 6, 9, 12, 15, 18, 21, 24, 27, 30

_____ Total score

Source: Lee Gardenswartz and Anita Rowe, *The Managing Diversity Survival Guide: A Complete Collection of Checklists, Activities, and Tips* (Boston: McGraw-Hill, 1994), 129–31.

TOOL TO ASSIST DIVERSITY CONSULTING TEAM PROJECT: ASKING GOOD QUESTIONS

Purpose

The purpose of this exercise is to illuminate meaningful questions that you can use to understand how diversity is seen within an organization. In diagnosing how an organization approaches diversity, it is helpful to assess the experiences and intentions of the leaders of the organization and those of members of its dominant and nondominant-cultures.

SAMPLE INTERVIEW QUESTIONS FOR LEADERS AND POLICYMAKERS

1. What have been the biggest benefits of having a multicultural workforce? What are the biggest problems and frustrations?
2. With an increasingly diverse workforce, what changes do you see in productivity? Interpersonal dynamics? Bottom line (e.g., training dollars spent on education)?
3. What challenges does this present to your organization?
4. What is your organization doing to help your managers meet these challenges? What do they need to learn to do differently?
5. How do you measure and reward your managers in this area?
6. What is your organization doing to enhance the upward mobility of nondominant-group members? What obstacles prevent this mobility?
7. What processes do you have to identify and develop a diverse pool of talented employees?
8. What does your organization do that reflects how it values cultural diversity?
9. What is your organization doing to accommodate differences in values, norms, and mores?
10. What made you decide to invest your organization's resources (time, energy, money) in making diversity development a priority? What results have you seen?
11. What organizational systems, practices, and policies present obstacles to fully developing and utilizing your diverse workforce?
12. If your organization does nothing to address the cultural diversity issue, what do you predict will happen?

SAMPLE INTERVIEW QUESTIONS FOR EMPLOYEES OF NONDOMINANT CULTURES

1. What do you like about the culture of this organization?
2. What do you find difficult about it?
3. What did you expect to find when you came to work here? What was your biggest surprise? Biggest joy? Biggest disappointment?
4. What kinds of experiences made you feel welcome in this organization? Unwelcome? What did you do to help the situation?
5. What is your professional goal? What do you hope to achieve here?
6. How has this organization helped you toward your goal? How could it help more?
7. Have you ever felt it was a mistake to come to work here? If so, what made you feel this way?
8. How have you been treated by bosses and coworkers?
9. How do you get along with people of other groups in the workplace?

10. On a scale of 1 to 10, how much do you feel a part of the organization? What needs to happen to make you feel more a part of it?
11. What is the most important thing the organization can do to help you adjust? What can you do?

SAMPLE INTERVIEW QUESTIONS FOR EMPLOYEES OF THE DOMINANT CULTURE

1. What have been the biggest changes in this organization the past few years?
2. What have been the biggest benefits of being part of a multicultural workforce? What have been the biggest problems and frustrations?
3. How does diversity in the workforce affect you? Your work group? This organization?
4. What has been the biggest "culture shock" for you in working with diverse groups?
5. What kinds of experiences make you feel comfortable with employees from different groups? Uncomfortable? What did you do to help the situation?
6. How have you been treated by employees of diverse groups?
7. What is the most important thing your organization can do to help members of nondominant groups adapt to this organization?
8. What is the most important thing these employees can do to help themselves adapt?

Source: Lee Gardenswartz and Anita Rowe, *The Managing Diversity Survival Guide: A Complete Collection of Checklists, Activities, and Tips* (Boston: McGraw-Hill, 1994), 160–161.

Notes

1. "Magic Johnson to Co-chair Diversity Committee," May 20, 2004, www.nascar.com/ 2004/news/headlines/official/05/20/mjohn-son_diversity/.
2. National Basketball Association News Wire, "Study: NBA is pro sports' best at achieving diversity," May 4, 2005, http://sports.espn.go .com/espn/wire?section=nba&id=2053236.
3. Jarrett Bell, "Group Seeks Diversity in NFL Front Offices," *USA Today,* March 2005, http://www.usatoday.com/sports/football/nfl/2 005-03-07-rooney-rule-expansion_x.htm.
4. "Sports Taking Aim at Diversity," http://racerelations.about.com/library/ weekly/ aa020801a.htm.

Index